CONTEMPORARY BRITISH STUDIO POTTERY

forms of expression

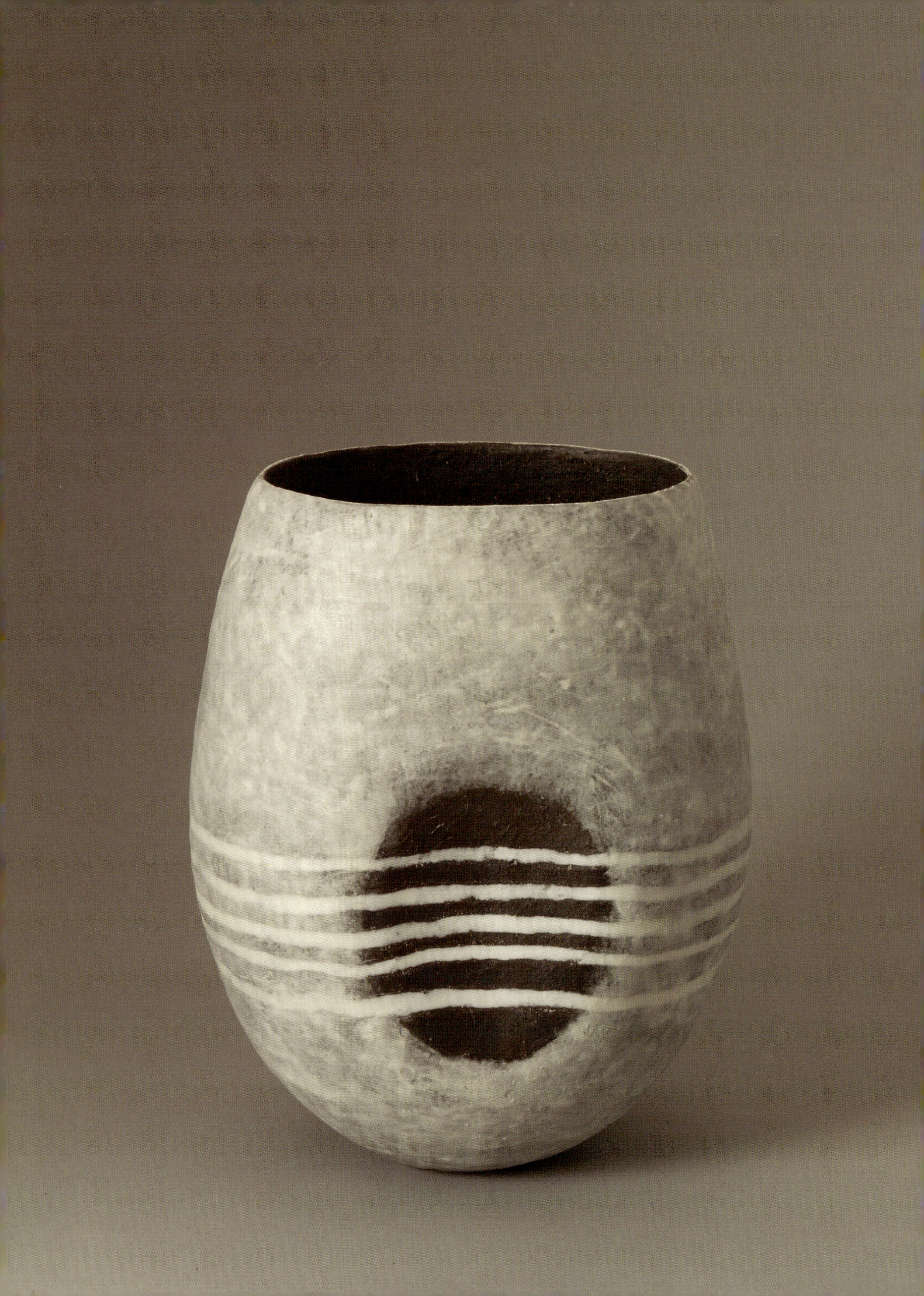

CONTEMPORARY BRITISH STUDIO POTTERY

forms of expression

Ashley Thorpe

THE CROWOOD PRESS

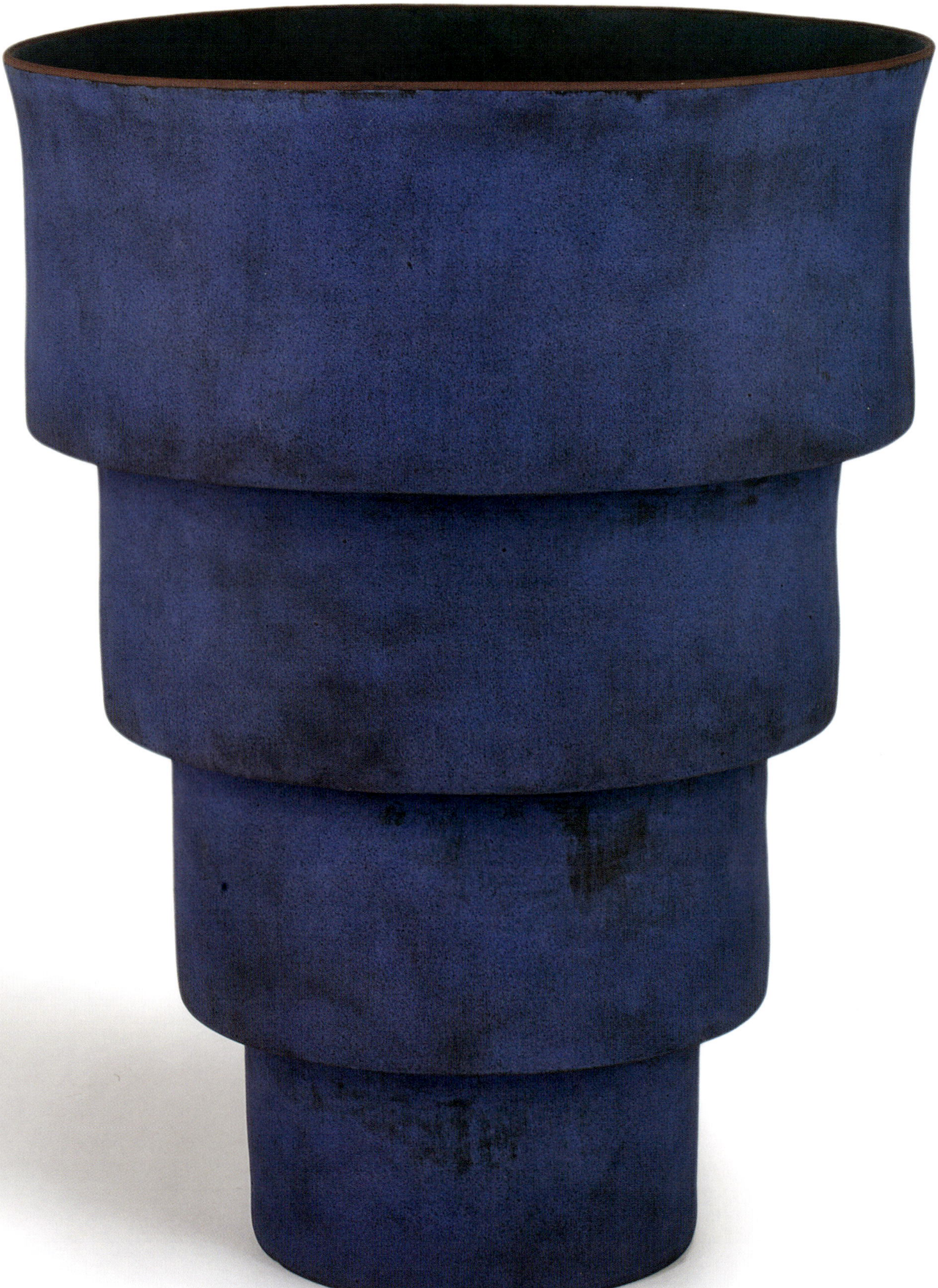

Contents

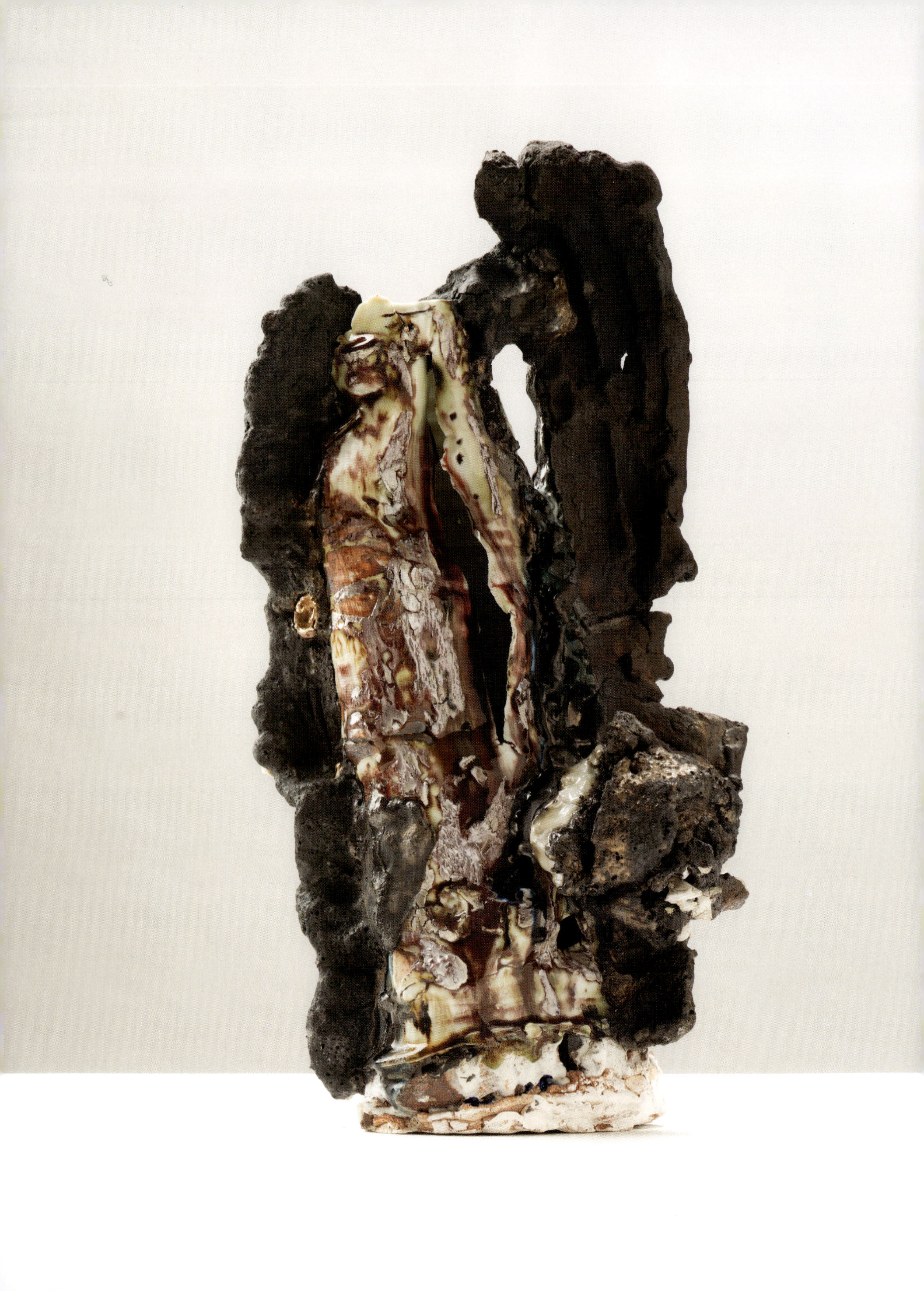

Introduction What is a pot and what is it not?

The 'vessel', it seems, is a contentious word in ceramics. As Laura Gray has noted, debates surrounding the validity of the term reveal 'tensions about the relative value of the pot, the vessel and the object, and the status between the useful and the useless in the art world.'[1] As Gray goes on to observe, the word 'vessel' brings to the fore anxieties about craft, its relationship to fine art, the relevance of utility, even accusations that ceramicists are guilty of self-aggrandisement.[2] The debate as to whether ceramics should be regarded as 'art' or 'craft' (even subject to the same kinds of criticism as fine arts) was particularly vehement in Britain in the 1980s.[3] Rather than being resolved, however, the debate simply fell to the wayside. When Grayson Perry won the Turner Prize in 2003, pottery was widely considered to have entered the world of British fine art, as if a trophy was all that was needed to iron out the polemics of the preceding decades.[4] Yet, as Perry admits of his own training, 'the main reason for not taking up throwing was that I wanted to avoid the signature ceramicist's skill because it would mark me too easily as a potter and I was clinging onto my newly minted identity as a contemporary artist'.[5] As Perry went on to observe, 'pottery *was* craft, not art, pottery was the business of skilled tradesman not gentleman academics, pottery was humble, small and domestic and seen as feminine.'[6] Indeed, Perry's work has readily exposed, rather than erased, the divisiveness of ceramic art/craft discourse.

Many of the artists included in my first book, *Contemporary British Ceramics: Beneath the Surface* (2021), made sculptures. This was a deliberate choice. I was interested in capturing the interdisciplinary nature of contemporary practice, and I wanted to focus on – what seemed to me at least – some of the less readily accepted branches of contemporary British ceramics. This necessitated moving across different formal concerns. However, makers of pots and vessels were still included; artists such as Alison Britton, Ken Eastman, Jennifer Lee, Carol McNicoll, Sara Radstone, and Martin Smith, were an integral part of the discussion because their work related to many movements, themes, and ideas. These included drawing, painting, film, modernism, postmodernism, architecture, history, identity, and belonging. From this interdisciplinarity, I was soon convinced that the impassioned arguments as to whether ceramics was or is fine art or craft were retrograde. Indeed, over the last forty years or so, and with the benefit of hindsight, I am left to conclude that the claiming of ceramics as either art or craft was not just futile, but a disavowal of the kinds of work produced.

Art or Craft?

In his excellent analysis of the history of the word 'craft', Paul Greenhalgh demonstrated how the meaning of the term shifted from the seventeenth century, partly in response to developing class politics. Indeed, the eighteenth-century philosopher Immanuel Kant (1724–1804) argued that:

> *Art* [...] differs from *handicraft*; the first is called *free*, the other may be called mercenary. We regard the first as if it could only prove purposive as play, *i.e.* as occupation that is pleasant in itself. But the second is regarded as if it could only be compulsorily imposed upon one as work, *i.e.* as occupation which is unpleasant (a trouble) in itself, and which is only attractive on account of its effect (e.g. the wage).[7]

For Kant, craft was produced for money, whereas art existed for its own aesthetic sake. Presumably art was not produced for financial reasons because it was either practised, or patronised, by the upper classes. Such collectors were perhaps less interested by the cost of the works they acquired, more the social and cultural capital of owning a collection. Craftspeople, presumably typified as lower class, needed to make a living from their wares because they had to put food on the table.

By the time of the late nineteenth century and the arrival of the Arts and Crafts Movement, craft was used to refer to any decorative art (an eighteenth-century catch-all term for all artistic practices excluded from 'fine art') that was non-industrial and community-produced, with the concomitant belief that such creative labour was for the common good.[8] Indeed, William Morris (1834–1896) defended craft in his 1882 lecture *The Lesser Arts of Life*, arguing that 'if our houses, our clothes, our household furniture and utensils are not works of art, they are either wretched make shifts or, what is worse, degrading shams of better things.'[9]

In the aftermath of the success of the Arts and Crafts Movement, craft became a more widely understood term. Craft became tied to anti-industrial discourses, and it was in this context that Bernard Leach (1887–1979) rose to prominence.[10] Leach became the dominating ideological force of the British studio pottery movement for much of the twentieth century. In *A Potter's Book* (1940), Leach suggested that 'a pot in order to be good should be a genuine expression of life. It implies sincerity on the part of the potter and truth in the conception and execution of the work.'[11] Such a view echoed William Morris; that the best pots should be consequential,

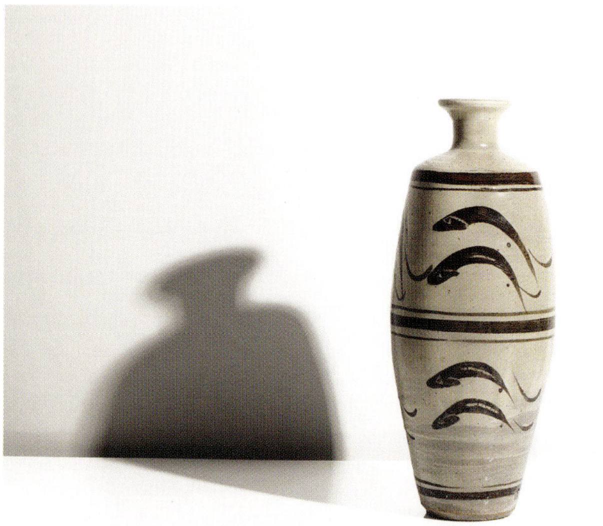

Bernard Leach, *'Leaping Salmon' Vase* (c.1960).

engaging us through sight and touching us through tactility. Yet, for Leach, such aesthetic experiences were tied to his universalist beliefs that art should inspire a cosmopolitan shared world culture of humanity. It is for this reason that Leach was such an ideological advocate for connections between 'East' and 'West'. After all, the bridging of cultures brought all of humanity together in the appreciation of a common aesthetic. Such ideas seem rather generous in spirit, and do not, in and of themselves, deem functional pots to be the worthiest. Nevertheless, his beliefs in artistic sincerity were inextricably tied to utility, where 'the form of the pot is of the first importance, and the first thing we must look for is [...] proper adaptation to use and suitability to material.'[12]

Such doctrinal thinking glossed over contemporaries who sought to align pottery with modernist fine art. In inter-war Britain, the work of William Staite Murray (1881–1962) had successfully situated pottery as a parallel activity to sculpture and painting. Regarded as antithetical to Leach's utilitarian artisanry, Staite Murray's solo exhibitions of pottery earned him critical acclaim, and by the 1930s he was exhibiting with the Seven and Five group of modernists (which included Ben Nicholson, Barbara Hepworth, and Henry Moore). Yet, as the 1930s wore on, influential art critics turned against Staite Murray's work for its apparent self-indulgence.[13] Following the dissolution of the Seven and Five group in 1935, Staite Murray emigrated to Rhodesia (now Zimbabwe) in 1939 and ceased potting.[14] In the decades that followed, Staite Murray's success in arguing for pottery as a mode of fine art expression was downplayed by Leach and his supporters.[15] Thus, the philosophical thrust of most British studio pottery became tied to utility.

Leach's philosophy was so prominent that it persisted in some quarters until the turn of the century. As late as 1998, the ceramicist and critic Peter Lane was still suggesting that:

> The form of a vessel often suggests that it can perform some kind of useful purpose in addition to the decorative aspects of its being. When vessels are primarily intended to serve as containers, that special function must be carefully considered and incorporated into the initial design.[16]

Lane was aware of artists who made pots that were not intended for use, for the volume was illustrated with numerous examples. Furthermore, all pots have 'useful purpose in addition to the decorative aspects of its being', making his distinction between a pot and a vessel obscure. In his concluding chapter, 'Traditions and Innovations', Lane nevertheless noted how, for some contemporary artists, 'utilitarian aspects in even the most familiar shapes of ceramic vessels are of little or no interest.'[17] Yet, by pushing the discussion of these artists to the final (somewhat shorter) chapter, they were still positioned as a departure from the mainstream. Perhaps in the 1970s and 1980s this might have been assumed by the casual observer, but by the turn of the century, the landscape was far more diverse.

The Turn to Painting

In the USA, things had proceeded very differently. In 1961, the important critic Rose Slivka articulated the impact of Abstract Expressionist painting on ceramic practice. Her observations were providential, and are worth quoting at length:

> Painting shares with ceramics the joys and the need for spontaneity in which the will to create and the idea culminate and find simultaneous expression in the physical process of the act. Working with a sense

> of immediacy is natural and necessary to the process of working with clay. It is plastic only when it is wet and it must be worked quickly or it dries, hardens, and changes into a rigid material.
>
> The painter, moreover, having expanded the vistas of his [*sic*] material, physically treats paint as if it were clay – a soft, wet, viscous substance responsive to the direction and force of the hand and to the touch, directly or with tool; it can be dripped, poured, brushed, squeezed, thrown, pinched, scratched, scraped, modeled; treated as both fluid and solid. Like the potter, he even incorporates foreign materials – such as sand, glass, coffee grounds, crushed stone, etc. – with paint as the binder, to emphasize texture and surface quality beyond color.[18]

The overlaps – and significant differences – that Slivka identified between painting and ceramics encouraged an understanding of how technique, form, approach, and treatment, could establish new modes of expression in clay. It is not that painting and ceramics were the same; more that they had overlaps that were fertile areas of investigation. By the 1960s, US artists such as Peter Voulkos (1924–2002) and then Ron Nagle (b.1939) had become leading names, capably demonstrating the expressive possibilities of new ceramic forms.

Such ideas arrived in Britain somewhat later and became hybridised with (and used as a response against) the prevailing Leach ideology. The pot would not be discarded, but it was considered that utility need not be the primary formal concern. In her important essay for *The Maker's Eye* exhibition held in London in 1982, Alison Britton observed how, in her curated selection of objects (which included ceramics, textiles, jewellery, glass, wood, and metalwork) she sought:

> to make a comparison evident between 'prose' objects and 'poetic' objects; those that are mainly active and those that are mainly contemplative. To me the most moving things are the ones where I experience in looking at them a *frisson* from both these aspects at once, from both prose and poetry, purpose and commentary. These have what I call a 'double presence'.[19]

In comparison to Slivka's observations, Britton's were somewhat more conservative, though it must be noted that Britton was reflecting upon her own curatorial choices, rather than agitating for the wider field. However, in time, the essay would do just that, being cited in arguments for new approaches to the pot in Britain as a conceptual and formal device. In her essay, she noted, for instance, how her emphasis on 'vessels' 'could be somehow inherent in the training of a potter', or a product of 'clinging to the residue of use as a justification', or even a recognition of 'vessels' as 'basic, archetypal, timeless.'[20] Nevertheless, whilst the pot was central to tradition, it did not mean it had to be 'traditional'. As an example, Britton explored the work of Andrew Lord in relation to painting, noting how his three-dimensional works 'retain some of the imprecision and loose, impressionistic quality of a two-dimensional representation.'[21]

Three years later, in 1985, the Institute of Contemporary Arts in London held the exhibition *Fast Forward: New Directions in Ceramics*. The accompanying catalogue included a range of essays by both critics and makers, but a passage by the critic Martina Margetts echoed and developed Britton's earlier essay. She asserted that 'usefulness, it seems, is absolutely *not the point*; the references are to everything except Modernism, which still seems to hold the ace card of Moral Superiority, as if purity of form = purity of thought; Modernism as this century's only Shared Symbolic Order.'[22] Such a statement not only offered a more explicit validation of Slivka's prophetic writing, but it also suggested that only once questions of utility have been cast aside might clay hope to enter the lofty domains of the sculptural and the aesthetic. Perhaps Margetts was responding to the more vehement critics of the time, such as Peter Fuller, who, as Tanya Harrod observed, 'demonised William State Murray, Hans Coper and Lucie Rie for encouraging a fine art approach to pottery and, in the case of Coper, for diminishing the importance of throwing.'[23]

Despite her intentions, Margetts's observation that modernism had been rejected in some ceramic practices from the 1970s and 1980s glossed over, rather than resolved, the awkward art/craft debate she sought to rationalise. Whilst Margetts highlighted how the modernist ethos of Bernard Leach had been questioned, no one seemed to observe that a logical extension of her argument at this time would be to similarly reject Lucie Rie and Hans Coper, whose modernisms had been construed as antithetical to Leach.[24] In general terms, Rie, Coper, and Leach were not all that oppositional in seeking a transcendent aesthetic for their work. Indeed, Leach famously gifted Rie a large white Korean Joseon Dynasty Moon Jar (now in the collections of the British Museum).[25] Perhaps this was tacit recognition that Rie's work, like his own, could combine 'East' and 'West' aesthetics in the search for universalist values, even if their approach to form was very different. Indeed, outside Europe, the strongest audience today for Rie and Coper is, in fact, in Japan. Thus, the apparent rejection of modernism in the 1980s and 1990s was somewhat contradictory, with Leach facing critique, but Rie and Coper receiving credit for fostering a whole generation of new makers.[26] In reality, as documented in Chapter 1 exploring the work of Magdalene Odundo, the rejection of modernism was selective and uneven.

A decade later, the exhibition *The Raw and the Cooked: New Work in Clay in Britain*, toured Britain between 1993 and 1995. Funded by the Crafts Council, the exhibition was curated by Britton and

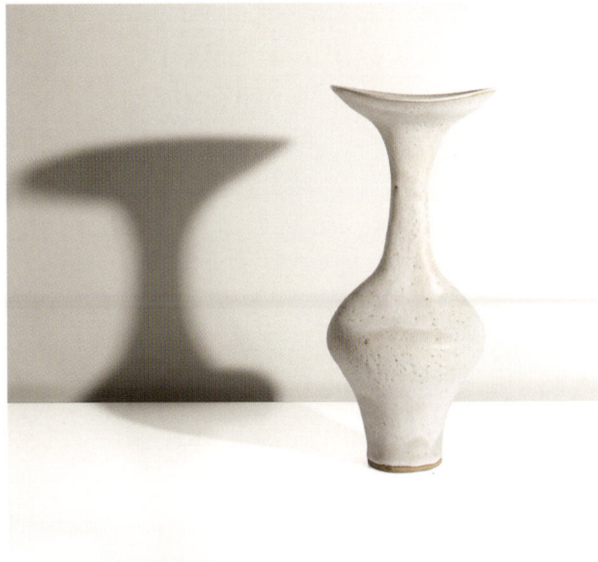

■ Lucie Rie, *Tall Vase with Flared Lip* (1979).

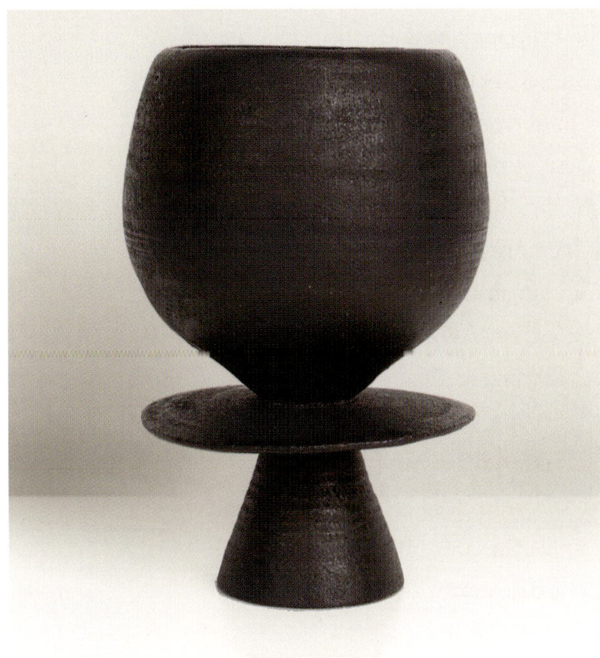

■ Hans Coper, *Cup on Foot with Central Disc* (1965).

Margetts. With a more expansive range of approaches, Margetts was able to confidently make her point:

> Clay is not a craft material but an authentic medium for sculpture. The works take myriad forms, in concept scale

> and meaning: the continuing exploration of the vessel form, fusing the languages of painting, sculpture and architecture in a physical language of its own, is balanced by works concerned with the ironical re-presentation of ceramic traditions; with figuration; with landscape (physical, mythological, metaphorical); and with identity.[27]

This constituted the strongest statement yet, for British-based makers at least, in support of the full plastic potential of clay. Margetts advocated for clay as a fine art material that should be respected in its own right; that is, if respect meant being freed from craft association. Indeed, Margetts even suggested that Hans Coper had now joined Bernard Leach on the reject pile for contemporary makers.[28] Yet, by erasing the craft roots of clay, Margetts short-circuited her own argument. Instead of agitating for the artistic virtuosity of all makers, she instead implied that only those who use clay as 'an authentic medium for sculpture' might transcend association with craft. What was meant by 'sculpture' was not explained. Such a position seemed to reinforce rather than deconstruct the art/craft dichotomy which, as the American jeweller Bruce Metcalf observed in 1997, was 'as if the two worlds spoke mutually incomprehensible languages, with no Rosetta Stone to establish translation.'[29] Yet, many of the works included in the exhibition by the likes of Gordon Baldwin, Alison Britton, Ken Eastman, Bruce McLean, Carol McNicoll, and Grayson Perry (to name just a few), were contingent upon audiences recognising how 'craft ideas', especially derived from domestic utility (that is, the pot), were being reframed in new ways. It was not that ceramics had escaped its 'craft' roots; nor was it as simple as reclassifying ceramics as 'fine art'. Indeed, the art/craft divide had been produced for ideological and economic reasons; arguing for pottery as a separate fine art practice simply reinforced the division. It was more that there was a recalibration of ceramics *as an expressive material in its own right and on its own terms*. The history, languages, demands, and predilections of ceramic forms were interrogated, but only to proliferate interdisciplinarity. To situate this expansion within a centuries-old craft/art dichotomy might have critiqued Leach, but with hindsight it seems to have missed the point. Ceramics was being celebrated as its own medium; its plasticity enabled it to take what it needed from any other discipline, artistic or otherwise.

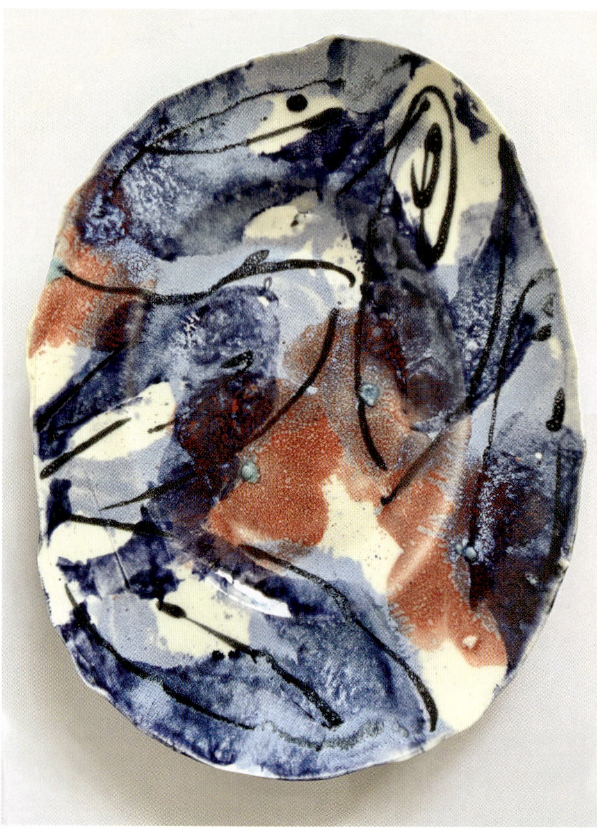

Janice Tchalenko, *Platter* (2016).
(Courtesy of Luke Tchalenko)

Even today, to suggest a move beyond the art/craft dichotomy risks being contentious. As Greenhalgh has observed of craft, 'the further it consolidated into classification – the more it became a naturalised and institutionalised signifier of a certain range of practices and attitudes – the less of a serious player it became.'[30] Indeed, as Tanya Harrod noted, by 'the 1980s [...] the word craft became a positive hindrance'.[31] Nevertheless, 'Craft' is an important word for many ceramicists, especially for those who trade in pots. Yet, an important definition of the word 'craft' is connected to skill; the myriad techniques of making, the ability to allow material to behave as itself, to compel it to take another turn, anticipate, or allow for surprise. Does craft define ceramics? No. It is true that ceramics is a technically complex discipline, and that these skills developed across history – so often lacking in fine artists who work in clay with little technical mastery – remain essential. Yet the fine arts – be it drawing, painting, or sculpting – also requires disciplinary craft, which must be mastered if a professional career is to be sustained. If fine art has 'craft', it follows that craft can also have 'fine art'. By 'fine art', I mean – in the Kantian sense – beauty, aesthetic pleasure, and personal expression. After all, Bernard Leach may have emphasised the importance of utility, but this did not preclude pots from becoming a vehicle for beauty. In fact, artistry was central to his ethos. As Leach observed in *The Potter's Challenge* from 1975, 'technique can be a good thing but not by itself.'[32] Leach insisted that pots should be beautiful, truthful, and individual. Above all else, he stated that 'the final word I would use as a criterion of value in the world of art, if I were reduced to a single word, would be the presence of *life*.'[33] For Leach, ceramic works – if they are any good – are the product of *both* craft and art.

Why does this matter? It matters because the question of whether ceramics is art or craft has rumbled on for decades, and it continues to have marked consequences on the contemporary. Johanna Drucker has convincingly argued how contemporary sculpture is dependent upon affect (the redeployment of materials into new contexts) and entropy (how conventional uses of material are eschewed).[34] In particular, she suggests that:

> Affectivity and entropy are intensified gestures of differentiation. Each defines a contemporary world of production and consumption that allows visual art to distinguish itself from mainstream consumer and material culture while still engaging with its very means. Rather than defining art as an entirely separate domain, affectivity and entropy suggest that fine art is a use, a way of working, a gesture of distinction, within the realm of material culture and of its objects, things, and stuff.[35]

In the contemporary period, such affect/entropy is often dependent on non-expert uses of material. In the case of ceramics, the affect of clay is aligned with the relative technical inexperience of the fine art artist, which is highlighted as a method of achieving authentic entropy. This means that ceramics in art must be distinguished from any association with its roots in craft (as argued by Margetts). The latter, in its mass-produced iterations, is deeply embedded in the material culture of the everyday. Tableware, for instance, is a product of, and literally a tool for daily consumption. By circumventing association with craft, clay can achieve authentic fine art entropy, legitimising it as a distinctive practice in the age of digital proliferation and mass manufacture. This is one means of accounting for the growing ubiquity of clay in the holdings of the contemporary fine art gallery, as well as the admittance of Grayson Perry into the world of fine art via the 2003 Turner Prize.

Given the above, it is not surprising that some trained contemporary ceramicists have chosen to downplay their skill (craft) so that they can exhibit a similar entropy as their fine art colleagues. As artists who have comparatively little technical understanding of clay occupy more and more space in fine art galleries, several trained ceramicists call themselves 'fine artists who happen to use clay', as though their choice of medium were a stumbled-upon accident. This is despite their advanced technical capability, and the fact that their work knowingly draws upon multiple aspects of ceramic history. Thus, the perceived difference between clay as 'craft' and 'art' material continues to have genuine impact on the careers of makers.

Astonishingly, Peter Dormer, writing twenty-five years ago, observed the same trend. He noted that although craftspeople:

> have many understanding admirers, they have not found themselves admired as much as other 'artists'. Potters do not earn the same regard as sculptors, for example [...]. The contradiction is that it appears to many intelligent craftspeople that they have to renege on craftsmanship to pursue their craft. The admirers of 'high art' are not interested in craft and the consumers of decorative objects and other trophies for the home do not see that high craft is really worth paying for. So what is a maker to do if he or she is to gain status and earn a living?[36]

Is this denial of the word 'potter' simply produced by what the ceramic dealer, critic, and historian, Garth Clark polemically described as an 'ego-driven envy [...] fueled by resentment that craft, while successful, was not as respected or as valued as the fine arts'?[37] Certainly such resentment persists in some quarters, though as many of the chapters in this volume evidence, the histories of ceramic production – understood as craft – are now being readily interrogated as part of studio pottery, and even circulated in fine art galleries. Nevertheless, as Clark suggests, as long as ceramics is seen to respond to fine art rather than vice versa, it will always be regarded as a discipline of secondary value.[38] Will this lingering sense of ceramic entropy lead to the ecstasy of new disciplinary value, or the gradual atrophy of skill?

Towards definitions

If it is to reach the former, echoing Clark, and responding to Greenhalgh's observation that the meanings of 'craft' have been subject to constant revision, criticism needs to play its part in documenting how ceramics is a vibrant and exciting interdisciplinary field of enquiry *of and for itself*. That means, to paraphrase Leach, finding the right language to evidence how ceramics is a field teeming with 'life'. In the catalogue for his curated exhibition *Pandora's Box* (1995) for the Crafts Council, Ewen Henderson (1934–2000) highlighted the significance of form as a central question. Selecting work for exhibition by makers such as Ian Auld, Gordon Baldwin, Bryan Illsley, Mo Jupp, Gillian Lowndes, Lawson Oyekan, Sara Radstone, and Angus Suttie, Henderson argued that ceramics demands 'a formal language, and we all have to have it I'm afraid. We can't converse without a verbal language and it's even more important in the visual language because people are less familiar with it.'[39] The pot, of course, remains central to this language.

But if considerations of utility are totally removed, is a pot still a pot in formal terms? What is the 'essential potness'? Are pots and vessels really the same? If not, where does one end and the other begin? Is one art and the other craft? There seems to be a problematic lack of precision about the language of ceramics.

Two years before *The Raw and the Cooked* exhibition opened, the critic John Houston published *The Abstract Vessel: Ceramics in Studio* in 1991. This short monograph was an attempt to give conceptual classification to the growing plurality of approaches towards ceramic form. For Houston, historicism was not enough; it was not simply that artists were returning to the ancient roots of pottery where aesthetic divisions between 'art' and 'craft' did not exist. Rather, he sought to analyse instances of contemporary work that demonstrated 'matters of stance and articulation where the artist's voice and the potter's form do not quite match; where the language is vivid but not entirely pottery-compatible: not authorized by pottery past.'[40] In sympathy with Margetts, Houston suggested that the disassociation between clay and craft was where 'the abstract vessel begins to be re-invented, made up, re-filled with more than the usual concerns of pottery.'[41] The 'abstract vessel' was thus the synthesis (preferably somewhat awkward) of pottery with non-pottery concerns. The results, Houston suggested, were 'abstract vessels certainly, but so rich in metaphors and analogies that our mental contexts are figured with a montage of kindred inventions, constructions, fictions – object-poems improvised in a cluster of tongues.'[42] Certainly ceramic objects can be poetic in the sense that they have a self-reflexivity beyond utility; Alison Britton had already argued this in her essay in *The Maker's Eye* in 1982, quoted earlier. But what does this reveal about the use of form?

Houston's recognition of the self-reflexive inter-disciplinarity of ceramics remains astute, but there is something of a lack of precision in the term 'abstract vessel'. His analysis includes figurative sculptures by Philip Eglin, where, Houston argues, 'the image of the body as the prime analogy of a form to render feeling is what transforms the abstract vessel into the thinking object.'[43] Yet, this expansive belief that figurative sculptures are abstract vessels, presumably because they contain space, effectively places most, if not all, non-functional ceramics into the formal sphere of the vessel. Eglin's work sometimes takes the form of a reconfiguration and innovative treatment of British ceramic history. Not all of his output relates to the pot, however, especially those works that explore figuration. These are ceramic sculptures. One of the issues with Houston's essay is that he uses the words 'pot' and 'vessel' interchangeably, making the notion of the 'abstract vessel' remarkably abstract.

In moving beyond the abstract, dictionary definitions offer an intriguing point of departure:

Vessel (noun)
A container, especially for liquid; a ship or large boat; a tube or duct for carrying liquid, e.g., blood or sap, in animals and plants.

Pot (noun)
Any of various domestic containers, usually deep round ones, used as cooking or serving utensils, or for storage.

Chambers Dictionary

From this, it is possible to deduce that pots are associated with domesticity and function, whereas a vessel is somewhat more expansive in form. Vessels comprise sculptural decisions that consider interior space as a question of containment; in particular, how interiority is confined by, and then released into, the exterior. This means that vessels have no overt relationship with the form of domestic pots. Pots may consider similar territory, but they have the additional frisson of filtering such sculptural investigations through forms associated with domesticity and utility, even if such associations are denied, or become replaced by other metaphorical resonances. It does not mean that functional pots are craft and non-functional ones are art; more that the emphasis on the self-evident, reflexive (poetic) nature of artistry is, as is always the case, dependent on the maker's own agenda, and how the end user chooses to deploy the object (that is, admire it on a shelf, use it, or both).

One might legitimately ask: why not simply call any pot that is sculptural and non-utilitarian a vessel? 'Vessel' certainly sounds grander than 'pot'. Indeed, some might feel that the description of work as a vessel helps to initiate the perceptive labour required from audiences, specifically recognition that there is more at stake than questions of utility. The problem here is that, at a fundamental level, *all* pots sculpt space, and a great many of the makers included in this volume make maximum use of this aspect in their work. There is, therefore, a risk that conflating 'sculptural pot' with 'vessel' diminishes the significance of form – especially the pot – and the development of precise ceramic languages.

In her essay for *The Raw and the Cooked*, Alison Britton (who refers to herself as a potter who makes pots) suggested how a pot can be:

> a form that is overtly hollow and frequently curvaceous, with a related interior and exterior appearance, [that] can very easily seem to be a metaphor for the human body or self. More angular geometric pots seem to relate to buildings, and perhaps sleights of scale and to an architectural sense of space. [...] More loosely amalgamated, highly fused, and geological-looking pieces readily make suggestions of landscape, pre-history, and forces of nature.[44]

Britton's definition highlights the interdisciplinary nature of pots. Pots can, and do, bridge formal connections between notions of utility (craft), decoration, painting (art), the technical history of ceramic production (craft) and contemporary sculpture (art). A pot is a form that can be pulled in multiple directions; one of its strengths is its malleability. Smuggling the formal language of the 'pot' into the 'vessel' risks denying the adaptation, extension, and individualisation of the formal languages of pottery that give a piece its significance. The vocabulary becomes obscured.

The remedy demands a significant shift in paradigm that runs counter to contemporary understanding, and even runs counter to several of the makers included in this book. The word 'vessel' is not automatically interchangeable with the word 'pot'. Rather, as the dictionary definition suggests, a vessel is a somewhat looser term; it is not anchored to forms associated with, or developed from, domestic utility but can float (like a sailing boat) on its own formal buoyancy. A vessel does not reference forms found in the domestic frame; it need not have the expansive curvaceousness and hollowness that Britton observes. Rather, it playfully arranges internal and external space into dynamic relational contours without recourse to the pot. Admittedly, a curvaceous pot is one means of exploring the relations between interior and exterior space, but importantly for the point being made here, it is not the only one. Tubes, for instance, are a recurring motif in vessels, perhaps a referent of blood vessels, which they nominally resemble. Once it is regarded as distinctive and independent from the pot, the vessel is a remarkably under-explored ceramic form. In Britain, some, though by no means all, examples of work by Gordon Baldwin (his boulder-inspired vessels), Sara Radstone (her boat-inspired caskets) and Lawson Oyekan – as outlined in the chapter on his work in this book – indicate the directions in which the vessel might be taken. To call these 'pots' is to distort what they really are.

Is it not the case, then, that a vessel is simply a kind of ceramic sculpture? Yes and no. Sculpture, as Laura Gray has appositely noted, is a nebulous term, capable of absorbing many of the contradictory approaches attributed to it. Indeed, as noted above, the three-dimensional quality of most ceramic work classifies it as 'sculptural', so what differentiates either the pot or the vessel from ceramic sculpture? Gray suggests that, despite its inherent complexity, 'form, space and material remain important for thinking about sculpture'.[45] Thus, if a pot has a curvaceous hollowness associated with (or derived from) utility, whilst a vessel uses other vocabularies to consider the flow between interior and exterior space, then – in another shift of paradigm – a ceramic sculpture emphasises exterior surface via an enclosed form. To reiterate the critique of John Houston's abstract vessel, a Philip Eglin figure is not a vessel, it is sculpture; sculpture that is formally different from a sculptural pot (for example, by Elizabeth Fritsch), and further different from a sculptural vessel (for example, by Gordon Baldwin).

It is important to point out that one form – sculpture, vessel, pot – is not worthier than another; they are simply different. Yet in acknowledging

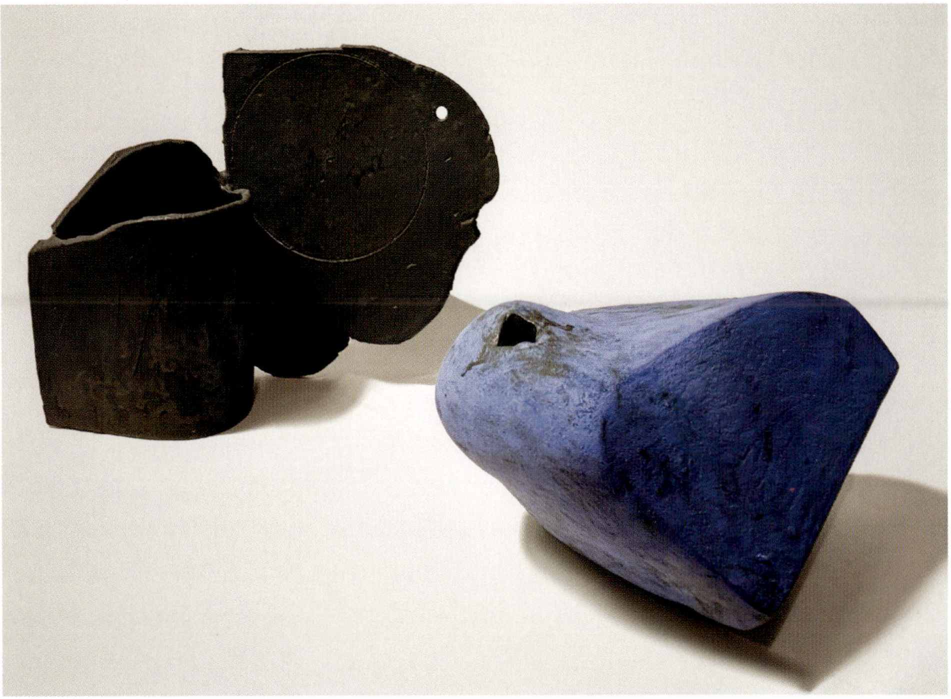

Millennium Cup (1999), a sculptural pot (left), and *Study for a Large Blue Vessel* (2002), a vessel (right) by Gordon Baldwin.

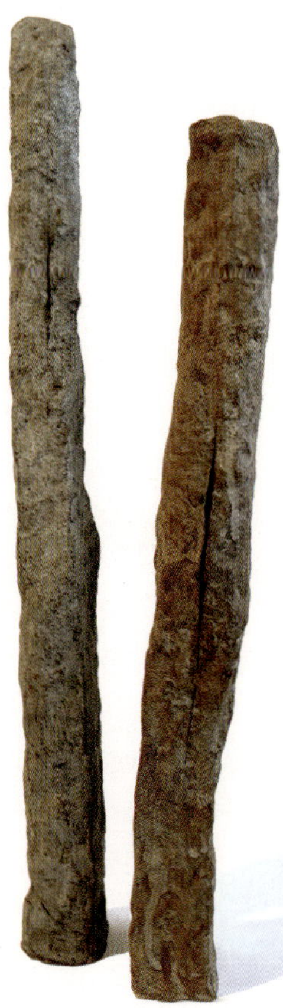

A pair of vessels by Sara Radstone, *Untitled* (2002). (Courtesy of Sara Radstone)

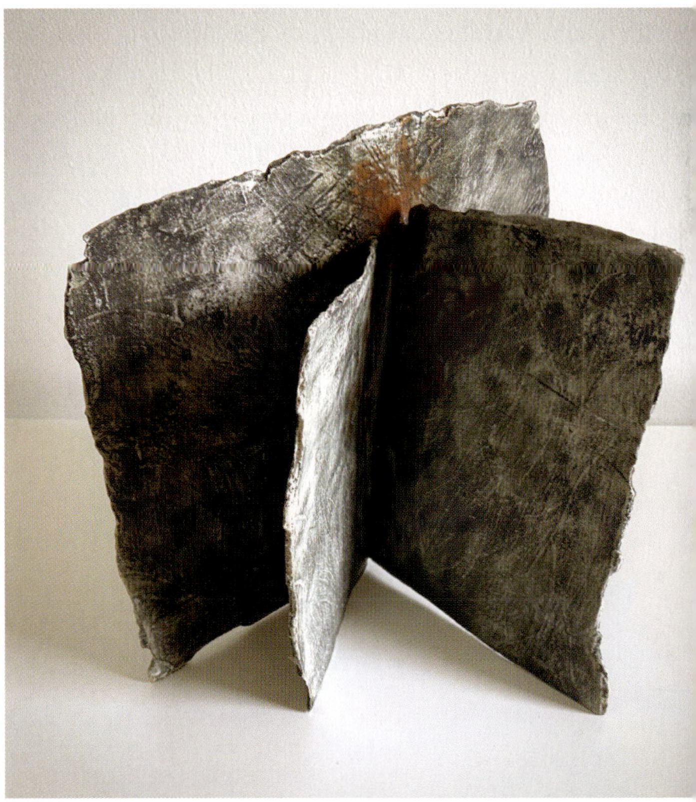

A ceramic sculpture by Sara Radstone, *Dark Folder* (2012). (Courtesy of Sara Radstone)

difference, there is perhaps the temptation to overstate them when they are by no means absolute. It is the job of artists to undermine formal categorisation at every turn. It is perhaps better, then, to consider these categories as having degrees of overlap, as operating on a continuum or sliding scale, where each work configures attributes of form into distinct kinds of dynamic relationship (*see* the diagram, The Continuum of Ceramic Form, for the principal arcs that might amalgamate categories). Much contemporary work hovers on the outskirts of, or sits across, categories – as pot-sculptures (perhaps the most common form described in this book) or vessel-sculptures. Theoretically at least, a work might even exhibit qualities of the pot, the vessel, and sculpture as resolved elements in the same complex composition (*see* the central axes across the shaded centre in the diagram below). Do these categorisations, and the attribution of a sliding scale, risk pushing analysis into subjective speculation? Perhaps. Yet, it is clear that ceramicists, whether they label themselves as potters, makers of vessels, or sculptors, do move between and across different

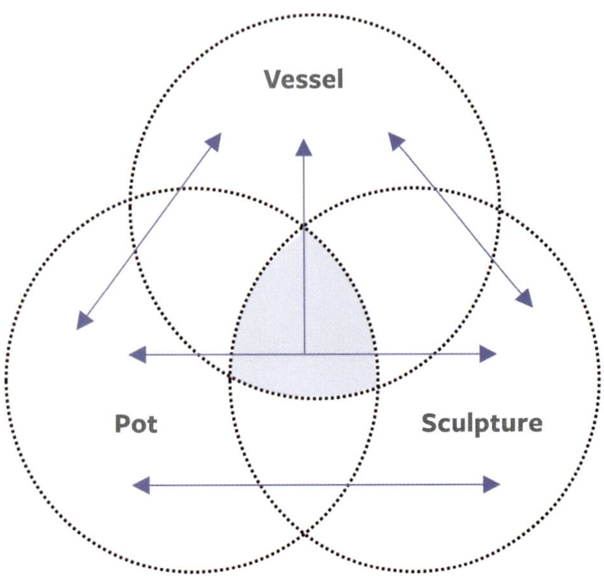

The Continuum of Ceramic Form: the principal axes between pots, vessels, and sculptures.

points of reference. My previous book, *Contemporary British Ceramics: Beneath the Surface*, was testament to this interdisciplinarity. As a natural extension of that project, forging a means to discuss movement across vocabularies of form is important, not only for the coherence of this volume, but also for the clarity and confidence of ceramics as a discipline.

The structure of this book

Given the above, it is clear that the structure of this book cannot follow the obvious format, namely the neat sub-division of chapters into potters that make pots, those that make vessels, and those that create sculpture. Such a categorisation might offer a satisfying straightforwardness, but it would be, quite simply, wrong. The pottery landscape does not work to such neat coordinates. Indeed, most chapters include examples of work that demonstrate how a potter moves between vocabularies in their work. The chapters that follow document how the languages of the pot, the vessel, and sculpture are (re)configured and (re)combined in the work of contemporary makers.

That said, where work is described as a vessel by its creator, that chosen term has been honoured in the writing. Some may feel that this undermines the ideas outlined in this introduction, and risks adding to the confusion. Personally, I feel it accurately reflects current ambiguity in describing ceramic form. If readers look at the terminology attributed to work more critically, this introduction will have achieved its aims. Further thoughts offered in the Afterword may also assist the discussion.

The chapters of this book can be read independently and non-chronologically. Yet, as reflected in its subtitle, *Forms of Expression*, the volume seeks to comprehend what is at stake in the decisions that have been made around form – the actual means of expression. For this reason, the volume is divided into six broad thematic sections, which highlight the central concerns of the potters included and facilitate comparisons between them. The first, *Formal Languages* (Chapters 1–3), introduces a methodology for the analysis of form inspired by Bernard Leach who, in *A Potter's Portfolio* first published in 1951, outlined the compositional structure of a pot. It emphasises how the constituent elements of form become utilised as an essential vocabulary for creative expression in contemporary work.

As noted earlier, William Staite Murray offered an alternative vision to Leach, aligning ceramics with the expressive plasticity of fine art. *Dialogues with Twentieth Century Art* (Chapters 4–8) presents four contemporary makers whose work might regarded as further developing Staite Murray's belief in the painterly and sculptural possibilities of the pot. Comparisons with Cy Twombly, Josef Albers, Barbara Hepworth, and Ben Nicholson are made not to imply the secondary status of pottery, but to evidence how pots exhibit equivalent decorative and sculptural expression through their own formal languages.

The third section, *Dialogues with the Eighteenth and Nineteenth Centuries* (Chapters 9–14), surveys a branch of the turn towards the postmodern that combines contemporary art with pre-Leach ceramic mass-manufacture and the circulation of its display. By drawing upon the aesthetics of Wedgwood, Spode, and Sèvres, these makers also offer a range of capital 'P' and lowercase 'p' political statements: from the denial of Britain's colonial past to a direct confrontation with it, and from the definition of studio pottery as necessarily 'handmade' to the embracing of the latest 3D printing technologies.

Pottery is, of course, concerned with tactility – the pressure of the fingers on wet clay and the touch of hands on fired objects. The fourth section, *The Tangible* (Chapters 15–17), explicitly focuses on the relationship between potter, pots, and purchaser, arguing that the pot is a singularly tactile vehicle for interpersonal connection. In contrast, *The Intangible* (Chapters 18–21) investigates how pottery expresses the ethereal, spiritual, and hypothetical, from the emotional landscape of the interior to the scientific theories that explain the laws of the universe. The final section, *Colliding Worlds* (Chapters 22–24), demonstrates how pots can reflect upon, and critique, our relationship with the natural world. Challenging the stereotype that pottery is simply a quaint and complacent activity, these works coalesce to warn us of the consequences of our ecologically unsustainable craving for natural resources.

The rationale for selecting who to include in this book was – as it always is – a personal one. For each potter I chose, I could easily have included another three. Nevertheless, as was the case with my previous volume, I have sought to include a mix of established, mid-career and emerging artists. Some of the potters are very much a product of the last decades of the twentieth century, but they form part of the contemporary ceramic landscape that connects the achievements of established generations with the evaluative concerns of the up and coming. In this sense, the volume represents a snapshot of a specific moment in time.

With this in mind, it must be asserted that the focus of this book on Britain does not infer that only British, British-based, or British-trained ceramicists undertake formal creativity, or that they automatically lead the world in their discipline. To spotlight Britain is simply a means to focus the discussion via the specific geographical context in which I live. Wherever possible, I meet the potter in their studio and discuss their work with them, and a focus on Britain is conducive to this process. No kind of ceramic neo-imperial British greatness, or post-Brexit superiority, is implied. All of the potters included were either born, currently live, or were trained in Britain. Beyond this, geography is irrelevant. Indeed, as the first chapter on the work of Magdalene Odundo attests, pots will always transcend boundaries.

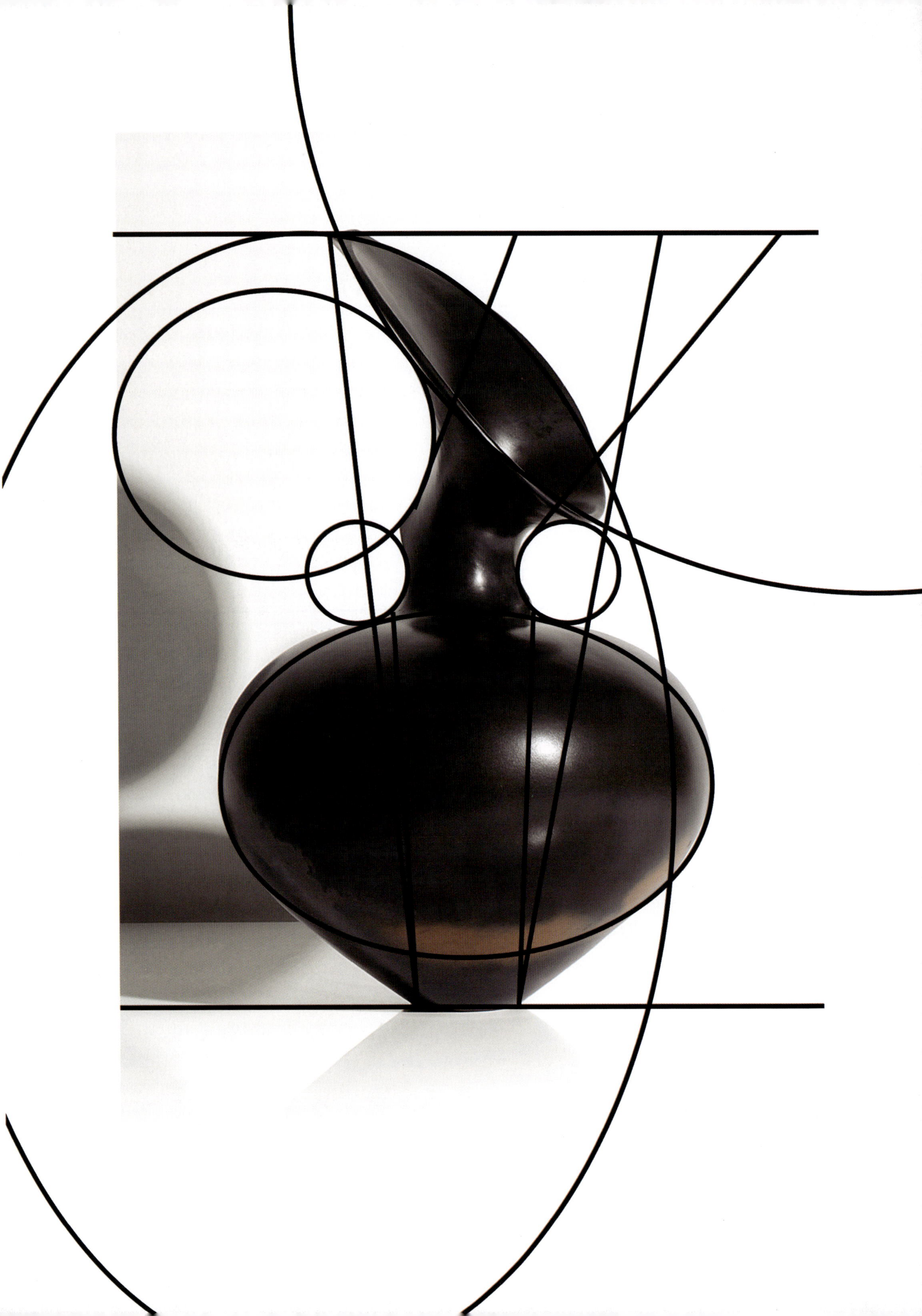

Formal Languages

Magdalene Odundo Glossolalia

> In my own work, my vocabulary is deliberately minimal. I do not want my pots to require lengthy explanation. I want them to feel empathetic, I want people to be able to understand them visually. For me, visual literacy, looking and noticing, is the most important thing. Viewers are welcome to imbue the work with whatever they want, but the words come second. The work, the vessel, must come first.[46]

To mark the end of the twentieth century, Dame Magdalene Odundo OBE produced a series of *Millennium Jugs* (as well as *Millennium Cups*) in white earthenware. Such unassuming domestically scaled pots might appear a curious introduction to the grander terracotta forms for which Odundo is internationally recognised. Yet, I begin with these inventive works because they exemplify key concepts that can be discerned elsewhere. The jug itself is formed with a rounded base and cannot stand by itself. A separate concave foot affords it a supported place to rest. Consequently, the jug can – if desired – be manipulated to stand at obtuse angles from its base, to tilt so that the symmetrical balance of the jug is disrupted. This interplay between symmetry and asymmetry is, as Emmanuel Cooper pointed out in his excellent assessment of Odundo's oeuvre, a central compositional concern in much of her work.[47] More significantly, as a piece made to commemorate the millennium, the jug points in two directions. The extruded handle curves away from the body in an upward direction, whilst the extruded 'spout' curves downwards away from the lip. The body of the jug is thus located at the interstice between these directions, redolent of the move between centuries, and symbolic of looking both backwards and forwards. Setting the jug into its base at one angle or another (either towards the handle or, conversely, towards the lip) implies a leaning towards history or the future, whilst the jug positioned upright (as photographed) emblemises attenuation to the present. Thus, the jug is a container of uncertainty and anxiety around moments of passage from one epoch to the next. The inability of the jug to stand without its concave base might even symbolise our need for rituals, and associated objects, to ground us during periods of transition.

Millennium Jug (1999) alludes to the wider liminality of Odundo's work; how it sits in and out of time. In museums, her pots blend effortlessly with examples of ancient ceramics from Africa or South America. Out of an interminable desire to comprehend the expressive potential of clay, the cultural and religious significance of pottery across thousands of years, pursued through decades of study, exudes from her fingertips. Yet, in the contemporary art gallery, Odundo's work commands its own presence and her instantly recognisable pots are internationally sought-after. Her forms curve across continents in every sense; she fashions visual patchworks that situate the present within the past and enmesh the present into the future. As with the *Millennium Jug*, her pots are Janus-faced, looking backwards and forwards from their own temporality.

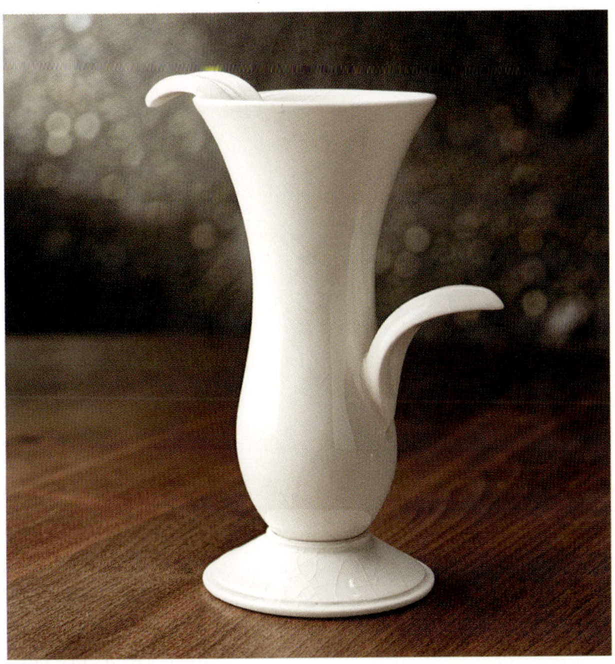

■ *Millennium Jug* (1999).

It is, however, axiomatic that pots transcend linguistic, religious, and cultural specificity. A look around the ceramics collection of any museum confirms this. What risks the prosaic becomes, in Odundo's hands, perceptive and enriching. Her emphasis on visual literacy implies an understanding of how the personal moves into the universal and back again. The perceptions of the artist are cast in the primordial visual language of clay for universal comprehension, but meaning is not a given; it is always context-specific, being inflected – accented – with a particular syntax in the moment of experience. Pots may possess a universal visual language, but meanings shift, are revised, or re-inscribed. Odundo challenges us to read visually. Interpretation comes later. But what is it, exactly, that we are being asked to read?

A clue to this lies in Odundo's early ceramic training. Born in Kenya, Odundo travelled to England to study at the Cambridge College of Art from 1971–73, and then the West Surrey College of Art and Design in Farnham from 1973–1976, where Henry Hammond (1914–1989) was the Head of Ceramics. Hammond, whose aesthetic was derived from Anglo-Orientalism, took his students on field trips, including to St Ives, where Odundo and her fellow classmates had the opportunity to meet Bernard Leach in 1974. Soon after, following a meeting with the Leach potter Michael Cardew (1901–1983), Odundo learned of the Abuja pottery that Cardew had himself set up in Nigeria, and travelled there to study for a few months in the summer of 1974. Then, in 1976, Odundo travelled to California and was able to see the Native American potter Maria Martinez (1887–1980) at work.[48] Even from this brief summary of Odundo's activities in the early years of her ceramic education (she later went to the Royal College of Art from 1979–1982), there is an obvious fascination with the transnational movement of potters, potteries, and pots.

It is no coincidence, then, that Odundo found sympathy with some of the internationalist and universalist ideas of Bernard Leach. As Odundo herself stated:

> Coming from a family where, for my dad, travelling had been a part of work, it seemed that Leach was describing a very enriching culture. [...] I thought the philosophy Bernard Leach was advocating, which I understood to be about being engaged in making objects or making art, was sound and relevant.[49]

Leach was a believer in the Bahá'í faith, a syncretic religion dating from the nineteenth century that seeks the realisation of a divine cosmopolitan world order. As Leach himself wrote, Bahá'í promised a unified world via:

> principles of independent investigation, [...] unity, [...] roots in justice, universal education, balance of religion and science, marriage of East and West, recognition of art, of the equality of men and women, the need of a common language, the abolition of both great wealth and great poverty, and, to these ends, of a universal parliament of man [*sic* ...].[50]

The cosmopolitanism of Bahá'í provided Leach with a philosophical and spiritual means of reconciling himself with his own sense of hybridity. Born in Hong Kong, and spending much of his life moving between Britain and Japan (and elsewhere), Leach recognised that Bahá'í offered a rationale for his practice, which 'was inextricably becoming rooted to two hemispheres', and that he considered placed him as 'a courier between East and West'.[51]

In *A Potter's Portfolio*, first published in 1951, and which was then subsequently edited into *The Potter's Challenge*, first published in 1975, Leach sought to expound upon the ability of pottery to communicate universally:

> The pot is the man [*sic*], he a focal point in his race, and it in turn is held together by traditions imbedded in a culture. In our day, the threads have been loosened and a creative mind finds itself alone with the responsibility of discovering its own meaning and pattern out of the warp and weft of all traditions and all cultures. Without achieving integration or wholeness he cannot compass the extended vision and extract from it a true synthesis.[52]

To provide a sense of how this synthesis was achieved, Leach included numerous examples of 'Exemplary Pots' which, aside from a few examples from Ancient Greece, America, and the Middle East, came from East Asia. To introduce these 'Exemplary Pots', Leach included diagrammatic analyses of two Chinese Song dynasty (960–1279) works: a vase and a bottle. The analysis of the vase, reproduced here, divides the form into different ratios, some documenting lines of correlation between the base and the rim, others exploring how compositional spheres exert control over mass and volume. By placing these illustrations before the reproductions of 'Exemplary Pots', Leach was clearly encouraging the reader to apply these ideas across the illustrations, and by extension, to their own practice.

In turning towards Odundo, it would be easy to overstate her connection with Bernard Leach's philosophy. Her relationship to Leach should be regarded as a general, if critical, sense of compatibility; Leach

Analysis of a Song Dynasty Vase by Bernard Leach. (Reproduced by kind permission of Profile Books)

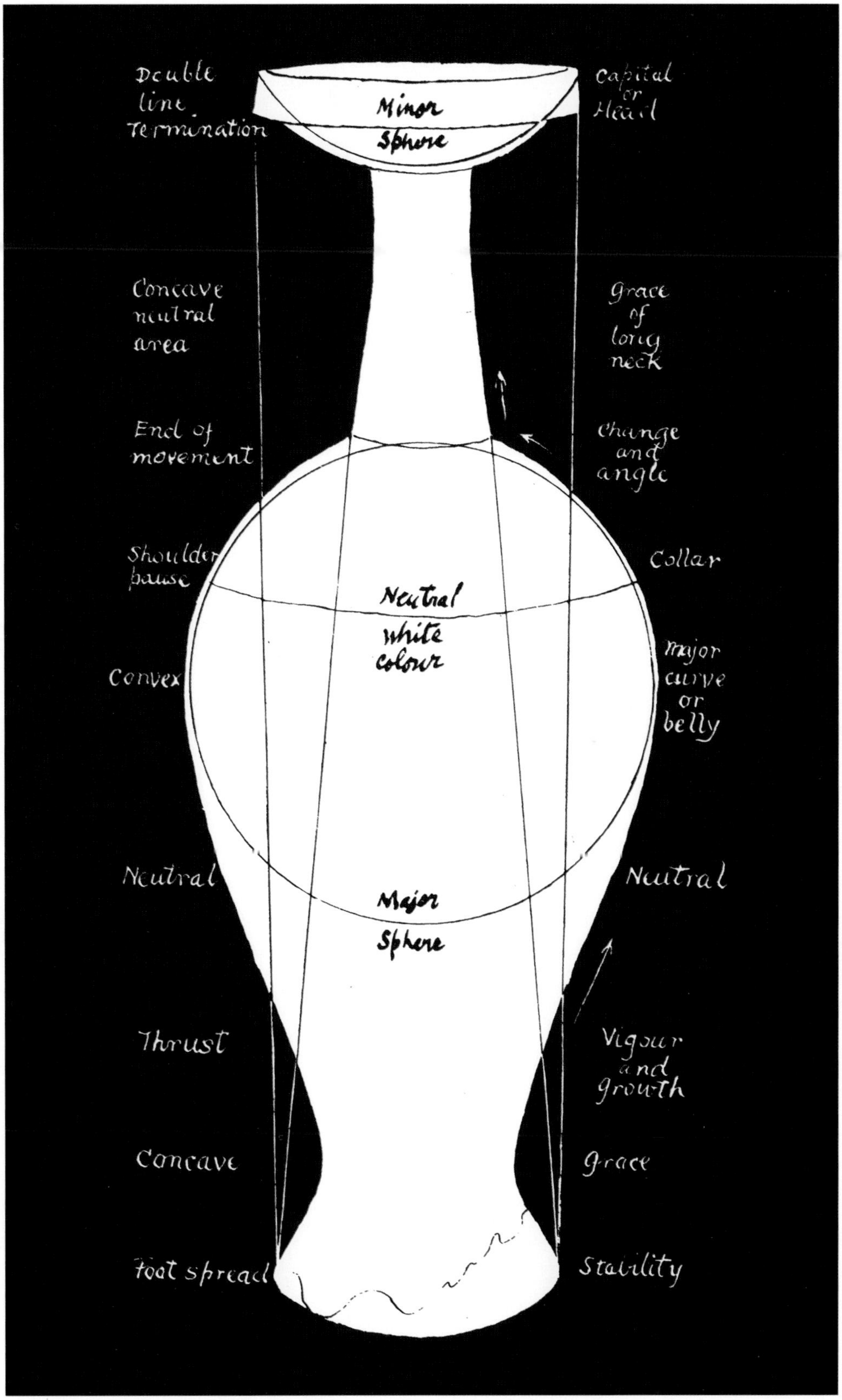

never taught Odundo. Nevertheless, in some of her work from the early 1980s, there is a stylistic fusion of form inspired by Abuja pottery and the black burnished pots of Maria Martinez. In the example reproduced here, Odundo has carved into the top section of the pot, creating a spherical pattern that both alludes to and disguises some of the compositional elements discerned by Leach. She has positioned the lines as being lower than – in parallel with, rather than as actual markers of – the 'major sphere' of the pot. This gives the feeling that the upper and lower sections are exerting pressure on one another, affording the work a dynamic presence despite its apparent simplicity.

The parallels between Leach's diagram and the early examples of Odundo's output as illustrated here may be superficial, but they nevertheless invite a more advanced application of Leach's terms of analysis to Odundo's compositional tendencies. To

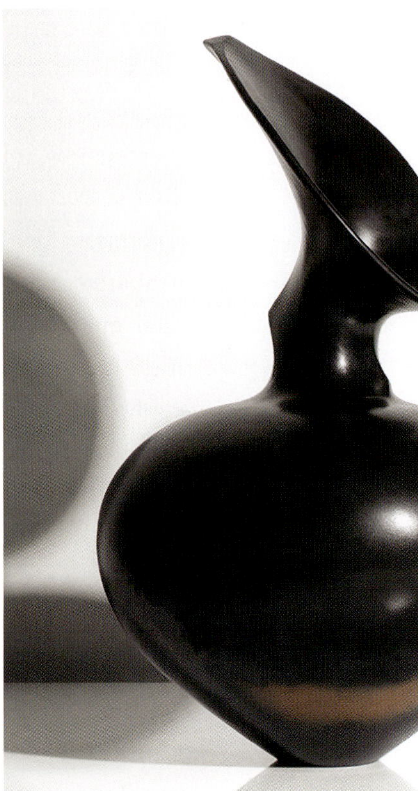

Angled Mixed-Colour Piece (1989).

this end, *Angled Mixed-Colour Piece* (1989) has been subjected to analysis in terms of spheres, arcs, and lines of ratio. Shapes have been applied on top of the image to demarcate the form. The photo has then been removed so that the shapes can be discerned in abstraction and with greater clarity. The pot has then been reintroduced by filling in the shapes so that the relationships between actual space (the body of the pot) and implied space (the way the form sculpts the space around it) can be observed. Finally, the image has been overlaid back on to the original photograph to facilitate dialogue between the two. The results of this process are as follows (the numbers relate to the diagram on page 28):

1. *Major Sphere.*
2. *Minor Sphere.* The minor sphere (the upper section of the pot where the rim is located) is extended and rounded, so much so that the principle of the sphere is almost inverted; the curved line faces outwards, away from the body of the pot, rather than inwards and towards it. The upper part of this line is elongated upwards and away from the body. This gives a dynamic accent to the minor sphere, the effect intensified by the elongated thickening of the exterior rim.
3. *Grace of Long Neck.* A compositional element that Leach problematically referred to as 'neutral', but by which he meant an area that 'may be the link which successfully relates two otherwise ambiguous statements of form'.[53] Here, Odundo utilises this principle to stunning effect through an angular shift, which is also related to the manipulation of lines of termination (see point 6). The neck becomes almost skeletal in its support of the minor sphere, giving the vessel an anthropomorphic sensibility.
4. *Full Convexity.* The point of full convexity is relatively wide, creating an ellipse in the major

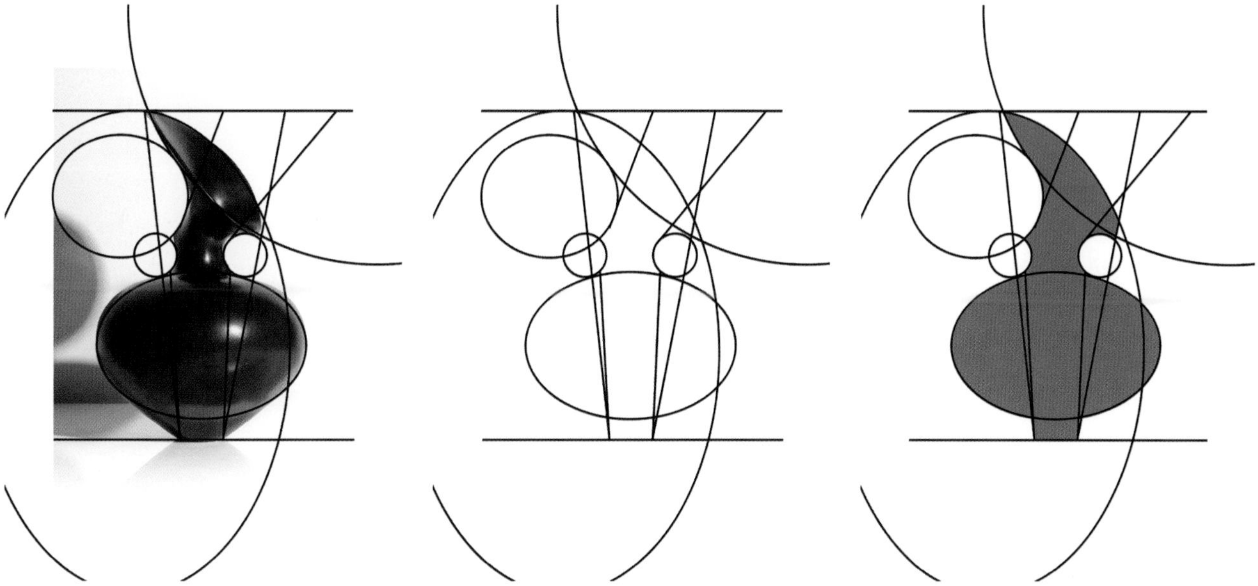

Stages in the analysis of *Angled Mixed-Colour Piece* (1989).

sphere. What could become an awkward form is deftly used by Odundo to balance the major and minor spheres, giving poise to the work.

5. *Thrust*. The narrowness of the base and the elliptical major sphere facilitate a strong degree of incline in the thrust section. This grounds the pot, even as it expansively asserts itself in space from its small base.
6. *Double Line Termination*. In both of the pots that Leach analysed, he described a 'double line termination' in which the curve of the minor sphere at the top is masked by an extended vertical section and extrusion that delineates the lip. Odundo masterfully elongates this double line. By pulling it downward, she resolves the impact of the angular shift in the neck of the pot. In formal terms, this pot really has two necks; a short one from the body to the first line of termination, and then a much longer neck which arcs from the first line to the second line of termination at the very top of the pot. Odundo manipulates these elements so that the 'grace of the long neck' appears where the double line termination might be, and vice versa. Such decisions demonstrate great compositional prowess in producing personal forms. This represents a clear example of Odundo speaking her own language.
7. *Concave Neutral Area*. Leach uses both this phrase and point 3 (grace of long neck) interchangeably. Interestingly, the elongation of the neck by Odundo means that a concave section *is* required as a distinct compositional element. Here, the concave neutral area carves out a circle in space, a shape that guides the eye towards the other circular lines (the major sphere [1]; the top of the minor sphere [2]; the elongated line of termination [6]; the treatment of the neck [3]). The centrality of this area in the overall composition of the pot is clear, especially in the skeletal process drawings used as the basis for this analysis, where the eye is repeatedly drawn to the small central circles. These circles around the neck of the pot have been materialised in many of Odundo's works. Here, they skilfully integrate external space into the internal substance of the composition.

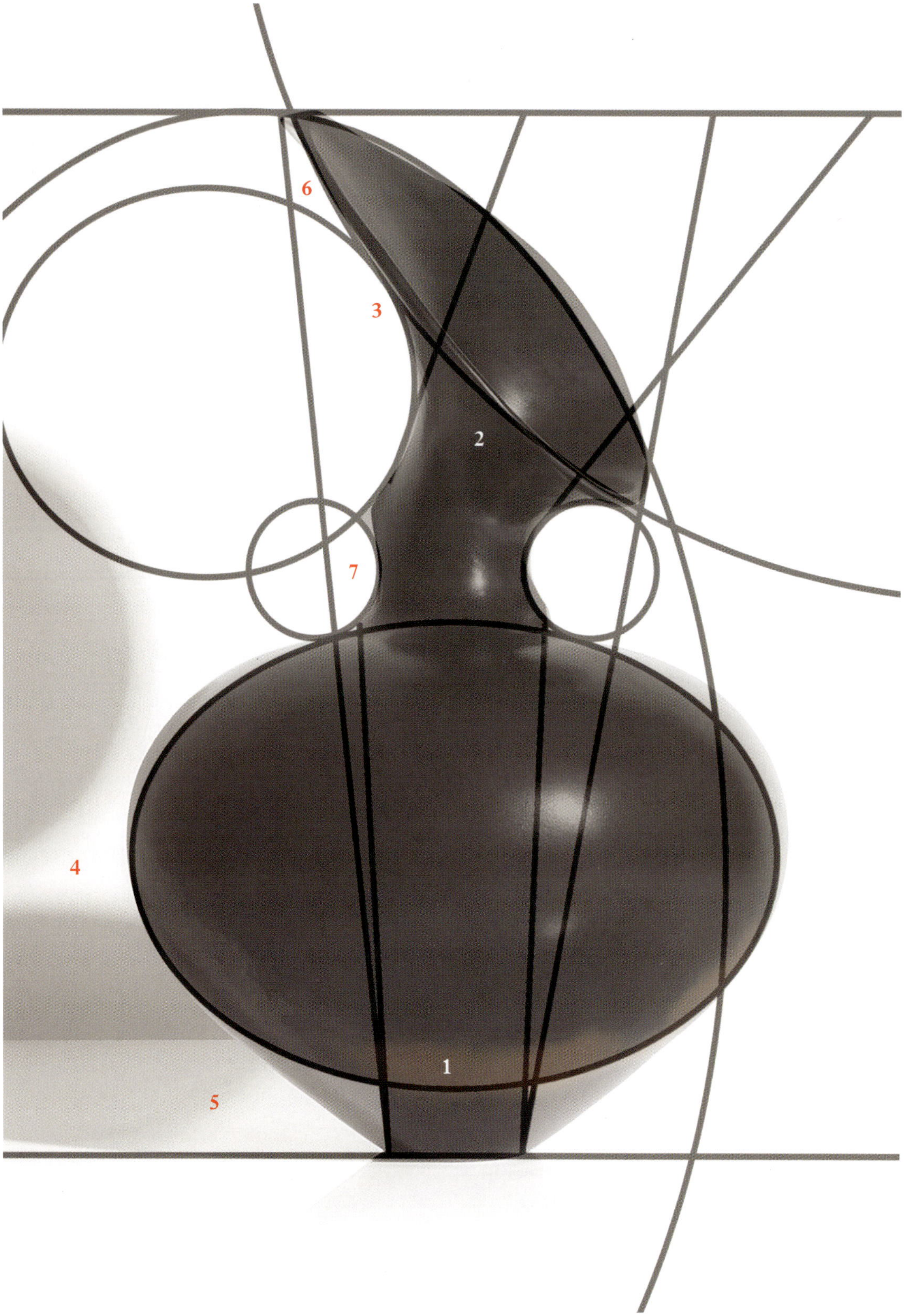

Angled Mixed-Colour Piece (1989) with lines of analysis. The numbers relate to points in the preceding text.

Taken as a whole, this analysis reveals Odundo's technical and aesthetic prowess, how she evinces an astonishing geometry and an imposing composition by creatively utilising the vocabulary of the pot.

Naturally, Odundo, as a visual artist, carefully examines objects. Examining is not the same as simply looking or seeing. Odundo's modes of examination probe beneath the surface to consider the anthropological relationships between civilisations and pottery. In this regard, her time exploring the collections of the Museum of Archaeology and Anthropology whilst studying in Cambridge in the early 1970s was especially formative. As Odundo has recalled:

> These were the first pieces I saw that combined the artistry of surface decoration and form, and I was intrigued, without knowing much about the culture. I am not sure that I really understood what the pots were about or had an interest in the meaning of them. My interest was the forms. I was amazed how clay encompassed objects that were universal.[54]

Tacit recognition of how humanity and clay have been wedged together has led to many of her pots exhibiting a trace of anthropomorphism. In *Angled Mixed-Colour Piece*, for instance, the minor sphere is akin to a head, supported – quite literally – by the neck of the pot. The full convexity – more commonly known as the 'belly' – adds to the sense of anthropomorphism, standing as it does on its base, or 'foot'. Yet, even in symmetrical works, such as '*Untitled*': *Mixed Colour Black Symmetrical Piece* (1989) and '*Untitled*' (1991), there is a sense of grace and stateliness suggestive of anthropomorphism. The elongated neck of '*Untitled*': *Mixed Colour Black Symmetrical Piece* is spinal, the curvature towards the rim suggestive of a neck, and the rim itself opening to a trumpet-like mouth. Such a composition draws attention to the interiority of the pot and its release into the exterior world, as though the pot were speaking out loud. The protruding additions to '*Untitled*' (1991) draw attention to the pot's shoulders. They read as abstracted adornments, akin to braided hair, with the elongated neck evocative of a headdress.

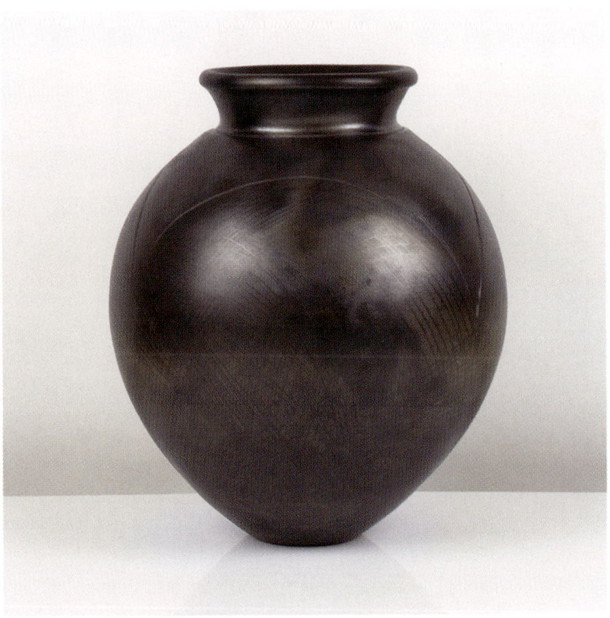

Early Vessel (c. 1980).

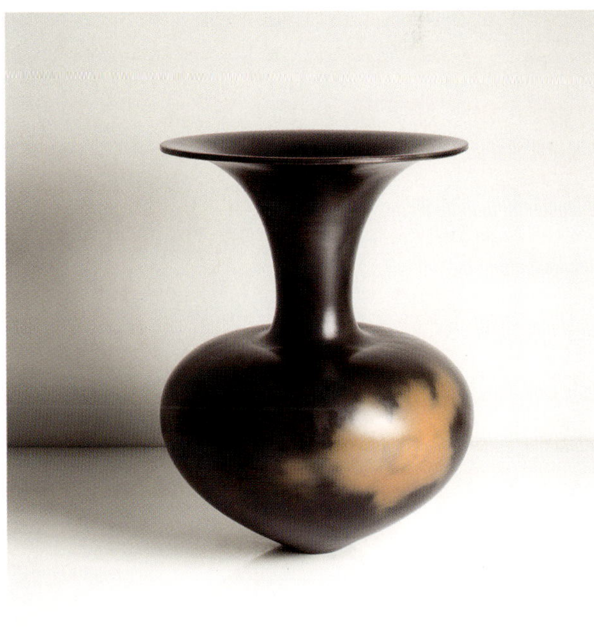

'*Untitled*': *Mixed Colour Black Symmetrical Piece* (1989).

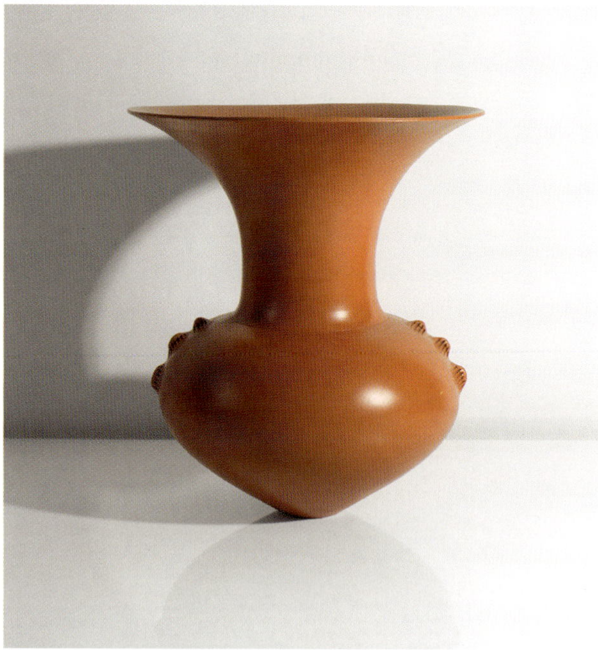

'*Untitled*' (1991).

Odundo's asymmetrical pots exhibit similar anthropomorphic qualities. The horn-like mouth of '*Untitled*' (1991) seems to shout, whilst the periscopic '*Untitled*' (1998) peers intently, keenly observing what is taking place around it. In both pots there is acute interaction between interior and exterior; a sense of looking, listening, and speaking. About what? Odundo's works are untitled for a reason. As described earlier, moving from the personal to the universal and back to the personal requires all participants to make meaning for themselves. To give a pot a title is to circumscribe its resonance and specify its applicability; whilst few things are truly universal, we are all capable of finding meaning in an object, even if we disagree as to what it is. To me, Odundo's work speaks of skill (her ability to evince commanding forms), ritual (the anthropological function of pottery), travel, trade, migration, and globalisation (Odundo's pan-global citation of form), the effects of imperialism, histories of enslavement, racism, and perpetual injustice (pan-global aesthetics as reflective of forced travel and migration), resistance, integrity, and equality (Odundo carving out space for her own expression). No wonder critics have sought to position Odundo as a black female artist whose work has created new spaces for non-patriarchal, global majority, expression. Yet, this is only one of the ways in which her work can be interpreted. Odundo makes striking pots; what they come to mean is out of her hands.

How, then, can Odundo's work be conceptualised without circumscribing it? I consider her pots to be visual forms of glossolalia: unintelligible utterances, often spoken under religious excitation (Chambers Dictionary). Her pots are unintelligible in the sense that their meanings are plural. Her work does not communicate a single intention, message, or thought. Neither are they straightforward documents of biography, travel, being African, black, a female artist, living in Britain, though her achievements have certainly demanded a long overdue critical space for the discussion of structural inequalities. Her language is more primordial than this, however. Her visual references are ahistorical and transnational, lying beyond the constraints of colonial English; indeed, of any language.

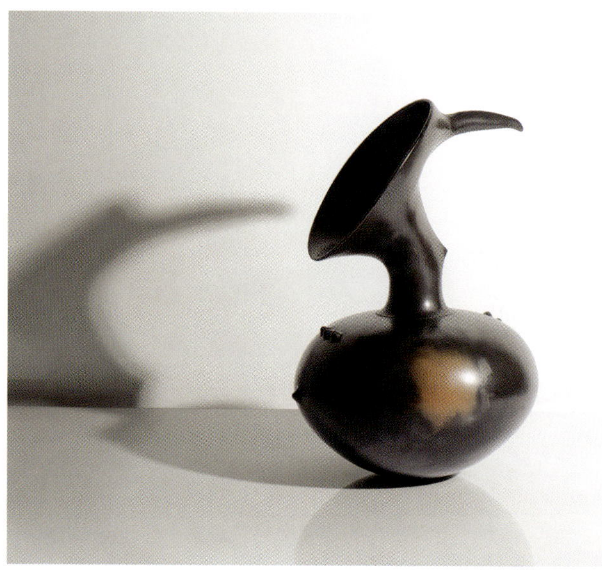

'*Untitled*' (1991).

As Odundo asserted in the quotation that opened this chapter, 'words come second'.

Her pots can also be considered as visual glossolalia because they arise from an understanding of the role of ceramics in rites and ceremonies across the world and throughout history. In her research concerning anthropomorphic pots in Africa, Odundo concluded that pots can be 'about the spirit without being spiritual.'[55] She further explained that:

> They were about celebration, appeasement and pleasing. They were the vessels from which the living partook and shared the passage of the dead person to continue with life among the ancestors; they were the chalices and fountains that offered sustenance for those rejuvenation ceremonies and the vessels that offered the gods the sacrifice.[56]

Such ongoing significance to rites of passage – as exemplified in *Millennium Jug* – afford pottery a resonance denied to other plastic arts like painting and sculpture. Pottery is bound to the mystery of liminality and change. As Odundo later asserted:

> I believe that vessels have a magical capacity and can amaze and astonish. They are the most important and fundamental objects on this planet and can be found in every society, and in every museum, on earth.[57]

Thus, her pots speak of the fundamental relationships between humans, the present and the past, the past and the future, the earthly, the divine, the living, and the dead. As glossolalia, they speak a visual language beyond any culturally marked system of meaning.

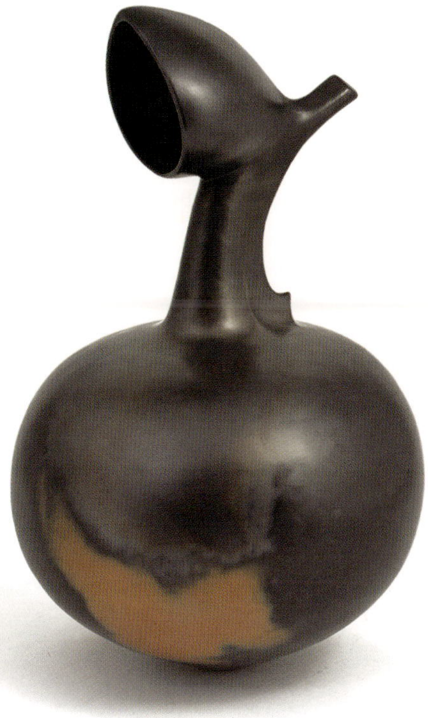

■ *'Untitled'* (1998).

Many British studio ceramicists in the latter half of the twentieth century patently rejected Bernard Leach's ideals. Critical writing from the period tells us that it was Lucie Rie and Hans Coper who were the pioneers, releasing artists from the quagmire of the doctrinal brown pots of Anglo-Orientalism. Odundo's work subtly challenges this narrative. She has paralleled Leach's search for universality whilst eschewing the dogmatic and restrictive. Her pots are minimally pure but not puritanical, deeply personal but openly universal. They are liminal: then and now, here and there. As visual glossolalia, they may speak in tongues, but in doing so, they are empowered to speak to us all.

Tina Vlassopulos Space for Imagining

> **Liminal:** relating to a transitional or initial stage of a process; occupying a position at, or on both sides of, a boundary or threshold (origin: late 19th century: from Latin, *limen, limin* – 'threshold').
>
> (*Oxford English Dictionary, 3rd edition*)
>
> Liminal entities are neither here nor there; they are betwixt and between the positions assigned and arrayed by law, custom, convention, and ceremonial. As such, their ambiguous and indeterminate attributes are expressed by a rich variety of symbols in the many societies that ritualize social and cultural transitions.[58]
>
> Just as when tribesmen make masks, disguise themselves as monsters, heap up disparate ritual symbols, invert or parody profane reality in myths and folk-tales, so do the genres of industrial leisure, the theatre, poetry, novel, ballet, film, sport, rock music, classical music, art, pop art, and so on, *play* with the factors of culture, sometimes assembling them in random, grotesque, improbable, surprising, shocking, usually experimental

> combinations. But they do this in a much more complicated way than in the liminality of tribal initiations.[59]
>
> (*Victor Turner*)
>
> Liminal rituals are transformations, permanently changing who people are. Liminoid rituals, effecting a temporary change – sometimes nothing more than a brief communitas [temporary community] experience or a several-hours-long playing of a role – are transportations. In a transportation, one enters into the experience, is 'moved' or 'touched' (apt metaphors), and is then dropped off about where she or he entered.[60]
>
> (*Richard Schechner*)

In anthropology, liminal rituals capture and express moments of change via a strong sense of being 'in-between'. For example, a marriage ceremony is a liminal event: individuals enter the ceremony as singletons and leave as a married couple. To enable this change to be publicly marked, the ceremony uses special places, symbols, and people. In Christian traditions, for instance, there is the 'giving away' of the bride, the public sharing of vows, the exchanging of rings, and the pronouncement of a joining in union. Such ceremonies take the bride and groom out of their everyday life and temporarily places them in a special setting, enabling their transitional status to be managed through the structure of the ceremony. At the end of the ceremony, the couple can resume their lives, the change in status now complete. A liminal event, therefore, is fundamentally concerned with addressing the 'in-between' modalities of life experience. Indeed, liminal events are everywhere: from birthday celebrations to funeral services, baby showers to court appearances.

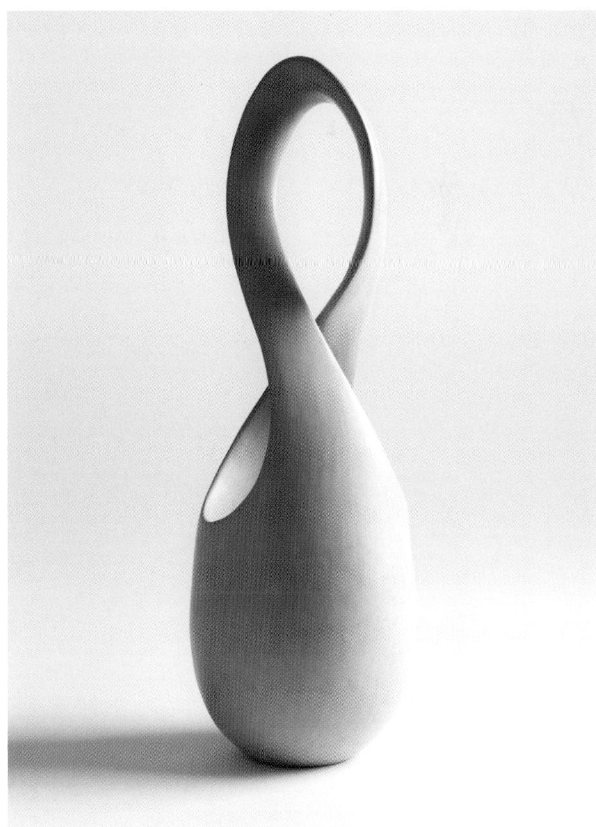

■ *Loop* (2022).

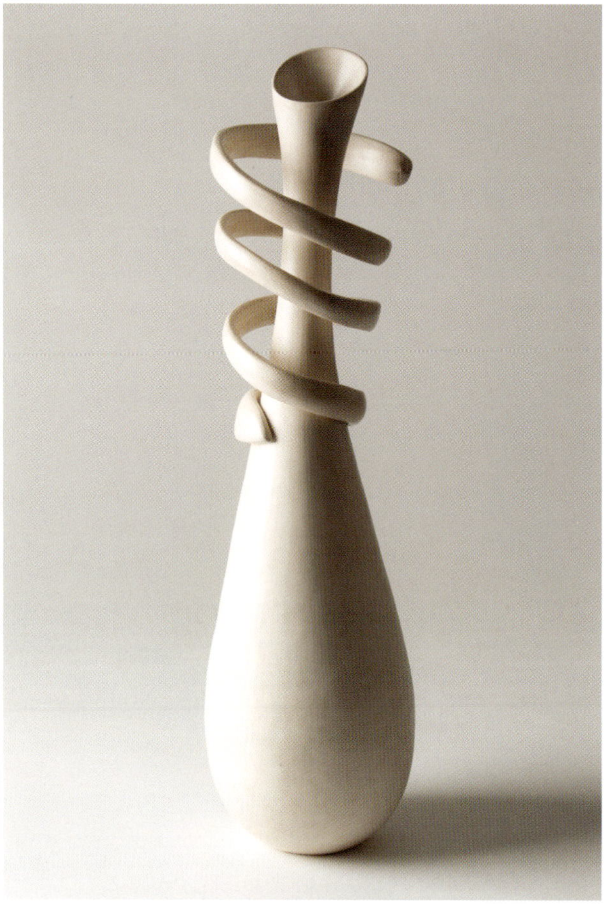

Momentum (2014).

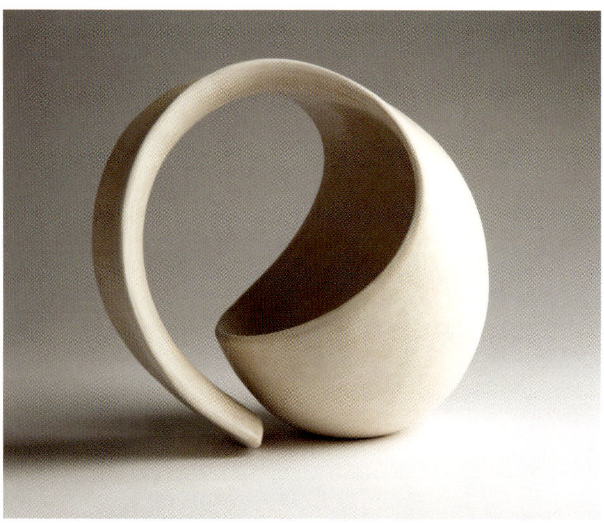

Toumba (2019).

The anthropologist Victor Turner also observed that some contemporary events, such as theatre and dance performances, were 'liminoid'; that is, facilitated a temporary rather than permanent transition and change in status. How? Not unlike a marriage ceremony, theatre performances take place in special spaces (theatres), use special symbols (props and costumes), and people (actors). Taken out of their everyday lives, audiences watch a performance to experience emotion cathartically without recourse to the real-life trigger. At the end of the performance, the audience leaves the auditorium to resume their normal lives. Any change in status was temporary.

I begin this analysis of the work of Tina Vlassopulos with a discussion of liminality and the liminoid for three reasons. Firstly, attendance at performances of music, classical ballet and contemporary dance afford Vlassopulos the mental space to create. Experiencing such liminoid events provides the artist with the freedom to think creatively, to enter a 'different head space' and formulate ideas. Although these performances are not the literal stimulus for her work – her sculptures are not representative of specific productions or performers – they nevertheless enable her to become fully present in the moment, released from all other preoccupations. Secondly, her work expresses a kind of ceramic liminality. Vlassopulos utilises the full expressive capacity and elasticity of ceramic as a medium to create forms that shift between conceptions of the pot, the vessel, and sculpture (as defined in the introduction). To categorise her work within only one of these forms would be to diminish its complexity. It exists betwixt and between categories. Her work – like many artists, in fact – is liminal in form. Thirdly, this elastic use of form dynamically charges the space around each work. In turn, this highlights how the appreciation of her ceramics – and by extension any form of art – requires entrance into a liminoid frame of aesthetic contemplation. To be moved by a work of art is to allow oneself to be both in, and apart from, the everyday stuff of life. Nowhere is this clearer than in ceramics, where pots can be both a practical part of the daily routine and a contemplative object.

Vlassopulos often develops her forms from the nominal shape of a pot, where the idea of spatial containment (which could easily be tied to a utilitarian pot if it were treated differently) is the fundamental generative structure. Once this base has been hand-built, however, the composition is extended into a wider spatial exploration of containment and release. This might be produced through the extension of the sides of the 'pot' section to form an architectural upper plane, as is the case with *Loop* (2022). This extension affords the work a sculptural presence, turning it into a sculptural pot. Elsewhere, in pieces such as *Momentum* (2014), the vase form is manipulated to suggest movement, the spiral spring-like addition akin to ribbons spun through the air, or arms stabilising a twirling body. Equally, the curved line of *Toumba* (2019) might refer to a body in motion, the foot of the sculptural pot evocative of the lower body, which then extends into an elegant flourish of a rounded torso ('*toumba*' means 'somersault' in Greek). Alternatively, the title might refer to the northern Greek Iron Age mound in the Toumba district of Thessaloniki in Greece, where excavations have unearthed important architectural relics and Bronze Age artefacts. *Toumba* might thus be a stylistic representation of how the earth's skin protectively shelters relics for later archaeological discovery. Vlassopulos deliberately chooses titles with multiple possible meanings.

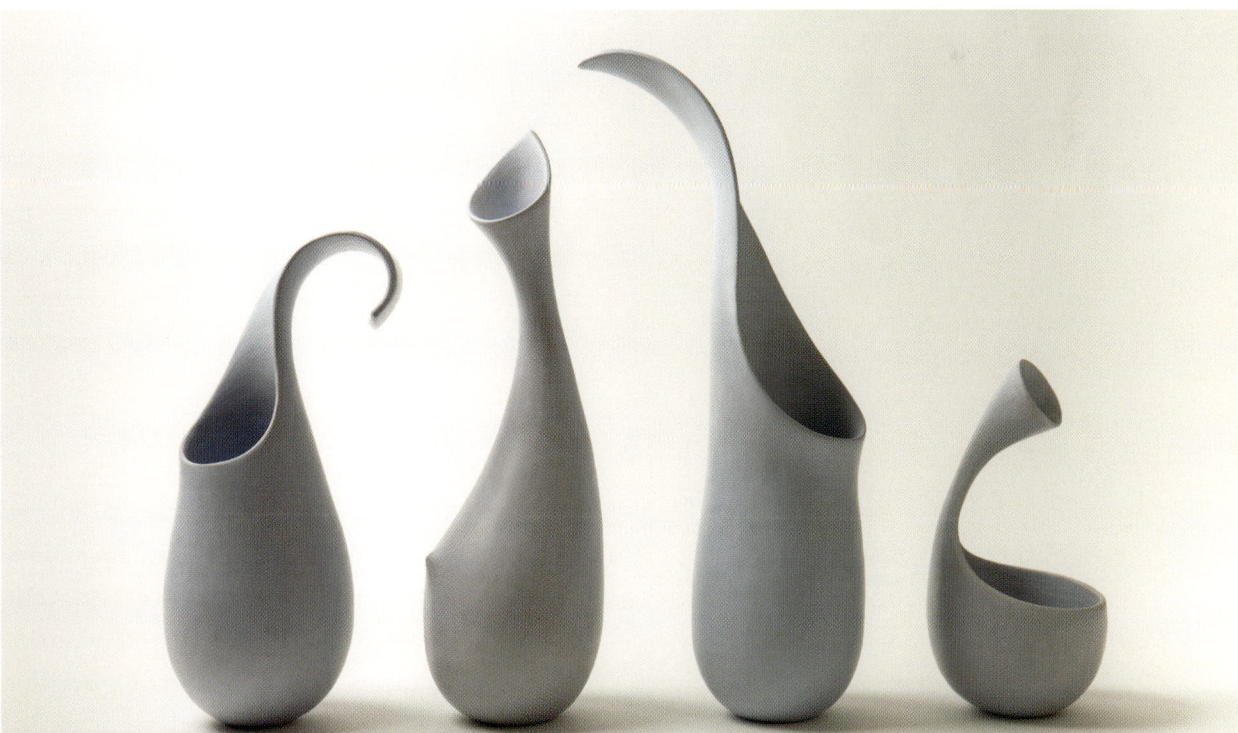

Blue Note (2015).

Compositional relationships between opened and closed spaces, elongated blades, and opening funnels, take on greatest resonance when observed as a group. In such installations, the spaces between works are activated as an integral part of the composition. For example, *Blue Note* (2015) is constituted by four forms – three sculptural pots and a sculpture. When taken together, they produce a complex multidirectional visual rhythm. If approaching the work from left to right (though it could easily be right to left), and following the accompanying silhouette diagram, the opening of the 'pot' section in the left-hand form (a vessel) pulls the eye leftward and downward, which is then offset by the curling blade of the upper section of the work, taking the eye upward and rightward. The impact of the curved blade of this upper section is caught in the dot of the lower body of the next form (a sculpture), its funnelled neck pushing the eye upwards again to the angled rim and on to the next form. The elongated blade of the third form dramatically takes the eye down to the base, the 'pot-like' opening serving to slow down the visual rhythm and ground the eye. Emerging from the base, the eye moves to the final right-hand form in the composition, which also gathers the eye at the base before projecting it out of a funnel-like top section towards the right. It is the interplay between high and low, and the speed of elongation and the slowness of containment, that initiates a visual dynamic akin to a musical composition. Hence the title, *Blue Note*, which is an allusion to the American jazz record label of the same name. In this sense, the sculptural elements can be construed as alluding to rhythm, pitch (the anchoring of bass lines and the airy lyricism of top notes), and instrumentation. As evidenced in the diagram that features only the contours of my perception of this group, the space between forms is activated as a kind of diminuendo (rather than a silence or empty space) to achieve tonal variation. As a consequence, space is used liminally: there is nothing materially present in the gaps between each work, and yet it plays an active part in our comprehension of the relationships between forms. In sculptural terms, space is both 'there' and 'not there'.

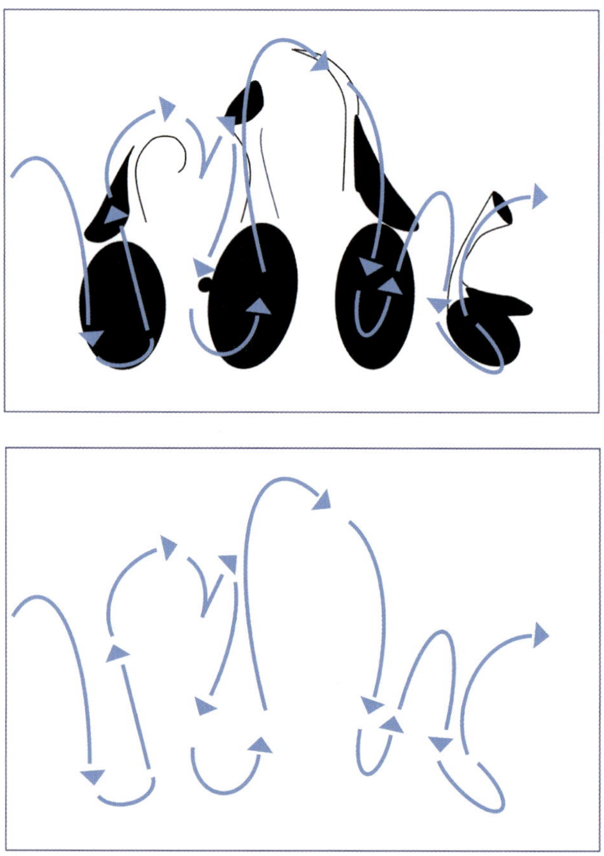

The author's perception of the visual flow across *Blue Note*, with silhouettes (left) and in isolation (right).

Other groupings are even more complex. *Composition I* (2022) is a series of solid sculptures developed from a relatively constrained series of motifs: 'S' shapes, inverted 'S' shapes, circles, implied circles, inward curves, and outward curves. Focusing on the lower sections for the purpose of this analysis, it can be discerned how each work rises from the ground utilising 'S' and 'Inverted S' motifs. When each motif is viewed in isolation, they can be seen to develop asymmetrically but in balance. The shapes

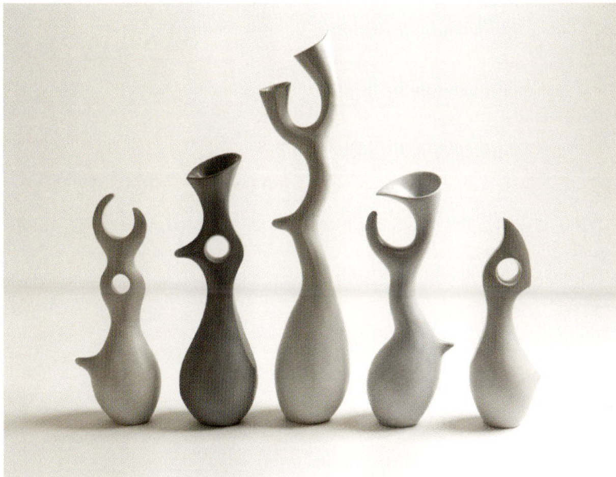

Composition I (2022).

are compressed to the exterior edges of the group, becoming elongated as they move towards the centre, and then weakening again as they move towards the opposite extremity. This produces an interlocking rhythm that affords the composition a spatial musicality. Although the approach of Vlassopulos is not strictly concerned with geometry, this developmental treatment of line nevertheless evokes Bridget Riley's exploration of the curve, which is made to expand and contract in the service of a pulsating image. *Composition I,* being a three-dimensional work, harnesses line to both sculpt material and carve different planes of space. The dynamism this produces is life-affirming, expressing the joys of music, dance, even athleticism.

Although it is not intended to be obviously figurative, the forms in *Composition I* could easily be construed as bodies aligned in space. Anthropomorphism might perhaps be implied in *Composition I,* but in the installation *Conversations with Friends,* exhibited at *Collect Open* in the Saatchi Gallery, London in 2019, it was self-evidently the subject. *Conversations with Friends* consisted of fourteen works, each named after, and somehow representing, one of the artist's close friends. Laid out at regular intervals like guests seated at a dining table, the installation drew attention to the domestic associations of clay, whilst reframing utility as a question of sculptural expression rather than practicality in enabling consumption. For instance, the central sculpture of *Portrait of Sophie* (2019) exhibits the contours of a vase but has no opening at the top: it cannot hold anything other than implied meaning. The rings placed around the centre of this form could almost be folded arms, as though it were an abstracted sculpture of Sophie herself looking down on the events below. Are the six smaller forms laid out in a row her children? Is she admiring them proudly, or is she exasperated? Are they different facets of her life laid out in an apparently orderly fashion? Or are

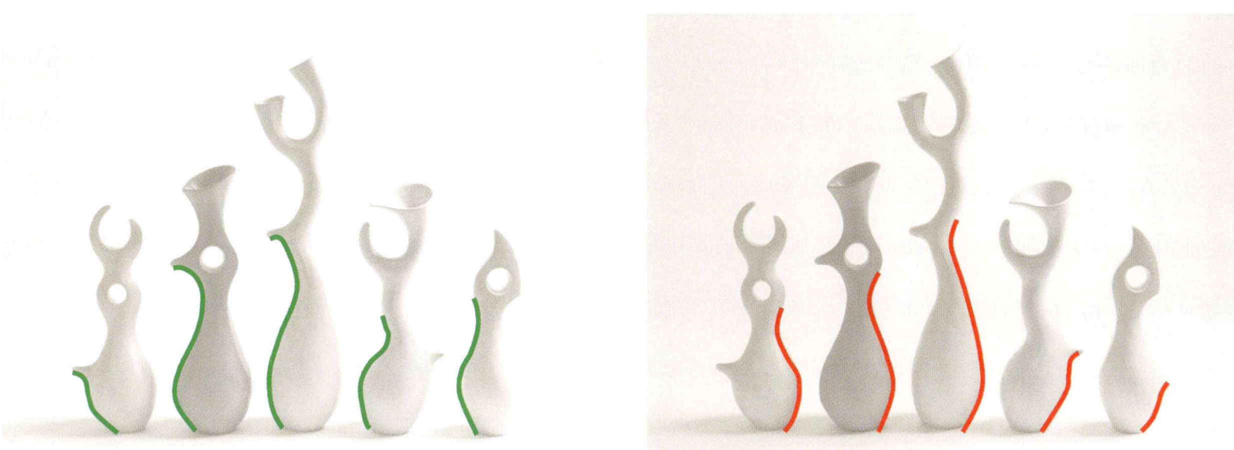

The development of 'inverted S' (left) and 'S' (right) motifs in *Composition I* (2022).

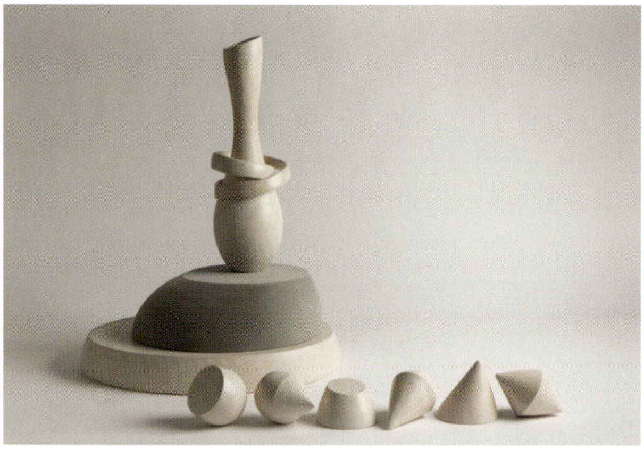

Portrait of Sophie (2019).

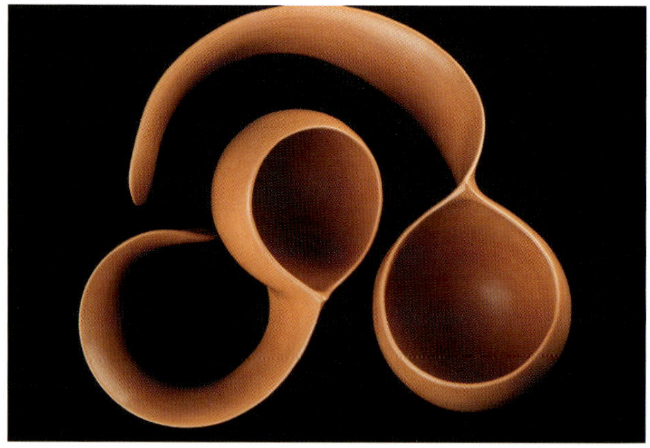

Embrace (1995).

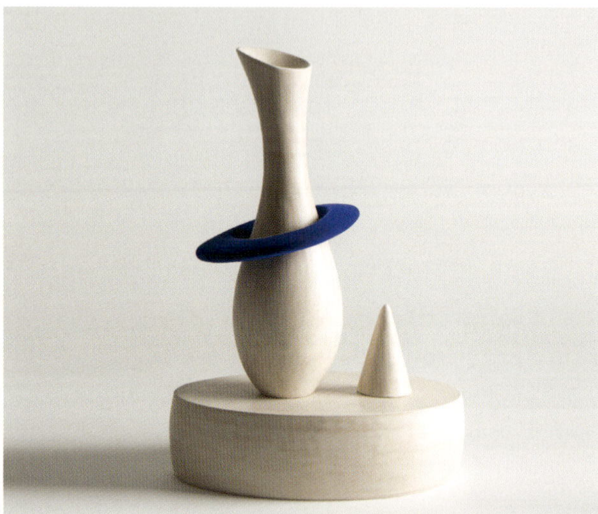

You know who (2020).

they secrets shared between the artist and her friend during their many years of friendship? As outsiders, we will never know. It would be impolite to eavesdrop on *Conversations with Friends* too closely.

A similar mystery hangs over a later portrait piece not included in the 2019 installation, *You know who* (2020). The implication of the title is that the person depicted is so obvious that it can be left unsaid. Yet, we, as the audience, do not know 'who'. One might speculate that it represents the artist herself: the central vase-like sculpture reading as a figure who, occupying their own space, contemplates a conical form in front of them. Is this Vlassopulos creating work in her studio? The central sculpture bears a ceramic disc covered with blue flocking, adding a different tactility to the smoothness of the clay surface. The significance of this is, again, unclear. Is it a neckerchief, an allusion to the favourite colour of the person represented? Or is it allegorical of some kind of state of mind, perhaps one that is freed to create? Only 'you know who' actually knows.

Whilst all this might leave audiences puzzling around intention, openness of meaning is precisely what makes Vlassopulos's work liminoid. Her forms are developed from the vocabularies of pottery, but they present as intriguingly ambiguous works. They exist in a kind of twilight: between the pot and sculpture, and thus the everyday and the realm of aesthetic contemplation. In this sense, the contexts in which Vlassopulos develops her work – the liminoid spaces of the theatre and concert auditorium – is imbued in each piece and resurfaces in the viewer. As spectators, we are positioned in a state of free play, assembling clues that might evidence our own understanding of what is being portrayed. Like the intervals between Vlassopulos's forms when arranged in pairs or in series, the spaces between people are also capable of being activated and energised by her work. Vlassopulos acknowledges this by leaving space for us to imagine.

Julian King-Salter Twists and Turns

The work of Julian King-Salter challenges and surprises. A largely self-taught potter – a friend showed him how to coil a pot when he was twelve – he has developed an individual and highly intuitive approach to form and surface. He began his career in 1983, setting up a studio in West Wales, before moving to Australia in 1999. After emigrating, King-Salter waited some ten years to make his first body of work (in the pottery of his son's high school). It was not until 2018, some nine years after, that he finally set up his own studio in South-east Queensland and recommenced serious production. He subsequently returned to Britain in 2020, establishing a new studio in the Staffordshire Moors, though his work is not concerned with the abstraction of landscape. His pots are more concerned with pots: how form is emergent, how intuition guides the application of glaze, and how the process of firing affords experimentation.

Perhaps surprisingly given the above, King-Salter is drawn to some of Bernard Leach's thoughts on form, specifically the vertical ratios between base, neck, body, and rim. As Leach wrote:

> The basic process of composition in pottery, as in other forms of art, appears to depend upon an intuitive perception of the way in which similar and dissimilar elements can be coordinated into a new whole. [...] Repetition and contrast, symmetry and asymmetry, major and minor, dark against light, convex and concave – these and many other dualisms have to be resolved in every pot by the catalytic effect of neutrals. By a neutral I mean a line, shape or color in which opposites have already come to an equilibrium.[61]

The essential qualities of a pot that Leach alludes to here could easily describe a work by King-Salter. Yet, the aesthetic of his work is a far cry from the Anglo-Orientalism of Leach. Although he may utilise some of these aspects in his work, King-Salter deploys them in the service of dynamic forms that evince a strong sense of movement. The analysis of

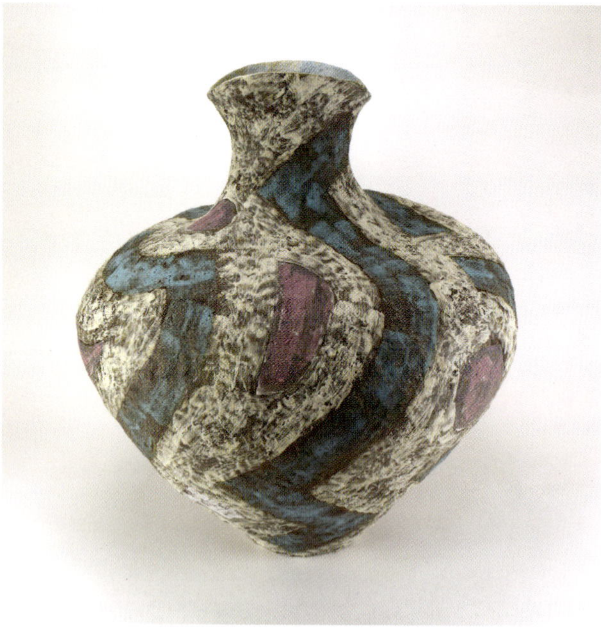

Large full eye top pot (2022).

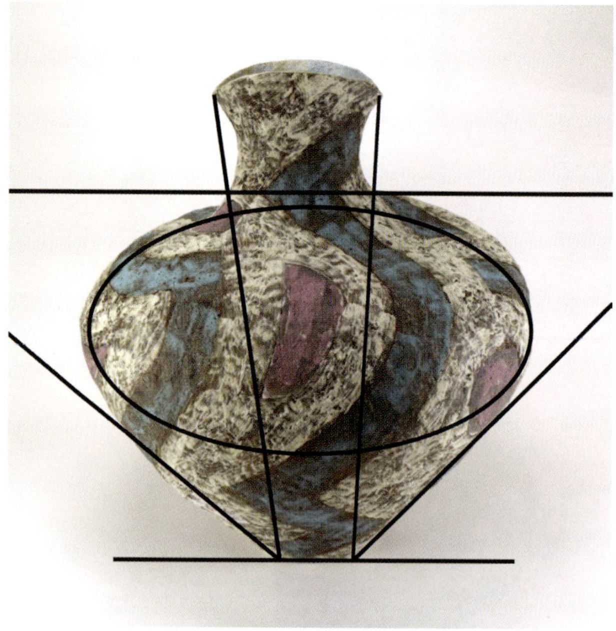

Large full eye top pot (2022) with lines of composition.

two of King-Salter's works using Leach's own observations of pot form (from the diagram on page 25) will illustrate how lines are never 'neutral'.

Large full eye top pot (2022) affords a pleasing sense of symmetry. The central compositional column expands from the base through the neck and up to the rim. This emergence is accentuated by the central major sphere, which is compressed so that the major curve of the belly of the pot extends outwards. The neck concaves inwards, providing counterpoint to the compression of the major sphere, but which also elongates the neck to provide grace and stature, an effect further accented by the curvature of the rim. What is distinctive – and stands as a quite radical departure from Leach – is how the application of glaze marks is informed by, but also departs from, the form. It might be expected, for example, that vertical marks would be utilised to draw attention to the compression of the major sphere or the elongated neck, uniting form with surface. However, King-Salter utilises a very personal and innovative vocabulary, breaking the pot into sections with thick vertical azure lines that accentuate the curve of the form via a series of loose zigzags. These lines draw attention to the major sphere, but they do so in a way that is surprising and arresting, providing a sense of flow. The visual texture of the mottled grey stone-like base seems to move down the form, the dark pink accents rotating across the major sphere at a vertical angle to animate it. As a consequence of these decisions, the composition of the pot dynamically moves between sculpture and drawing, between a conventional rounded pot and an abstracted painting.

In contrast, *Duet of pots* (2009) alters the relationship between base, neck, and rim so that the two pots tilt. As before, the central compositional column expands as it moves up the pot, but the inclusion of two major spheres provides King-Salter with room for greater sculptural expression. The curves of the pot have been developed into expressive 'S' shapes which, on the right-hand sides as shown here, are interrupted by a concave semi-circle, or a 'bump' produced by the intersection of the spheres. These decisions animate not only the pots but also the

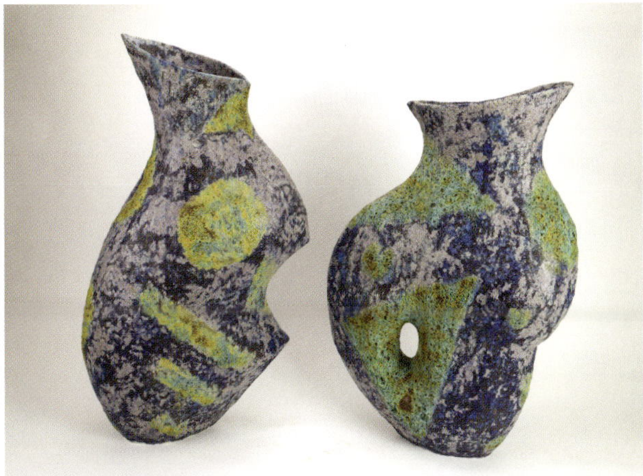

■ *Duet of pots* (2009).

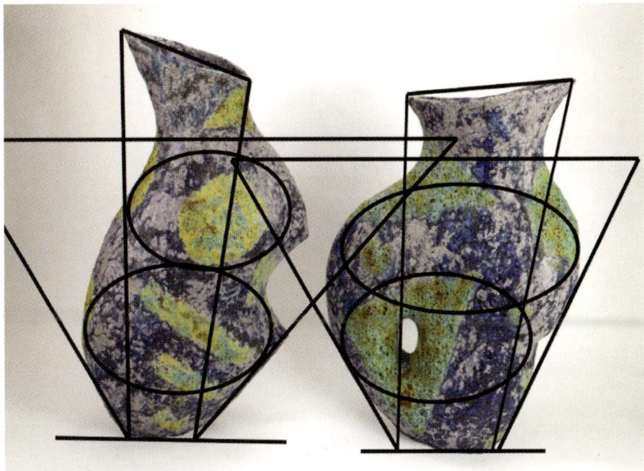

■ *Duet of pots* (2009) with lines of composition.

spaces between them, carving an hourglass-like silhouette into space that cements their relationship as a pair. Glaze subtly reinforces these compositional decisions; circles and triangles are located across the centre of some major spheres, whilst others are modulated by diagonal strokes, or the placement of shapes to their extremities.

Critics may feel that King-Salter's approach produces forms that lack the presence of, say, the smooth and stately pots of Magdalene Odundo, or the dynamic interplay between form and surface that typifies the work of Elizabeth Fritsch. However, such comparisons are unhelpful. Although King-Salter explores some of the same conceptual territory as these artists, his response to the problem of form is uniquely his. To put it another way, nobody makes pots like King-Salter. He exudes a freedom that is possible only by eschewing advanced formal training, yet his self-imposed rigour and relentless desire to discover new terrains emerges only from a lifetime of working and a strong technical understanding. Art school training, it might be surmised, would have been detrimental to his approach.

King-Salter's output is diverse, even though his forms arise from the development of specific techniques and formal ideas that are used repeatedly. To this end, he often works in series, producing four or five works that investigate a particular creative impulse. From this, certain groupings or pairings will emerge. Sometimes, as with *Two-sided diptych* (1998) and *Two-sided diptych* (2019), pots from a series 'find' each other and make more sense as a pairing. For instance, the waiving lines of *Two-sided diptych* (1998) repeat symmetrically and asymmetrically. Their appearance at shared and divergent angles is evidence of how King-Salter's exploration of the curvature of form – and its augmentation through surface marks – was predetermined as a series, yet spontaneous in the peculiarity of its iteration. Mirroring resolves these two works into a pair, which also activates the space between them as an important fixing rhythm. *Two-sided diptych* (2019) suggests a similar concern, this time with triangular 'teeth' slowing down the ability of the eye to read and process form, a tempo that is contrary to the rapidity of the adjacent curves to the exterior. The space between the two pots is again significant, the triangles producing spatial rhomboids that serve to anchor the composition. Yet, once they are applied as glaze, the triangles pick up speed again, vaulting the eye from one side of the work to the other. It is in the precise interplay between form and surface that the dynamic power of King-Salter's works is to be found.

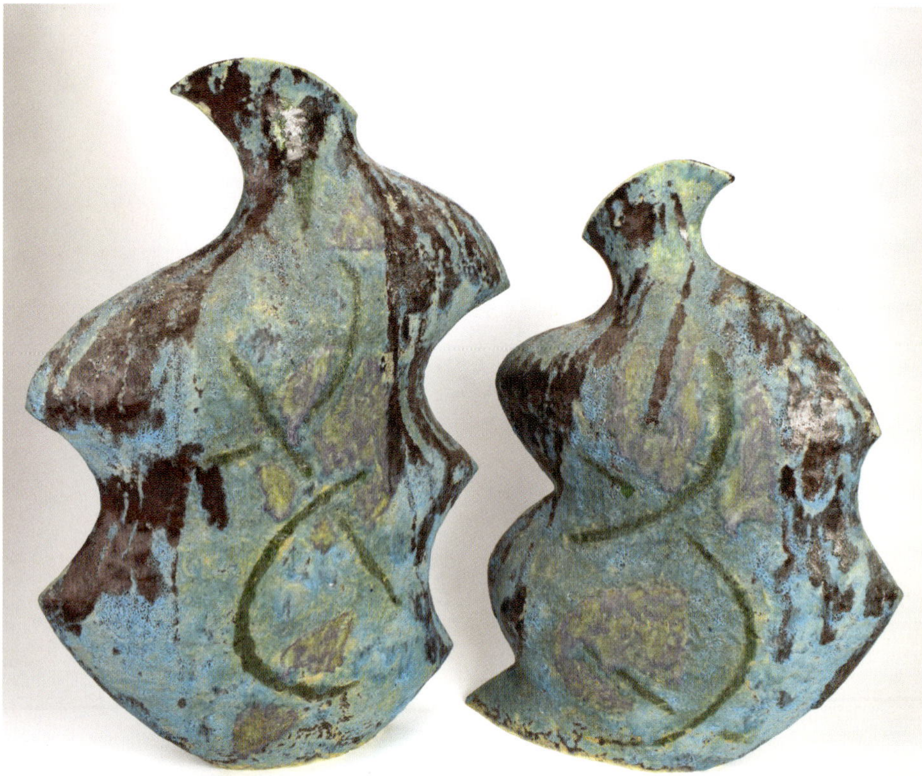

Two-sided diptych (1998).

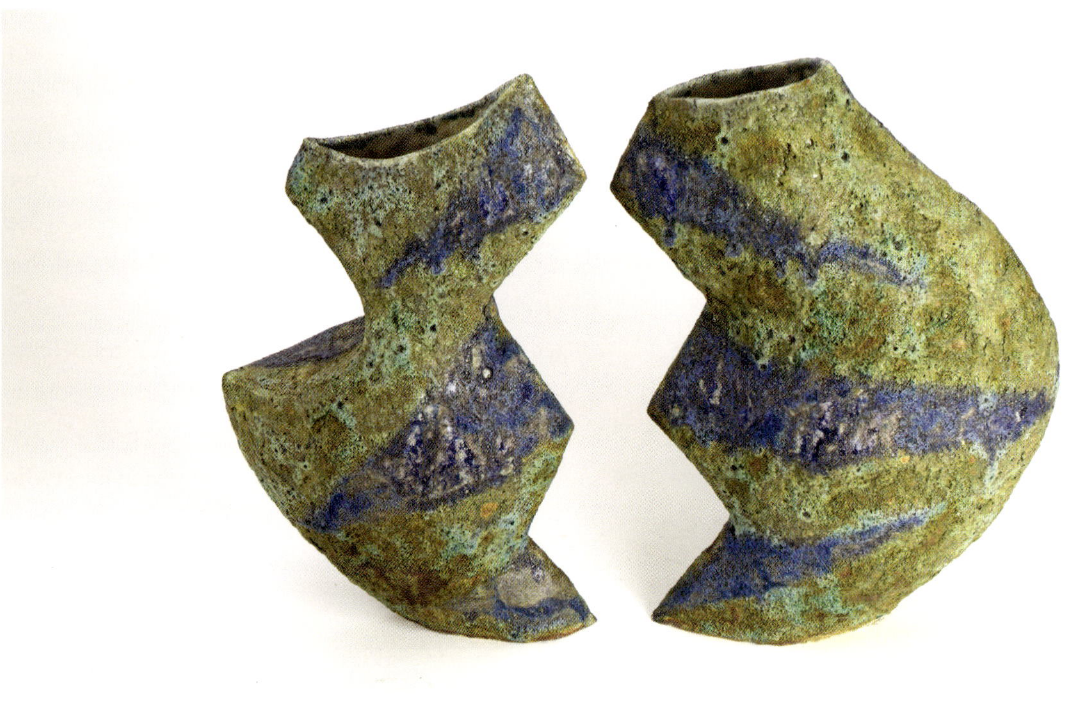

Two-sided diptych (2019).

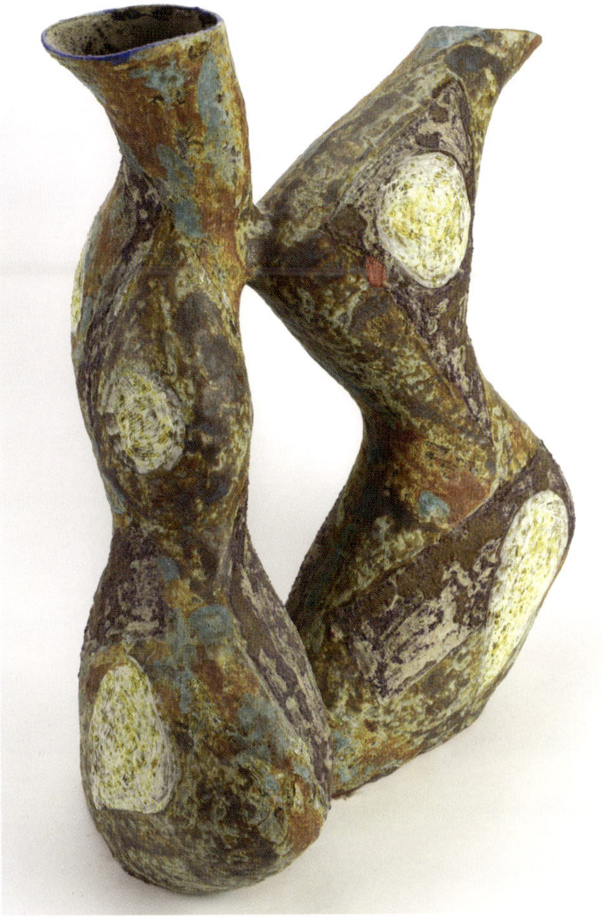

Dancing pot (1990).

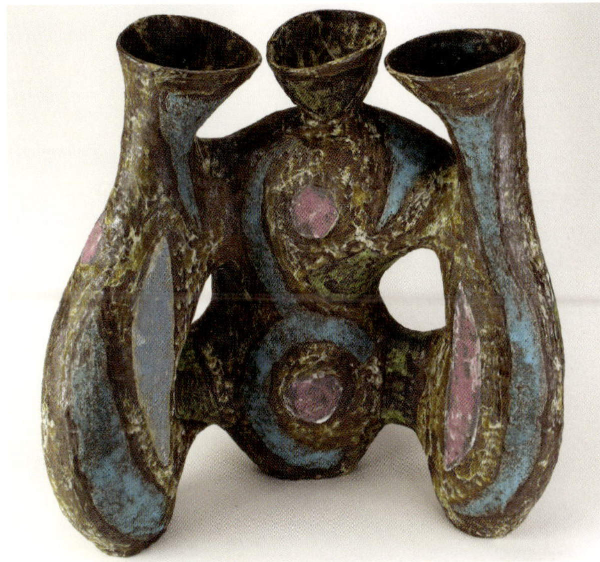

Hugging pot (2022).

Other pots might begin as individual pieces, but as they evolve, demand to be merged. *Dancing pot* (1990), for example, consists of two leg-like pots that are fused at the top and bottom. The work necessitates scrutiny from all directions like a piece of sculpture, the central space dynamically transforming the relationships between sections of the pot body. The central space is far from 'empty': it echoes both elements of the form and the off-white shapes that adorn the surface. The interplay between these elements becomes a kind of dance, a tacit recognition that both form and surface sculpt complex relationships between spaces.

If *Dancing pot* hinted at anthropomorphism via the invocation of limbs, other works present as human bodies more overtly. *Hugging pot* (2022) is a conjoined composition that speaks of relations between members of a family, or of friendship, or of both. The decorative patterns resolve the piece as a group, but they also demarcate individual entities, a decision reinforced by their alluding to the vertical relationship between the base and the rim. By invoking the human body, King-Salter harnesses the prehistoric symbolism of the pot, the dependence of our bodies on water, the survival of the family, and, as a consequence, our species. Indeed, some of King-Salter's works look as though they could have been recovered from an archaeological excavation, even though his approach to design is steadfastly personal.

King-Salter's pots are documents of transience, of being immersed in the creative act and responding to the demands of a particular work as it arises in the moment. In some instances, a piece may sit in the studio for many months, even years, before being re-glazed and re-fired. Multiple firings can produce surprising effects – not so much in terms of happy accidents – but in the accretion of unexpected hues and tones that afford each work inimitability. *Tall vase* (2020/2022), for instance, has a rich surface colouring created by the

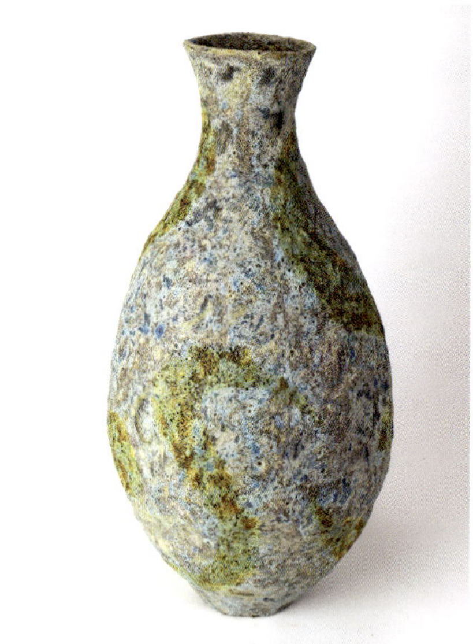

Tall vase (2020/2022).

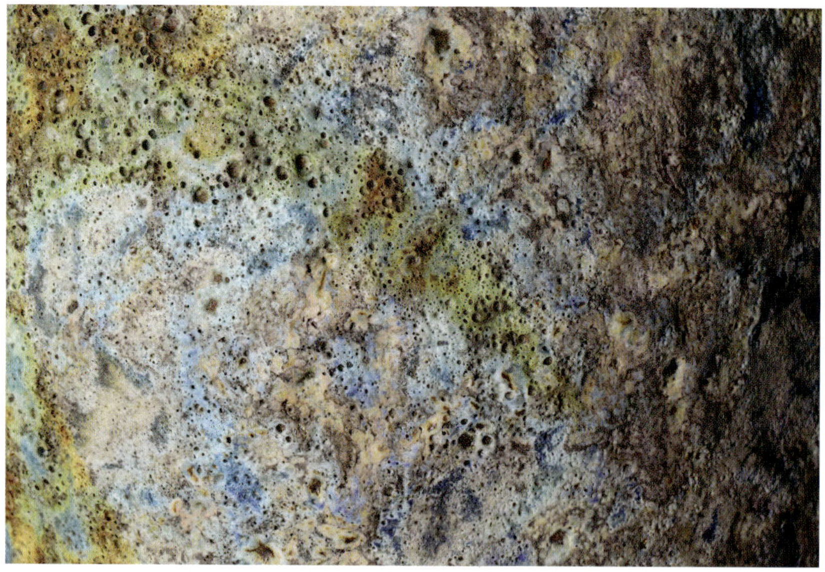

Tall vase (detail) (2020/2022).

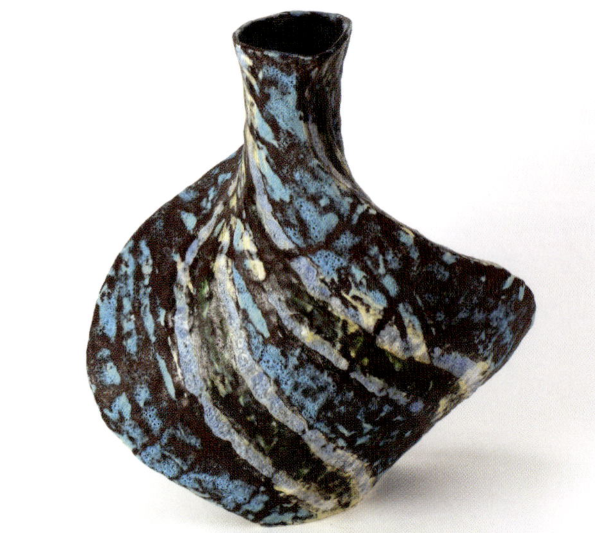

Dancing twisting pot (2022).

mingling of glazes in the kiln. The effect of mixing these glazes was of course anticipated, but the precise areas of their mixing, and the extent of their interaction, was determined by heat. The outcome is a soft volcanic patterning composed of a myriad of mottled colours, which adorn the surface like a lava bed of flowers.

Unsurprisingly, King-Salter's pinched pots always have the same starting point: the base. Yet, whilst the

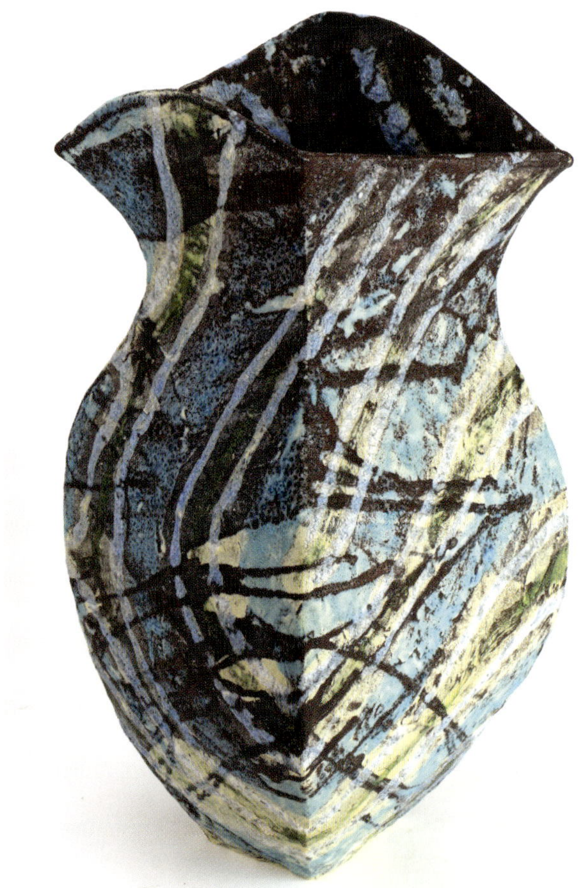

Four-sided breastbone pot (2022).

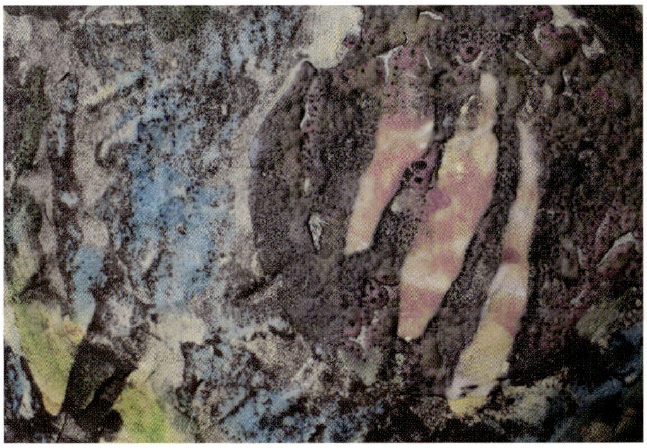

▌ *Wide indented pot* (detail) (2022).

four sides of a square base, for instance, might begin in a certain direction, the contours of the form will be made to twist and turn as it develops. *Dancing twisting pot* (2022) demonstrates the nature of this twisting, the work spiralling up like a whirling blade. The lines of glaze are developed from, and re-enforce, this twist in form, coalescing to provide speed to the implied movement of the pot. *Four-sided breastbone pot* (2022) was developed in the same series as *Dancing twisting pot*, but the turn of the pot produces a perceptual effect. If one of the edges faces directly towards the viewer (as shown here), the pot appears to foreshorten, the wide expanse of the pot body sitting at odds with the small base and concave neck. The forward-facing edge presents as less of an 'edge', more like a kind of crease. This effect is intensified by the glaze marks, where lines run across the edges of planes in different layers – white, light blue, and a darker blue produced by its mixing with a darker glaze. Although the application of glazes might at times appear haphazard, these drips and splodges are highly anticipated. Such control stems from the development of technique, for King-Salter handles the run of glaze like a highly skilled action painter.

Naturally, glaze distortions occur in the kiln, but these moments of experimentation and discovery are significant to King-Salter's process. Although he undertakes glaze tests to ascertain the exact hue that will be produced, he prefers to allow the kiln to dictate the ways in which glazes may come to blend. *Wide indented pot* (2022) is a perfect example of this, where the firing has caused the glazes to combine into a rich yet relatively flat surface that is almost akin to screen-printing. Sky blue gives way to azure, black becomes grey, yellow-green darkens to emerald. Such instantaneous reaction of the glaze to the heat of the kiln exemplifies King-Salter's general approach: the bringing together of all the elements of pottery to respond to the circumstances of a given moment in time.

Over a period spanning forty years, King-Salter has produced highly distinctive pots whilst avoiding repetition. He has absorbed Leach's observations of form but used them for his own unique and personal vision. He is a naturally gifted and intuitive potter, whose ability to conjure impressive forms and glaze combinations has been discovered only through decades of methodical working. Commendably, King-Salter has no truck with trends and 'isms'. Like his pots, his strength lies in his own twists and turns.

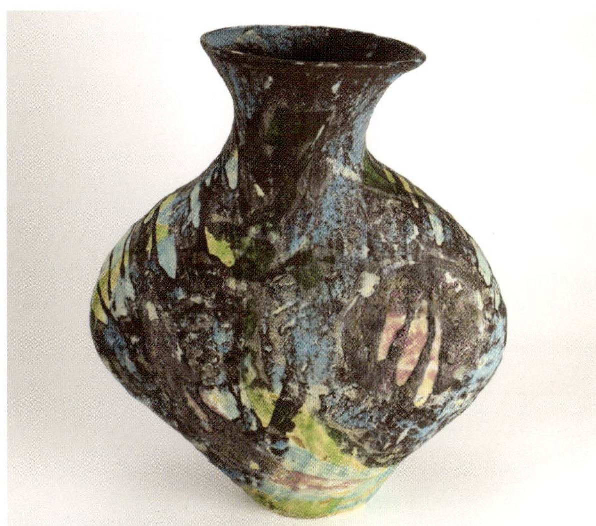

▌ *Wide indented pot* (2022).

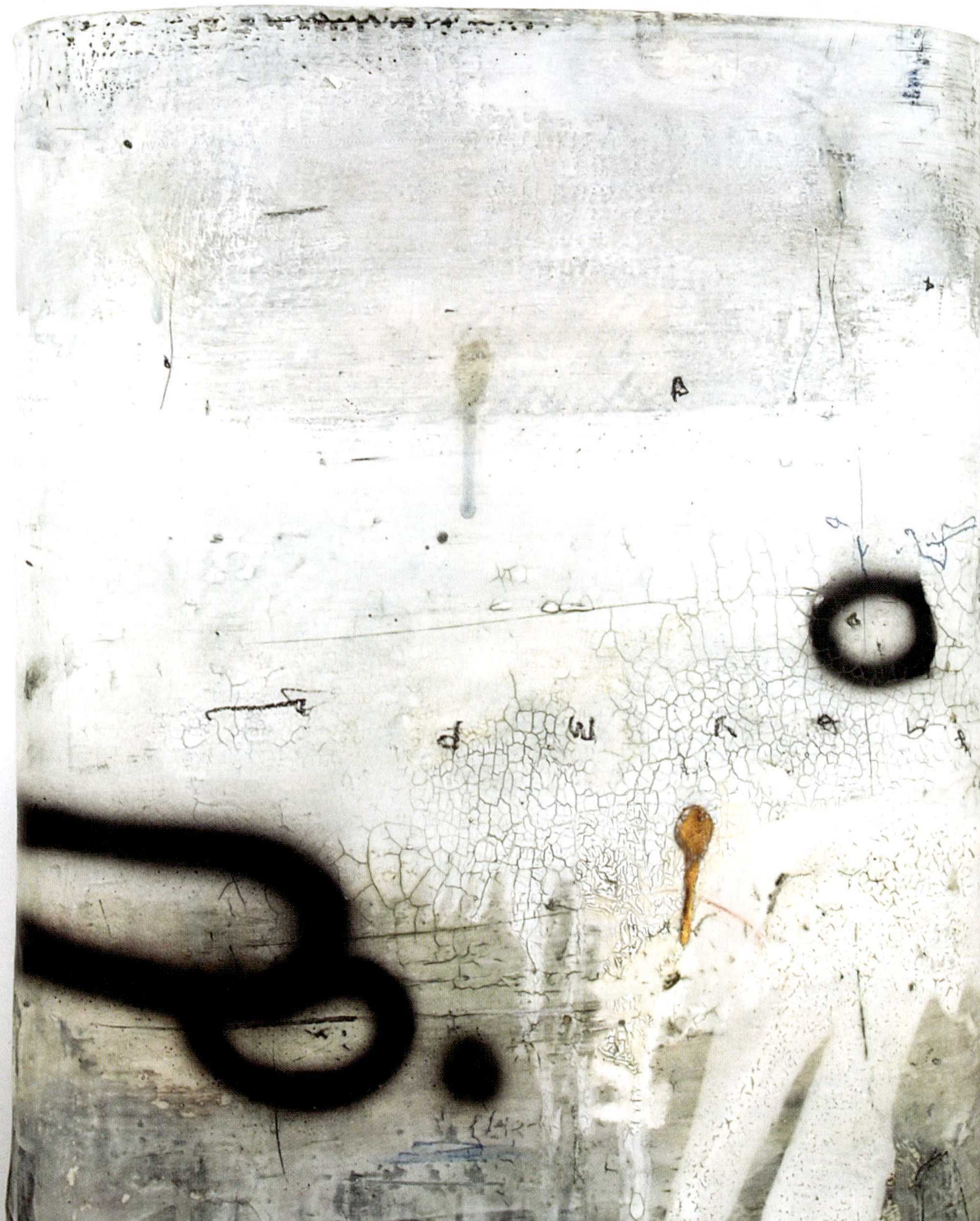

Dialogues with Twentieth Century Art

Dan Kelly In Contrast

> Consider a white patch against a homogenous background. All points on the patch have a certain common 'function' that makes them into a 'figure'. The figure's color is denser and somehow more resistant than the background's color. The borders of the white patch 'belong' to the patch and, despite being contiguous with it, do not join with the background. The patch seems to be placed upon the background and does not interrupt it. Each part announces more than it contains, and thus this elementary perception is already charged with a ***sense***. The objection will be raised that if the figure and the background are not sensed as a whole, then they must surely be sensed in each of their points. This would be to forget that each point in turn can only be perceived as a figure on a background. When Gestalt theory tells us that a figure against a background is the most basic sensible given we can have, this is not a contingent characteristic of factual perception that would, in an ideal analysis, leave us free to introduce the notion of impression. Rather, this is the very definition of the perceptual phenomenon, or that without which a phenomenon cannot be called perception. The perceptual 'something' is always in the middle of some other thing, it always belongs to a 'field'.[62]
>
> (*Maurice Merleau-Ponty*)

In his 1945 book *Phenomenology of Perception*, the philosopher Maurice Merleau-Ponty (1908–1961) sought to rationalise how we, as human beings, inhabit our world. He rejected the philosophy of René Descartes (1596–1650), whose influential philosophical statement proposed that 'I think therefore I am' (*cogito ergo sum*). Instead, Merleau-Ponty argued that existence is predicated on experience, produced through interactions between the individual and the world in which they live. The implications of this shift were significant. Descartes' 'I think therefore I am' became insufficient, for it assumed that existence was independent of interaction with the exterior world. To be, all one has to do is think. As a developmental corrective, Merleau-Ponty argued that our existence is fundamentally relational; it is produced by the individual responding to the world around them, a world which also responds to the individual.

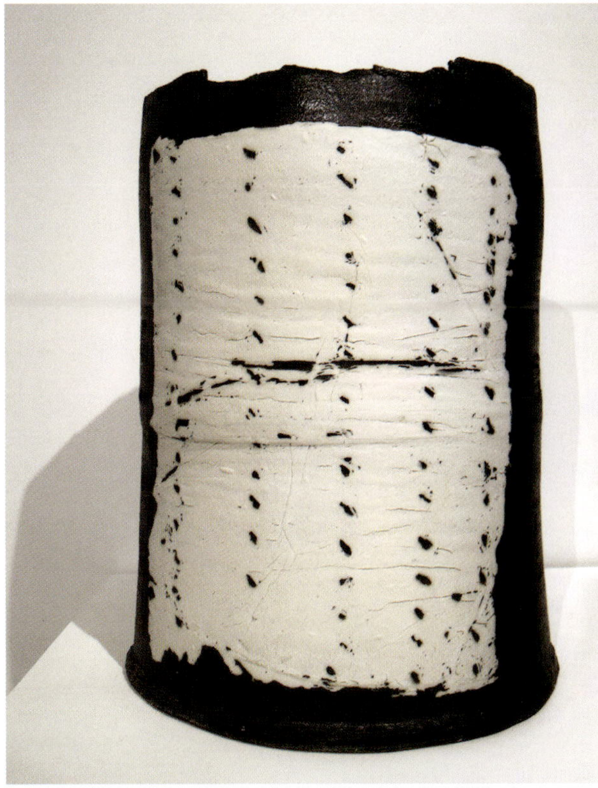

Large Pot (2015).

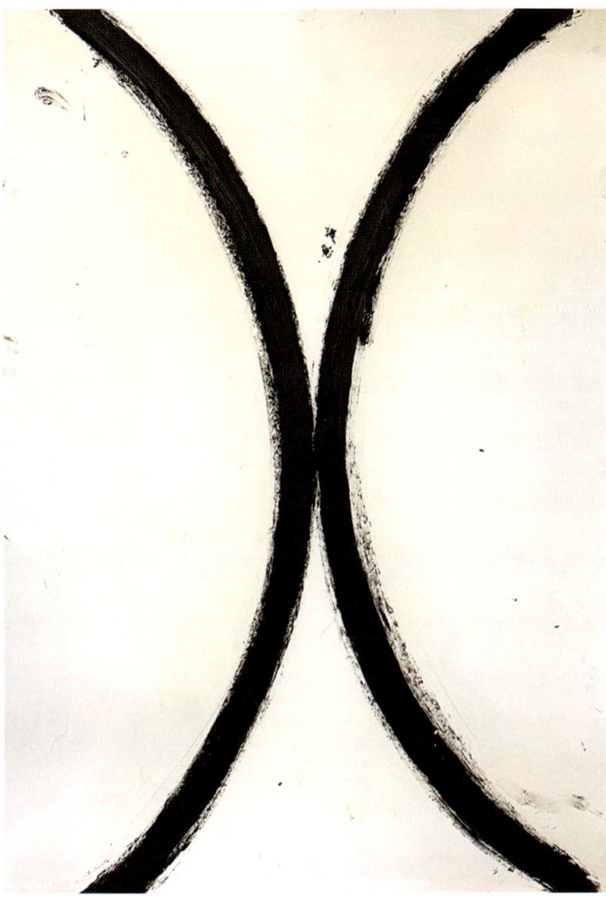

Co-exist (2019).

Because of this, Merleau-Ponty placed significance upon the creation and experience of objects. To use the body to create something – whether that is a thrown pot or an abstract expressionist painting – is to demonstrate 'how habit has its abode neither in thought nor in the objective body, but in the body as a mediator of the world.'[63] To throw a pot is to bring the body into contact with the exterior, to sense with touch the spinning clay, to use sight to bring it into shape, to smell the damp earth as it moves into form, to hear the spinning of the wheel. Once fired, the pot remains an experiential object to be seen, touched, and used. The quotation that opens this chapter highlights how our perception of objects is always relational. To see an object is to recognise its place in a context (or what Merleau-Ponty calls a 'field'). A pot cannot be discerned without registering its relationship to the surface upon which it sits, the wall that lies behind it, or the other pots that might stand next to it. Contrast enables our perception of objects.

The work of Dan Kelly revels in contrast through a predominance of black and white tones. Such contrast maximises perception, but it does so for specific reasons. Pots, as containers, shape space. They are dependent on a 'skin' to delineate the inner space of the pot from the external space of the world. Yet, when we look at a pot, we can only see half of it at any one time: its three-dimensions prevent us from observing all the surface at once. To be able to observe all sides of a pot, it would have to be flattened out as a sheet of clay; the consequence of such flattening being that the pot would no longer be a 'pot'. Pots are thus curious objects: they are three-dimensional, but they are only observable as curved planes that could easily be perceived as two-dimensional.[64] Kelly's work tacitly recognises this. The dark monotones that are the hallmark of his pots are astutely perceptual. Set against a lighter background, the range of blacks and coppers Kelly deploys serve to heighten the sense of the pot as an object drawn in space. Yet, these dark monotones absorb light in different ways. Whilst a

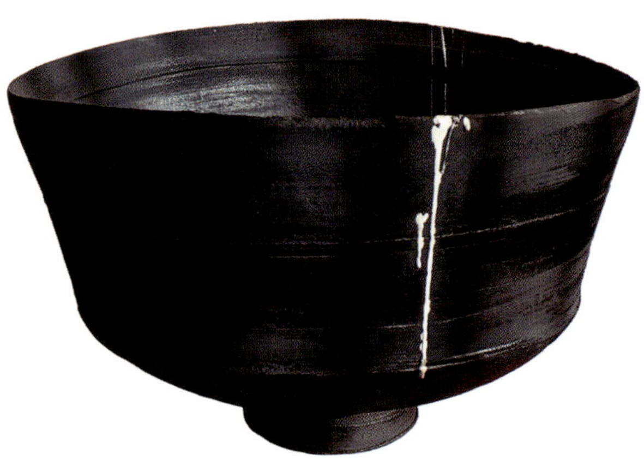

Bowl (2017).

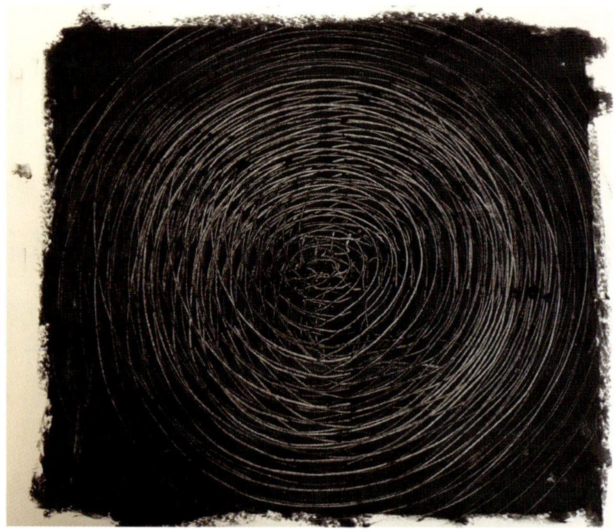

Rotations (2020).

glossy glaze on porcelain might enable light to reflect across the form, rendering it as an object that the eye can more readily perceive in three dimensions, matt black glaze across earthenware might absorb light, flattening the sense of form. Kelly plays with the possibilities this creates, pitting the three-dimensionality of form against the flattening effect of a monotonal surface.

Kelly paints as well as pots, but the above analysis infers that the distinction between these two spheres of activity might be blurred. Indeed, some of his paintings utilise contrast to provoke questions of perception. In *Co-exist* (2019), do we see two circles, or two curved 'v' shapes, or both? In *Rotations* (2020) two concentric circles spin, pulling the eye across dizzying lines as it seeks to order the image. The visual speed of these lines is analogous to a pot being thrown in front of us. Both images infer a kind of perspectival depth at odds with its two-dimensional reality. This visual juxtaposition connects his paintings to his pots, where similar visual questions are provoked by the application of white glaze across the surface. Marks may range from a square canvas-like painting, as can be discerned on *Large Pot* (2015),

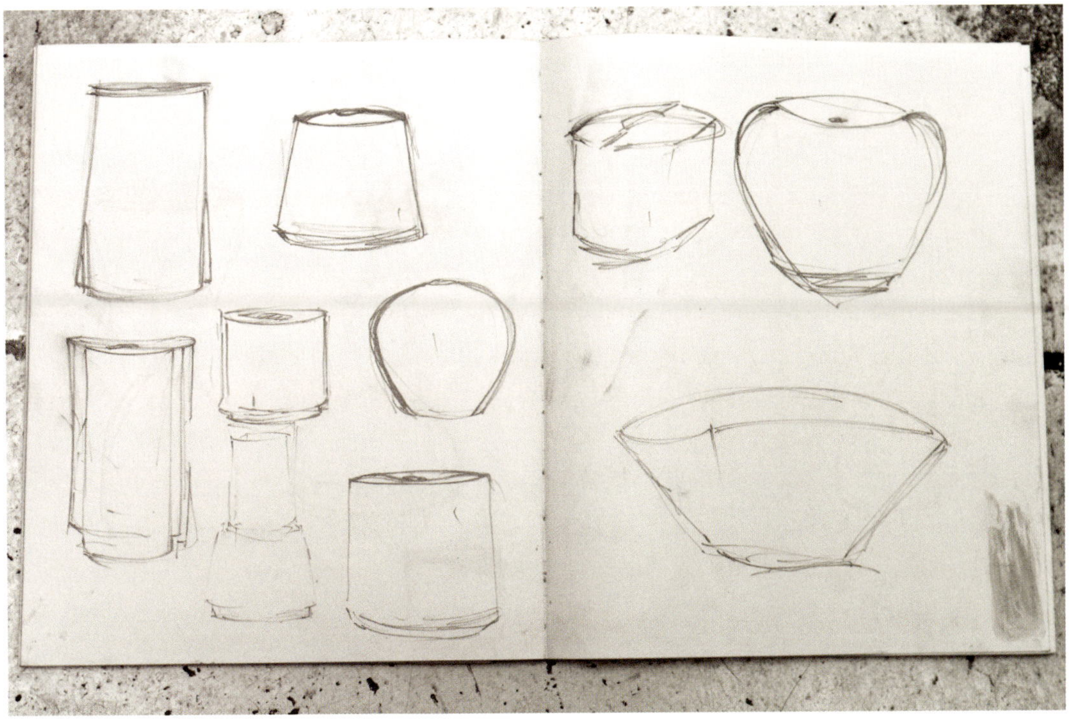

Sketch Book (2010).

to a lightning-like streak of white that runs vertically down the form, such as on *Bowl* (2017). These marks provide a sense of movement to animate the form. Yet, this animation simultaneously provokes recognition of the curvature of the pot form as perceivable only from one angle, one 'semi-flattened plane'. In this sense, Kelly reminds us that pots are always perceived as both two- and three-dimensional objects.

I contend that this relational understanding is central to Kelly's practice, as evidenced in the drawings he makes to refine form. His vocabulary is rooted to three basic shapes: the cone, the cylinder, and the sphere. Such limited choice may appear restrictive, but as with any constraint, restriction demands creativity and innovation to avoid repetition. Kelly's pots are always distinctively his, yet two works are never the same. This is undoubtedly a result of his prowess as a thrower, in particular, his ability to manipulate form as it evolves on the wheel, to create a pot that has a rightness according to its own emerging

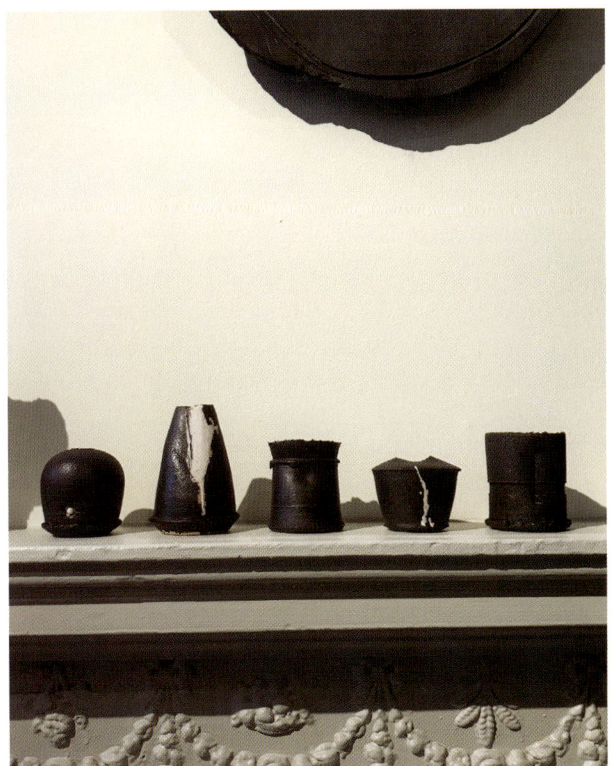

Small Vessels (2022).

proportions. Interestingly, his drawings capture the way in which we perceive pots, as partial elevations which require our imagination to model the hidden aspects. Like the actual pots, these drawings use lines to suggest three-dimensional objects, even though we read the spaces around and within the lines as flat, two-dimensional, paper.

Perhaps this interest in dimensional juxtaposition stems from Kelly's brief training in technical drawing when he was younger, and his continued interest in architecture. Kelly has spent most of his life living in South London, and it is tempting to read his pots as a reflection of the high-rise buildings that populate the urban landscape. After all, buildings are also constituted by planes (walls), which are manipulated into interior and exterior spatial volumes. And, like a pot, our view of a building is always partial; our imagination constructs the back elevations we cannot see. Certainly, when his pots are arranged in series, they could easily stand for the shapes of the urban landscape. Yet, this seems a rather literal reading. If the urban does bleed into Kelly's works, it is as much through mechanisation, particularly the interior of car garages, than the architecture of the skyline. In fact, some of Kelly's pots have been inspired by exhaust pipes, and some of his painterly marks (on both pots and paper) respond to the tread marks and oil spills on the garage floor.

If architecture is manifestly present in Kelly's work, it is explored through the prism of the anatomical

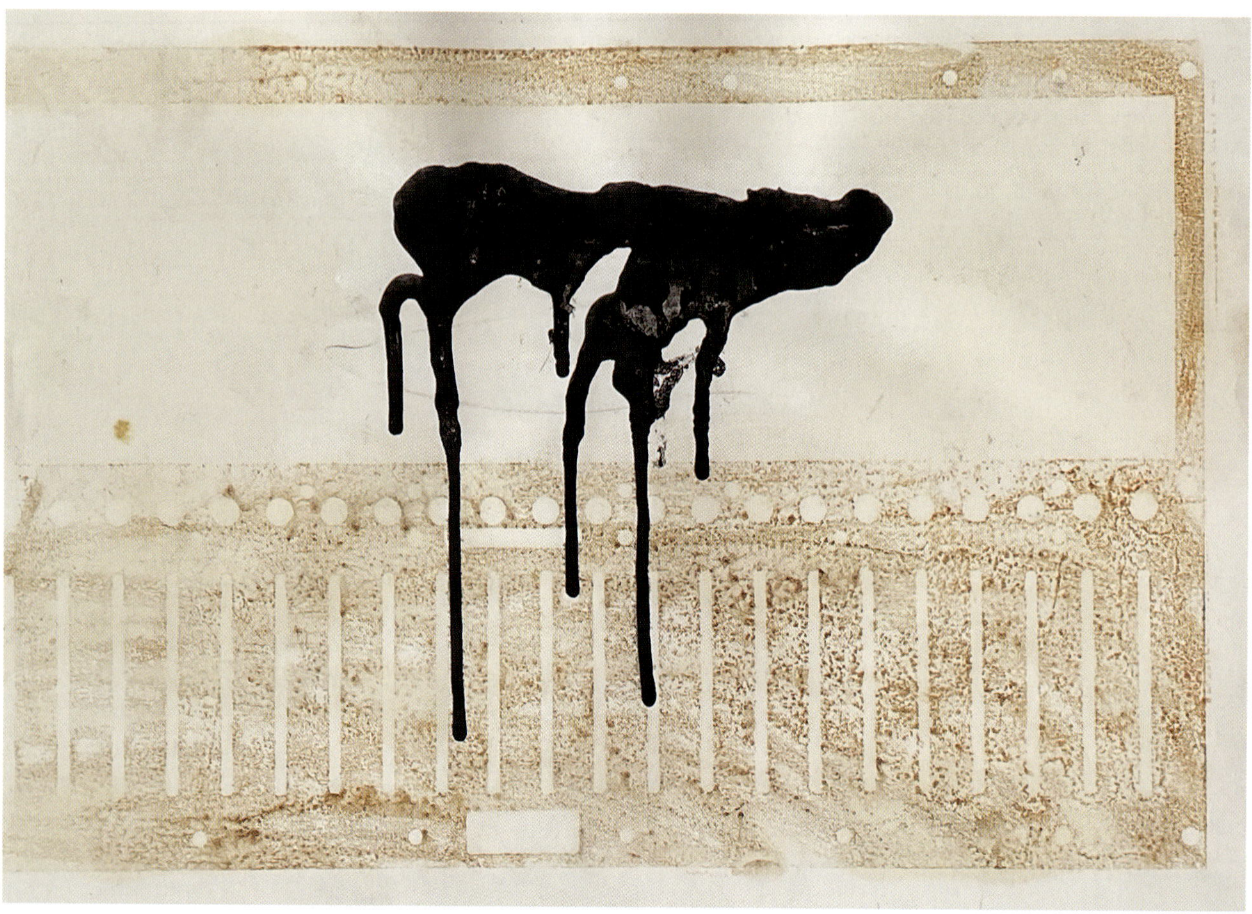

■ *Ilustro* (2021).

Duce (2011).

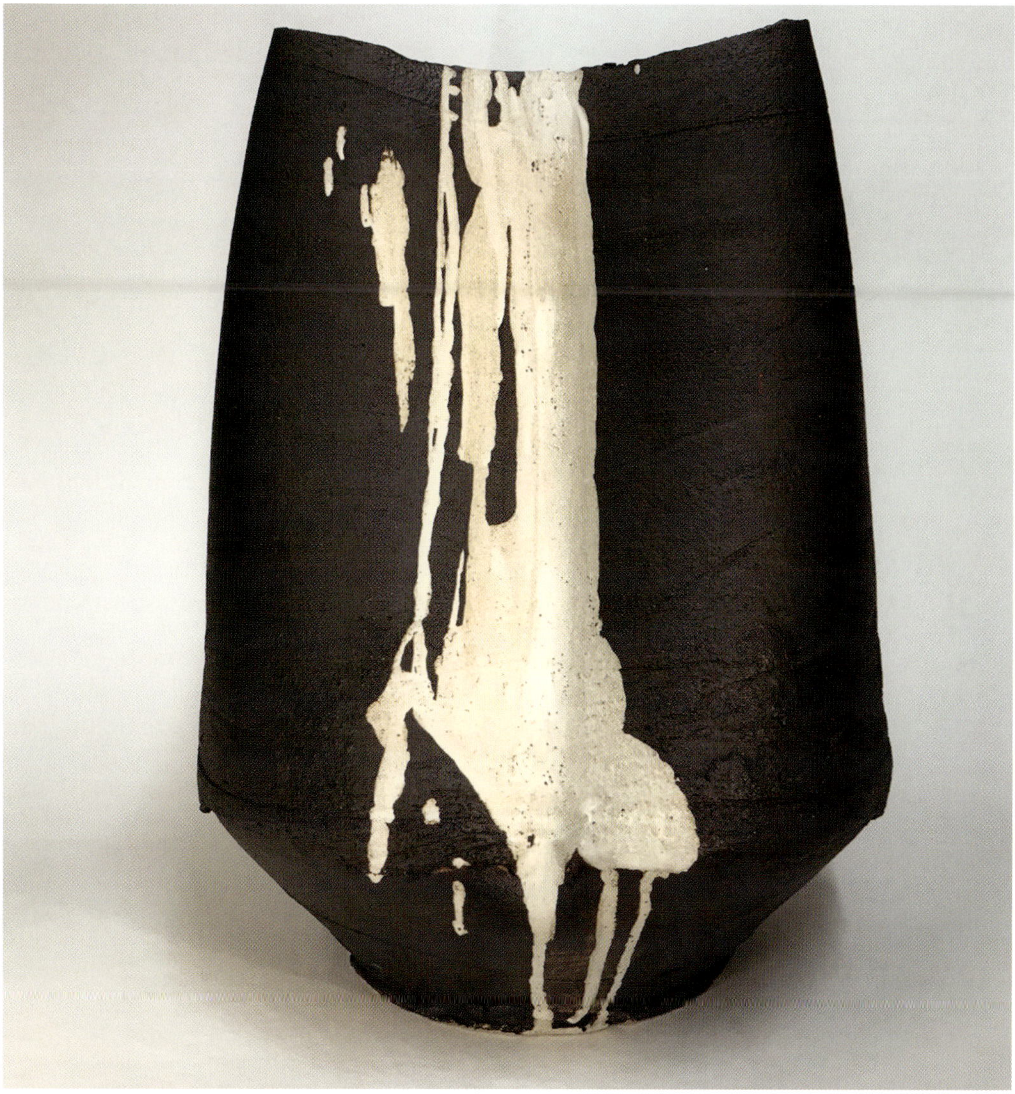

structure of the human body. As Kent Bloomer and Charles Moore have observed in their analysis of the body and architecture:

> The most fundamental organizing principle in the formation of our body image is that we unconsciously locate our bodies inside a three-dimensional boundary. This boundary surrounds the entire body and demarcates our 'inside' personal space from our 'outside' extrapersonal space. It is an unstable boundary subject to events both inside and outside the boundary.[65]

Such analysis accords with Merleau-Ponty's thesis that we exist through the relational interplay between our individual bodies and the world around us. Kelly utilises the same architectural metaphor to explore how the pot can symbolise the body. This is perhaps most discernible in terms of form, such as in *Figure in Three Parts* (2002), where a cone shape has been manipulated into an abstracted head, trunk, and lower body. Anthropomorphism is more than a visual phenomenon, however. The division of interior from exterior space associates the body with the home, and with the pot. Such alignment constitutes an anthropological commentary on

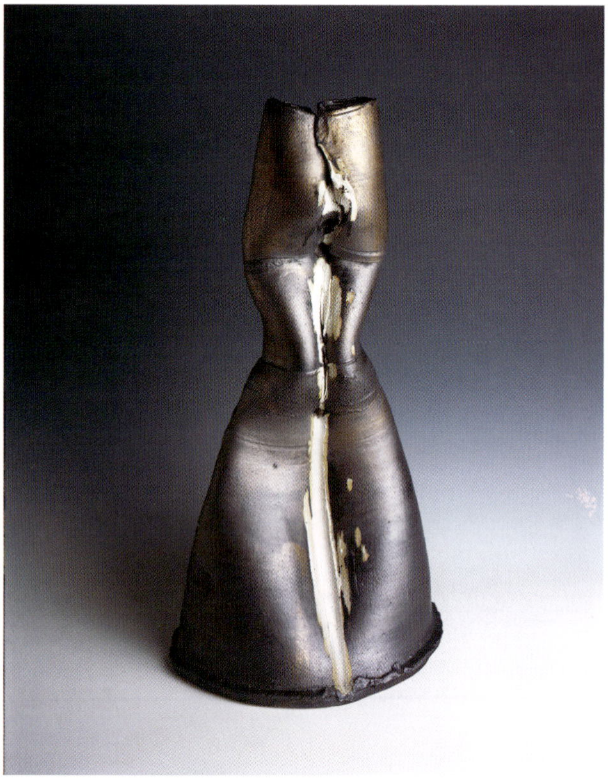

Figure in Three Parts (2002).

the relationships between pottery, domesticity, and the development of human civilisation. Perhaps pots are symbolically totemic because they enable us to touch history, to place our fingers on a surface that our ancestors shaped thousands of years ago.

In this sense, Kelly's pots (if not all pots) expound the phenomenology of perception as theorised by Maurice Merleau-Ponty. They highlight how the creation of pots is a relational activity: clay is shaped by the potter, who is themself shaped by the world around them. Each potter combines these two aspects into a distinctive relationship, empowering them to take an individualised approach to a form that has a history spanning tens of thousands of years. Yet, pots are also relational in terms of dimensions; the throwing of a pot creates a three-dimensional form that cannot be perceived simultaneously in its totality. Thus, a pot is always an implicit drawing in space. Only by understanding its relationship with its surroundings are we able to evince dimensions that we cannot see with our imagination. Even as we move around a pot, our visual memory must map what it has seen with what it sees in the here and now. We process and map the surface to fill in the gaps. Kelly's utilisation of the pot surface as a kind of canvas for abstract expressionist marks in glaze highlights how our perception of a pot is limited to one aspect. Of course, in contrast, Kelly's two-dimensional paintings have no need for such mental spatial conjuring, but they nevertheless produce sensations of depth that are at odds with their flattened surface. In *RWB* (2022), the overlaying of marks creates the impression that the image is produced through a series of interlocking planes that move across one another. Two-dimensions allude to three-dimensions, and three-dimensions allude to two-dimensions. Kelly uses contrasting tones to highlight the contrasts of form, evidencing how painting and pottery are separate, but closely related, activities. For, as Merleau-Ponty observed, all contrasts are out of necessity relational.

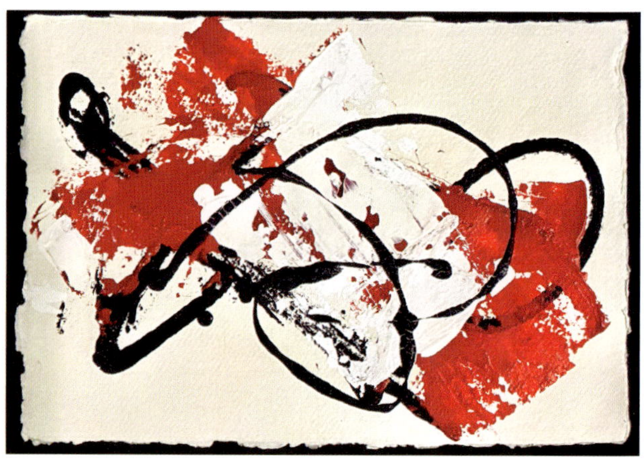

RWB (2022).

Elizabeth Fritsch
A Responsive Eye

On 25 February 1965, *The Responsive Eye* opened to the public at the Museum of Modern Art, New York. The exhibition, which featured work by ninety-nine artists from fifteen countries, brought together examples of optical and kinetic art – painting and sculpture that was concerned with the experience of looking rather than the documentation of a subject (such as a landscape or still life). In the accompanying catalogue, William C. Seitz hailed the exhibition as a bold assertion that fine art was now a self-referential medium capable of exploring perception itself:

> Before the advent of abstract art a picture was a window through which an illusion of the real world could be viewed, and a statute was a replica. Non-objective painting and sculpture defined a work of art as an independent object as real as a chair or a table. Perceptual abstraction – its existence as an object de-emphasized or nullified by uniform surface treatment, reflective or transparent materials, and a battery of optical devices – exists primarily for its impact on perception rather than for conceptual examination. Ideological focus has moved from the outside world, passed through the work as object, and entered the incompletely explored region area between the cornea and the brain.[66]

The cultural impact of *The Responsive Eye*, which featured artists such as Josef Albers (1888–1976), Agnes Martin (1912–2004), Ellsworth Kelly (1923–2015), Bridget Riley (b.1931), and Victor Vasarely (1906–1997), was immediate and far-reaching. Optical patterns soon made their way onto fabrics and into department stores, becoming synonymous with London fashion designers such as Mary Quant (1930–2023) by the middle of the 'swinging sixties'.

It was in this era, in 1966, that Elizabeth Fritsch first started making ceramics. Yet, her emergence did not coincide with the op-art craze. Attending the Royal College of Art from 1968–1971, the fashion world had long since moved on by the time she held her first solo exhibition at the Crafts Council exhibition space in London in 1974. Yet, her work had an immediate impact, being regarded as a serious self-referential engagement with the materiality and languages of clay. In analysing her work through some of the central concerns of *The Responsive Eye*, I seek to situate Fritsch's output in the broader history of twentieth-century modern art. In fact, her work demands such an approach, for the best of her vessels stand as a masterful interweaving of ceramic and fine art vocabularies. In this regard, it is important to note that Edward Lucie-Smith connected Fritsch's work with Modernism, specifically Cubism and Futurism.[67] Yet, for me, her achievement is more than the flattening of form. It is a series of complex decisions that critically engage with Abstract Expressionism and realise the implications of optical and kinetic art from the 1960s.

Of course, *The Responsive Eye* did not concern itself with ceramics: the selection of exhibited works was entirely comprised of painting and sculpture. In his essay, Seitz naturally confined his analysis to these two spheres of artistic activity. He thus observed some of the tendencies of optical art:

> Stripped of conceptual association, habits, and references to previous experience, perceptual responses would appear to follow innate laws, limited though our understanding of them may be. The eye responds most directly when nonessentials such as freely modulated shape and tone, brush gestures and impasto are absent. These means muffle and distort the purely perceptual effect of lines, areas, and colors.
>
> All forms of representation, even ideographs, signs, and symbols, also alter or deflect whatever is innate in vision. (Horizontal lines and shapes tend to be avoided by perceptual painters, for example, because they suggest landscape.) The eye needs only the slightest clue to link an abstract shape to some past association with actual objects and space.[68]

According to Seitz, total abstraction was necessary to achieve purely perceptual effects. A self-evident problem for the participation of ceramics in this kind of practice is that one of its most important languages – the pot – is steeped in symbolic meanings of utility, domesticity, and civilisation. Any attempt to draw attention to modes of perception in a purely abstract sense will inevitably be compromised. Does this exclude Fritsch's work from the sphere of optical art? No. In fact, Fritsch demonstrated early on that such associations did not inhibit optical effects. Indeed, the manipulation of the viewer's perception could be contingent upon conceptual association, especially with regard to volume and mass.

On this point, it is interesting to note that Fritsch appeared to be at ease with the domestic associations of the pot from the very beginning. Most of the photos taken of her in the mid-1970s – and subsequently for that matter – were in her domestic studio. Fritsch was photographed seated on a rocking chair next to a large sash window or leaning against a chest of drawers upon which examples of her work were placed, or at what appeared to be a dining table, pinching together a piece whist her son played on the floor by her side. Perhaps such photos were making a subtly feminist point; women could have both successful artistic careers and raise families. Whether this was an accurate picture of studio life is not really the point. In the images she presented to the public, Fritsch appeared totally at ease with the existence of her pots in the domestic sphere.

It is all the more significant, then, that the impact of her work was tied to a rejection of utility. Like those of her tutor Hans Coper, Fritsch sought out the sculptural potential of form. Moreover, she manipulated perceptions of volume and mass through the interplay of formal contours and the application of lines and areas of colour. An important early example of this approach can be found in *Pocket* (1974), a work featured in her first solo show at the Crafts Council in Waterloo Place, and subsequently chosen by Alison Britton for her selection in *The Maker's Eye*, held in the same space in 1981. Here, the manipulation of perception is reliant upon an interplay between form and surface. When viewed from the front, the lip of the pot is lower to one side, leading the eye to consider its curvilinearity as a fully opened circle, when it is in fact a compressed oval. The unglazed line around the rim draws attention to this composition, turning it into a kind of drawing in space. The diagonal lines that taper around the pot flatten its sense of volume, disguising the fact that the piece is significantly larger at the bottom of its body than at the top. This compositional feature is discernible when the work is viewed from the side. From this perspective, the interplay between line and form shifts; the diagonal lines augment rather than disguise the irregularity of the body. Here, Fritsch utilises the curve of the form to produce perceptual effects, to give tempo

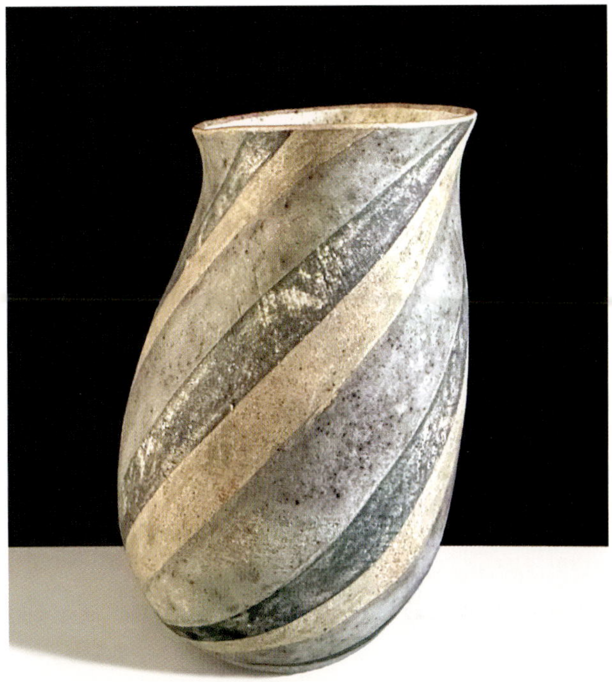

Side view of *Pocket* (1974).

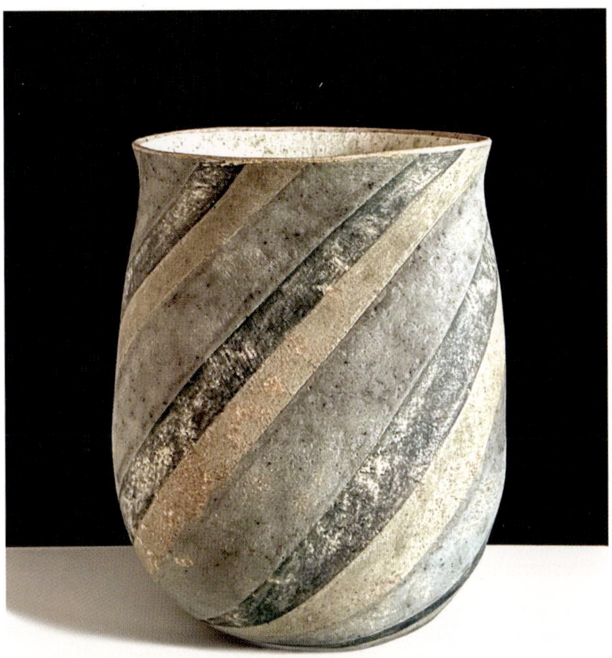

Pocket (1974).

to the surface. There is a strong sense of a static contour down the left-hand side of the pot (as photographed) receding away with increasing rapidity as the eye moves to the right (thereafter, this form was titled by Fritsch as 'blown-away'). There is, in this work, a masterful manipulation of how the eye perceives form and decoration.

By understanding how line and form work with and against each other, Fritsch was able to address some of the concerns documented in *The Responsive Eye*. Indeed, Seitz's observations on how paint could be used to manipulate perceptions could easily describe some of Fritsch's work:

> Today, with a vastly expanded and brightened battery of pigments at his [*sic*] disposal, the painter can work with a palette enlarged by another order of perceptually created images, simultaneous contrasts, after-images and other effects, some of them as dynamic as any produced by physical motion. Hard

> edges can be made to soften, wave, and fluctuate; flat bands can be modelled perceptually to appear like Doric fluting; and because of periodic fatigue, or 'bleaching' of color-sensitive cones in the retina, luminous shapes, purer and more brilliant than the painted shapes that generate them, can be made to appear, disappear and reappear at another location in a rhythmic cycle. From these aggressive confrontations of hues, to smaller and more numerous units that pulsate with faster rhythms, down to pointillism that neutralizes opposites rather than intensifying them, an uncatalogued range of possibilities can result from simultaneous contrast and fusion.[69]

Fritsch's *Spout Pot from Tlön* (1984) offers an apt illustration of how 'flat bands can be modelled perceptually' and 'luminous shapes, purer and more brilliant than the painted shapes that generate them, can be made to appear, disappear and reappear at another location in a rhythmic cycle'. The green stripes that run across the outer body of the pot exert the form in three-dimensional space. This sits at odds with the brilliant blue background which has also been applied to the interior of the pot, a decision that makes the form hover between two- and three-dimensions. This pot was, as Peter Dormer observed, a creative response to the 1947 Argentinian short story *Tlön, Uqbar, Orbis Tertius* by Jorge Luis Borges (1899–1986), in which the material world is denied by the inhabitants of the fictional Tlön.[70] More importantly, however, the interaction of colours also produces an optical effect. Where lines intersect, the eye registers faint black, yellow, or white lines. These optical effects give the pot a sense of fluctuation, as it shimmers between the fictional world and material reality.

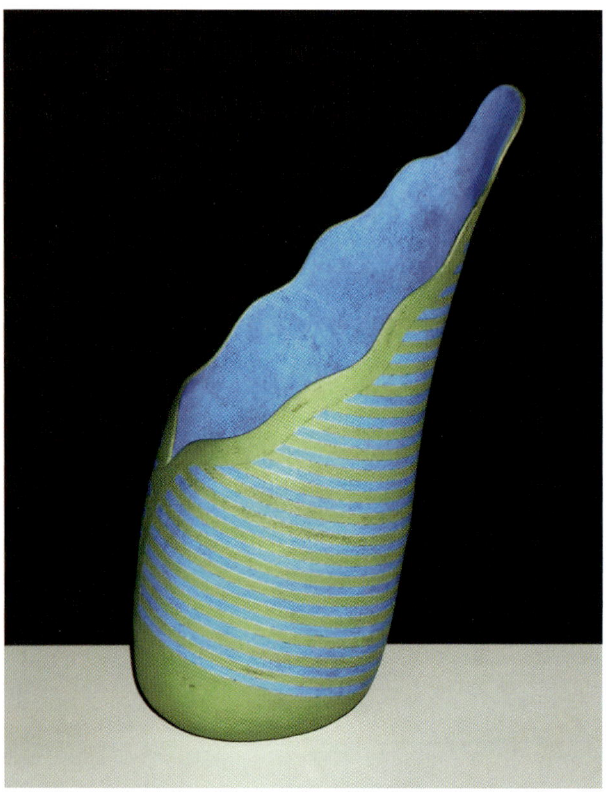

■ *Spout Pot from Tlön* (1984).

Some of Fritsch's works are titled as optical objects, such as *Optical Cup and Saucer* (2008), a flattened chalice-like form that uses rectangles painted in perspective to suggest interior volume, almost like an X-ray. The rectangle as symbolic of volume was vigorously pursued across subsequent work, either as rhythmic elements relating to music (*Jazz Piano pots*, 1975), as a means of modulating form via tempo across a flattened vessel surface (*Blown Away Vase, Dynamic Structure of the Third Dimension*, 2008), or of suggesting the opening out of interior space (*Blown Away – Collision of Particles*, trio of vases, 2008). Yet, the tendency to place emphasis on the surfaces of her work leads attention away from her formal experimentation. In 2000, as an apparent corrective (and emerging from a desire to create radically different forms[71]), Fritsch exhibited uncharacteristically plain vessels, many of which explored the ziggurat, at Galerie Besson. Entitled *Memories of Architecture (Part II)*, the works indeed seemed a radical formal departure. Yet, they are also entirely consistent with

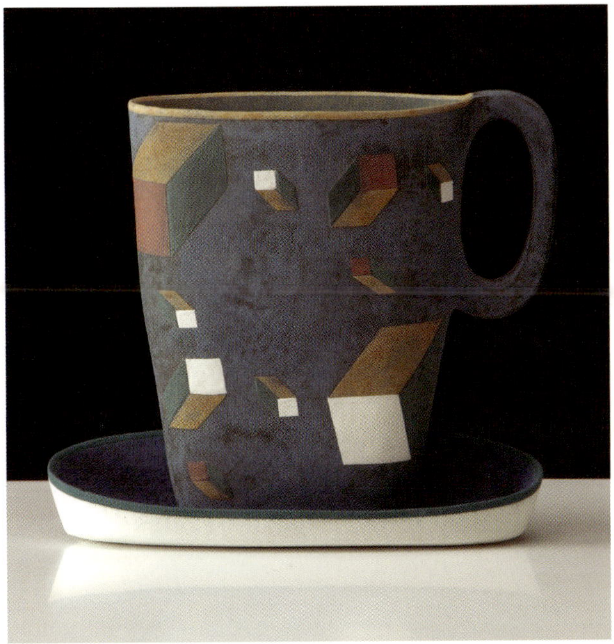

Optical Cup and Saucer (2008).

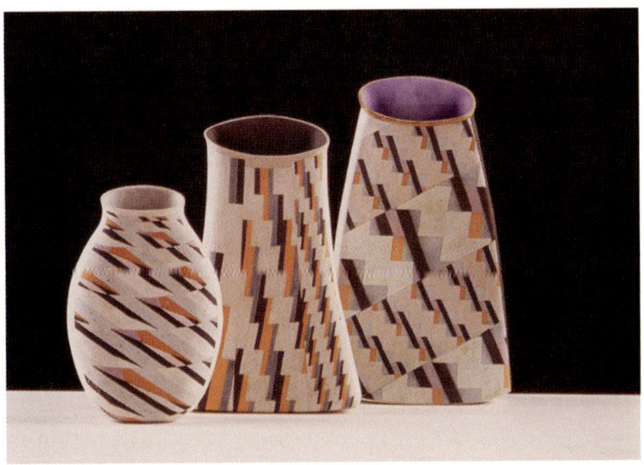

Jazz Piano pots (1975).

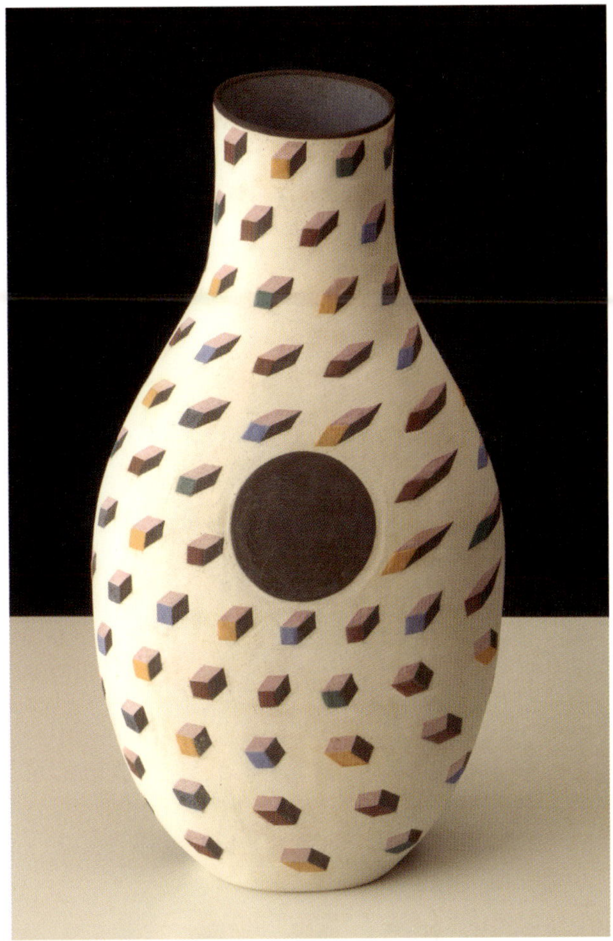

Blown Away Vase, Dynamic Structure of the Third Dimension (2008).

Fritsch's deployment of the rectangle as a signifier for mass. In *Big Ziggurat* (1999), for instance, the elliptical exterior appears to flatten, so that the eye considers the interior of the work as being in the shape of an ellipse rather than a circle. More importantly, each section seems to float above the other, offering a sense of lightness to what is, in fact, a substantial work measuring 40cm (15¾in) in height. Here, it is the form itself that creates the optical effect, a disconnect between material reality and perception. These architectural works are thus a different iteration of the same critical investigation of the architectural mass of pots.

Fritsch has become internationally renowned for expanding the vocabularies of studio ceramics. She explores how the optical sensation of mass can be manipulated through the treatment of form and surface. Whilst some might view her approach as being rather narrow (much, though not all, of her output has consisted of pots and vases) this seems a necessary constraint. Fritsch is concerned with documenting the impact of differences of pattern, colour, and the

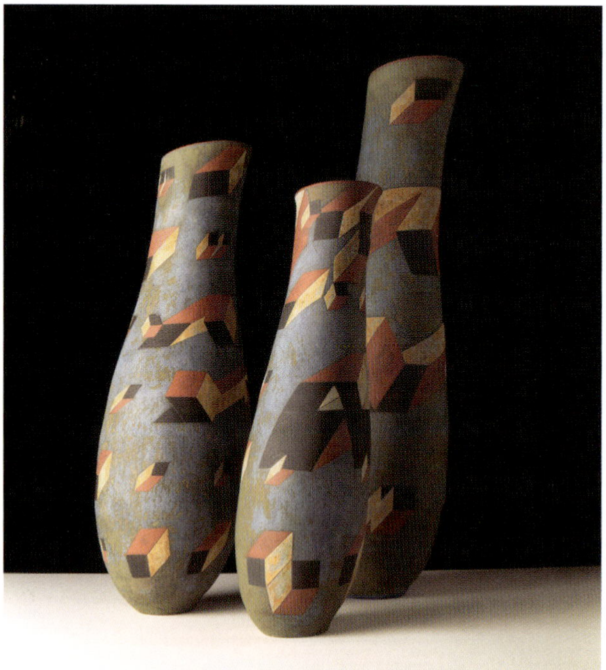

Blown Away – Collision of Particles, trio of vases (2008).

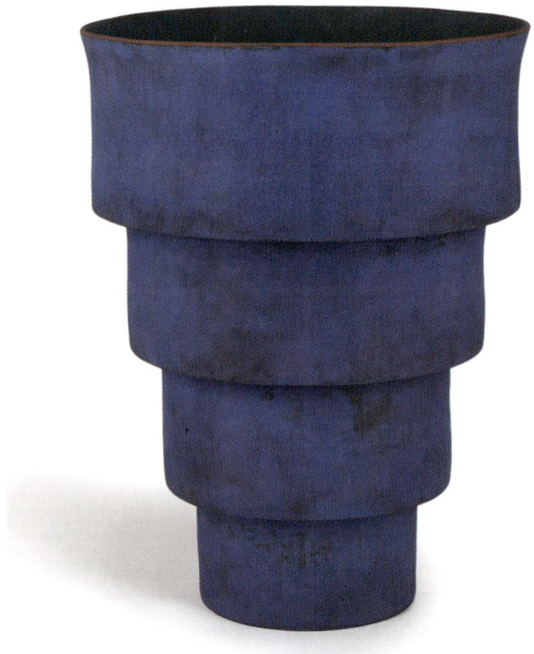

Big Ziggurat (1999).

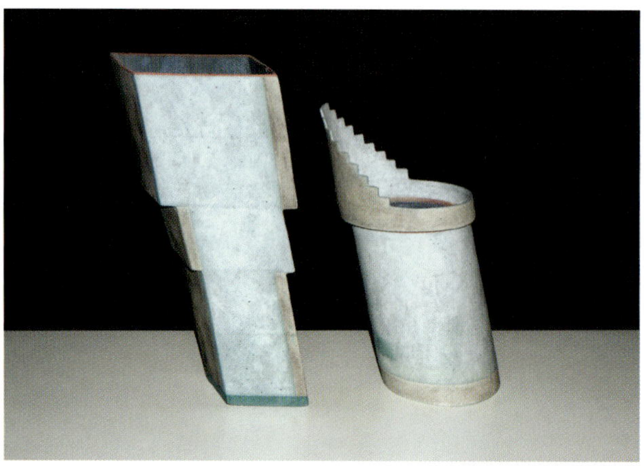

Memories of Architecture (1998).

undulations of the handmade form, and how these coalesce as perception. To criticise Fritsch for the use of a narrow range of forms is akin to criticising Bridget Riley for using the stripe, or Josef Albers for using the square. Perhaps the issue here is that Fritsch's achievement is less understood as rooted to self-referential questions of material perception, broadly in line with the concerns of other optical artists, but with important differences of material emphasis. Perhaps this arises from peculiarly British reservations about blurring the categories of fine art and craft. Yet, it is also clear that in the fullest sense of what ceramics has to offer, Fritsch has drawn from many categories to produce work. She is at once aware of the inherited languages of the medium yet has remained open to its interdisciplinary potential. On her own terms, and as a ceramic artist (one that encompasses art and craft ideas), Fritsch should be regarded as an important figure in one of the most internationally significant artistic movements of the twentieth century.

Sam Hall
The Muse of Fire

For the American painter, sculptor, and photographer Cy Twombly (1928–2011), art was self-referential. Putting paint on canvas did not, for instance, automatically mean the depiction of a subject or the description of feelings. Rather, as he asserted in a statement about his practice in 1957, marks were simply the culmination of emotion, thought, and the impulse to make:

> To paint involves a certain crisis, or at least a crucial moment of sensation or release; and by crisis it should by no means be limited to a morbid state, but could just as well be one ecstatic impulse, or in the process of a painting, run a gamut of states. [...]
>
> Each line [...] is the actual experience with its own innate history. It does not illustrate — it is the sensation of its own realization. The imagery is one of the private or separate indulgencies rather than an abstract totality of visual perception.
>
> This is very difficult to describe, but it is an involvement in essence (no matter how private) into a synthesis of feeling, intellect etc. occurring without separation in the impulse of action.[72]

Such self-referentiality moved beyond the image as description to place emphasis on the aesthetics of paint as a material, and painting as a process.

The ceramicist Sam Hall is equally concerned with process. His pots are simply a by-product of enquiry. In fact, he begins at the point where most ceramicists end: after the firing. In its fired state, work is appraised, altered, and then refired: a process repeated until the work is deemed satisfying. Even then, Hall's opinion can change, and a piece once considered complete will be amended and refired. There is no limit to the number of firings a work will endure. Sometimes the next stage will reveal itself only after months, perhaps even years, have passed.

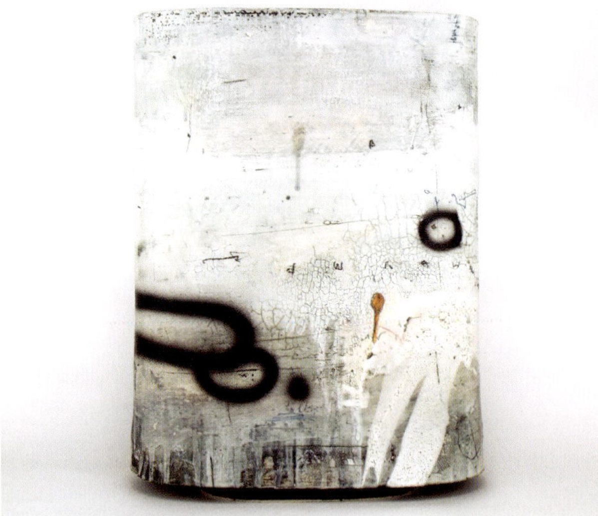

Large Form with Black (2017).

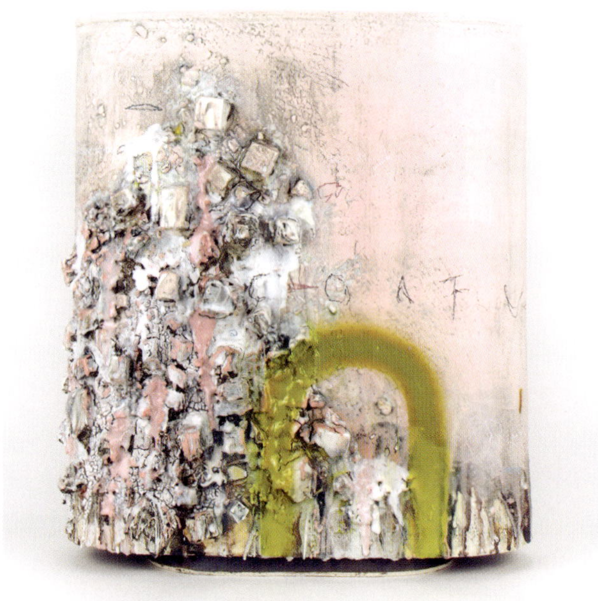

CORF (2019).

What exactly is he looking for? I asked Hall this rather thorny question, and it was indeed difficult for him to answer. His work is instinctual: there is no formula in terms of surface composition, even if there are recurring visual motifs resulting from his working in series. In parallel with Twombly, Hall's work is bound to innumerable decisions that coalesce over time, and which principally speak of themselves. If the results of his searching are hard to define, Hall could pinpoint more readily what he now found unsatisfactory: obvious visual reference to the Cornish landscape, something that looks too self-conscious or seems imitative of other artists, and a smooth minimalism that would likely appeal to the interior design market. Treating the surface like a canvas is important to Hall, and this explains his preference for flattened forms. Staring at a blank canvas like a painter, Hall makes a start on his pots with a few marks, and out of the first firing, more questions arise: how can balance be achieved? What is the relationship between viscosity and thinness, elaboration and minimalism, fast and slow, and filled and unfilled space?

It is clear, even to the casual observer, that the interdisciplinary nature of ceramics is important to Hall. His work exemplifies how drawing, painting, and sculpture can become the central components of pottery. However, a closer examination reveals how these elements are carefully deployed to evince the elusive sense of balance he strives for. *Large Form with Black* (2017), for instance, unites different tempos; the apparent stasis of horizontal strokes offers a counterpoint to the movement of the vertical strokes that run down the side of the pot. Circles and dots, comprised of solid black lines, anchor the composition, pinning together what would otherwise be diverse background colours and textures. Smooth areas of glaze are tempered with crackled sections, and opacity is balanced with lucidity.

CORF (2019) explores similar ideas, but with a heightened sense of balance between coarse texture and smooth contour. The left side of the pot is covered with cubes of material which dissolve into layers of glaze. In contrast, the smoother side to the right undulates between soft grey and fleshy pink. The two parts – rugged and soft – are brought into dialogue via a yellow arch that functions as a focal point for the composition. To achieve such balance in paint would be difficult enough. To do so on a pot that will be fired numerous times is an altogether different kind of achievement.

Many of Hall's works feature fragments of illegible writing. Sometimes the letters are recognisably from the Roman alphabet, other times they seem akin to the Greek or Cyrillic alphabet, whilst yet others appear as indecipherable hieroglyphs. In his analysis of Cy Twombly's use of lettering in his paintings and drawings, Kirk Varnedoe observed that 'the evocation of graffiti seemed to speak at once of uncensored, expressive personal urgency and of objective engagement with a common, social language; to be of today and yet agelessly ancient.'[73] An identical ambivalence can be found in Hall's use of script. *Small Form* (2020), for instance, horizontally aligns lettering with two solid black marks – a semicircle and a dot – which could almost have been applied with spray paint. The spatial relationship between these two elements, in particular the fact that the black dot obscures one of the letters, suggests that the writing came first and was subsequently 'graffitied' over. This provides a sense of totemism, that the pot conveys earlier languages that have since been altered or erased. This could be emblematic of the ever-shifting development of language, evidenced by a constant revision of dictionaries. Ultimately, it documents nothing more than Hall's own process: his sense of layered decision-making, and the production of pots as an activity that takes considerable time but must coalesce into a single moment of appreciation.

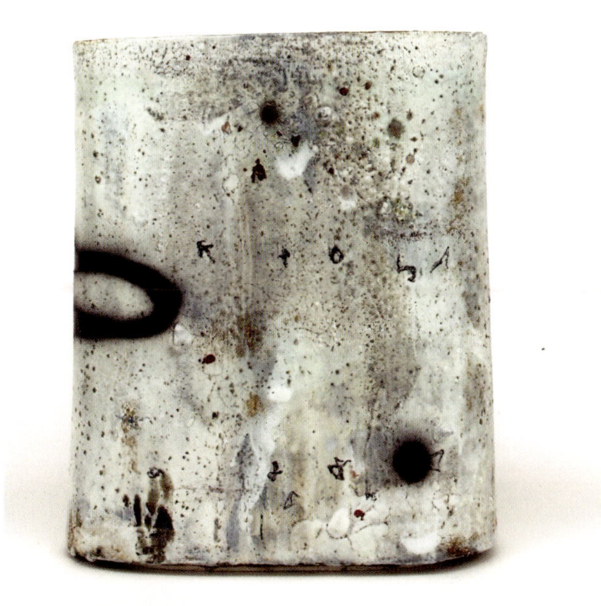

■ *Small Form* (2020).

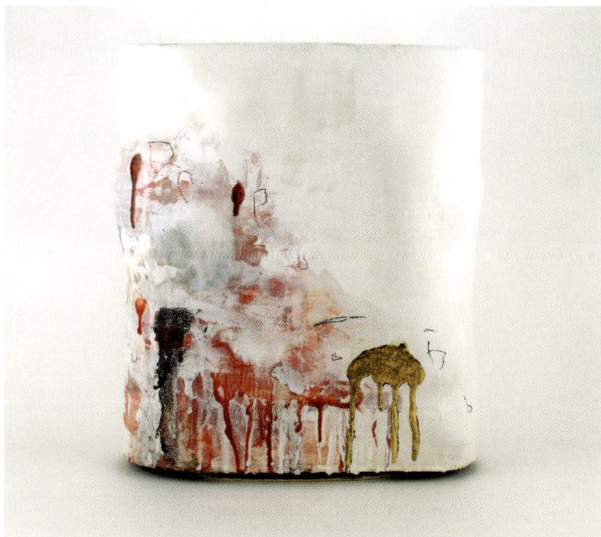

■ *Gold Cloud* (2018).

In contrast, the lettering that perpendicularly descends across the surface of *Gold Cloud* (2018), constitutes a porous border between the coloured section on the lower left and its lighter yellow/white background to the upper right. Once again, this invites several speculative narratives, from the significance of language in defining one nationality from another to language itself as a marker of civilisation apropos the rawness of nature. Like Twombly, Hall's use of writing marks his work as both modern and primordial, as a totem of civilisation via the pot, and

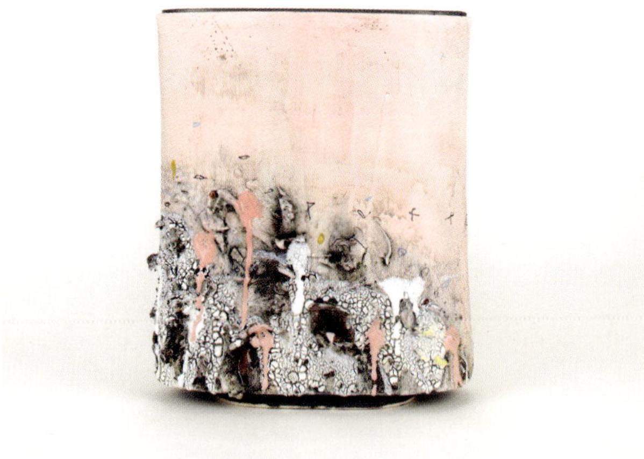

▮ *Flat Form Pink* (2020).

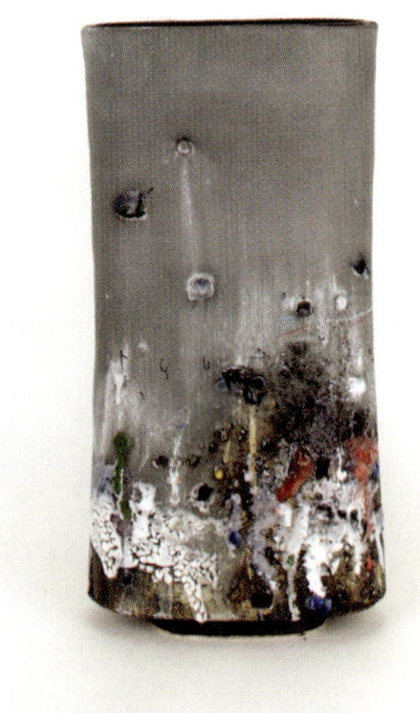

▮ *Tall Form Grey* (2020).

its subsequent palimpsestic re-inscription as contemporary art object.

Hall does not have a formula, but he certainly has compositional tendencies which relate to form, for it needs to be remembered that these are three-dimensional objects rather than flat canvasses. Many pots have a black interior of a density that seems to absorb light, a stark contrast to the vividity of the exterior. This 'emptiness' is redolent of the self-referential nature of the work: it 'contains' no secret ideological messages for the viewer to decode. The sense of internal absorption is often amplified through the application of layers of texture to the exterior, usually across the lower half of each work. This decision not only visually anchors each piece to the ground, but also alludes to containment. As representative examples, both *Flat Form Pink* (2020) and *Tall Form Grey* (2020) evoke a sense of gravity, as though the black hole of the interior were pulling matter down the side of the pot towards its base. Paradoxically, this creates a self-referential compositional frame where the exterior communicates something of the force of interior space, specifically the vertical sense of containment in each pot, and how the contents itself might rest once held inside.

The significance of containment is also explored in Hall's tea bowls. Inspired by his admiration of Anglo-Japanese pottery (especially the work of potters such as Mike Dodd), these bowls are more obviously three-dimensional than his expansively flattened forms. The roundedness and smaller scale of the tea bowl has enabled Hall to explore different compositional tendencies. Although some bowls, such as *Tea bowl* (2020), utilise a vertical topology that speaks to his larger works, others, such as *Tea bowl 2* (2021), are quite radically different. Hall's investigations into balance are reframed to cross the work horizontally, the addition of found pieces of rock functioning as both a handle and a compositional counterweight that literally pulls the form and surface texture away from the central cavity. The smoothness of the white-blue areas on *Tea bowl* (2019) create both visual and tactile dissonance to the coarse additions, the hand acutely aware of the texture as the bowl is held. Even where there is a toughness across the entire bowl, tension between viscosity and fluidity remains. The glaze run that has become a kind of supporting 'leg' on *Tea bowl 2*

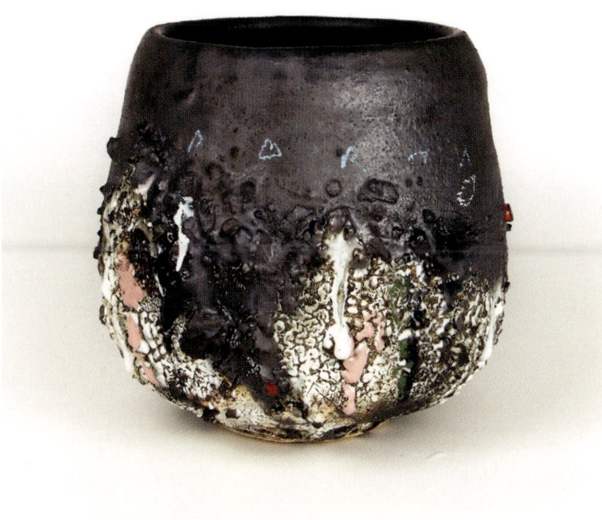

Tea bowl 1 (2020).

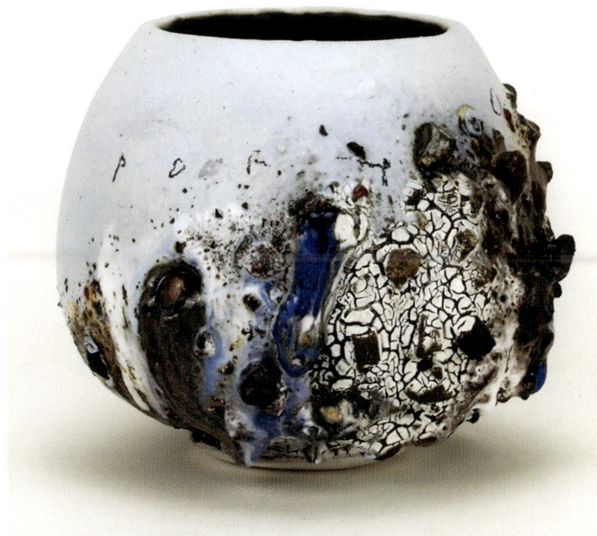

Tea bowl (2019).

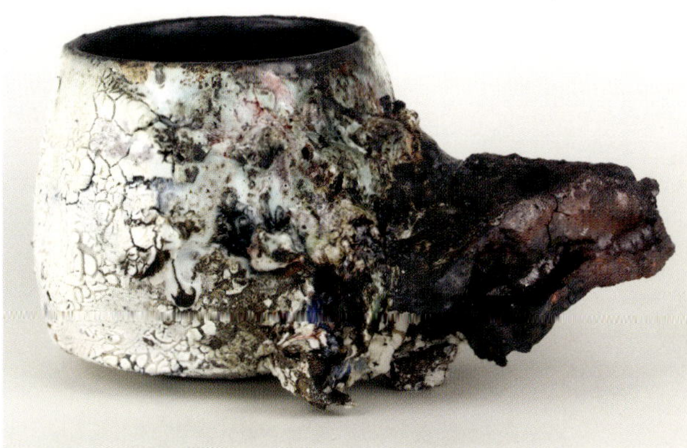

Tea bowl (2021).

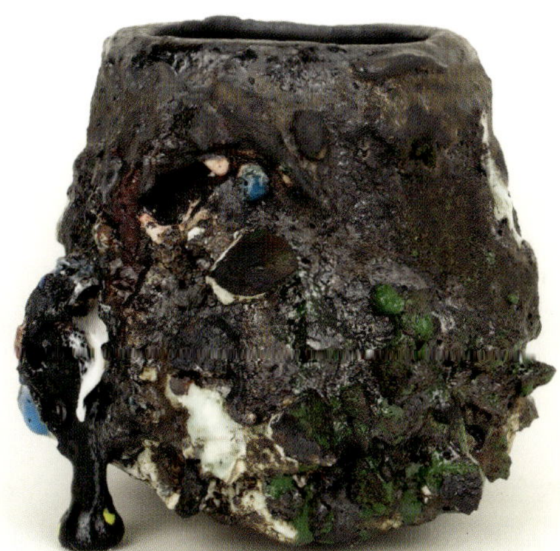

Tea bowl 2 (2020).

(2020) highlights the density of the surface; the gap between the body and the 'leg' demonstrating the weight of accumulated layers. Although products of the same general process, Hall's tea bowls are powerful because they are immediate and rugged. Their impoliteness commands attention.

If Hall's pots are documents of process, the studio as the site of production is necessarily interwoven with the object. Of course, the studio – particularly the way in which space directs process, the archiving of work, and the revealing of new avenues for exploration – is central to all artists. As the cultural geographer Jenny Sjöholm has observed:

> There is an archival character to the modern art studio; but, in contrast to the studio as a space where things are hidden and put into storage, the studio is an archive that can be highly vivid and bring certain

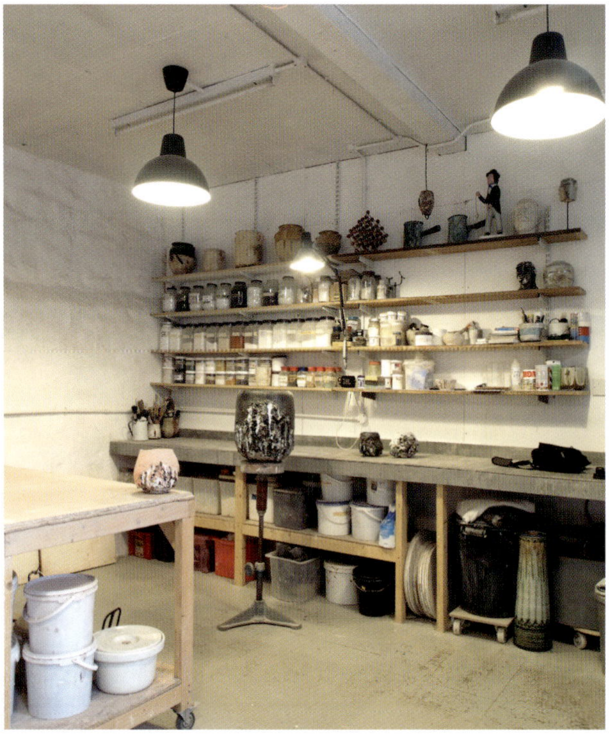

The Interior of Sam Hall's Studio (2012).

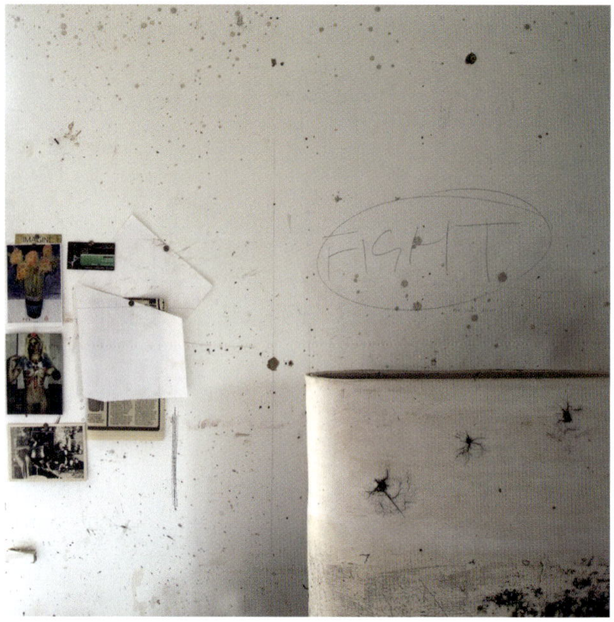

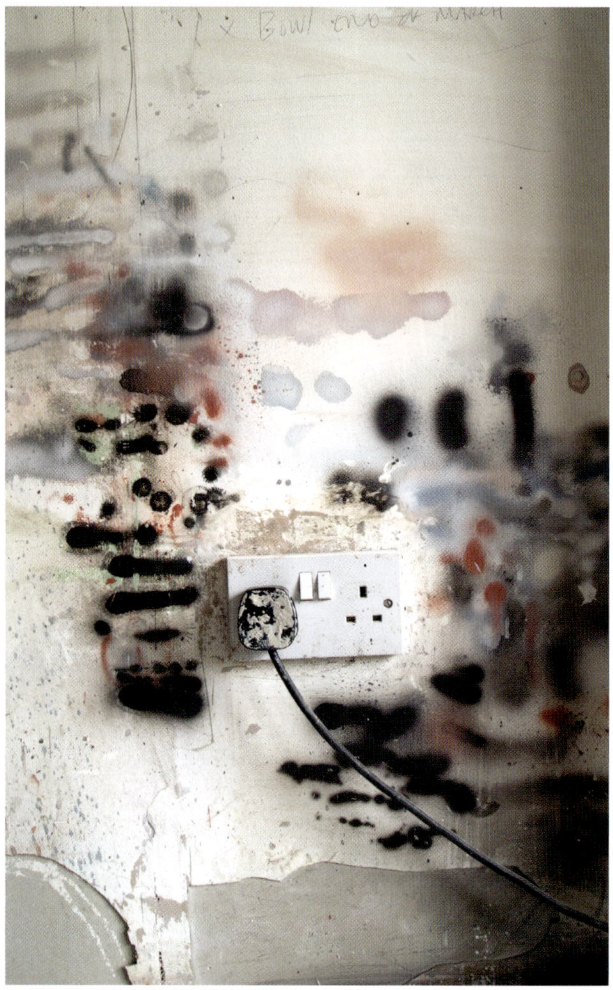

> potentialities. The archive points to the importance of material and stores of knowledge, and not momentary flashes of genius, to the artist. It points to the importance they attach to storing and logging their careers and development. [...] These processes and the collections, categories and archives that root them in the space of the studio offer artists a potential to, in the future, develop new work, as well as being a way in which they move through the past and forward in their practice. The personally set up active archives of artists are like tool sheds, feeding further exploration and understandings.[74]

Similarly, of the German-born British-based artist Mariele Neudecker, the curator, designer, and critic Greer Crawley has observed how her:

> archive like her studio is a territory made up of sediments and strata, residues and deposits. In both

> locations we see the artist as itinerant cartographer and her archive and studio as event-filled and autobiographical topographies. The marks, traces and imprints that are found there are itineraries of her wanderings. Records of her thinking and memories in pixels, graphite, paint, oil, gouache are indicative of a desire to reflect the immediacy of her experiences; the textural, visual and aural sensations of being elsewhere.[75]

The 'sediments and strata, residues and deposits' that Crawley speaks of are central to Hall's studio, which is equally redolent of the 'tool shed' identified by Sjöholm. Exactly like his pots, Hall's studio is a container – albeit for process – produced through layers of accumulation: of technique, experience, ideas, forms, tools, and glazes. As the photographs show, his studio resembles his pots; as a product of planning, decision-making, archiving for later use, and the layering of materials. Unlike his pots, however, the studio is not a work to be finished but an open-ended process, a continually working-in-progress. It is the dialogue between Hall and his studio that produces his pots, the latter akin to a diary in ceramic form, from which extracts are released into the world. In this sense, the studio is a symbiotic instrument: it is shaped by Hall, but it also shapes his creative process. Indeed, studios are spaces that demand a certain kind of scrutiny, a focus on creation, an attenuation towards practice. Interestingly, the word 'studio' is developed from the Latin word 'studium', which means desire, zeal, pursuit, and study. 'Studium' is itself derived from 'studere', to strive, desire, to busy oneself with something. Linguistically, the studio is bound to the focusing of behaviour: it is not an inert space but a negotiated and dialogic one. It speaks to the artist who must respond to its call, even as it inanimately submits to the artist's will.

Hall's self-referential pots and tea bowls are the products of a conversation between himself and his studio. They are fragmentary documents of impulse let out into the world. Perhaps surprisingly, given this, there is a strong sense of place in his works. This is not allusion to the Cornish landscape or a specific coastline, but to the studio as the site of process. The interweaving of smooth and rough contours, of lucid and blurred textures, seem to speak of the ups and downs of process, of Hall's 'fight' – the word is written on the wall of his studio – to create. Though ceramic processes are always fraught with failure, Hall's poetic work confirms that the kiln is, to quote Shakespeare, 'a muse of fire, that would ascend the brightest heaven of invention.'[76]

Sara Flynn
Drawn to Life

> Abstract drawing has always been for me a particularly exciting adventure. First there is only one's mood; then the surface takes one's mood in colour and texture; then a line or curve which, made with a pencil on the hard surface of many coats of oil or gouache, has a particular kind of 'bite' rather like incising on slate; then one is lost in a new world of a thousand possibilities because the next line in association with the first will have a compulsion about it which will carry one forward into completely unknown territory. The conclusion will be reached only by an awareness of some special law of harmonics induced at the beginning with some second line added to the first. Suddenly before one's eyes is a new form which, from the sculptor's point of view, free as it is from the problems of solid material, can be deepened or extended, twisted or flattened, tightened and hardened according to one's will, as one imbues it with its own special life. The whole process is opposite to that of drawing from life.[77]
>
> (*Barbara Hepworth*)

Drawing and sculpting have long been regarded as necessarily parallel activities, even if a sculptor's drawings are nothing more than a private and preliminary means of investigating form.[78] Barbara Hepworth (1903–1975) produced drawings, paintings, and prints alongside her sculptures, and her analysis of the ways in which these practices might overlap is insightful. For Hepworth, a drawn line could be understood as sculptural, as a kind of incision into space. Relationships between lines were considered as developmental, with their true impact discerned only in the actual act of making. Her belief that a line could be 'twisted or flattened, tightened and hardened' suggests that they have the capacity to deliver sculptural presence; that a line could be made to advance or recede, and even pulsate in simple or complex rhythms.

The work of the Irish ceramicist Sara Flynn explores the sculptural potential of line. Her vessels might even be regarded as three-dimensional drawings. From her Belfast studio, she produces pieces in which the scalpel acts as her pencil, her linear curves dividing interior from exterior space. The results are ceaselessly inventive vessels that explore specific kinds of formal language. Like Hepworth, Flynn has become acutely aware of how the placing of one line in relation to another opens up new realms of possibility. Her approach is guided by a mixture of design and instinct, an experiential understanding of how porcelain might behave, but also excitement in the discovery of the unexpected during the process of making.

Like a sculptor, Flynn often makes thumbnail sketches of form. Although drawing is a private activity – primarily a means for her to explore form without recourse to porcelain – the images are nevertheless revealing of her thought process. They document her preoccupation with formal refinement, specifically how the placing of one line in relation to another creates a new possibility, which is then captured in a subsequent drawing. Shading draws attention to the fact that these are three-dimensional works upon which the fall of light will be significant. Although the expanses of unshaded sections leave room for considerations of glaze, they also suggest a flatness, a kind of foreshortening, which gives her work a finely engineered sense of spatial ambiguity. Ultimately, Flynn's drawing is an act of investigating the linear flows that will constitute a composition in advance of its making. Yet, once in the moment of creating work, she will respond to what is happening

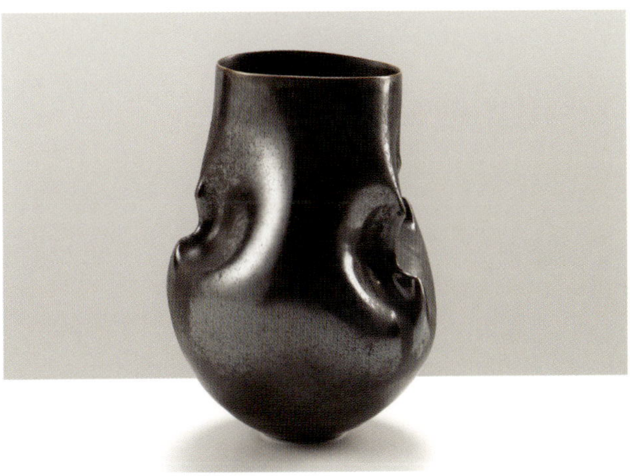

Triple Hipped Vessel (2012).

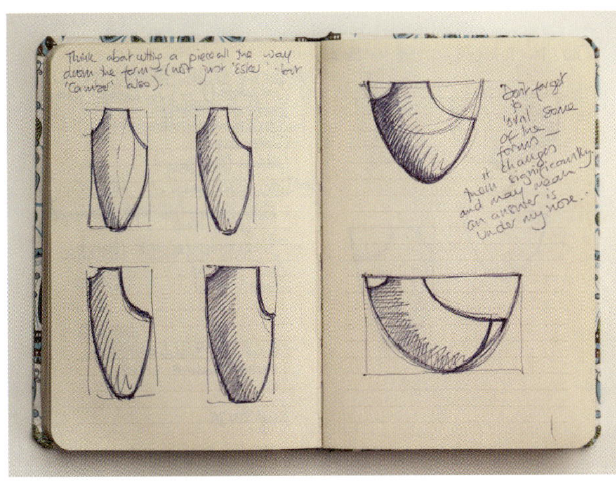

Studies for *Spine-Camber Vessels*.

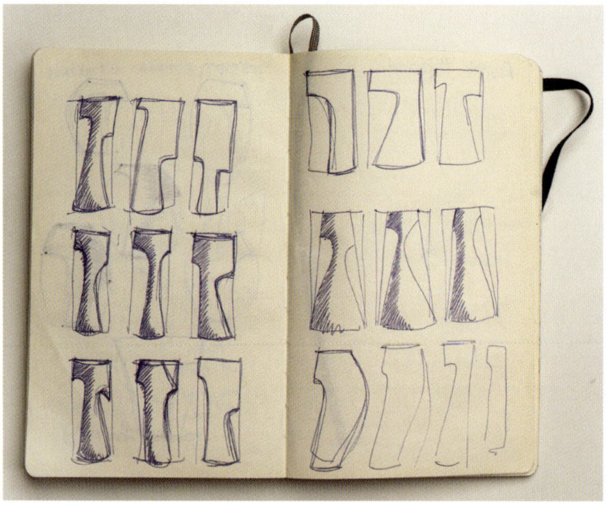

Studies for *Flection Vessels*.

in front of her, looking at how porcelain responds to the form she seeks to impose upon it, and making alterations as she goes so that there is a strong sense of material resolution.

In fact, there is a strong sense of being 'in the moment' in all of Flynn's work. She begins the process of sculpting by throwing pots in porcelain, seeking a form that has an appropriate sense of mass for the composition she will pursue. Throwing is, itself, an act of linear sculpting; the walls of porcelain that rise from the wheel from the pressure of the hand cut through space to form an interior. Throwing, to paraphrase Hepworth, constitutes the drawing of the very first sculptural line. Expression becomes predicated on where Flynn places the second, and any subsequent, lines. Acts of cutting and pasting transform the singular line of the vessel into a polyvalent statement of sculpture. By responding to the lines as and when she makes them, as opposed to uncritically realising a pre-determined design, she can produce forms that balance complexity with simplicity, that somehow capture the immediacy of their creation. One is always left feeling that the artist was fully mentally present at each stage of making. Processes of problem-solving and compositional refinement produce works that both surprise and satisfy; they push the eye around form at different speeds, drawing attention to the three-dimensional curvature that encloses space within, and resists spatial pressure from without. It is as though her works are being formed, glazed, and fired in front of us.

Flynn's vessels are not abstracted representations of the natural world. Titles, such as *Flection*, *Shoulder*, *Camber*, *Ipseity*, *Esker*, *Line*, and *Inner-cut*, might evoke the human body or landscape, but they are deployed because they help to draw attention to the dynamic qualities of her forms. The lines that constitute each piece twist and pinch with startling angularity, but these exist only to give the sculpture expressive potency. When examined from different angles, such contours can produce very different effects, sometimes extending, sometimes supressing, the sense of an interior space. The intersection of these contours activates a compositional tension that Flynn skilfully resolves. This is how works such as *Spine-Camber Vessel* and *Esker Vessel* (both 2014) command presence; they have a rhythm that is taut because it is both angular and smooth. The shiny white surface of these pieces implies movement, leading the eye towards the spatial presence of the work. Yet, the play of light across the surface (alluded to in her drawings) gives them a strong sculptural

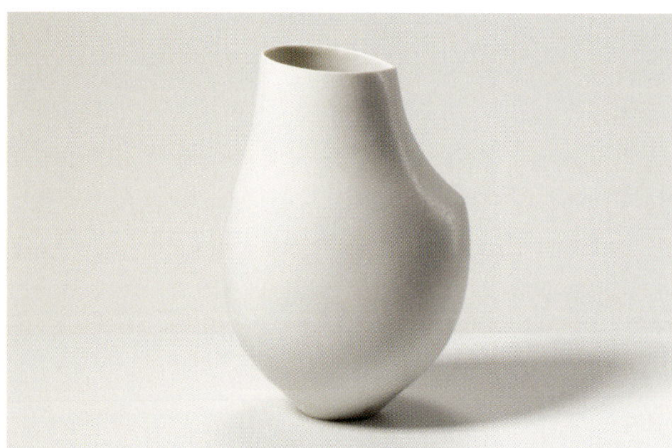

Spine-Camber Vessel (2014).

presence. To my mind, pieces such as *Esker Vessel* (2014) express the same material sensuousness as a Hepworth sculpture in marble.

For Flynn, colour is symbiotic to the composition of form. Decisions around glaze might be based upon the form produced, or a form might be created to enable a specific glaze to behave in a particular way when fired. Naturally, these decisions affect how light is reflected or absorbed, enabling surface undulations to stand out or recede. The knowledge required to anticipate such effects has been gained only through rigorous glaze testing, and by understanding how glaze recipes will behave when applied to different kinds of form. Certainly, this is where Flynn demonstrates her supreme technical mastery. *Triple Hipped Vessel* (2012), for instance, utilises the reflection of light to draw attention to the compressions that constitute the form, thereby highlighting the three-dimensional curve of the surface. This activates a visual pun on the name – the concave shape emphasised by light serves to evoke a female torso with 'hips'. There is a richness of colour, almost akin to a patina, that breaks down to a pointillist-like combination of inflection upon detailed scrutiny of the surface. Each piece has a strong presence when examined close up as well as from afar.

Rims and feet are equally important compositional facets. They are end points, a kind of sculptural full stop, that serve to connect the form with the surface. They are rarely perfectly circular, and in darker works such as *Flection Vessel* and *Ipseity Vessel* (both 2018), the porcelain body is allowed to show through. This decision gives each piece a strong sense of vertical completion, paradoxically encouraging the eye to read the form horizontally. Some pieces, such as *Ipseity Vessel*, feature matt black interiors, turning the rim into a kind of black hole that seems to pull space inwards. Others, such as *Flection Vessel*, have shiny interiors, giving the impression that interior

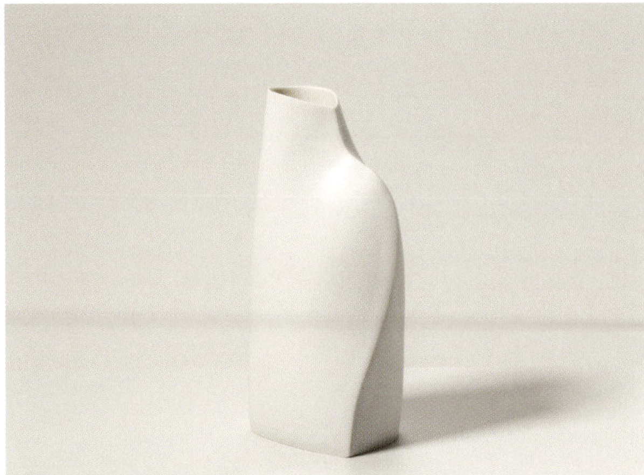

Esker Vessel (2014).

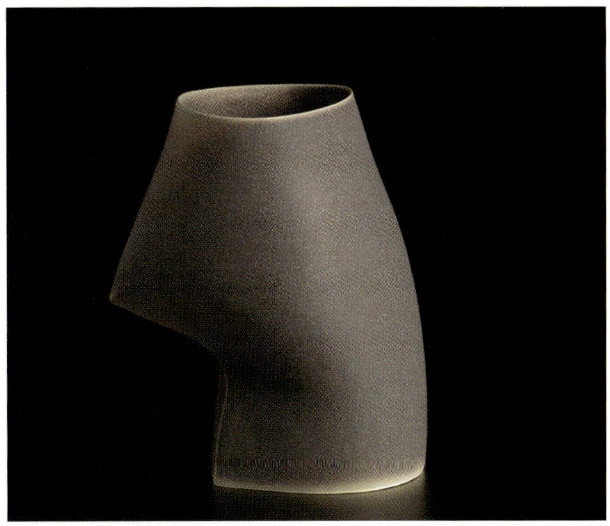

Flection Vessel (2018).

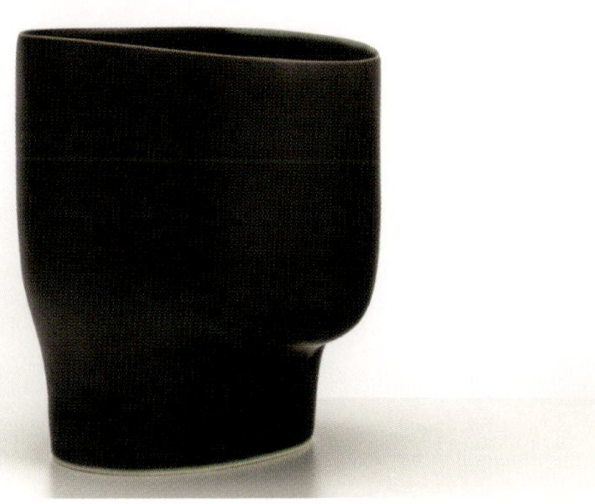

Ipseity Vessel (2018).

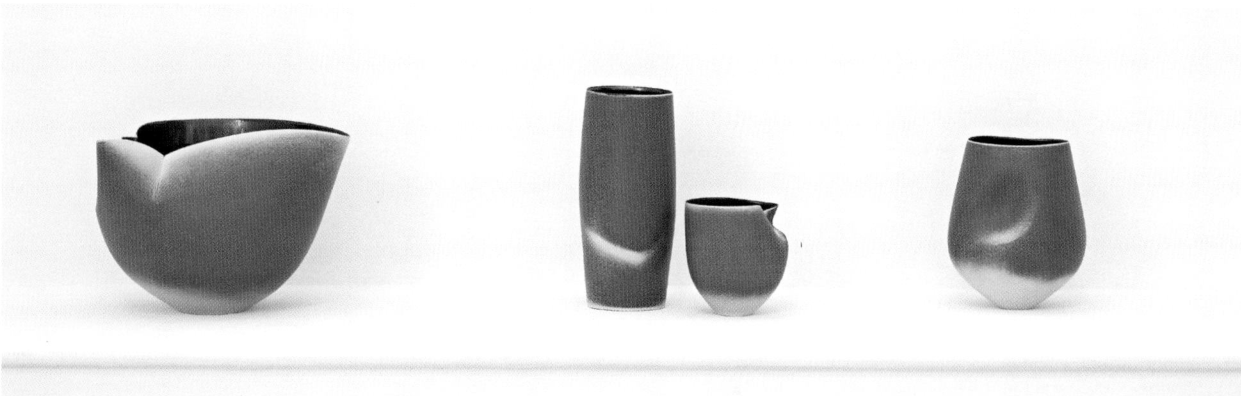

■ *Flection Bowl, Ipseity Vessel, Spine-Camber Vessel, Camber Vessel* (2020).

space is being ejected from the vessel body. Form, colour, and surface are always carefully resolved. The result is a poised vessel that implies movement between internal and external space. In short, they seem to breathe.

The unification of form, colour, and surface treatment is powerfully caught in a series of works in which the glaze was applied as a spray. The rich green-grey glaze that flashes across *Flection Bowl, Ipseity Vessel, Spine-Camber Vessel,* and *Camber Vessel* (all 2020) appears to flatten each piece. This sensation is at odds with the light green foot and rim, which highlights the three-dimensionality of each form. Further sculptural lines appearing in light green, either to the rim or across the vessel body, draw attention to undulation, rendering a three-dimensional line into an apparently two-dimensional canvas. Such visual games cause the eye to twist and turn across the complexity of the composition, even whilst the richness of glaze and apparent simplicity of form conjure a gentle calmness. In such work, Flynn demonstrates her highly refined understanding of how light can shape form but has here fixed it in glaze for the sake of the spectator. Through their interplay between two and three dimensions, these pieces evoke her preparatory drawings, though they are resolutely sculptural works.

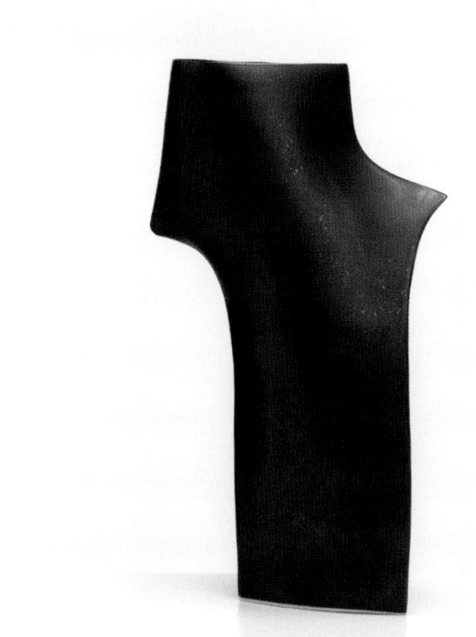

■ *Flection Vessel* (2020).

Even the apparently flattest of forms, such as *Flection Vessel* (2020), have great sculptural presence. This is in part derived from the fact that, rather obviously, they can be held when physically encountered. Tactility is an integral part of the experience of Flynn's ceramics, and even the most precariously balanced

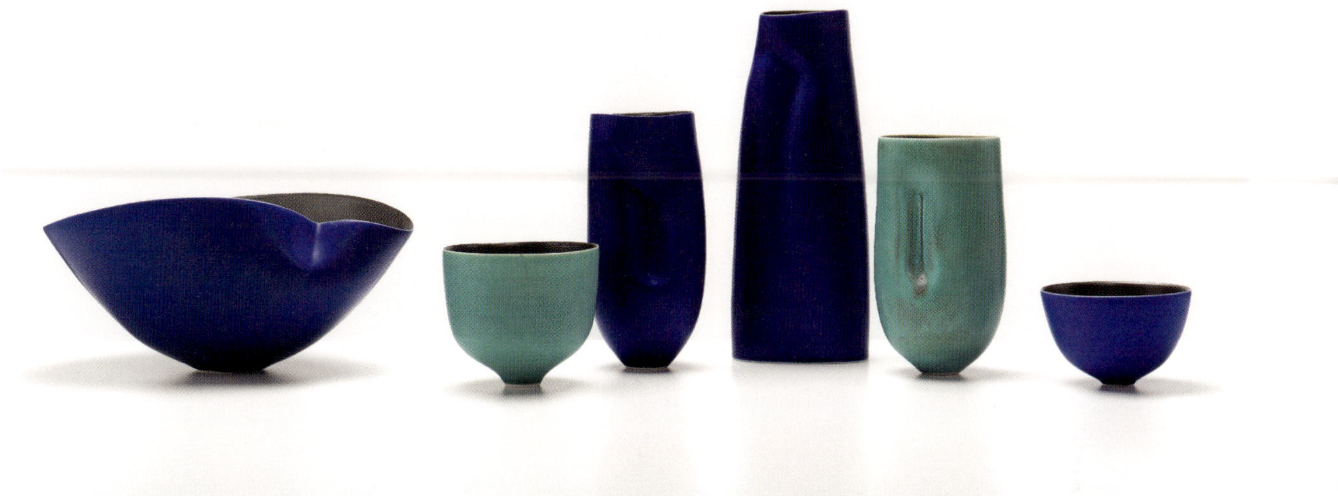

Vessel Group (2020).

form retains a strong sense of weightiness to the base. Of course, this is a practical outcome – it prevents the work from tumbling over and is undoubtedly a product of its throwing – but it is also a compositional decision that pertains to mass. For example, *Flection Vessel* seems to grow vertically from the ground, only to twist and turn via perpendicular joints that shape the interior into a diagonal. The smoothness of the surface enables light to reflect this angularity, and the mass of the vessel appears to be manipulated to move across multiple elevational axes (vertically, horizontally, perpendicularly, diagonally). The eye registers one mass, but the hand feels a different one as it handles the form and recognises that the weight is firmly located in the base. This illustrates how Flynn pushes porcelain in all directions, manipulating the visual and physical sense of its mass, as well as its spatial properties across two and three dimensions.

Taken as a whole, Flynn's work exudes a masterful knowledge of how the different elements of a vessel can be powerfully combined. She uses a formal language derived from the history of ceramics to produce elegant sculptures, and each piece stands as an investigation of the sculptural possibilities of curved lines. When her work is displayed in groupings, its full richness can be seen. Beautifully resolved contortions move the eye across different compositional ebbs and flows, from the horizontal to the vertical, and from a two-dimensional contemplation of surface to a three-dimensional recognition of form. Such comparison enables a stronger appreciation of how she engages with different sculptural questions and yet produces a resolved set of answers. Ultimately, Flynn's work captures the fluidity and stability of porcelain as a material. Her works look as though they might melt, or that touch could leave an imprint or distort their delicate surfaces. Yet, these are robust, grounded, and resolute sculptures that Flynn has carefully drawn to life. As referential of nothing beyond the language of porcelain, her work constitutes a powerful celebration of what this material can do.

Julian Stair
On the Table

This *Attic Red-Figure Skyphos* (a pot used for the consumption of alcohol) dates from 460–450BC. It is adorned with the motif of other pots: a cooking pot, a wine jar, and a jug are placed in an interior setting as a type of early 'still life'. The design transforms the skyphos into a kind of self-referential meta-pot where form is also subject. The depiction of a woman drinking from a similar bowl to the bowl itself (a subversive act in a domestic setting where the consumption of alcohol was a male social activity) suggests that the ripest appreciation of this pot comes at the moment of its use. As such, it conveys the significance of pots as multi-sensory objects: they are concerned with sight, sound, taste, touch, and smell.

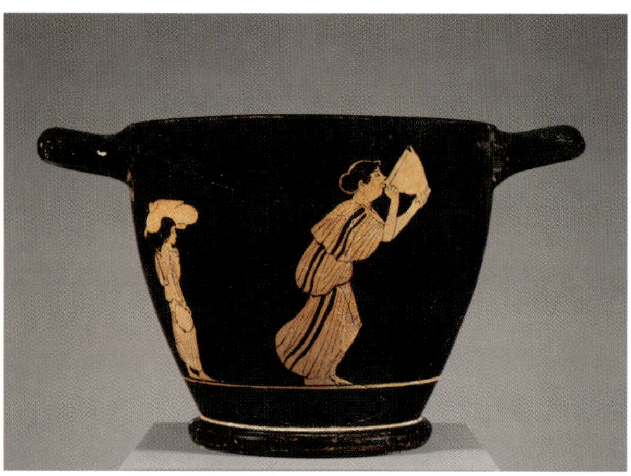

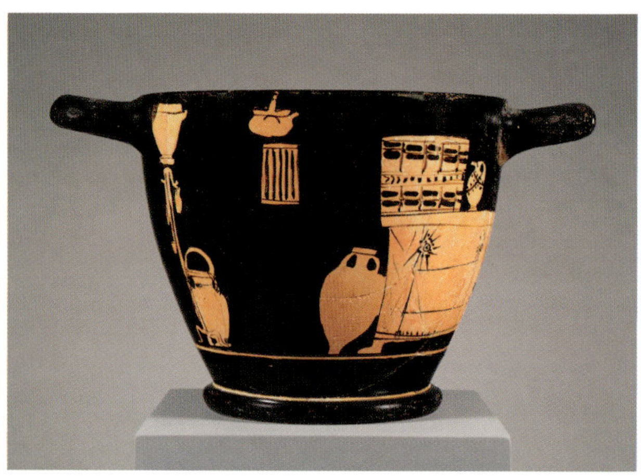

Attic Red-Figure Skyphos (460–450BC).

Yet, when considering ancient Greek pottery, the rather tired arguments discussed in the introduction resurface: should ceramics be classified as art or craft? As Brian Sparkes has observed in his study of these ancient pots, 'emphasis has been placed on the art-historical aspect; the vases have attracted the art-market approach (as well as the art market), even though Greek vases do not seem to have been considered, at the time of their making, as works of art, as objects to be admired in their own right.'[79] The contemporary classification of ancient works as 'art' is at odds with academic insistence that these pots were accorded no such status in the period they were made. Today, ancient Greek pots are displayed in museums, placed on plinths, and framed by vitrines that demand aesthetic rather than tactile appreciation. Yet, this change in status, which occurred across the twentieth century,[80] serves only to highlight the paradoxical attitude taken towards the classification of ceramic objects. If ancient Greek pots are now art museum objects, claims for clay as art or craft have nothing to do with the material itself, as some critics cited in the introduction claimed. Instead, status is produced by market driven economics seeking profit from the finite availability of work. This is a force so influential that it can produce a kind of historical revisionism: 'humble pots' from ancient Greece can be transformed into totemic markers of Western civilisation.

Of course, pots have long been a fine art subject, appearing in still life paintings from the fourteenth century onwards. For instance, Diego Velázquez (1599–1660), Jean-Baptiste Siméon Chardin (1699–1779), Henri Matisse (1869–1954), Georges Braque (1882–1963), and Pablo Picasso (1881–1973) have long revealed the expressive potential of pots to fine art audiences.[81] Some of these later artists influenced twentieth-century British abstract painters such as Ben Nicholson (1894–1982), whose exploration of the architecture of jugs, mugs, and goblets was a central motif in his work. In this respect, it is noteworthy that Nicholson exhibited alongside the artist potter William Staite Murray (1881–1962) at Beaux Arts in London in 1927, the latter refuting Bernard Leach's diktat that utilitarianism had to be the primary concern of pottery. Possibly influenced by Staite Murray's own love of Chinese porcelain, Nicholson expressed admiration for what he perceived to be an enduring sense of aesthetic reality in decorated Chinese vases:

> In writing Herbert recently a letter which I did not in the end post, I found myself putting out an idea that what I am interested in in painting is in *realizing an experience* and not at all in *making a painting*. It's something to do with creating an *enduring reality* based on an experience of living which is by no means purely visual but is a rhythm arrived at by means of *all* the senses. In my work I don't want to achieve a dramatic arresting experience exciting as that can be, but something more enduring – the kind of thing one finds say in the finest Chinese vases or in the Cézanne apple paintings.[82]

In sympathy with my analysis of the *Attic Red-Figure Skyphos* described above, Nicholson also found in Chinese porcelain a transcendent multi-sensory aesthetic experience.

Such admiration of Chinese pottery was nothing new of course. The British appreciation of porcelain can be traced back to the first Chinoiserie craze in the seventeenth century. Perhaps Nicholson's fascination arose from his interest in so-called 'Primitivism' – the disavowal of developed Western painting conventions – which he had found in the work of the retired fisherman turned painter Alfred Wallis (1855–1942). Certainly, Nicholson's interest in Chinese porcelain paralleled other Western developments in modern art that were invigorated by contact with Asian art, such as the opening up of Japan during the Meiji

Restoration, which enabled the export of Japanese *ukiyo-e* woodblock prints and influenced French Impressionism, as well as, later, Bernard Leach's veneration of Japanese ceramics. In any case, from 1933 to 1934, Nicholson worked on designs for a coffee service for Foley China (E. Brain and Co) in Staffordshire, which was produced in bone china and exhibited at Harrods in London in October 1934 (prototypes for which are now in the collections of the Victoria and Albert Museum). Even though Nicholson's design bore many similarities with his paintings of the same period, this did not push the craft of ceramic production into the domain of fine art.[83] After all, this project was first and foremost a design commission.

Yet, when I look at some of Ben Nicholson's still life works, especially his etchings, I am reminded of the work of Lucie Rie (1902–1995). There is no causal connection in terms of art history, yet I observe how the sgraffito lines on Rie's cup and saucer echo Nicholson's scoring, his etchings made by drawing into steel plates with a sharp implement. Indeed, they share the utilisation of lines to sculpt space in an almost architectural manner, animating flattened planes into highly resonant and arresting compositions. As with ancient Greek pots, Rie's work

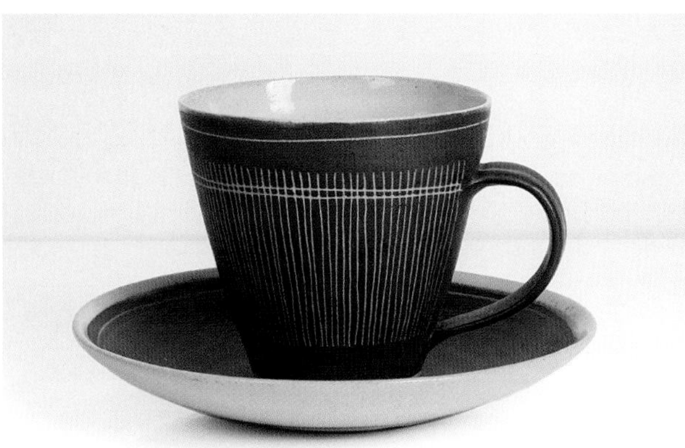

Cup and Saucer by Lucie Rie and Hans Coper (c.1958).

has been increasingly subject to museumification; the only function of much of her functional pottery now is to be observed through glass. Rie's work was expensive whilst she was alive and, since her death, market prices have gradually risen (at the time of writing, the auction record for Rie stands at a whopping £171,000 for a footed bowl). However, during her lifetime, Rie refused classification as either tradition or modern, art or craft. She was simply a potter who made pots:

> If one should ask me whether I believe to be a modern potter or a potter of tradition I would answer, I don't know and I don't care. Art alive is always modern, no matter how old or young. Art theories have no meaning for me, beauty has. This is all my philosophy. I do not attempt to be original or different. Something to which describe I am not clever enough [*sic*], moves me to do what I do.[84]

Rie remained consistent with the priorities of European modernism, where, as Peter Apsden has noted, 'purity of form and technological innovation were, crucially, allied to function'.[85]

I have begun this assessment of the work of Julian Stair with these wider examples for three reasons. Firstly, like the *Attic Red-Figure Skyphos* described above, Stair draws upon the meta-pot, of situating the pot as both form and subject in his work. Such comparison with the *Attic Red-Figure Skyphos* also seeks to locate his approach as arising from an interrogation of ceramic history. Secondly, as will be demonstrated below, Stair has always been concerned with the sculptural possibilities of line, making both Ben Nicholson and Lucie Rie instructive points of reference. Thirdly, he emerged into the profession in the late 1970s, when heated debates about the categorisation of studio ceramics as either 'art' or 'craft' was at its height. Yet, like Rie, Stair obstinately refused to be pulled into any one category. The history of the pot as a tactile and functional object, the sculptural possibility of the pot, the visual appeal of surface, and the arrangement of form into a compositional tonality, are all equally important to him. In this sense he is, like Rie, simply a potter who makes pots. Yet, if one eye is focused on the wheel, the other has been scanning debates about art and craft for the different ways in which his work might be framed. His art history PhD thesis, which focused on the development of studio pottery criticism across the twentieth century, enabled Stair to contemplate how his work might be conceptualised from different perspectives. The 'ceramics as art or craft discipline' debate is not irrelevant to Stair; it is just that, by assiduously investigating how ceramic form sculpts space, he acknowledges that both are always on the table.

For his degree show in 1977, Stair produced a series of works that manipulated perceptions of containment – an approach that evokes the work of Ben Nicholson, where flattened planes were created through the manipulation of lines that could also be simultaneously recognised as three-dimensional forms, such as a cup or a goblet. In these early works, Stair successfully deployed trompe l'œil effects to evince volume and perspective. *Freestanding Reliefs* (1977) are strong examples: the reliefs – as the name suggests – are flattened forms meticulously carved and shaped into perspective to imply volume. In contrast, the *Shadow Pots* (1981) produced just a few years later used marks on a three-dimensional form to foreshorten them, to produce the sensation of a three-dimensional object becoming two-dimensional. Although they might be regarded as rather literal in comparison to later investigations, they nevertheless allude to questions that have remained central to Stair. How does form inhabit space and how can sensations be manipulated? How can preconceptions around the categorisation of ceramics be challenged and augmented? How does user interaction facilitate the creation of meaning?

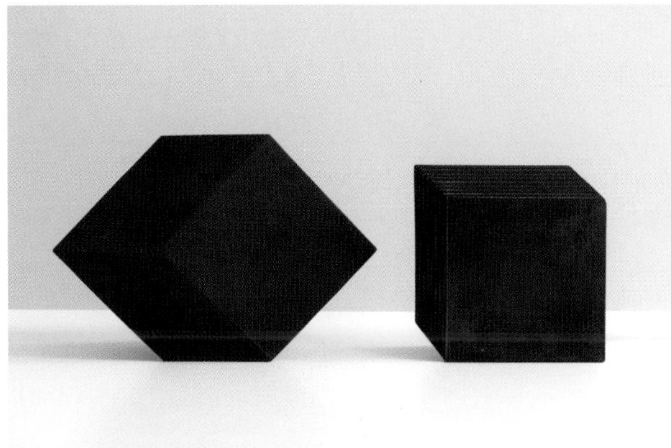

■ *Freestanding Reliefs* (1977).

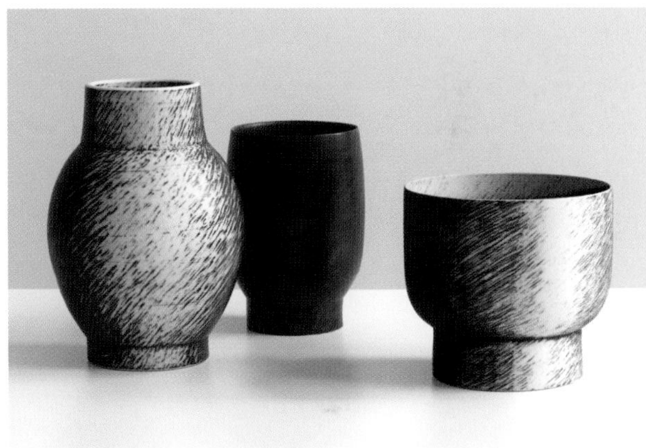

■ *Shadow Pots* (1981).

Subsequent work further interrogated how interactions between form and surface could affect perception. *Small Jar, Waisted Jar, and Bowl* (1984) utilise marks that, by interaction with the three-dimensional form of the work itself, create an illusion of movement. The *Bowl*, for example, appears to spin at rapid speed. In compositional terms, the vertical marks break the rhythm of the horizontal marks, yet they intensify the feeling of momentum because they suggest directions of travel. These concave vertical marks are repeated to the interior, making the bowl appear to rotate clockwise. The *Waisted Jar* spins like a cotton spool, the white horizontal band in the middle squeezing the waist inwards. The waiving lines of the *Small Jar* afford a sense of emergence and

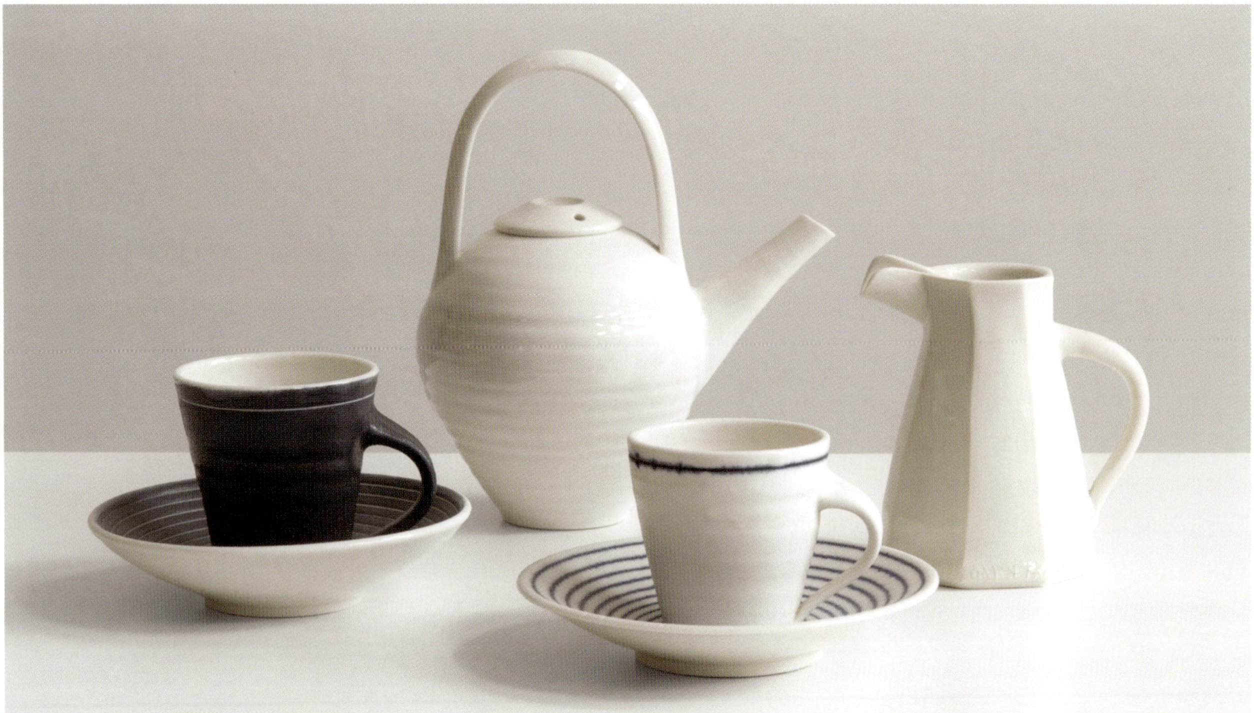

Teapot, two Cups and Saucers, and Faceted Jug (1990).

growth, which amplify the opening and closing of the form itself. In these works, form and surface have been placed in careful dialogue to manipulate sensations of space via quasi-optical effects.

By the late 1980s, Stair began to feel that he had pushed line as far as it could go, whilst forms were becoming too complex. Following a trip to the USA in 1988 (which included some experiments in wood-fired stoneware), he returned to explore how domestic forms could be perceived as sculptural statements through a more minimal aesthetic. In earlier transitional work, this entailed using marks to draw attention to form. Redolent of sgraffito by Lucie Rie, concentric circles were applied to saucers to amplify shape through repetition (an approach also utilised by the painter Bridget Riley). A line drawn around the rim of a cup highlights how the rim itself actively sculpts space. The extrusion of handles on teapots and the faceting of jugs enabled light to activate sensations of the form as still life sculpture. Thus, the shadows on the *Shadow Pots* could be highlighted through form alone, without the need for additional marks.

This understanding led to a stronger sense of the power of form. *Two Cups on a Ground* (2001) draws attention to cups as intrinsically sculptural objects;

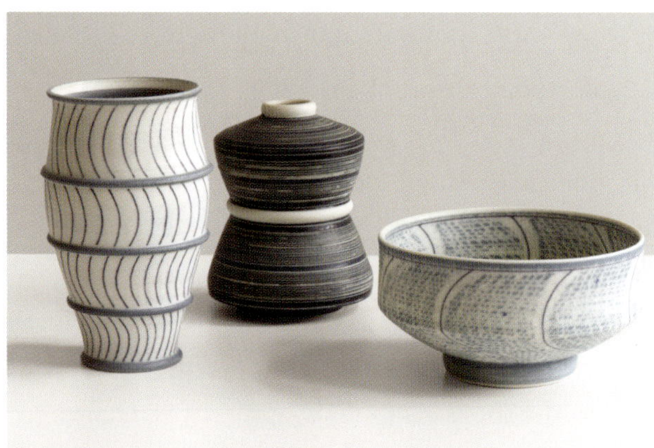

Small Jar, Waisted Jar, and Bowl (1984).

that cups need to contain space before they can contain anything else. Stair also began to explore tone, achieved by the use of different materials, as part of the same composition. The glazed white porcelain cup reflects light differently to the black unglazed stoneware cup; the white is more reflective, and shadows are less apparent, yet despite the black being more absorbent of light, shadows heighten our sense of the form. Akin to the plinth for sculpture, grounds 'contain' objects by giving them a resting place. Like the ancient Greek pot placed in the museum, here the ground elevates the significance of the cup. Quasi-ceremonial, as though they belong in some kind of tea ceremony, these works draw attention to the significance of daily activities, specifically the celebration of food and drink as something essential to all humanity. Like the *Attic Red-Figure Skyphos*, Stair's work connects all the senses.

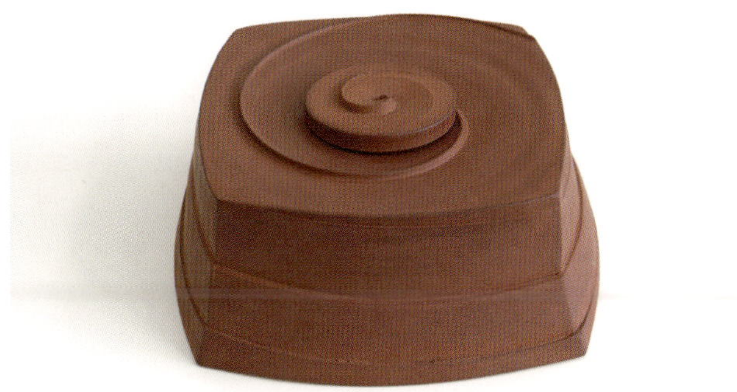

Caddie (1998).

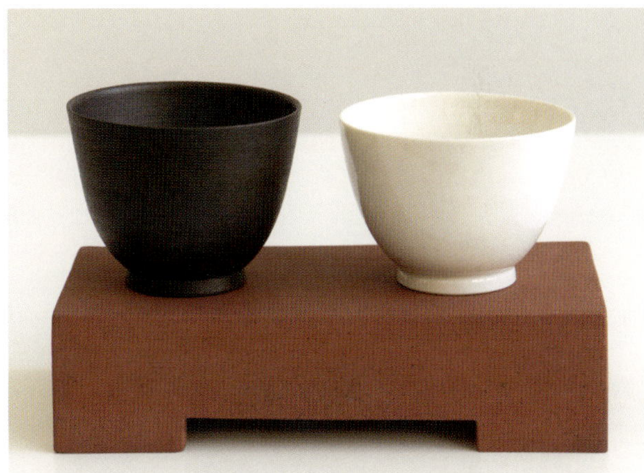

Two Cups on a Ground (2001).

A particularly significant form to develop from the work on grounds was the caddie. The caddie is perhaps most associated with tea leaves, yet the elevation of a caddie on a ground once again afforded it a special status, as if it were a ritual object. This inevitably provokes analysis of its broader symbolism in rituals for containment, as a holder for the remnants of life, and as a metaphor for the human body. Indeed, in different times, places and cultures, there have existed sarcophagi, tombs, coffins, and urns, all of which contain and commemorate the dead, and prevent contamination with the living. Stair's anthropological understanding of this significance led to *Quietus* (2012–2014), an exhibition shown at MIMA Middlesborough, the National Museum in Cardiff, Winchester Cathedral, and Somerset House in London. *Quietus* consisted of numerous works, including *Columbarium* – an installation of 130 cinerary jars developed from the caddie form – as well as sarcophagi, and large jars thrown to resemble the contours of the human body. One cinerary jar was especially symbolic of death: it was partly made from, and made to contain, the ashes of Stair's uncle-in-law, Lesley Cox. The exhibition of these works in different locations – art galleries and cathedrals – signalled how Stair used ceramic practices to reunite artistry and religion, an aspect readily apparent in the tomb monuments that provided a visual counterpoint to Stair's works when they were exhibited in Winchester Cathedral.

Quietus also included a number of *Monumental Jars* that, constructed in sections to rise to the height of a person, inferred relationships between the human body and the pot: both are containers of liquid and mass, exhibit the contradictory qualities of fragility and resilience, and are constituted by

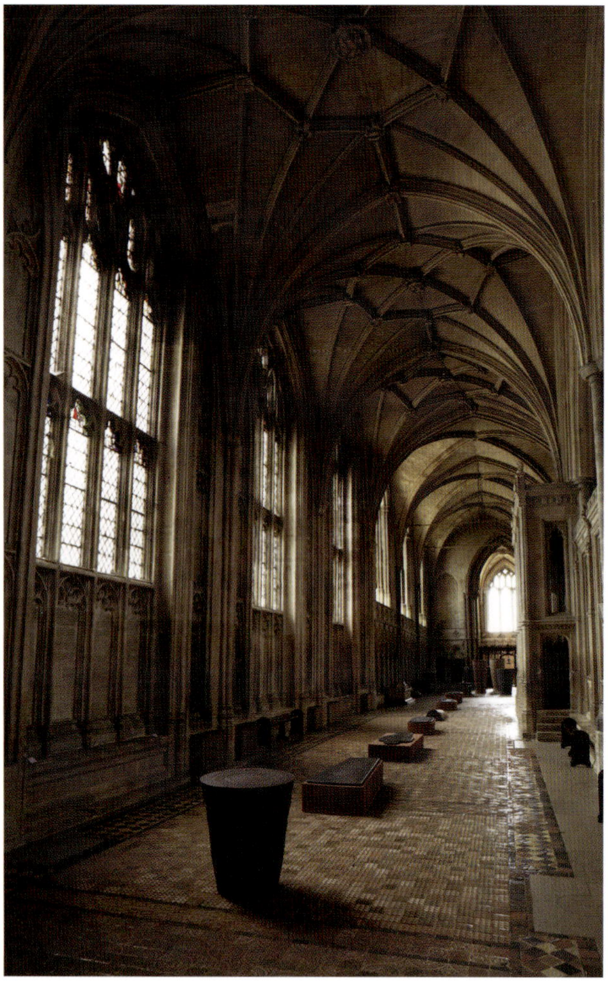

Quietus in the Presbytery Aisle of Winchester Cathedral (2013).

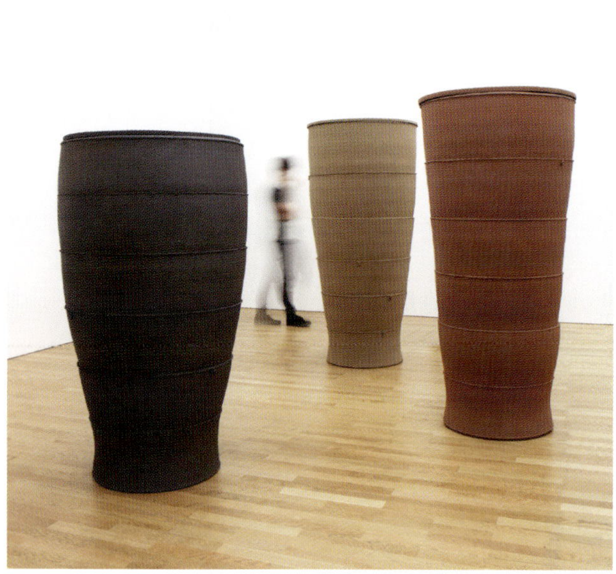

Monumental Jars VIII, XII & *X*, mima (2012).

'skins' which divide interior space from the exterior world. These works led Stair to further investigate questions of monument and the status of the pot. In *Equivalence* (2018), held at the Corvi-Mora gallery in London, monumental cups, mugs, and jugs were placed in the centre of a white gallery space, whilst smaller works on wall-mounted grounds were hung around the gallery walls. The architecture of the white space meant that the works became meta-pots in dialogue with themselves. Perceptions of form were foregrounded. If the proportions of a mug are scaled up and placed in a white gallery space, is the work fine art sculpture or pottery? Visitors were invited to question the delineations between art and craft based upon form, context, and scale. Stair seemed to propose that the containment of space exists in both fine art sculpture and craft, enabling ceramics to hover between the two. Interestingly, the same conceptual questions surfaced in works from Stair's degree show in 1977.

To be equivalent does not mean to be the same, however. Stair has consistently sought to shift perceptions about ceramics: its form, status, and meanings. This includes reference to movements in fine art and sculpture, especially modernism, but also to the history of pottery as an essential facet of civilisation – the pot as a totemic marker of humanity, and the modernist pot as broadening out the aesthetics of British studio ceramics. He has successfully exploited the ambivalence of categorising ceramics: that cups can be a subject of the loftiest kind of fine art, yet resolutely attached to the earthy realities of death; aesthetically contemplated as sculpture yet used unpretentiously in the everyday stuff of life. If

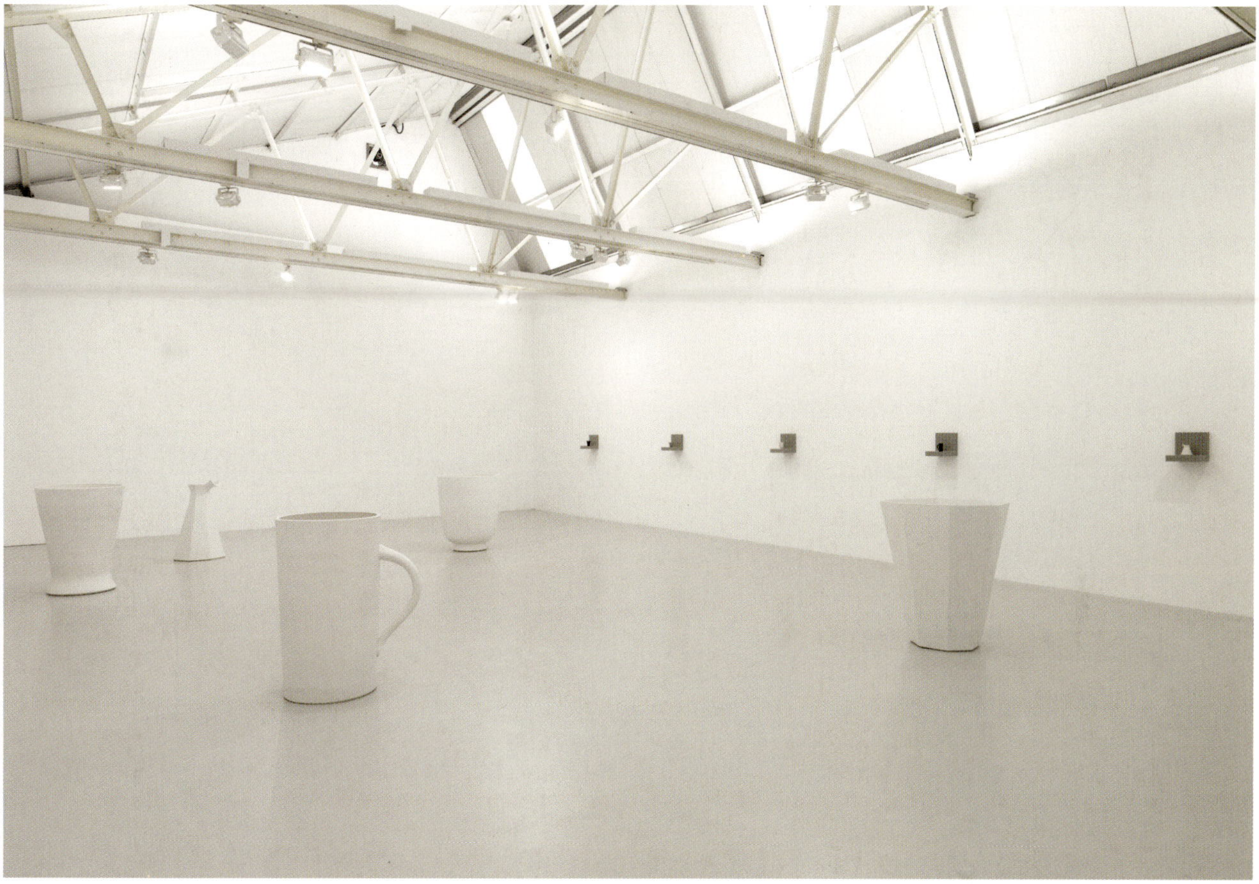

Equivalence, held at Corvi-Mora, London (2018).

there is a developmental thread across his forty-year career, it is the assertion that ceramics, despite its interdisciplinarity, should be treated on its own terms according to its own parameters and referents. His work is more than the aesthetic pleasure of fine art; yet it is also more than the essential utilitarianism of craft practice. For Stair, ceramic practices are themselves powerful modes of expression. His work is a reminder that clay services our most basic needs and our grandest aesthetic ambitions.

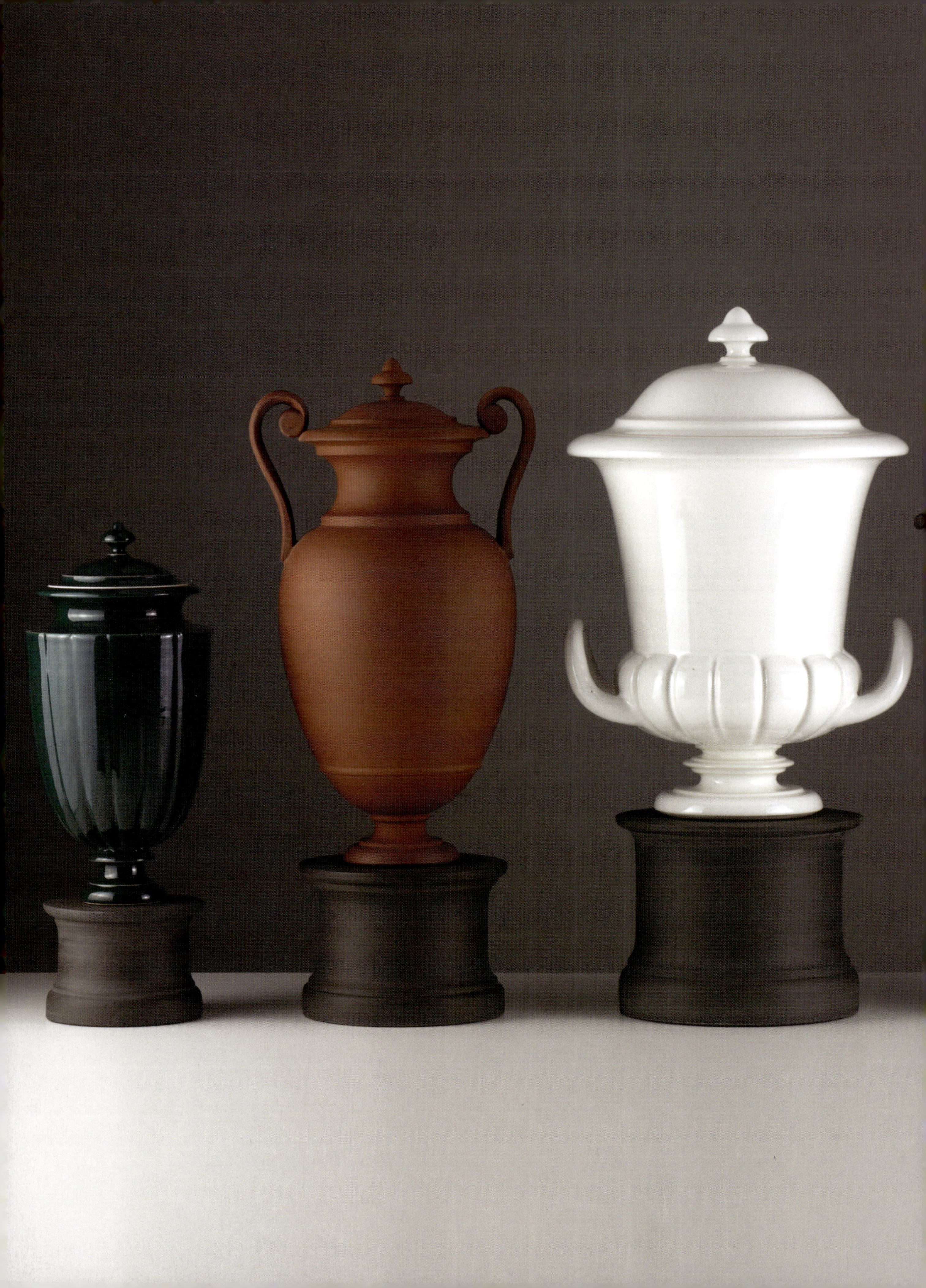

Dialogues with the Eighteenth and Nineteenth Centuries

Jo Taylor
Re-Collections

> **collect** (verb): to bring or be brought together, to gather; to build up a collection of a particular type because of an interest in or enthusiasm for them; to call for something, to fetch, to pick up; to get something from people; to calm or control oneself, to get one's thoughts etc under control.
>
> (*Chambers Dictionary*)

Jo Taylor's work is inspired by the aesthetics of the European baroque and French rococo, as expressed in seventeenth- and eighteenth-century architecture, interior design, fine art engravings, and ceramics. This interdisciplinary interest has been forged through visits to English country houses, where baroque ceramic objects were collected, displayed, and used. Interestingly, this means that the ornate aesthetics of her work is as much a response to the wider social history of ceramic collecting as it is to design. As Tamara Préaud has noted in her analysis of French Sèvres porcelain:

> In the hothouse environment of social distinction, the ideal host or hostess was one who could bring inspiration to the art of dinner-giving and creativity to the art of dressing a table; one who could plan a dining experience that would satisfy the palette, the mind, and the eye. [... Sèvres] porcelain served as nothing less than a symbol of the transforming power of human creativity in taking a humble ingredient like clay and fashioning it by hand and mind into something rare and lovely.[86]

By the middle of the nineteenth century, Sèvres 'ranked among the most sought-after of porcelain, conferring upon its owners respectability and taste'.[87] Whilst some British ceramic artists – most notably Neil Brownsword – have sought to document and safeguard ceramic factory manufacturing processes in their practices, few have concerned themselves with the other end of the spectrum – the context of the collector. In an approach that seems quite distinctive, Taylor references both the histories of factory production – the significance of moulding, throwing, drawing, painting, and sculpting skills to the creation of Sèvres porcelain – as well as the social histories of ceramic consumption, and combines them in her practice as a studio ceramicist.

For Taylor, the once private dining and sitting rooms of the wealthy, now open to the public, offer an abundance of inspiration. An ornate design on a section of coving or panelling might catch her eye, which will prompt her to focus on a detail by drawing it out on paper. These drawings are not mere recordings (photography can do this); they are a means to look with concentration, to collect the mind, and focus the eye. Looking at Taylor's volumes of drawings, I am reminded of pattern books – style books produced by ceramic factories to document the standard ware produced as part of a specific collection. Taylor's 'pattern books' are themselves collections, but ones that respond to, and in some ways have sympathy with, the collecting impulse that drove the wealthy to amass art collections and ornate furnishings. Taylor collects references in the same way as those wealthy patrons before her: touring, seeing, feeling, and collecting.

However, unlike its factory namesake, the drawings included in Taylor's 'pattern-books' are not a means to reproduce forms; hers are a means of collecting ideas for development. Once in the studio, the drawings facilitate the recollection of looking. They seem to be less about recovering the structure of the decorative object and more about what was important in observing it at all. Taylor's drawings are abstractions, extracting interior architectural detail into observations of line and curve. Drawing is, after all, an intrinsically abstract activity, where the three-dimensional world is isolated from its wider context for closer inspection, and then abstracted on to the flattened two-dimensionality of paper. Indeed, one notes how the drawings exhibit definite rhythms, where shadow is strategically used to notate the significance of lines in creating compositional flow. This emphasis gives each drawing a sense of shape

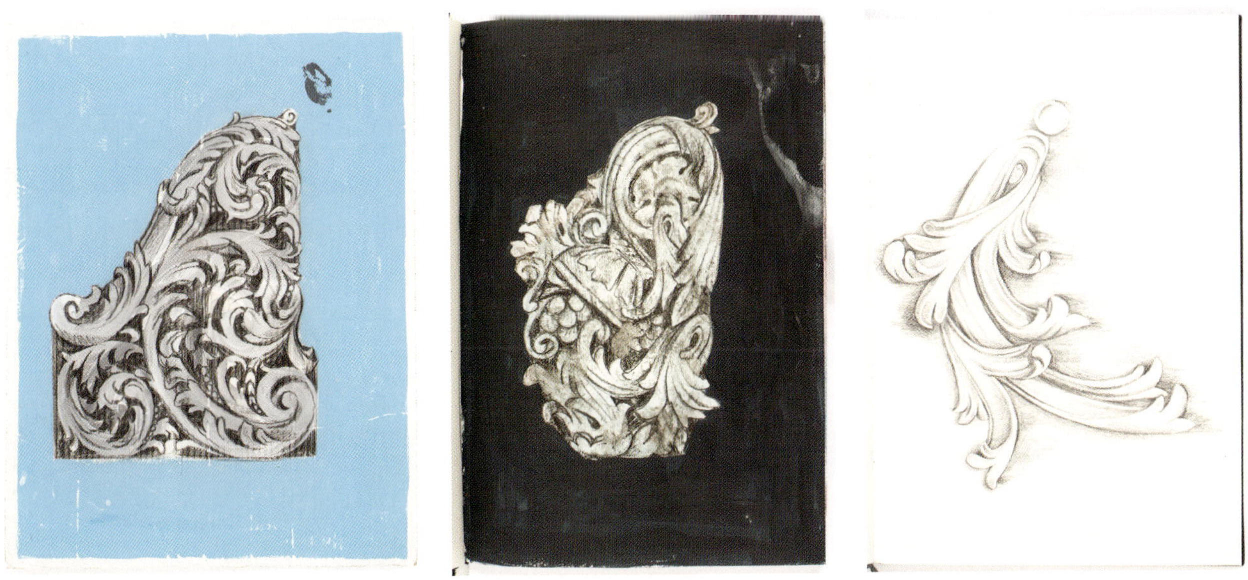

Drawings from Marchmont House residency (2021).

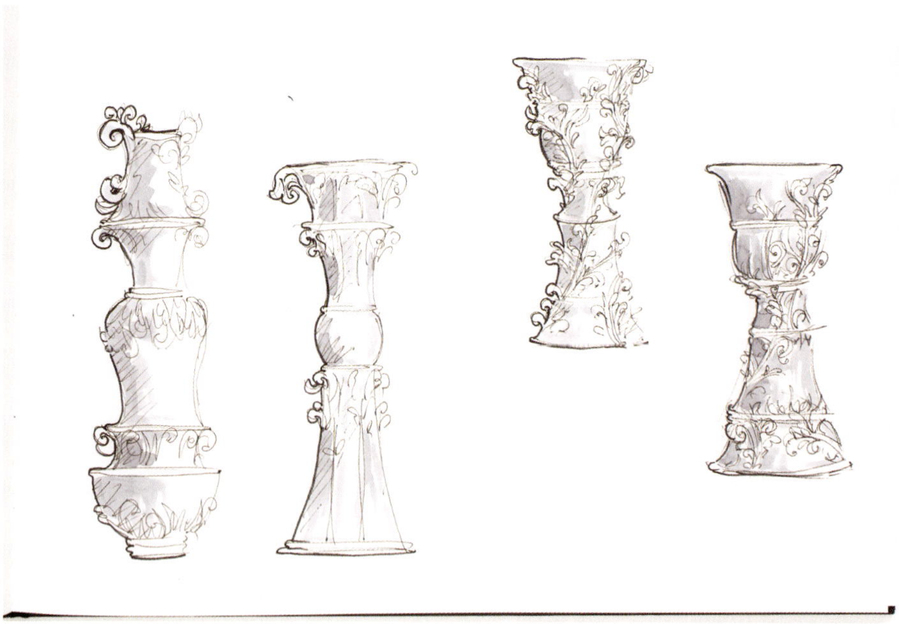

Sketches for Promenade Forms (2021).

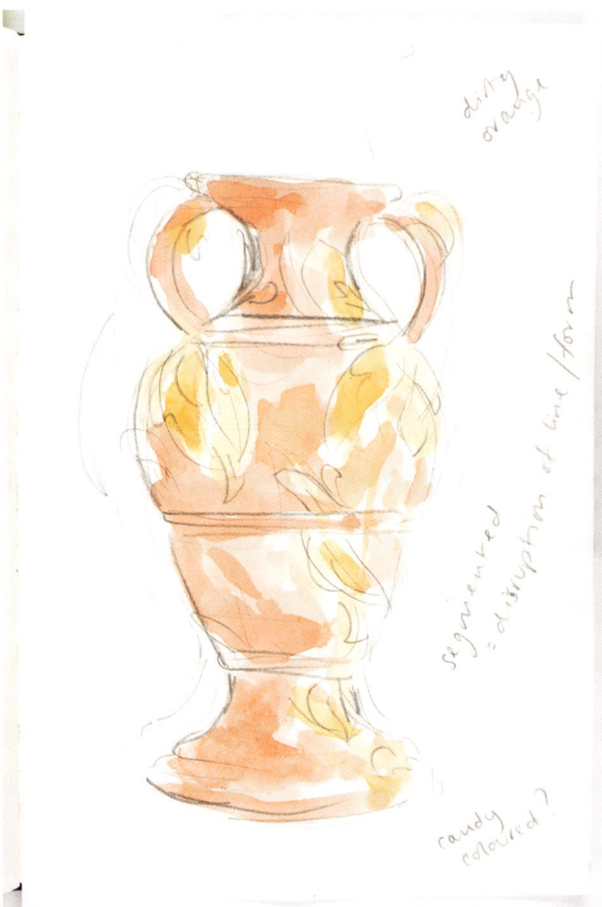

Sketch for Architectural Vessel in Orange (2021).

in relief: of three-dimensional forms waiting to be released from the page, absorbed as inspiration, and rearticulated in three-dimensions as individualised marks in clay.

Before embarking on the production of a piece, Taylor will make preparatory sketches of the intended form. In some sketches, such as *Sketches for Promenade Forms* (2021), the clarity of outline found in her detailed drawings returns, calling attention to the contours of form in silhouette. This approach highlights her concern for the sculptural qualities of pots; how sections might interweave to create rhythmic occupations of space via the direction, angle, and interaction of curves. Interestingly, whilst there is an intense focus on the overall form, the ornamental detail of each work is often vague. This is especially the case with *Sketch for Architectural Vessel in Orange* (2021), where form and colour are outlined, but ornate detail is only loosely alluded to by pencil lines and watercolour marks.

For Taylor, then, once the design idea is formulated, the actual process of creation is instinctive. Sections of the pot are usually thrown sequentially,

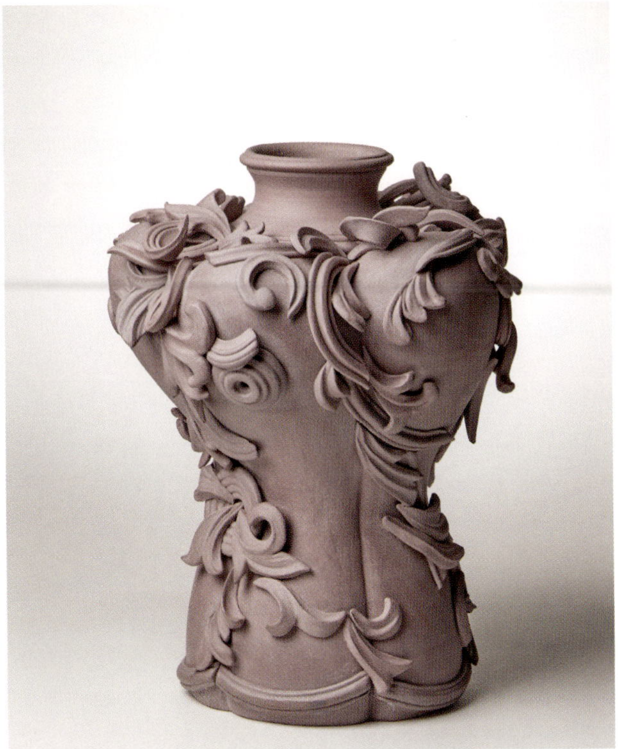

Vari Capitelli VIII (2020).

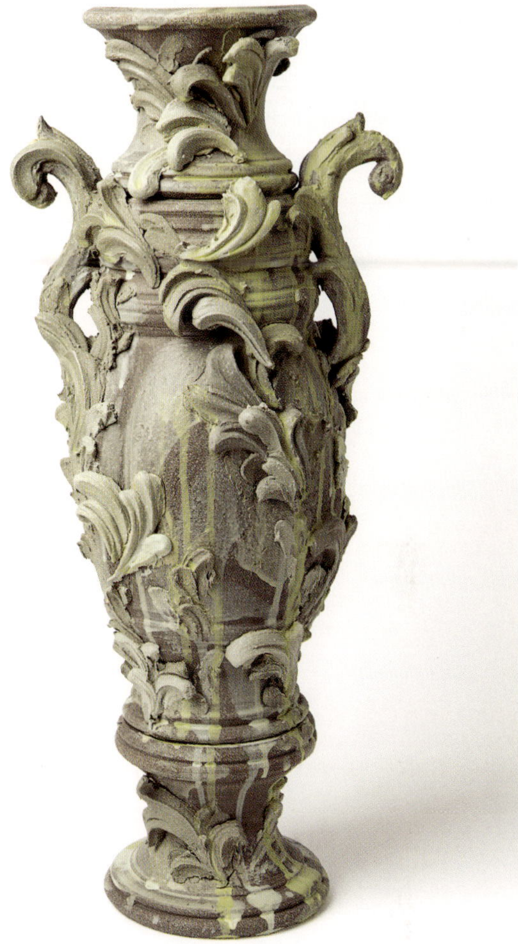

Lichenesque (2021).

the result of one section informing her approach to the creation of the next. Once the form has been completed, decoration will be applied to the exterior with much spontaneity. Such an intuitive approach enables the abstraction and internalisation of her stimuli through drawing to now be redeployed as her own visual language in clay. A cumulative process of making also enables her to judge the overall composition as it progresses. She can consider whether the work is balanced, has movement, and crucially, interweaving rhythms that sustain interest. By combining two- and three-dimensional processes, and balancing planned composition with responsive instinct, Taylor draws together elements of the pot and ceramic sculpture, the factory and the artist's studio, in surprising ways.

As noted above, the aesthetic of Sèvres porcelain might inspire Taylor's approach to form, particularly her preference for ornate handles, generous bodies, and slim feet, but her sources of inspiration span across the seventeenth and eighteenth centuries. Some works, such as *Vari Capitelli VIII* (2020), reference the architectural prints of Giovanni Battista Piranesi (1720–1778), whose depiction of sweeping archways and interlocking staircases are echoed in Taylor's composition. In *Lichenesque* (2021) the variations of green are redolent of Wedgwood's jasperware, but the glaze runs suggest the rearticulation of historical material that is central to Taylor's practice. This work seems to imply that pots accrue meanings through their contexts of display, contexts that alter as fashions and modes of spectatorship change. The

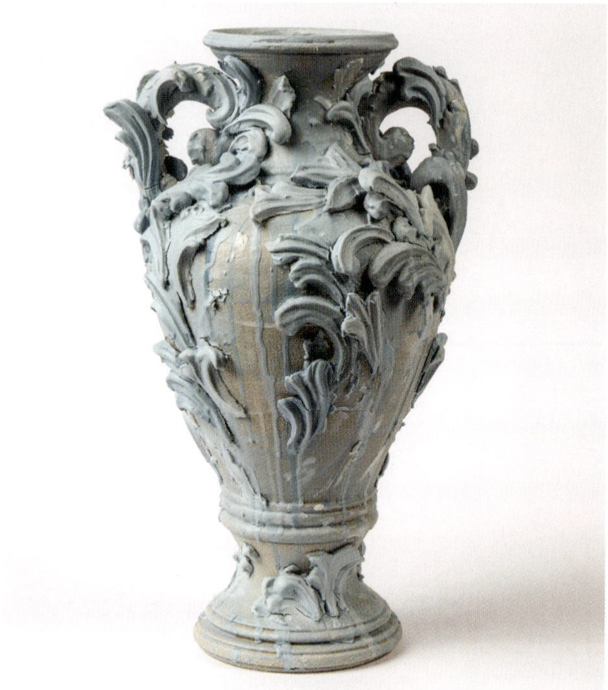

Archaeology of Surface (2021).

high-class status of British factory-produced ceramics became compromised in the twentieth century when many important factories went into decline, and where value gradually shifted towards certain studio ceramic artists such as Hans Coper and Lucie Rie. The glaze runs on this pot imply the fluctuating movement of the status of ceramics, perhaps even a sense of aged decay, of a past splendour trickling away from factory ware because of the changing fads of contemporary fashion. In *Archaeology of Surface* (2021) the application of green-blue ornaments evokes a similar kind of acculturation, where the interior décor of the country house has become so associated with Sèvres forms that the architecture appears to have fused itself onto the pot. These are functional pots, but they are also meta-pots; they offer commentary on the shifting social status of ceramic forms as a part of interior design collections.

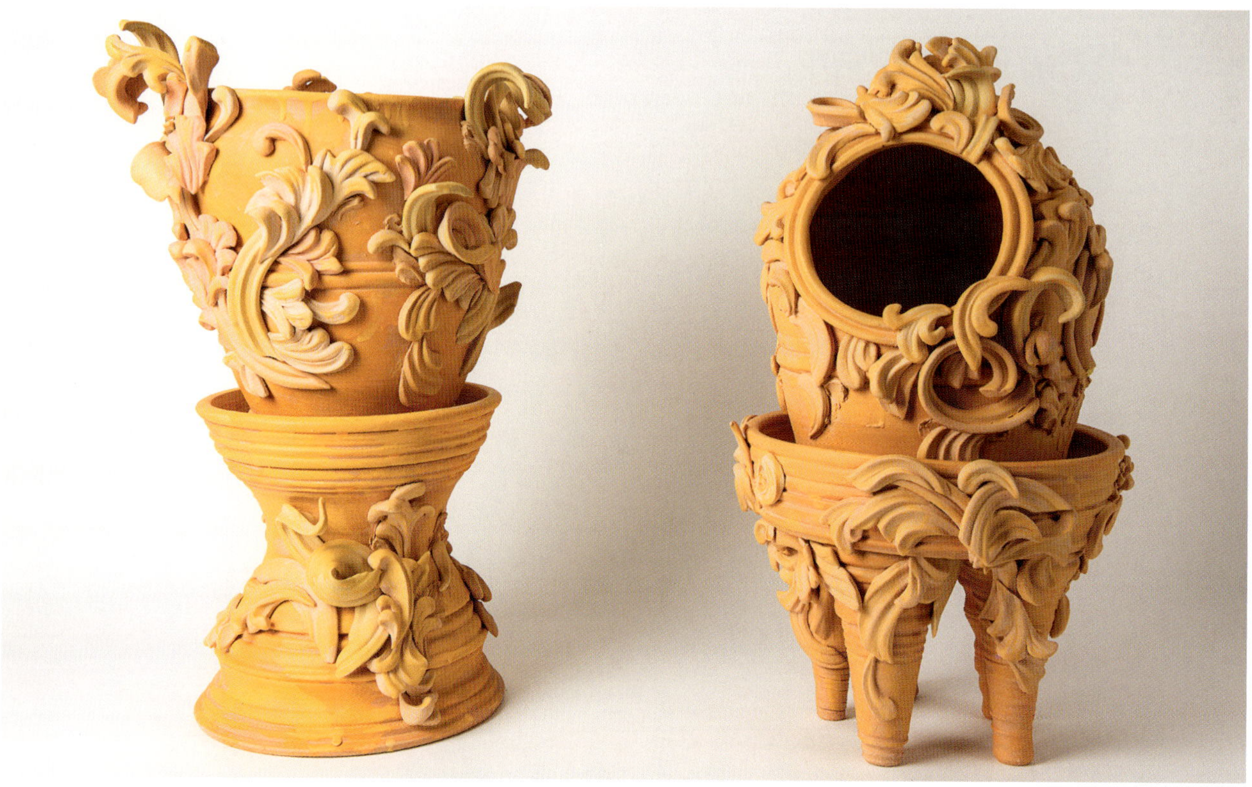

Jardiniere I and II (2021).

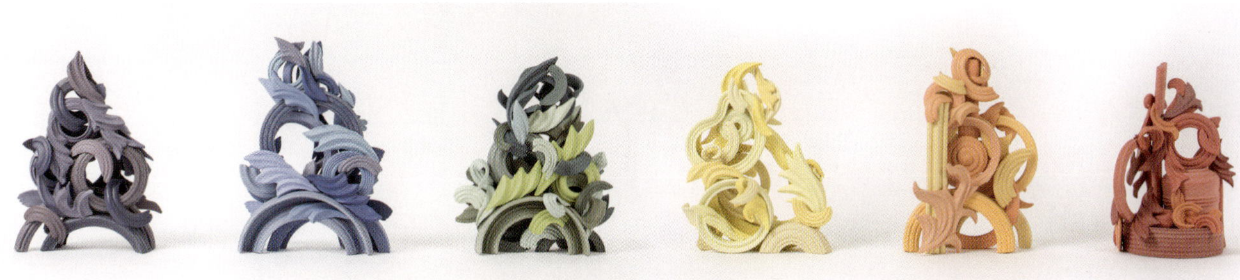

Pride and Joy (2017).

Whilst some of her works reference the blues, whites, and greens of the ware produced by factories such as Wedgwood, Taylor's palette also extends to rich reds, oranges, and yellows. Naturally, these colours give the pots a different temperament, but they also subtly draw her use of form away from historical referents to become resolutely contemporary works. *Jardiniere I and II* (2021) are functional planters with generous rims and study feet, but they also succeed as standalone works of sculpture. Ornamental patterns seem to grow around the form like ivy, even emerging from the mouth of *Jardiniere II*, not unlike the plant it may come to contain. Through the uses of bright colour, Taylor rearticulates the unapologetically eye-catching designs of Sèvres for the contemporary, proposing that pots can still make a significant statement as interior design.

Whilst pots are important to her output, Taylor also makes innovative sculptures produced from thrown, hand-formed, and moulded elements. Although they have no reference to utility, these ornamental sculptures connect with vessels because the containment and release of space are integral to their composition. The *Pride and Joy* (2017) series of sculptures are developed from thrown elements, which are cut and altered as necessary to become bridge-like supports or circular enclosures upon which other compositional elements – moulded or hand-formed – depend. Captivating to observe, the *Pride and Joy* series are also political. They are a celebration of the diversity of life, of different states of being, echoing the rainbow colours of the gay pride flag. As a celebration of a 'coming out' story, this series suggests that people should be treated with the preciousness of ornaments, no matter who they are.

Taylor's approach to sculpture exemplifies how she herself is a kind of collector. She collects ornamental references which, via collected thought and the recollection of observations, are quoted and rearticulated. Each piece – pot or sculpture – stands as a collected postmodern assemblage (or 're-collection') of vocabularies and techniques absorbed from ceramic history, design history, the status of the luxury ornament, throwing, hand-forming, moulding, drawing, architecture, the factory, the studio, sculpture, and the pot. The ability to combine such diversity and yet retain a strong sense of individual aesthetic identity is uncommon. There is a sense of joyousness in her work. Like Sèvres, Taylor's work aptly demonstrates 'the transforming power of human creativity in taking a humble ingredient like clay and fashioning it by hand and mind into something rare and lovely.'[88]

Matthew Warner
Status Symbols

Jug. The word calls to mind a pot with a handle and a spout designed to hold and pour liquid. You know what a jug is because you have seen and used one before. But despite this familiarity, your comprehension of a jug is totally different to mine. This not only pertains to style and form (the aesthetics and utility of design) but also to disparities in how we perceive value. A factory-produced jug may be priceless to me because of its status as a family heirloom, its only value resting in its emotional relationship to memory, but it may mean nothing to you. Conversely, a rare antique jug that you own could seem remote to me because of its economic value, its ornate design decrying utility and only signalling your wealth. Indeed, a rare Tobey jug can cost as much as £65,000, a mass-produced second-hand jug in a charity shop can cost less than £1.

Despite the familiarity of form, our responses to a jug are diverse and context-specific: they are shaped by our experiences, histories, associations, even our mood at the time of encounter. As the anthropologist Howard Morphy has argued:

> People who use works of art, interact with works of art, respond to works of art, do so with some background of knowledge and experience which may include detailed knowledge of the artwork itself and of innumerable previous interactions involving it, or similar objects. Likewise, people respond to the physical properties of an artwork, to the complexity of its composition, partly in the context of the moment but also in the light of a history of viewing artworks and other things. Their viewings are influenced by how those experiences are interpreted in relation to their cultural background, their religious beliefs, their social status or gender and so on.[89]

Following Morphy's lead, jugs can be viewed as anthropological objects that reveal how facets of social identity are negotiated and recognised in the moment they are encountered. This meaning is generated both from external social cues we have learnt over time (for example, how we understand social class), but also from our own experiences of, and relationships to, those cues (whether we perceive the jug to represent the class to which we feel we are a part, or those of another). Each person combines these cues in different ways, and so the experience of a jug is unique to each of us.

If all our experiences are different, how do we come to agree on the special status of a jug? The answer to this lies not in the object itself, but in a complex set of relationships that exist around it. As the sociologist Erving Goffman has observed:

> Status symbols provide the cue that is used in order to discover the status of others and, from this, the way in which others are to be treated. The thoughts and attention of persons engaged in social activity therefore tend to be occupied with these signs of position. It is also a fact that status symbols frequently express the whole mode of life of those from whom the symbolic act originates. In this way the individual finds that the structure of his [*sic*] experience in one sphere of life is repeated throughout his experiences in other spheres of life. Affirmation of this kind induces solidarity in the group and richness and depth in the psychic life of its members.
>
> As a result of the circulation of symbols, however, a sign which is expressive for the class in which it originates comes to be employed by a different class – a class for which the symbol can signify status but ill express it. In this way conscious life may become thin and meagre, focused as it is upon symbols which are not particularly congenial to it.[90]

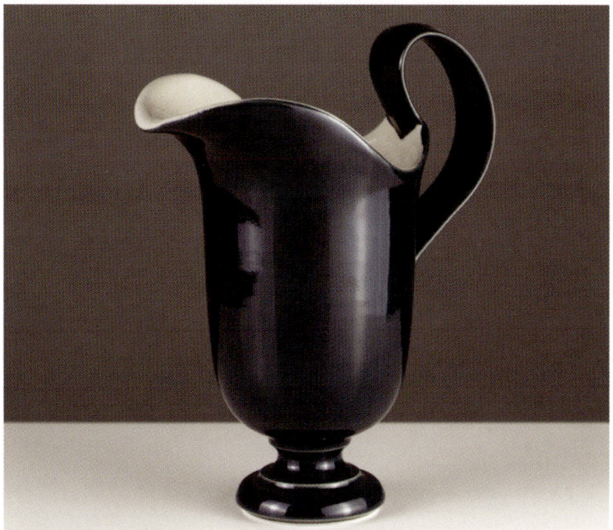

Small Jug (2021).

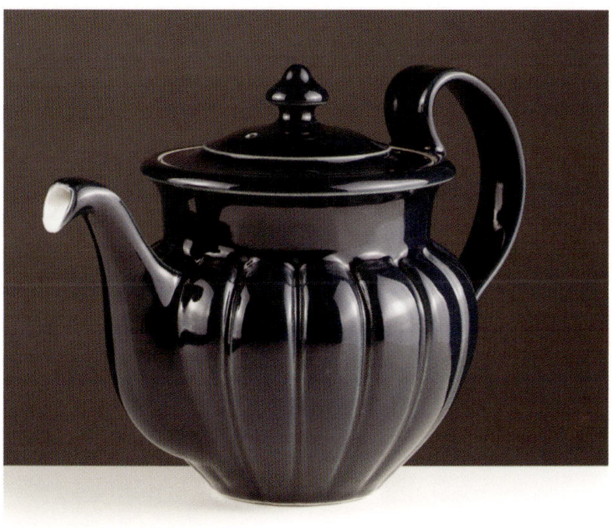

Fluted Teapot (2022).

For Goffman, status exists as a group mentality that can be discerned through, for instance, the symbolism of objects, usually in finite supply and thus with high economic value, considered as part of a series rather than in isolation. Indeed, one object by itself is not sufficient to convince other members of a group that an individual is of the same status. Symbols are used contingently and relationally to cement status through association. To give an example, you encounter a Sèvres porcelain jug on a dining room table, seen as part of a country manor tour next to a 'do not touch' sign. The jug exhibits value because a) it is in a country manor house, which is associated with the aristocracy, and is thus itself a symbol of class; b) the house is part of a tour and so functions as a kind of museum display. That the jug is on show on the dining room table suggests that it is already valuable and worthy of attention; c) other people have come to see it on the tour, signalling group affirmation of the rarity of the experience; d) there is a sign saying 'do not touch', so it must be precious; and e) if you have ceramic knowledge, the fact that it is labelled as Sèvres might mean it is worth several thousand pounds. All of these markers, however, are extrinsic to the jug. In the above description, I have not actually revealed any details about the form of this jug. Rather, I have offered a description of a network of external associations that combine to assert how the object is afforded status.

If this contextual network does not cohere, the status assigned to the object would appear 'thin'. To use a different example, upon visiting a friend for coffee, you see a small jug sitting on the dining table with a sign that reads 'do not touch'. Upon enquiring, you are told that this ornate jug once sat in the ornament cupboard of a grandmother and is now a treasured possession that children are not allowed to touch. In this context, the mechanics of display seem excessive; it exhibits what Goffman describes above as 'a class for which the symbol can signify status but ill express it'. Whilst the lack of touching here concerns the symbolic preservation of a lost loved one and a concern for familial heritage, the mode of public display is disproportionate to the rarefied status it has been attributed. Thus, status symbols read like words in a sentence; they are only effective when chained together to produce legible meanings.

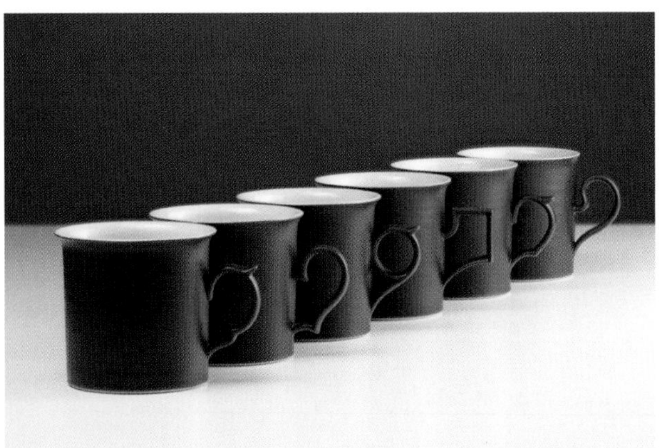

Six Coffee Cups (2021).

The work of Matthew Warner investigates these shifting contexts in the production of social meaning by creating pieces that reference motifs from Sèvres and Wedgwood. In part, these vocabularies are deployed to reframe British ceramics beyond the Anglo-Japanese aesthetic that Bernard Leach, the 'Father of British studio pottery', advocated in the early twentieth century, and which has cast a long shadow ever since. As an earlier point of reference, Warner interrogates the work of Josiah Wedgwood (1730–1795), the 'Father of English Potters', who established the Wedgwood Company in 1729. He developed new production techniques and designs that were soon patronised by Queen Charlotte (1761–1818), wife of King George III (1760–1820), and then other heads of state.[91] Wedgwood thus transformed British pottery from a folk practice into a luxury commodity. Meanwhile, in France, with the support of King Louis XV (1710–1774), the Vincennes porcelain factory was established in 1740, before being moved to Sèvres at the behest of Louis XV's mistress Madame de Pompadour (1721–1764). Purchased by Louis XV in 1759, the factory developed new porcelain techniques, most notably the European recipe for hard paste porcelain, which afforded the final work greater resilience when exposed to hot liquid. The ornate rococo and then neoclassical styles of Sèvres were widely admired across Europe, purchased by royal houses and the aristocracy, and frequently given by the French court as diplomatic gifts. The connection with royalty and the aristocracy provided both companies with a reputation for luxury goods, but whilst the Sèvres factory has managed to navigate the passage of time through constant innovation, Wedgwood went into administration in 2009. Although the factory was rescued by a US-based investment company, some production was moved to Eastern Europe and Indonesia. Wedgwood was then sold again to a Finnish consumer goods company in 2015. Whilst the rarer pieces from both companies sell for tens, if not hundreds of thousands of pounds, more common works can sell for just a few pounds, with pricing further complicated by the existence of forgeries. Thus, the status of both brands as the producers of luxury objects fluctuates quite markedly in the contemporary market.

Warner explores this ambivalence by challenging us to associate our experiences of social class with ceramic form. The ornate handles and full bellies of his jugs, and the poised spouts and crown-like lids of his teapots, speak to the aesthetics of Sèvres and Wedgwood, evoking the royal collections or manor houses in which we might expect to encounter them. Yet, for the majority of the collectors of Warner's work, the context of display will be more commonplace. Indeed, whether his work is used on a daily basis, only on special occasions, or as an ornament to be admired, alters the symbolic status of the work. The more a piece is used, the less status it has. For instance, the daily use of a Warner teapot normalises it, but infrequent use activates the symbolic status of the pot as evidencing the occasion as special. In accordance with Morphy, the status of Warner's work lies in how we associate form with occasions for use.

Warner produces pieces that sit at two extremes of price depending on size and implied utility. The smaller works, such as mugs and jugs, are at the cheaper end of the range perhaps. This indicates that these forms are designed for use rather than as ornaments. Yet, his mugs exhibit a formal ambivalence by uniting two frames of reference. The mugs are thrown with very straight sides, giving them an almost bucket-like appearance that suggests maximum volume for contents. This robust shape is offset by ornamental handles, which are much finer, and seem delicate. The deployment of these two vocabularies indicates that there is something worthy in the drinking of tea or coffee in mugs, perhaps relating to socialisation or friendship. Yet, it also alludes to the

Garniture III (2020).

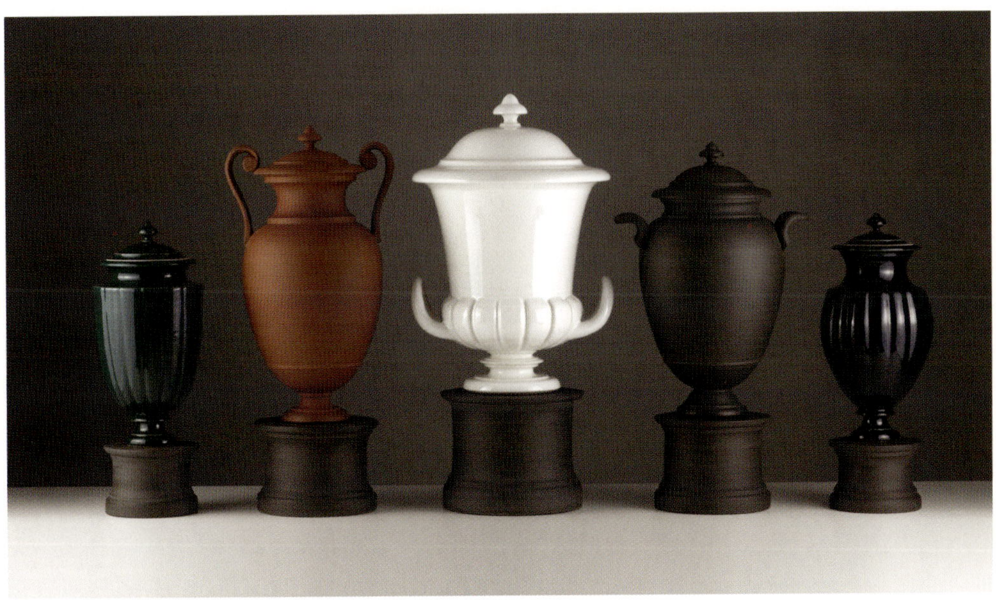

fact that a Wedgwood mug can be purchased for as little as a few pounds, the great luxury brand now selling at a knockdown price.

At the other end of the price spectrum are his magnificent urns, evidencing Warner's outstanding skills as a thrower. Warner elevates the status of his Wedgwood-inspired urns further by placing them on plinths. This additional height adds a slight sense of pomposity to each work, as though they are self-aware of their own status as a rarefied ornament, even looking down on other kinds of ceramic form that have their base directly touching the supporting surface. The decision to render these urns as plain evokes the differently coloured jasperware urns of Wedgwood, yet their presentation as a group of five works gives them a lofty symbolic status; these are urns produced by only one artist (rather than a factory), requiring many hours of design, labour, and advanced technical understanding. Indeed, the skill required to produce these pieces is impressive, even as they exude an understated quietness.

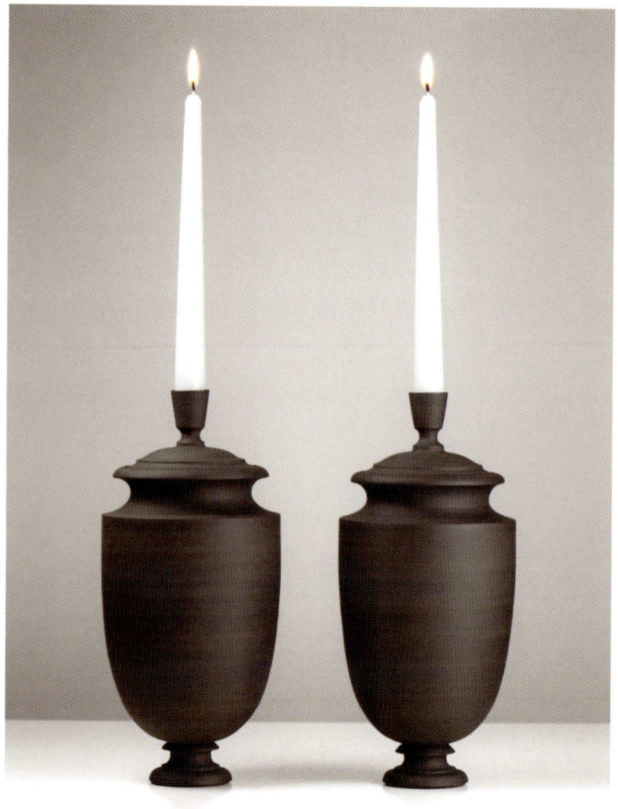

A Pair of Candlestick Vases (2021).

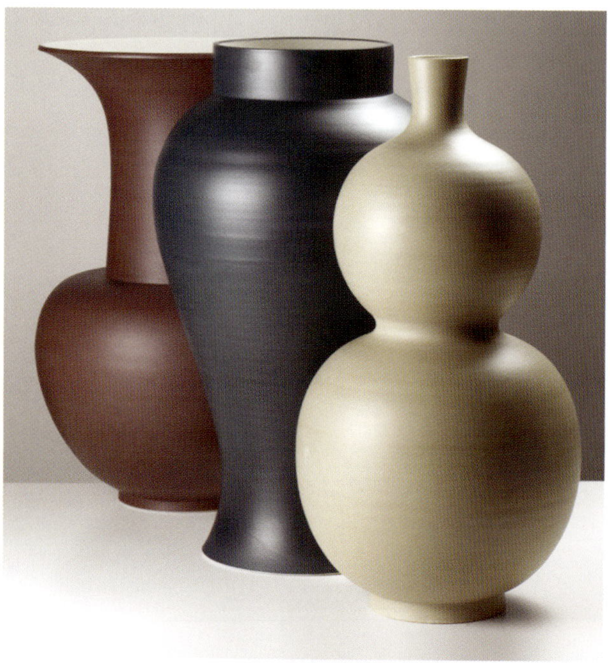

Three Large Vase Forms (2021).

Ambivalence is captured in the self-aggrandising plinths and sculptural forms, which contrasts with the serenity and unobtrusiveness of the plain surface. Wedgwood, Warner seems to imply, occupies an ambiguous position in contemporary ceramic practice; a symbol of luxury that has fallen foul of shifting twentieth-century tastes and the globalised economics of mass-produced chinaware.

The base of a form – the way a piece contacts the surface upon which it rests – is of key importance for Warner. Vases that exhibit a wider base appear more grounded, robust, and somehow more approachable as objects. Although the forms remain satisfyingly ornamental, the smooth contours seem less fastidious, more direct, a little more informal. In contrast, other vase forms (such as *Candlesticks*, 2021) sit on more ornamental feet, as though they rest on tiptoe, uncomfortably touching the surface that is beneath them in every sense. Both types of form are beautiful, but they exhibit markedly different vocabularies. Collectively, they establish an innovative connection between the contemporary and pottery from the eighteenth century. This is achieved via a playful mixing of postmodernism (the sampling of motifs) and modernism (the sleekness of form).

If Bernard Leach casts a long shadow over the practice of British studio pottery, Warner argues that the same should apply to Josiah Wedgwood. Warner's predilection for creating works that are matt black (often with a glossy black interior) turns form into silhouette, echoing Wedgwood black jasperware, but also offering a parallel reading as symbolic of Wedgwood's erasure as a source of ceramic inspiration for studio potters. The ambivalence of Wedgwood's relevance to the contemporary is also caught in Warner's ingenious and knowing deployment of certain aspects of form which, in turn, trigger associations within us about class status. A teacup may have an ornate handle suggesting value, but the relatively simple body and absence of a saucer – the latter as though the cup were once part of a tea service that has been split up and sold off – undercuts such grandiosity. Teapots are arranged in rows as though they are on display as treasured ornaments, the crown-like lids invoking royal patronage. Yet, reading the absence of colour as symbolic, these ornaments are just that: ornamental teapots devoid of purpose, little more than shadows of their former selves.

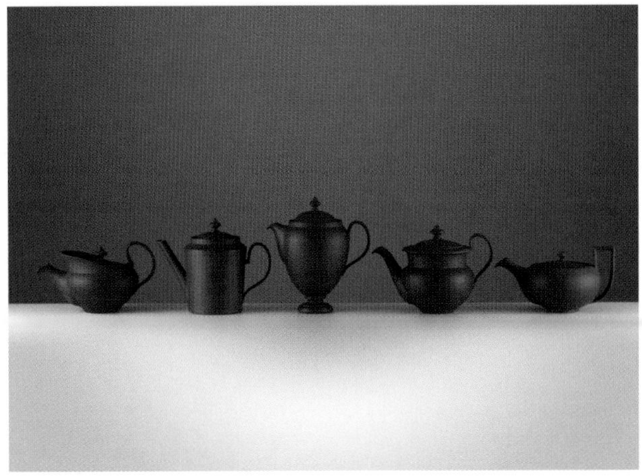

Five Teapots (2020).

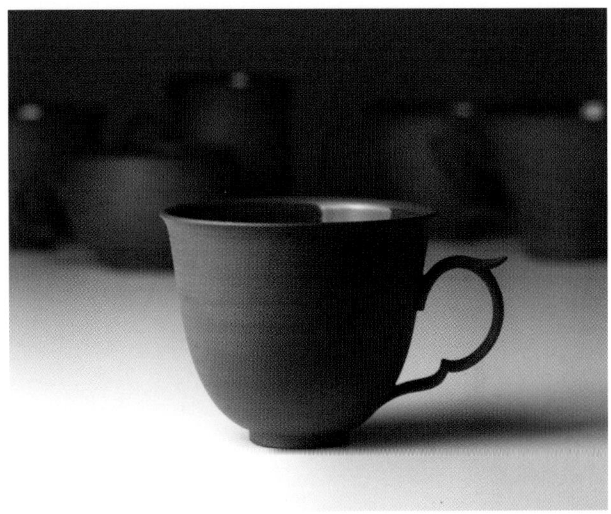

Teacups (2021).

Matthew Warner is an intelligent and gifted maker, but more than this, his work stands as an innovative investigation into the social history of ceramics. He offers an anthropological study of pottery as it pertains to social class, charting the shifting forms and fortunes of pre-twentieth century ceramic vocabularies. His pieces are context-dependent, yet the absence of decoration places them in a liminal time frame; they are both in and out of the contemporary period, and the time in which the design motifs were first produced. Through this individual mixing of styles and approach, he activates a critical commentary about form whilst empowering each work to be reactivated by the context of its contemporary display.

Paul Scott
Breaking with Tradition

In his analysis of landscape painting in Western art, Malcolm Andrews argues that:

> A 'landscape', cultivated or wild, is already artifice before it has become the subject of a work of art. Even when we simply *look* we are already shaping and interpreting. A landscape may never achieve representation in a painting or photograph: none the less, something significant has happened when land can be perceived as 'landscape'.[92]

Looking at land as 'landscape' demands a certain approach to seeing, one that involves aesthetic reasoning about composition, balance, and beauty. Strangely, this means that our appreciation of landscape is not natural; the very idea of framing land as 'landscape' is itself ideological, a product of learned convention.[93] Consequently, when we come to look at a drawing or painting of a landscape, the image we see is not an objective representation of nature but an artificial representation of an artificial way of seeing.

If the concept of landscape itself is an ideology, whose ideology does it follow? The cultural geographer Gillian Rose has asked the same question of her own discipline:

> recent work on landscape has begun to question the visuality of traditional cultural geography [...] as part of a wider critique of the latter's neglect of the power relations within which landscapes are embedded. Some cultural geographers suggest that the discipline's visuality is not simple observation but, rather, is a sophisticated ideological device that enacts systematic erasures. They [...] have argued that it refers not only to the relationships between different objects caught in the fieldworker's gaze, but that it also implies a specific way of looking. They interpret landscape not as a material consequence of interactions between a society and an environment, observable in the field by the more-or-less objective gaze of the geographer, but rather as a gaze which itself helps to make sense of a particular relationship between society and land.

> They have stressed the importance of the look to the idea of landscape and have argued that landscape is a way of seeing which we learn; as a consequence, they argue that the gaze of the fieldworker is part of the problematic, not a tool of analysis. Indeed, they name this gaze at landscape a 'visual ideology,' because it uncritically shows only the relationship of the powerful to their environment [...].[94]

For Rose, gazing at the landscape is a kind of 'visual ideology' that rests upon a particular kind of power. It asserts a subjective point of view that erases other kinds of looking. Indeed, applying the notion of 'visual ideology' to the history of landscape painting in Western art simply reinforces the assumption that most images were made from the perspective of white heterosexual men. Painting the landscape is akin to an act of ownership, of the dominant power capturing in paint all that they survey. How might this 'visual ideology' of the landscape in Western art be highlighted and deconstructed?

The work of Paul Scott investigates the power dynamics at play in the creation of decorative transferware – which often romantically depicted the landscape – by deconstructing and reconstructing images. Transferware was developed in the middle of the

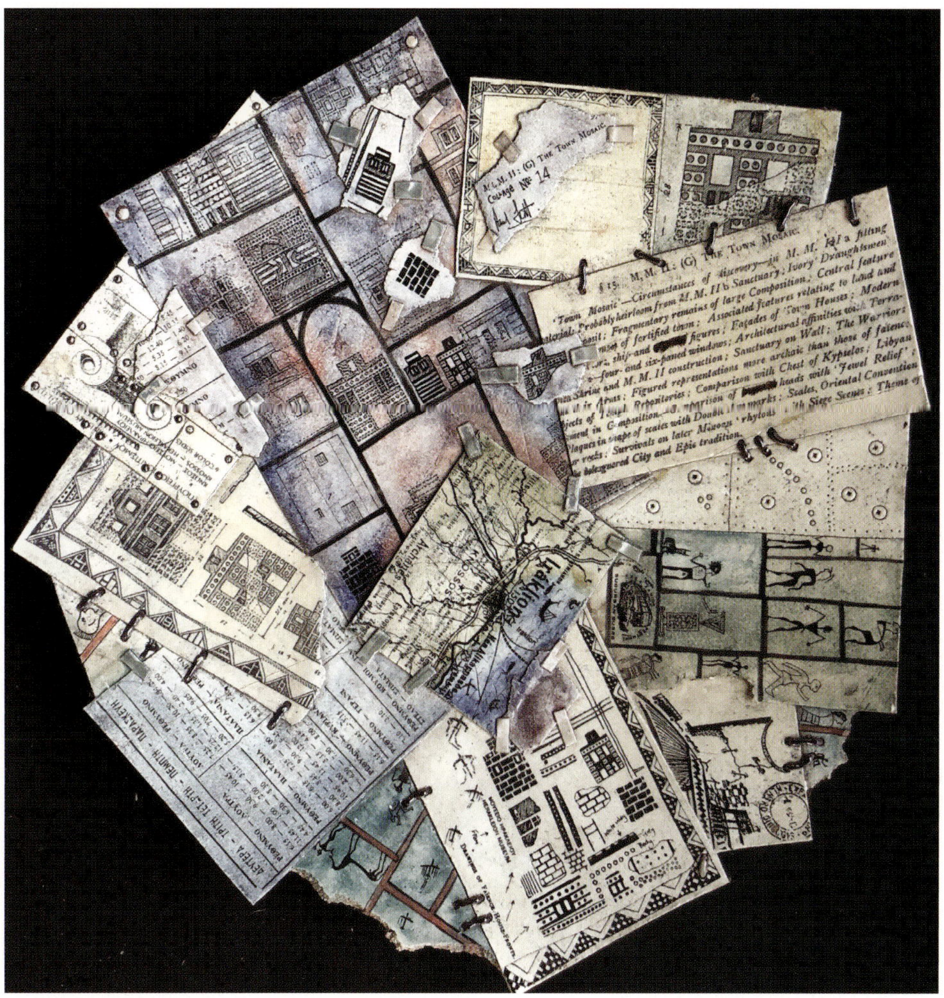

The Town Mosaic (1989).

eighteenth century, first being used on a mass scale by Robert Hancock (1731–1817) at both the Bow factory in London and the Worcester factory, before it spread elsewhere. As the domain of largely white male artists, questions of power and erasure in transferware are central both to Scott's methodology and his aesthetic. In particular, he is drawn to transferware that has cultural significance either in Britain – such as the Willow Pattern – or in export – such as the darker blue and white wares that became popular in the USA. Scott critically investigates the ubiquity of circulation, destabilising assumed historical narratives, and refashioning works (often literally) with new kinds of imagery that foreground social, economic, and political acts of erasure. This enables Scott – himself a white heterosexual male – to disrupt the flow of imagery from the past to the present, to take account of racial and gender power dynamics, and to repurpose narratives surrounding the development and meanings of transferware to offer a reflexive critique of its own history.

Even in early work, Scott sought to challenge the notion of a monolithic narrative using ceramic collage. *The Town Mosaic* (1989) refers to a collection of majolica tiles dating from between 2000–1700BC held in the Heraklion Archaeological Museum in Crete. The tiles, likely a local development of an Egyptian practice, mostly depict houses, whilst others show plants, people, and animals. Some of the tiles were reproduced in graphic form on Scott's collage, alongside transfer prints of a reference text explaining the tiles, a map of Heraklion, and fragments of tickets and receipts. In one sense, Scott's collage is a kind of travel scrapbook, a fixing of fragments from a memorable trip. Yet, it also describes the layering of history within a town, and how archaeology is dependent upon piecing together scraps of information to build a sense of a lost way of life. Consequently, Scott's *The Town Mosaic* is emblematic of memory, of how the past is pieced together from fragments.

Memorialisation was also central to *Free At Last* (1990), a three-sided work that commemorates the freeing of Nelson Mandela (1918–2013) from prison following a twenty-seven-year prison term for conspiracy. Across Scott's three-sided form (which one might speculate refers to the unification of

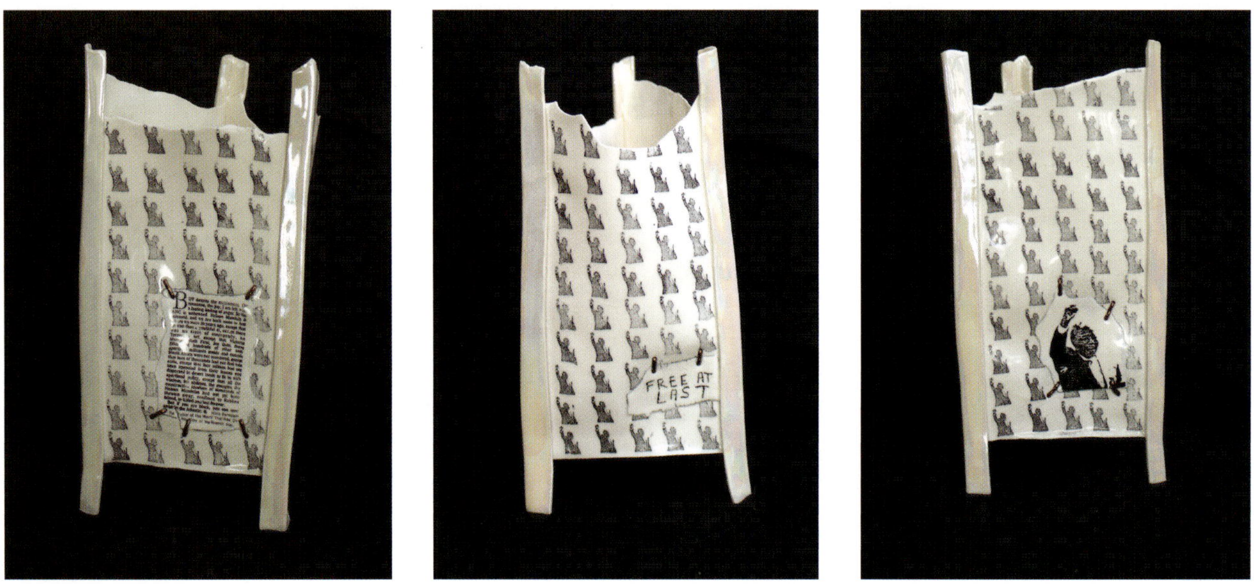

Free At Last (1990).

the nationalist government's apartheid classification of three races: 'Whites', 'Blacks', and 'Indians and' 'Coloured' people), the iconic image of Mandela raising his right arm as he walked to freedom on the 11 February 1990 is reproduced. Akin to a free-standing noticeboard, the work features an additional image on each side: a larger picture of Mandela, the text 'Free At Last' and, most significantly, a quotation from apartheid activist Hilda Bernstein (1915–2006), which asserts anger about the ways in which Mandela's release enabled the apartheid government to gloss over past and ongoing injustices. In what would become an important sense of ambivalence in Scott's work, *Free At Last* commemorated the release of Mandela, even as it cast doubt on whether genuine freedom was being achieved.

Scott recalls developing a political sensibility early on in his life, and whilst much of his work is political, all pieces are produced from an emotional response to the subject. *Free At Last* is an important work in that it articulates complexity rather than the convenient soundbite of the headline. Scott pursued this desire

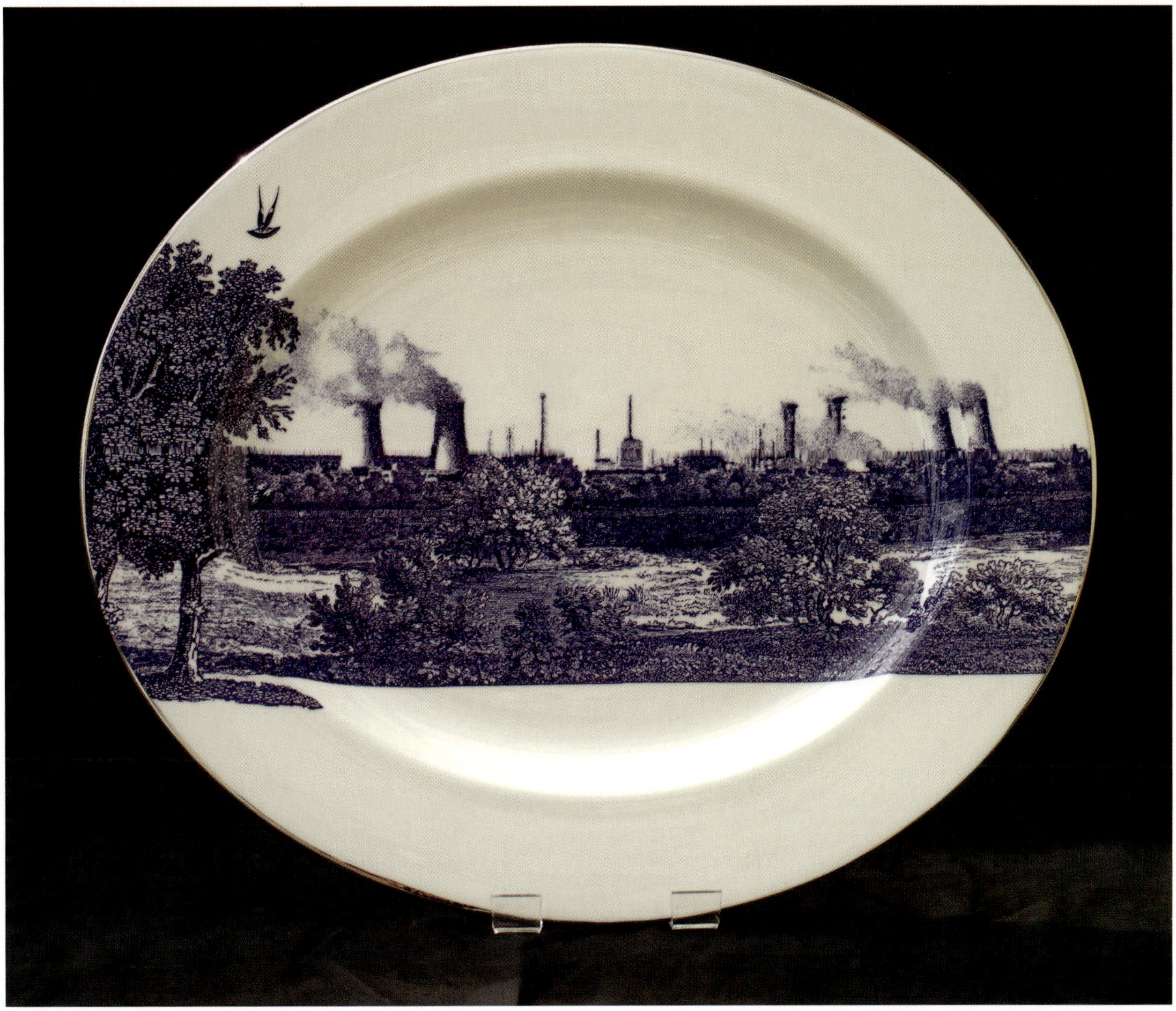

Seascale Pigeon No: 5 (1998).

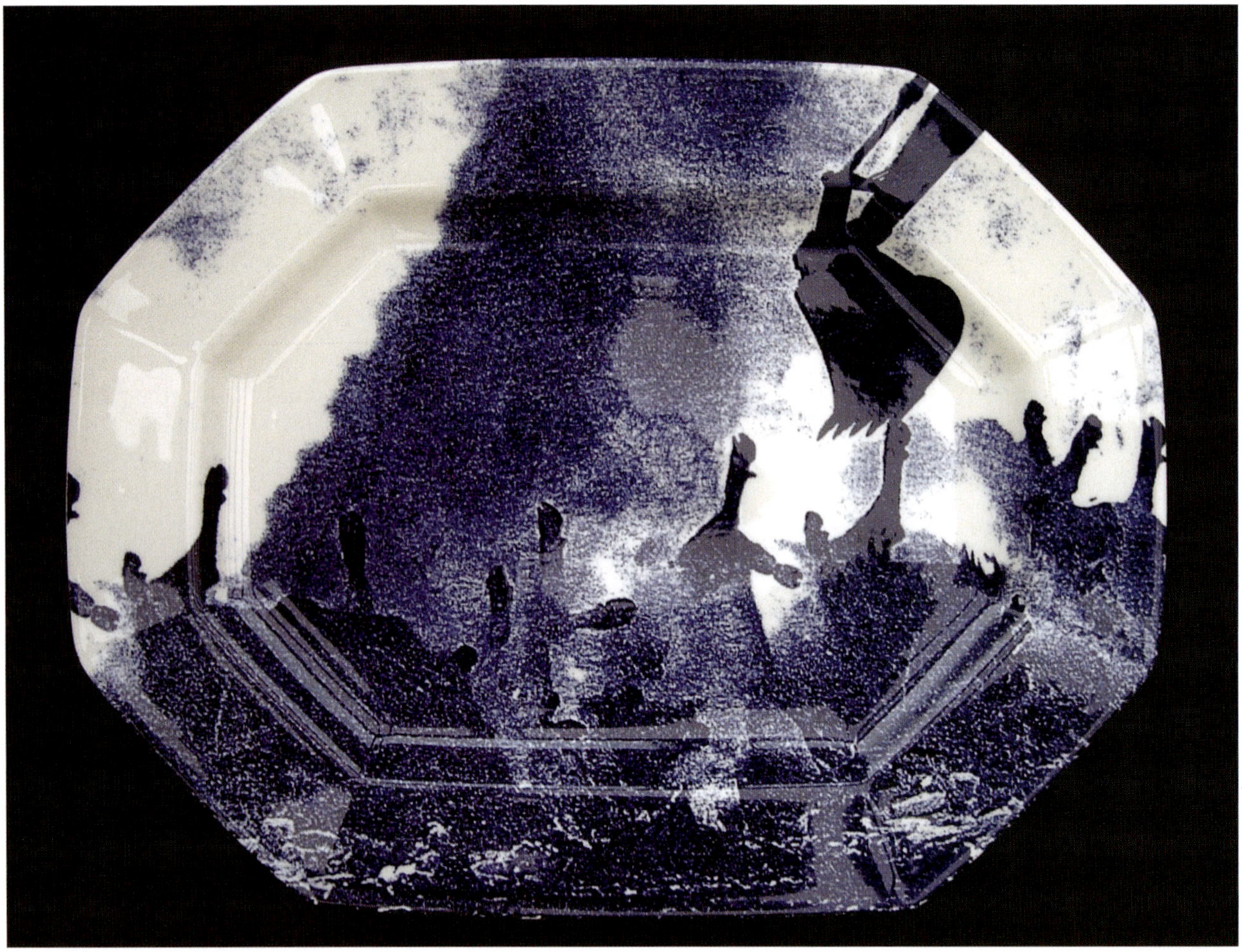

Foot and Mouth No: 5 (After MacLeod, Darwell and May) (2001).
(Courtesy of Paul Scott)

to confront the uncomfortable nature of reality in subsequent work, where more attuned skills and the development of new technologies for printing bespoke short-run ceramic transfers led to a series of groundbreaking works. *Seascale Pigeon No: 5* (1998) refers to the incident in February 1998 where 150 pigeons living near Sellafield were found to be highly radioactive. In total, 700 pigeons were culled, with low levels of radiation confirmed at a house in Seascale where the birds were regularly being fed. As a response to this alarming event, Scott designed a plate that situated Sellafield amidst idyllic flora and fauna. Disconcertingly, a pigeon flies outwards, directly towards the viewer.

Specially designed plates are often produced to commemorate. Usually, the events memorialised are joyous occasions, such as weddings, births, significant national anniversaries or ceremonies. Scott subverts the conventions of the commemorative plate to ensure we remember the parts of history that, perhaps, members of the Establishment would rather we forgot. If *Seascale Pigeon No: 5* (1998) commemorated a radiation leak at Sellafield, *Foot and Mouth No: 5* (2001) memorialises the 2001 outbreak of the highly infectious foot-and-mouth disease amongst cattle. In an attempt to contain the disease, some 6 million cows and sheep were

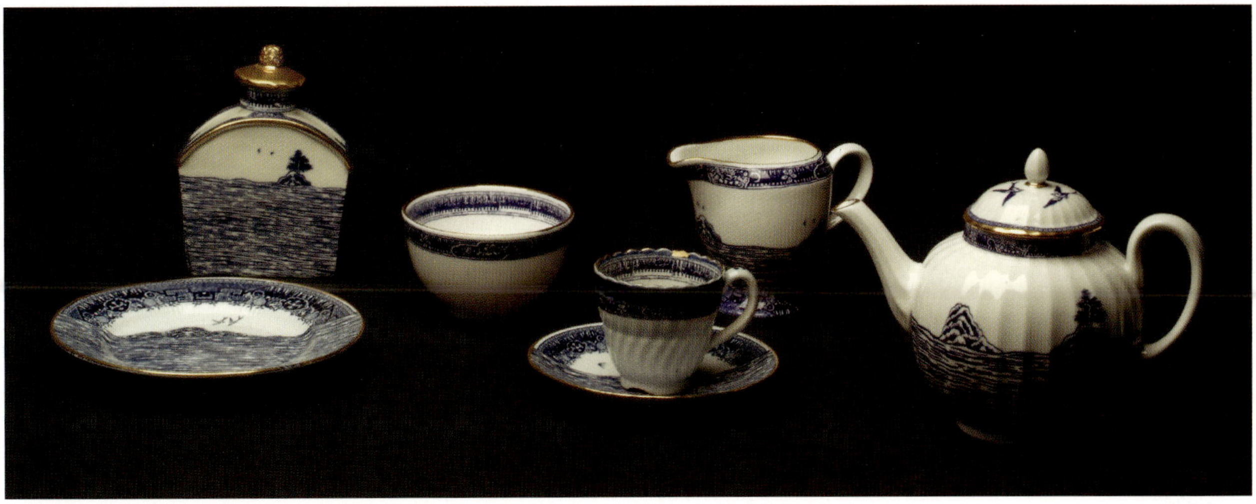

The Cockle Pickers Tea Service (2007).
(Photograph by Paul Scott)

slaughtered. When I visited Scott in his studio in Cumbria – the worst affected area in the country – he described the intense smell of rotting flesh during this time. The Ministry of Agriculture, Fisheries and Food had to monitor all culls, and with insufficient staff to cope with the scale of the crisis, piles of dead animals were left out in the summer heat. Flies swarmed for weeks whilst the carcasses waited to be burned. Scott's series of *Foot and Mouth* plates documents this visceral reality by showing the animals as they burn, their hoofs raised upwards like chimneys (symbolic of the impact of the disease on farming as an industry), as a digger moves to lay yet another animal on the fire.

Scott's empathetic desire to immortalise what is hidden from view led to the production of *The Cockle Pickers Tea Service* (2007). On 5 February 2004, twenty-three illegal Chinese immigrants, many of them from Fujian in southeastern China, were drowned in Morecambe Bay whilst picking cockles at low tide. The tragedy highlighted how the world's poorest, under the illusion of searching for a 'better life', are exploited by people traffickers. *The Cockle Pickers Tea Service* consists of a teapot, caddie,

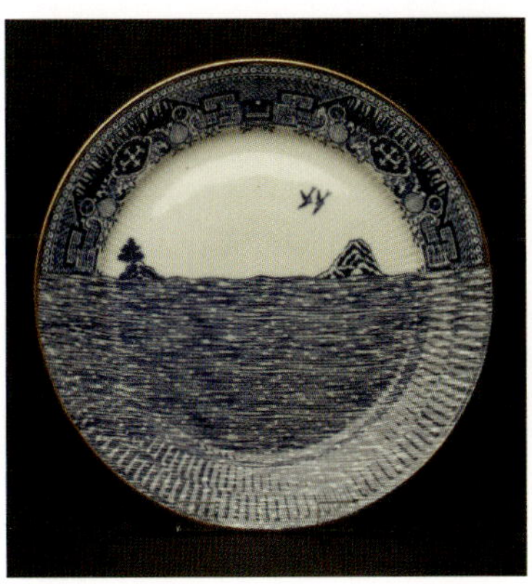

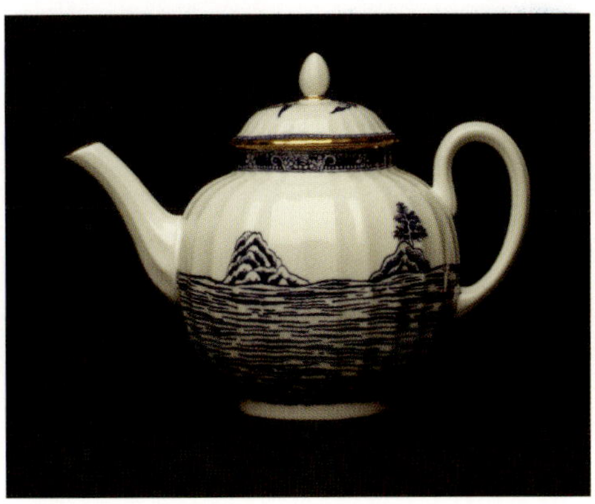

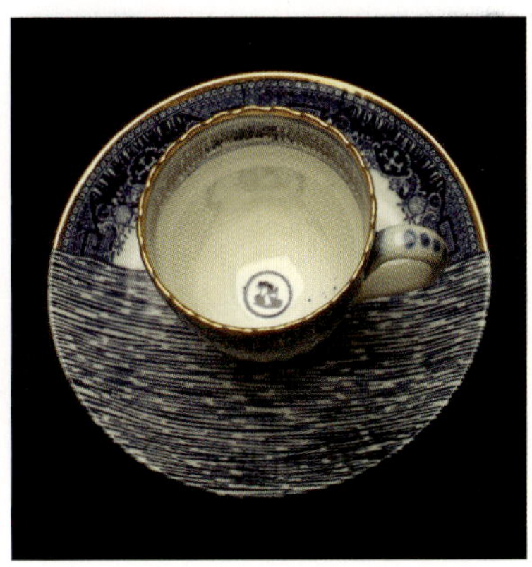

Plate, Teapot, and Cup and Saucer from *The Cockle Pickers Tea Service* (2007).
(Photographs by Paul Scott)

milk jug, sugar bowl, and cup and saucer. Drawing on a mixture of pre-existing teapots, bowls, cups, and dishes made by Royal Worcester and Royal Copenhagen – as well as a specially commissioned tea caddie – the famous Willow Pattern design from the early nineteenth century was altered so that it was mostly submerged under water. Although a tea service might seem an odd tribute to the victims, Fujian is a famous tea-producing province. The set also references the famous British idiom 'not for all the tea in China', a phrase used to describe something where the personal cost of an act is deemed too high. To contextualise the trafficking of the Chinese cockle pickers with the history of British involvement in the slave trade, the interior of the sugar bowl, the cup, and the neck of the caddie, depict enslaved Africans laid out in rows, as represented in the famous 1788 engraving of the slave ship *Brookes*, published by the Society for Effecting the Abolition of the Slave Trade (formed in 1787). Indeed, the desire for sugar in tea sustained plantations, and thus the eighteenth-century slave trade.[95] Even by 2021, the tea industry was still utilising child and forced labour in tea plantations in parts of Western Uganda and Sri Lanka.[96] The submerged landscape in *The Cockle Pickers Tea Service* thus symbolises

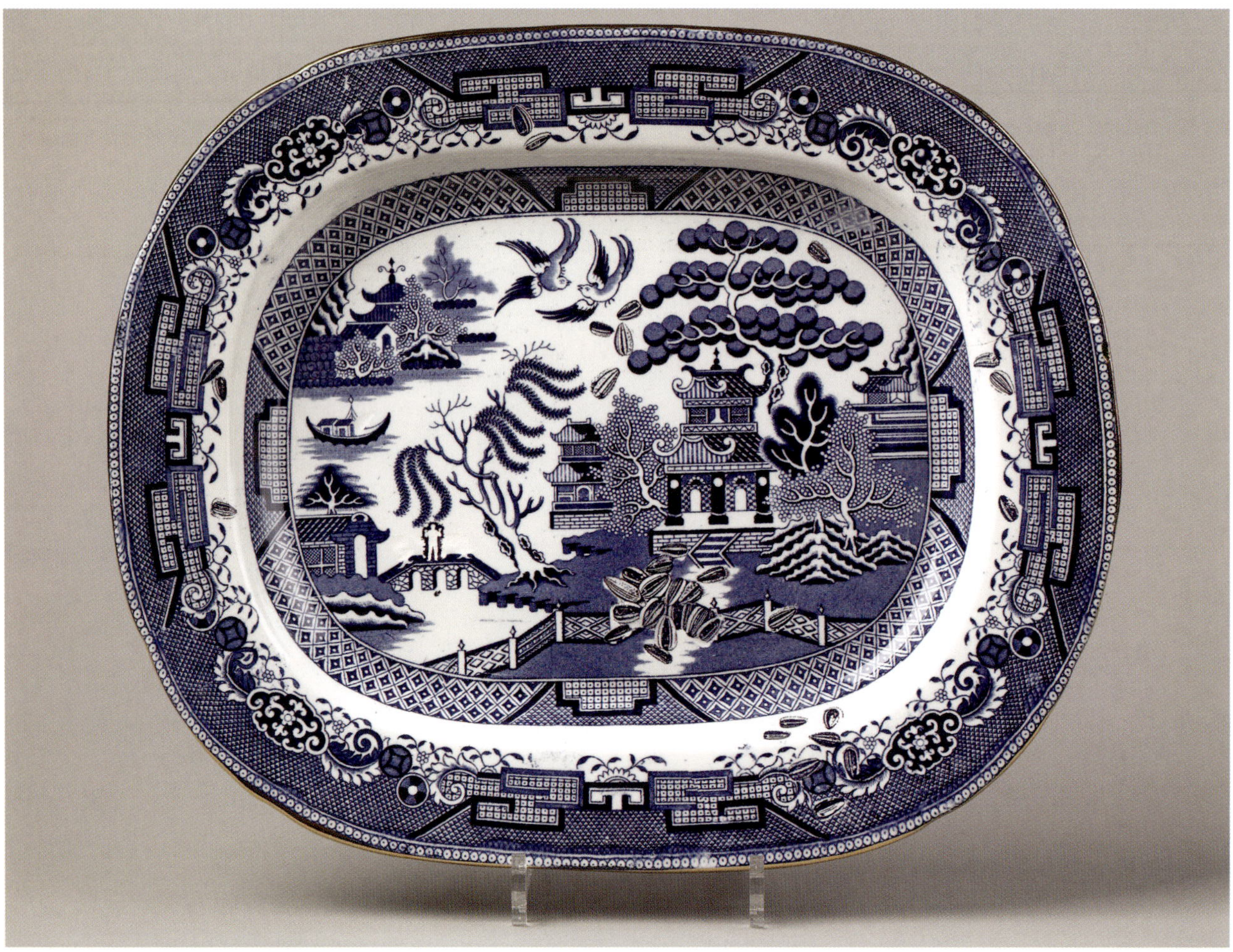

A Willow for Ai Weiwei (2011).
(Courtesy of Paul Scott)

what we, as consumers, choose not to see about the products we buy.

The Cockle Pickers Tea Service utilised existing factory-produced service ware, and this might lead some to believe that if Scott is not making his own forms, he is not a 'proper studio potter'. Yet, as evidenced by several essays in this book, the rich history of factory-produced British pottery is being utilised within studio practices, even if it remains something of a marginal activity.[97] Scott produces either one-off pieces or works in small series (the equivalent of fine art print editions) using vocabularies and techniques derived from a masterful understanding of ceramic transferware. He may use mass production techniques, but his works are not mass-produced. He makes far less in one afternoon than, for instance, a production potter might throw. One practice is not more worthy than the other, but it is important to acknowledge how the vitality of studio ceramics rests upon its diversity. Furthermore, Scott's alteration of existing antique pieces might anger those who believe that older works of pottery should be revered. Yet, if Scott is to break with tradition, then tradition literally needs to be broken down and formed anew. In some instances, utilising antique objects enables history to materially figure in the work. Breaking these objects down and reforming them – rather than imitating antiques for the same purpose – becomes key.

Some of the most compelling works that Scott has made were formed from antique plates. *A Willow for Ai Weiwei* (2011) was made in response to the arrest of Ai Weiwei at Beijing International Airport on 3 April 2011. The internationally recognised Chinese artist was held by the government for eighty-one days under the charge of committing 'economic crimes'. Scott took a small number of Willow Pattern plates and erased the three figures on the bridge and the single figure on the boat. Crucially, Scott's disappearances take place in a world where things are not what they seem. Although the Willow Pattern purported to be Chinese pottery, it was really an imitative design by Thomas Minton (1765–1836), probably first produced in Stoke-on-Trent around 1780. To convince buyers of the authenticity of the Willow Pattern, mythological stories were circulated about its meaning, culminating in 'The Story of the Common Willow Pattern Plate', published in *The Family Friend* magazine in 1849. Thus, in Scott's work, Ai Weiwei has disappeared in a landscape swirling with misinformation and lies, a direct critique of the Chinese government's ruse for his arrest. Scott refired the plates with additional transfers of sunflower seeds (a reference to the ceramic *Sunflower Seeds* exhibition at Tate Modern in 2010) and an outline of Weiwei executing his work *Dropping a Han Dynasty Urn* (1995). Scott thus draws a parallel between Weiwei dropping an antique vase and his own altering of an antique plate.

When the 9.1 magnitude Tōhoku earthquake struck the eastern coast of Japan on 11 March 2011, the world watched in horror as almost 20,000 people lost their lives to the ensuing tsunami that devastated entire towns. The tsunami also damaged infrastructure at Fukushima Daiichi Power Plant, causing several reactors to melt down. Radiation was released into the air and water, leaving the town uninhabitable, possibly forever. Scott's *Fukushima No: 2* (2014) utilises a Willow Pattern platter, actually produced in Japan in the 1960s, as the basis for the work. Purchased online, the platter was broken in the post. Its arrival in pieces provided the impetus for *kintsugi*, a Japanese process of repair where lacquer mixed with gold is used to join the pieces, rendering the breaks clearly visible and part of the history of the work. Rather than undertaking a straightforward *kintsugi* repair, Scott decided to include a section from Katsushika Hokusai's (1760–1849) famous giant wave print *Kanagawa oki nami*

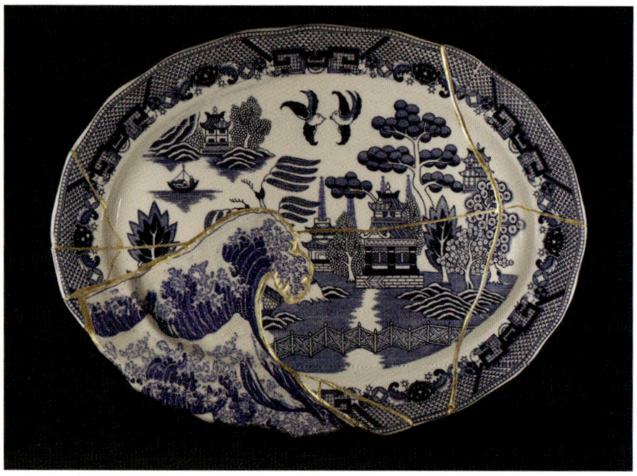

Fukushima No: 2 (2014).

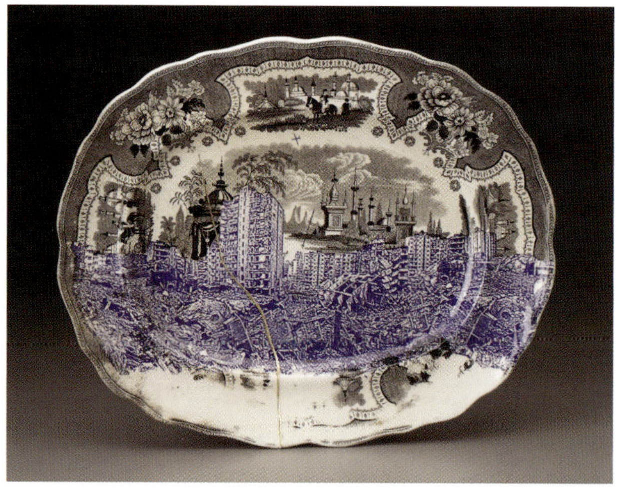

Palestine, Gaza (2015).
(Courtesy of Paul Scott)

ura (*Under the Wave off Kanagawa*, c.1830–32) in the composition. The result is a work that memorialises the disaster, but also speaks of rebuilding and renewal.

Palestine, Gaza (2015) juxtaposed the mid-nineteenth century romanticised image of Palestine by the Stoke-based pottery William Adams IV and Sons Pottery with the contemporary reality of Gaza's destruction by Israeli bombs. The horse-drawn carriage which was the focus of the original Adams composition is now masked by collapsing tower blocks and a sea of debris. A large crack, sealed with *kintsugi*, runs down the dish. This small feature provides the work with enormous power; redolent not only of fracture but also fragility, as though Palestine's existence hangs by a tiny thread.

Some works by Scott necessitated the creation of new images from old. *Bombs Over Baghdad* (2003/2007) was developed from the Stanbul Pattern made by the Gustavsberg factory in Sweden. The Stanbul Pattern, like the Willow Pattern, is a conglomerate imagining of the Middle East for the purposes of the European market. Scott digitally manipulated the pattern so that the palaces of Saddam Hussein appear in the border, along with ornamental bombs. Smoke emerges from the main image of the city, as helicopters and fighter jets roar through the sky. The deliberate smashing of the plate symbolises the effect of the Iraq War, begun in 2003, and which in 2007 saw the US deploy an additional 20,000 military personnel into the country, part of President George Bush's ironically named New Way Forward strategy. Yet, the people in the foreground of the image continue with their lives, seemingly oblivious to the carnage that surrounds them. Plates are a symbol of domesticity, and civilians must continue with their lives as best they can, even as their homes collapse around them. Equally, for the purposes of propaganda, governments frequently downplay the impact of military action on their country. The fact that, here, the figures are broken in two suggests that the struggle is indeed real.

Destruction of a different kind was evidenced in *Italian Sampler No: 4* (2021). The plate is decorated with salvaged decals from the Spode factory in Stoke-on-Trent, which ceased manufacturing in 2008, and was subsequently taken over by the Portmeirion Group in 2009. Opened in 1776, the Spode factory was one of the largest potteries in Staffordshire and was at the forefront of developing transfer printing. In 1816, Josiah Spode II (1755–1827) launched the famous *Blue Italian* range, which, despite a brief lull in production in the twenty-first century, has been revived and is still manufactured today. *Italian Sampler No: 4* (2009) fragments the iconic landscape of the *Blue Italian* range – the sheep on the riverbank, the castle, and the ruins – to capture the declining fortunes of the once-thriving factory. The loss of a factory represents the dispersal of technical knowledge and skill, design histories, as well as machinery. The calculated 'misprints' of *Italian Sampler No: 4* capture this scattering of history.

If anything is constant in Scott's diverse body of work, it is the use of historical imagery to speak to the concerns of the contemporary. His expert

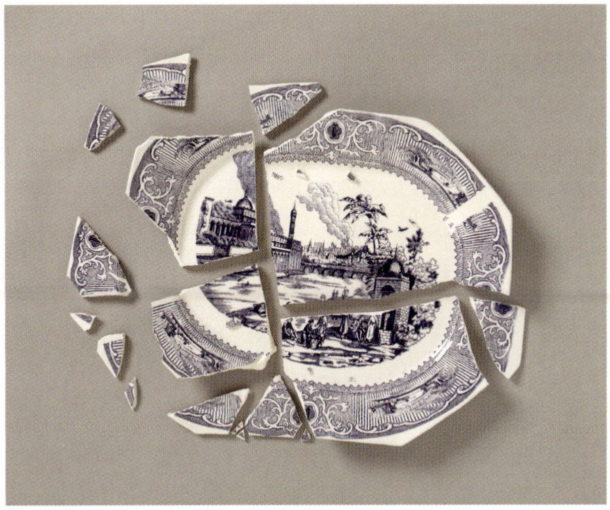

Bombs Over Baghdad (2003/2007).
(Courtesy of Paul Scott)

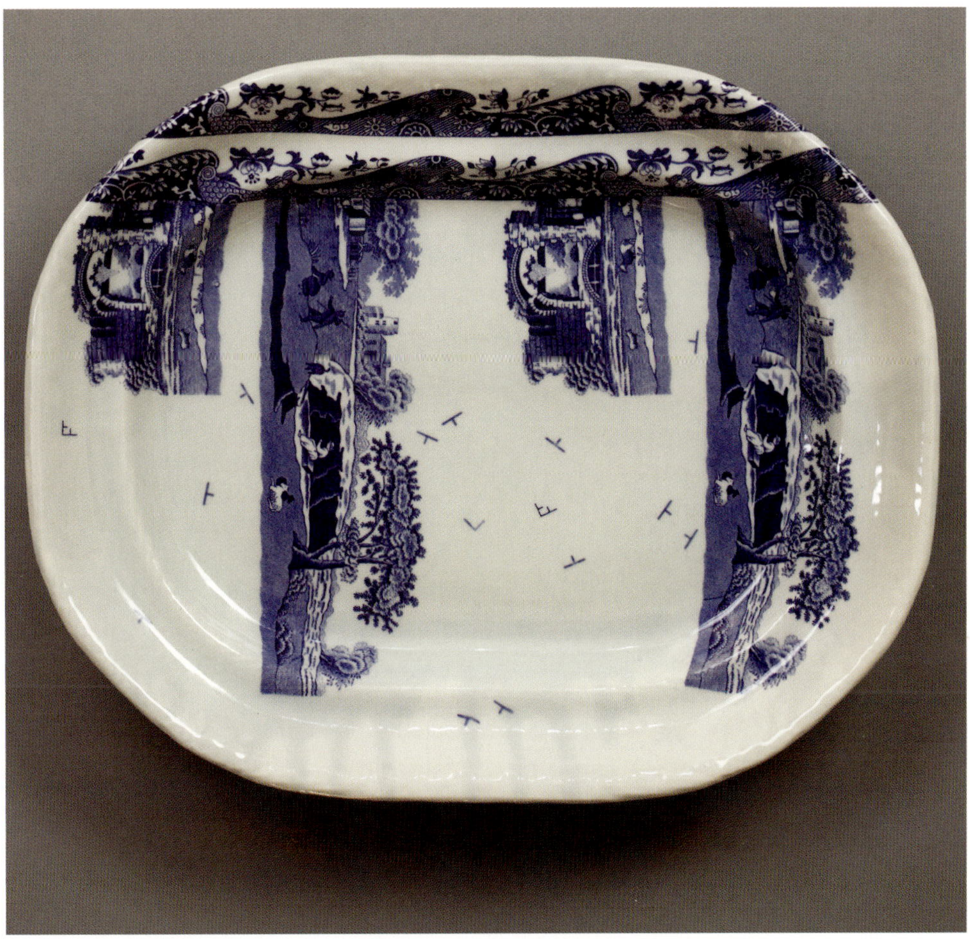

Italian Sampler No: 4 (2009).

understanding of images, their place in ceramic history, and the extent of their global circulation, is adeptly deployed to make 'visual ideology' visible and open to critique. His *New American Scenery* series, for instance, engages with the history of export ceramics from Staffordshire to the USA. Transferware in dark blue was especially popular in America, and British factories sought to engage this export market with the production of pots to order, many of which featured American landscapes. *New American Scenery: Souvenir of Portland; Or, Black Lives Matter (After Killen & Howard)/Trumpian Campaign No: 5* (2021) repurposes an early twentieth-century commemorative plate of Portland, Oregon. The work engages with the Black Lives Matter protests that took place in the city between May and October 2020 following the murder of George Floyd (1973–2020) by police officer Derek Chauvin. Following an executive order by President Donald Trump, federal law enforcement from around the country arrived in Portland in July 2020, despite protests having been largely peaceful. Ensuing arrests by federal law enforcers, many accused of not wearing identification and using unmarked vehicles, reignited protests. Mothers gathered outside the federal courthouse to protect protestors from law enforcers, whilst video evidence documented the beating of stationary protestors who posed no obvious threat. Scott's *Souvenir of Portland* erases pictures of the Hotel Portland (demolished, now Pioneer Courthouse Square) and Union Depot (or Portland Union Railway Station) and replaces them with armed law enforcers shrouded in smoke. What was once an anodyne commemorative plate is now an emblem of the government suppression of protest.

New American Scenery, Sampler Jug No: 8 (After Stubbs) (2021) is developed from a nineteenth

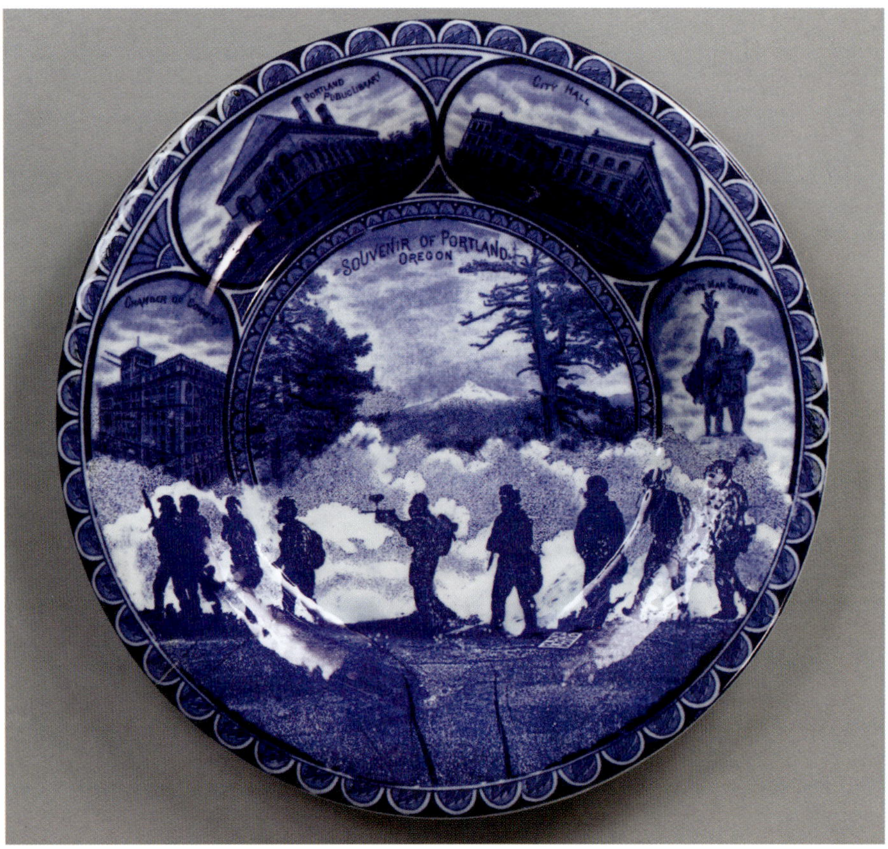

New American Scenery: Souvenir of Portland; Or, Black Lives Matter (After Killen & Howard)/Trumpian Campaign No: 5 (2021).

century factory practice where images from smaller works were deployed across a much larger piece, sometimes for the purposes of glaze testing, other times to create a large imposing work for the purposes of exhibition. In his series of *Sampler Jugs*, Scott combines both aspects of the practice, using smaller images that appear on his other *New American Scenery* works, but which nevertheless coalesce into a balanced design appropriate for exhibition. Standing at almost 40cm (15¾in) tall, *Sampler Jug No: 8* features, amongst other images, the armed law enforcers from the *Souvenir of Portland*, a photograph by Ryan Vizzons titled *Defend the Sacred* (2016), which depicts Native American Mega Mae Plenty Chief, Lakota Oyate, on horseback seeking to defend the Standing Rock reservation from damage by the construction of an underground oil pipeline; and a portrait of the Native American rights activist Leonard Peltier, who was unjustly imprisoned for aiding and abetting murder in 1977 and remains in prison at the time of writing despite calls by Amnesty International for his release. The collaged jug – which recalls the aesthetic of *The Town Mosaic* – communicates the injustices committed by government and big business, and their effect on the individual and the disempowered in contemporary America.

Naturally, Scott's interventions in history will, themselves, soon be historical. Yet, ceramics have been utilised for commemoration precisely because of their longevity. Scott's work captures the visceral realities of disaster and injustice so that the emotional impact of these moments is preserved. Moreover, by exposing the 'visual ideologies' at work in transferware, Scott demonstrates how pottery was the social media of its day, with all the selectivity, manipulation, and falsification that can be associated with the platform. He highlights the flaws in its algorithms, exposing the white, male, heterosexual ideologies that lurk in the undergrowth of the benign landscape. As an iconoclast, Scott breaks, with tradition.

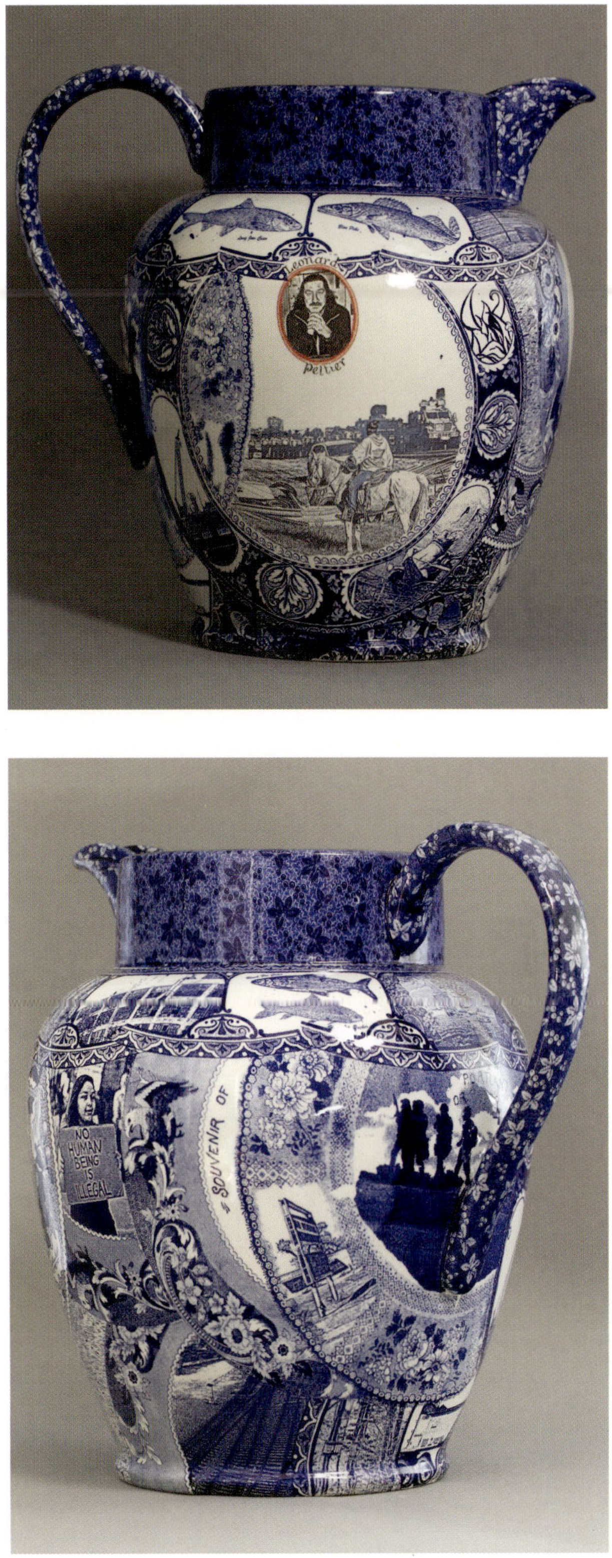

New American Scenery, Sampler Jug No: 8 (After Stubbs) (2021).

Stephen Dixon
Satura

In Latin, the word *satur* translates as 'full' or 'fullness'. In its feminine form – *satura* – the word means 'medley' (as in the phrase *lanx satura*, 'a full dish of various kinds of fruits'). However, by the post-classical age, *satura* had also garnered the modern meaning of 'satire'. The reasons for this change have been contested by etymologists. B. L. Ullman argued that the contemporary meaning of *satura* as 'satire' actually originated in the word *saturae* (a staged performance consisting of a 'medley' or 'miscellaneous' items), and was only later collapsed into *satura* following its use by the Roman poet Quintus Horatius Flaccus (65–8BC), better known as Horace.[98] Theodore Kharpertian, however, suggested that this usage did not occur until much later, when, at some point in the Middle Ages, *satura* became confused with the word *satyr*, a genre of humorous plays from ancient Athens.[99] Certainly, Stephen Dixon's satirical pots speak to the fullest etymological meanings of *satura*. His is an aesthetic of miscellaneous imagery that harnesses poetic allusion to humorously critique social and political figures. His pots are collages that draw upon diffuse metaphors, ranging from the Old Testament, classical sculpture, Hollywood films, and popular music, to satirise the rich and powerful.

Dixon's approach is strongly influenced by the aesthetic of satirical prints; from the 'modern moral subjects' of William Hogarth (1697–1764), through the prints of James Gillray (1756–1815), Thomas Rowlandson (1757–1827), and George Cruickshank (1792–1878), to the contemporary cartoons of Steve Bell, Gerald Scarfe, Ralph Steadman, and photocollages of Cold War Steve. However, given that *satura* has been etymologically linked to performance (as *saturae*, performance 'medley', and as *satyr*, humorous plays), as a theatre academic, I cannot help but notice that melodrama took hold of the English stage in the early to mid-nineteenth century, at around the same time that satirical prints reached maturity. The first 'English' play to be labelled as a melodrama was Thomas Holcroft's (1745–1809) *A Tale of Mystery* performed in 1802 (although it was in fact a translation of

René-Charles Guilbert de Pixérécourt's (1773–1844) *Cœlina ou L'enfant du mystère* first performed in Paris in 1800). As a dramatic genre, melodrama emphasised excesses of emotion, sensation, and spectacle. Feelings were the primary drivers behind action, which took place in a clearly defined moral universe. Good always triumphed over evil.

This change in theatrical style was not universally welcomed, however. A satirical print entitled *The Monster Melo-Drame* and attributed to Samuel De Wilder, appeared in the January 1808 edition of the *Satirist*. The image depicted a deformed lion (symbolic of Britain) with three necks, each featuring the head of an iconic theatre practitioner (playwright Richard Brinsley Sheridan, 1751–1816, and the actors Joseph Grimaldi, 1778–1837, and John Philip Kemble, 1757–1823). This gigantic hybrid beast was depicted trampling across 'Shakespeare's Works', whilst a group of contemporary playwrights suckled on its teats. As David Mayer and Michael Gamer have observed of this print:

> While we do not know their identities, we can assume that the *Satirist*'s subscribers, like many Britons in these years, were experiencing social confusion and, in some instances, a threatened loss of status. Their towns and cities were changing, and these changes were reflected and dismayingly perceptible in their theatres. The growth rate of Britain's cities materially contributed to this perception of a growing merchant and middle class edging a gentry schooled in the classics into a diminishing minority, the *Satirist*'s readers amongst them.[100]

Although here pitted against each other, I propose that melodrama and satirical prints offered parallel responses to social disorientation. Both sought to strengthen and clarify communal morality in the face of shifting social and cultural mores.

For the nineteenth century was marked by a prolonged sense of antagonism between tradition and modernity. Uncertainty about the outcome of the Napoleonic wars in the first decades of the nineteenth century gave way to economic uncertainty, greater class consciousness, and economic and political reform. William Gladstone (1809–1898) ushered in a model of executive leadership that nevertheless espoused liberalism, where individuals were guided towards communal belonging via a shared Christian moral compass.[101] Meanwhile, the moral superiority of Gladstonian liberal capitalism (as working towards benevolence rather than personal greed) was palpably at odds with the reality of industrial exploitation and working-class slums, just as scientific discoveries concerning the evolution of species undermined religious creationism.[102] Both melodrama and satire generated shared points of communal reference that could gloss over, or draw critical attention to, the contradictions of the age. As Peter Brook has observed in his analysis of melodrama:

> Melodrama does not simply represent a 'fall' from tragedy, but a response to the loss of the tragic vision. It comes into being in a world where the traditional imperatives of truth and ethics have been violently thrown into question, yet where the promulgation of truth and ethics, their instauration as a way of life, is of immediate, daily, political concern.[103]

In such destabilising times, both forms drew upon parallel aesthetics of emotion, excess, exaggeration, and spectacle to evince narrative clarity. As Brook has further suggested, in melodrama:

> Nothing is spared because nothing is left unsaid; the characters stand on stage and utter the unspeakable, give voice to their deepest feelings, dramatize through their heightened and polarized words and gestures

> the whole lesson of their relationship. [...] The world is subsumed by an underlying manichaeism, and the narrative creates the excitement of its drama by putting us in touch with the conflict of good and evil played out under the surface of things – just as description of the surfaces of the modern metropolis pierces through to a mythological realm where the imagination can find a habitat for its play with large moral entities.[104]

Melodrama contained both myth and modernity – religious faith and science. Plays were set in the land of fairy tale or in the smoky depths of the industrial metropolis, and told tales developed from a clear-cut theological morality whilst utilising the latest technologies to stage ever more spectacular performances. Similarly, satirical images referenced both myth and modernity via fantastic and grotesque beasts where, for example, a diminutive devil might chomp on a large foot, as in James Gillray's famous 1799 print *The Gout*, or the latest clothing fashions could produce weirdly deformed body shapes, as in George Cruickshank's *Monstrosities* etchings. These 'fantastical' beasts were distributed by presses who, by virtue of developments in transportation and printing technology, could reach larger audiences in greater quantities and at cheaper prices. In both genres, representations of the contemporary were rendered excessive and grotesque via reference to mythical imaginaries mined from the past.

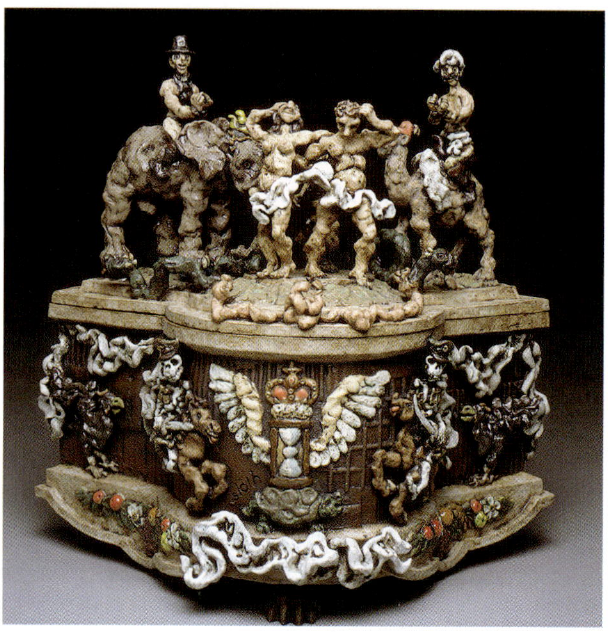

Momento Mori (1991).

Dixon's parabolic work is produced from both two- and three-dimensional approaches, from both transfer prints and modelling, slab building and casting. In this sense, his pots can be positioned as an aesthetic hybrid, as existing between the grotesqueness of satirical prints and the emotional excesses of melodramatic theatre. For example, the earlier piece *Momento Mori* (1991) – part of a series of works inspired by Hieronymus Bosch's (c.1450–1516) painting *The Seven Deadly Sins and the Four Last Things* (c.1500) – takes the form of a lidded box. The lid becomes a kind of 'stage' upon which the central figures of Adam and Eve preen and dance amongst the clouds, even as worms of decay wriggle around their feet. An elephant, symbolic of the Republican Party of the USA, and a camel, emblematic of Arab oil states, stand guard, though the hands of their riders are bound together. A relief to the exterior of the box shows a timer running amidst emblems of the establishment, the approach of dead generals on horseback, and hovering vultures. The feet of the box itself are claws, as though all the characters are riding atop a demonic beast. Although *Momento Mori* arises from a specific observation of neo-imperialism and class politics in eighties Britain, it offers a broader political point; the rich will always exploit their power and access to resources even as they stare death in the face. As global warming increasingly threatens our ecosystems, this observation is as saliant as ever.

Living In The Past (1992) draws a historical parallel between two royal couples: King Charles III (then Prince of Wales) and his relationship with

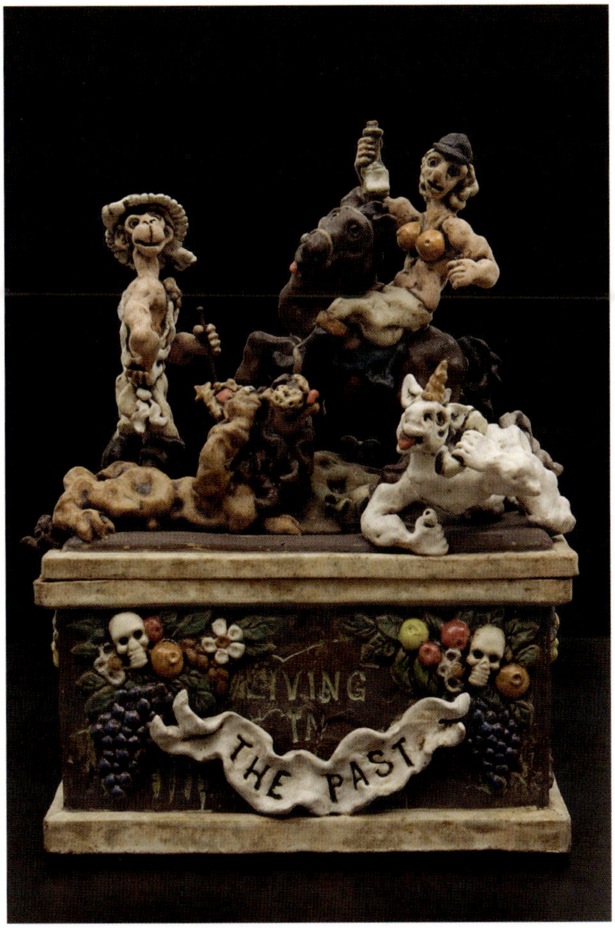

Living In The Past (1992).

Camilla Parker-Bowles whilst married to Princess Diana (1961–1997), and the earlier liaison between King Charles II (1630–1685) and his mistress, the actress Nell Gwyn (1650–1687). In Dixon's work, Gwyn is depicted naked on horseback, whilst Charles wears a safari suit. The suit is similar to that worn by Charles III when climbing Uluru with Diana as part of the couple's first royal tour to Australia in 1983. For the occasion, Diana sported a dress designed by Singaporean designer Benny Ong, leaving Charles' choice of safari suit jarringly symbolic of colonial longing. Despite occurring only two years after their marriage, the tour increased media speculation about the difficulties facing the couple. Below these two figures, a lion and a unicorn, emblems from the Royal Coat of Arms, look on at the couple in dismay. The unicorn listens to a conversation on the telephone, an allusion to 'Camillagate' (where a transcript of a tapped phone call between Charles III and his then mistress Camilla was leaked to the press in 1993, scandalising the Establishment). As with *Momento Mori*, the relief around the box alludes to decay; skulls nestle amidst the fruits of abundance. In an image that could have come straight from one of James Gillray's prints, Dixon satirises the monarchy for lacking the exemplary morality it is expected to exemplify.

The meticulous planning and hours of labour required to make Dixon's early works left him with little room for experimentation. A turn towards slab-building and transfers (including the development of his own transfer and screen-printing processes when he began working at Manchester Metropolitan University in 1998) enabled his process to be refined. Slabs of clay could be treated like paper, and the

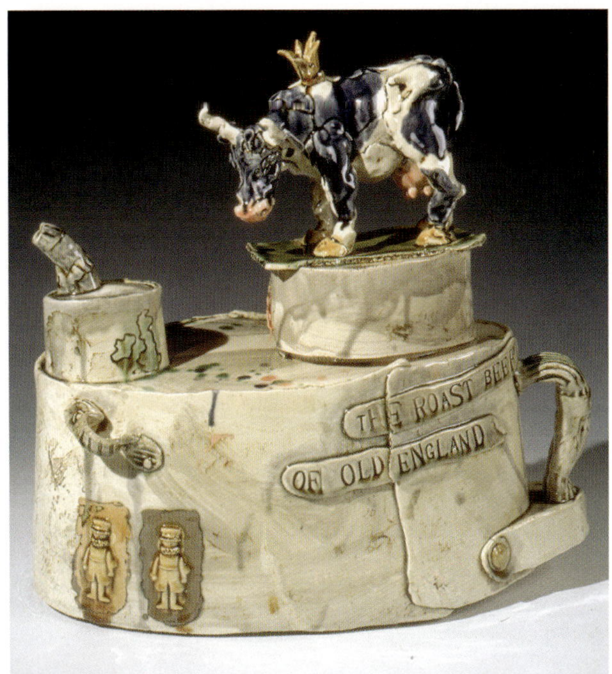

The Roast Beef of Old England (1997).

application of transfers brought Dixon's work closer to printmaking. Yet, the lids of his pots were retained as stages for figuration, often showcasing the primary subject matter of the work.

The Roast Beef of Old England (1997), for instance, takes its title from Henry Fielding's (1707–1754) patriotic ballad, first performed in 1731, and frequently sung in theatres thereafter. It became so popular that it was subsequently used by Hogarth as the title for his 1748 painting *O the Roast Beef of Old England* (*The Gate of Calais*). Dixon utilises this patriotic nostalgia to critique the British government's handling of the neurodegenerative disease BSE (Bovine Spongiform Encephalopathy). In 1990, at the height of the first outbreak amongst cattle, the MP John Selwyn Gummer famously fed his daughter a beefburger in front of the assembled press. Scientists had already shown that BSE could infect other species of animal, and by 1994, people were beginning to show signs of infection by developing variant Creutzfeldt-Jakob Disease (vCJD). In fact, the daughter of one of Gummer's friends, Elizabeth Smith, tragically died from vCJD in 2007. In 1996, the European Union banned all imports of British beef, a ban that lasted until 2006, and which was dubbed by the British media as a 'Beef War'. Dixon's work takes the form of an oil can, a pot used to oil machinery, and thus an emblem of the role of imperialist nostalgia in keeping the machinations of the Establishment running. A cow with a crown on its back stares towards a map of the British Isles and Ireland, whilst Beefeaters – a pun on meat consumption – line up along the base.

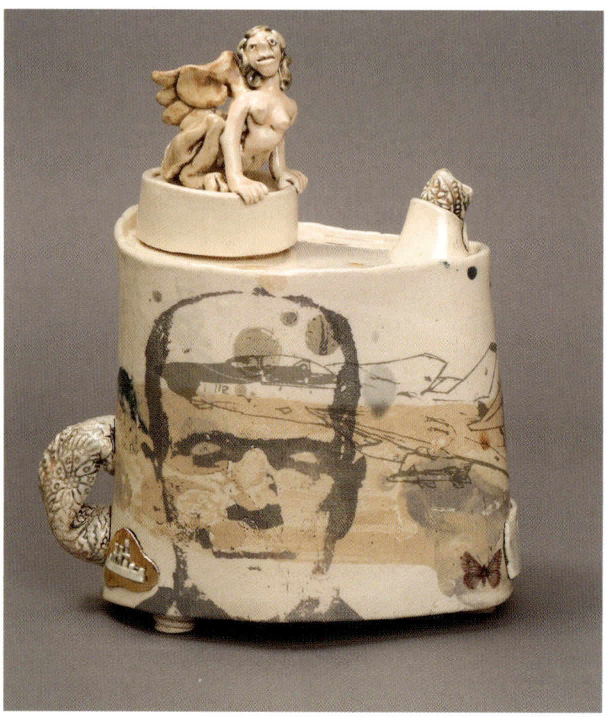

▌ *The Sphinx* (2003).

A later work, *The Sphinx* (2003), demonstrates even greater refinement in approach. In classical mythology, sphinx are treacherous and merciless creatures, killing those who cannot solve their riddles. Here, Dixon has sculpted a sphinx as symbolic of the Labour Government led by Tony Blair, sitting atop a teapot, a cosy emblem of domesticity. A fighter plane rushes across the side of the pot, a reference to the 2003 invasion of Iraq. The plane flies across an image of Frankenstein's creature played by Boris Karloff in the 1931 film. Frankenstein's creature is a theatricalised emblem of the monstrous (it was, coincidentally, produced as a melodrama for the stage in 1818 – the same year in which the novel was first published), which here symbolises Saddam Hussein (1937–2003), who was initially supported by Western powers during the Iran–Iraq war (1980–1988). The US Defence Secretary Donald Rumsfeld (1932–2021) met with Hussein in December 1983. Yet, as Hussein increasingly asserted Iraqi self-interest in the years that followed, some twenty years later Rumsfeld was calling for an invasion of Iraq under the pretext of preventing the deployment of (non-existent) weapons of mass destruction. As an ambivalent symbol of perpetrator and victim, the image of Frankenstein's creature seems to answer the riddle of

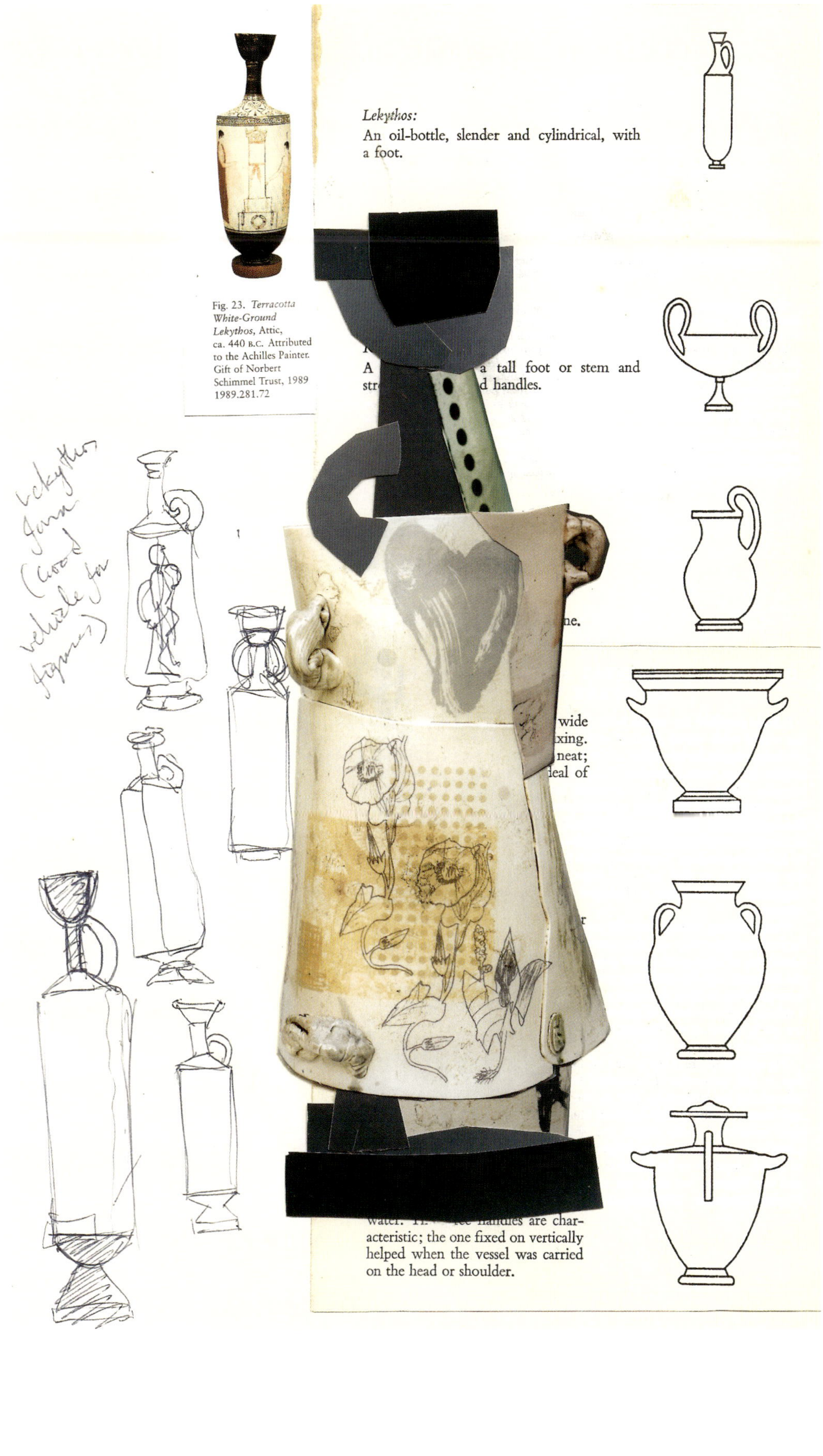

Lekythos (2004).

the sphinx with another question: what morality is there in tyranny and war?

Dixon's ceramic collages are always carefully considered and planned. *Lekythos* (2004) is a page from his sketchbooks, demonstrating how historical references are redeployed in contemporary contexts. A lekythos, for instance, is an ancient Greek container for olive oil or other kinds of oil. In *Paradise Lost* (2008), the lekythos is recontextualised within the narrative of the 2003–2011 Iraq War, the symbolism altered to signify a container for crude oil. On the lid of the pot, Dixon has sculpted Tony Blair as a tinpot soldier. He lies extended in a pose reminiscent of Adam in Michelangelo's (1474–1564) Sistine Chapel fresco (1508–12), reaching out to touch God. Yet, there is no divine hand reaching out in return; instead, he lies there naked, with chainmail and a teacup on his head, holding a gun. The side of the pot features a drawing of Thomas Lawrence's (1769–1830) oil portrait of The Duke of Wellington (1769–1852) completed around 1815–16. Blair seems to imagine himself as part of a long line of right-wing Establishment military heroes. Any hope for a truly alternative, leftist, political vision is lost.

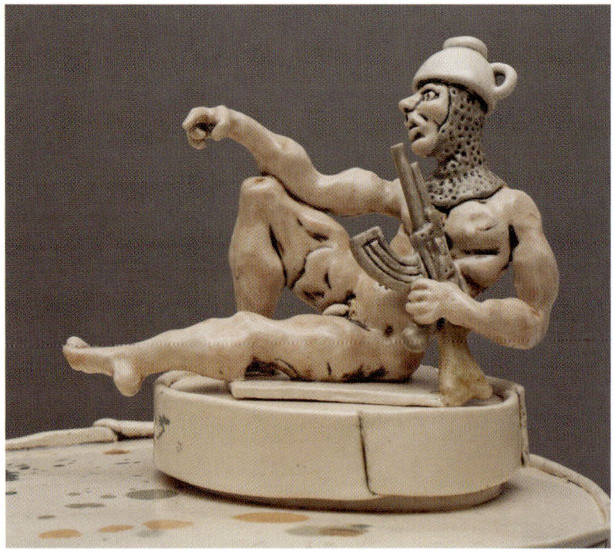

Detail from *Paradise Lost* (2008).

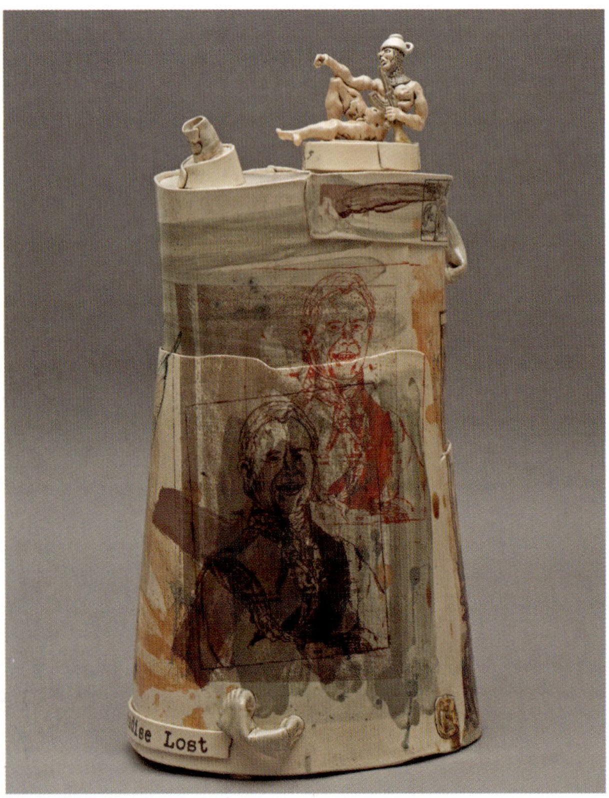

Paradise Lost (2008).

Dixon's growing fascination with the possibility of digitally manipulated imagery led to a renewed interest in the production of plates, works that were less concerned with sculptural form and more with visual design. *21 Countries* (*Grenada*) (2003) is from a series of plates inspired by a 2002 *New Internationalist Magazine* article, which observed that the USA had bombed twenty-one countries since the end of World War II. Each of Dixon's twenty-one plates – all of which are now in the collections of the Museum of Modern Arts and Design in New York – alluded to one of these countries, the designs relying on visual metaphor to make their point. Grenada became independent from Britain in 1974, but less than a decade later it was invaded by the USA. Instigated in 1983, *Operation Urgent Fury* was a four-day incursion, launched under the pretext that Cuba (apparently at the behest of Soviet Russia) was helping Grenada to build an airstrip for military use. The plate features a drawing of the marble sculpture *Laocoön and His Sons*, which was excavated in Rome in the early sixteenth century. The sculpture describes how snakes were sent by Poseidon to kill Laocoön and his family for exposing the falsehood of the Trojan Horse, the wooden sculpture that concealed a secret army which successfully crushed the city of Troy. The inclusion of the image alludes to the wafer-thin ruse used by the US military to justify the attack. The singer Britney Spears is also pictured at the 2001 MTV Video Music Awards, where she famously danced with a Burmese python. At once symbolic of the disposability of US popular culture, the appearance of Spears perhaps also alludes to exploitation, where Spears' treatment under her conservatorship undermined the 'wholesome' American values she was supposed to exemplify.

Dixon has long been drawn to the form of the oil can. The sketchbook page *Oil Cans (With Portraits)* (1996) documents Dixon's earliest explorations of the oil can form, juxtaposing drawings of the Qatari elite with oil cans, not only metaphors of their wealth, but also their freedom of movement (as a transportable object, the oil container can be taken – or exported – almost anywhere). Recent work has returned to the oil can, interrogating it as a symbol of power and wealth. *Ferretto Italiano* (2022) takes the form of a moulded oil can in tin-glazed earthenware, its aesthetics loosely inspired by Italian majolica pottery from the Middle Ages. *Ferretto* is Italian for 'wire', referenced on the can as a fence, a symbol of incarceration and defence. Fences delineate borders, and because of recent history, articulate national anxieties concerning refugees and migration. Italy saw some 150,000 refugees cross from North Africa during the Syrian refugee crisis of 2015, though the route had long been used by people smugglers, whose overladen boats capsized all too often in the Mediterranean Sea. Italy has

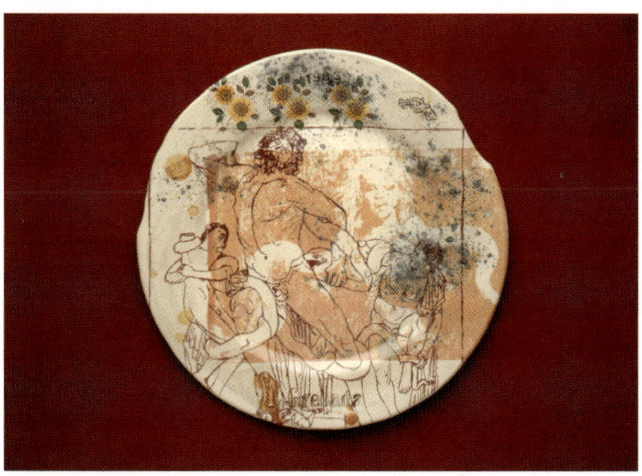

21 Countries (Grenada) (2003).

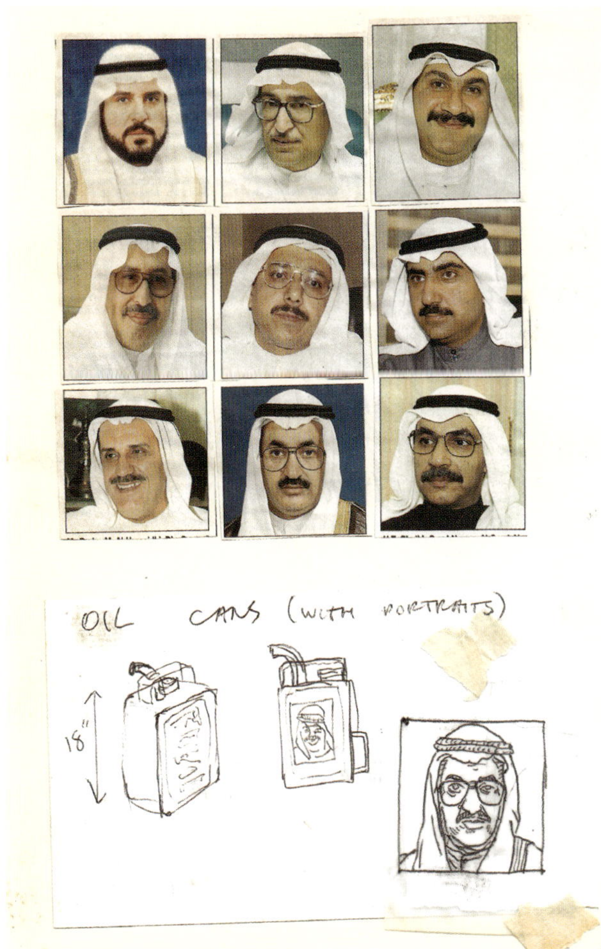

Oil Cans (With Portraits) (1996).

an ambivalent relationship with Non-Government Organisations (NGOs) seeking to provide aid to refugees and illegal migrants. In 2022, Andrea Costa, the President of Baobab Experience (an NGO set up in 2015 when tens of thousands of migrants passed through Rome), risked being sentenced to prison for eighteen years for aiding and abetting clandestine immigration. In the end, he was acquitted. In a gesture of solidarity with the dispossessed, *Ferretto Italiano* features a drawing of the bronze figure of *David* (c.1440s) by Donatello (c.1386–1466), the figure representing David from the Old Testament, who takes on the mighty Goliath and wins. The other side of the can features a bird, symbolic of migration, as well as the word 'passenger', a reminder that oil cans, like countries, facilitate flow as well as containment. *Ferretto Italiano* is an important work for Dixon, representing a shift in emphasis away from critiquing the powerful towards representing the powerless.

Like satirical prints, Dixon's exaggerated figures utilise historical motifs to invite a critique on contemporary issues. Yet, the flattened tops of his pots are akin to stages; his figures are grotesque actors whose self-conscious melodramatic gestures communicate their villainy. Like melodrama and satire, Dixon's pots do not simply represent the world. The intensification of sensation produced through exaggeration renders deeper meanings explicit. Such amplification enables traits to become observable, inviting – even soliciting – wider critique. As Brook observes in a passage that could easily stand as a description of any of Dixon's works:

> The narrative voice is not content to describe and record gesture, to see it simply as a figure in the interplay of persons one with another. Rather, the narrator applies pressure to the gesture, pressure through interrogation, through the evocation of more and more fantastic possibilities, to make it yield meaning, to make it give up to consciousness its full potential as 'parable.'[105]

Dixon's pots are, in this sense, anthropological parables. Political in content (like satirical prints), they are nevertheless driven by feelings (like melodramatic performances). Dixon must feel, be moved by a predicament, to create work. As pots that critique the powers that shape humanity for the worse, they are indeed *satura*: satirical, poetic, composed from miscellany, and akin to dramatic performance. Speaking to the past, present, and future, Dixon's expressive pots are indeed 'full'.

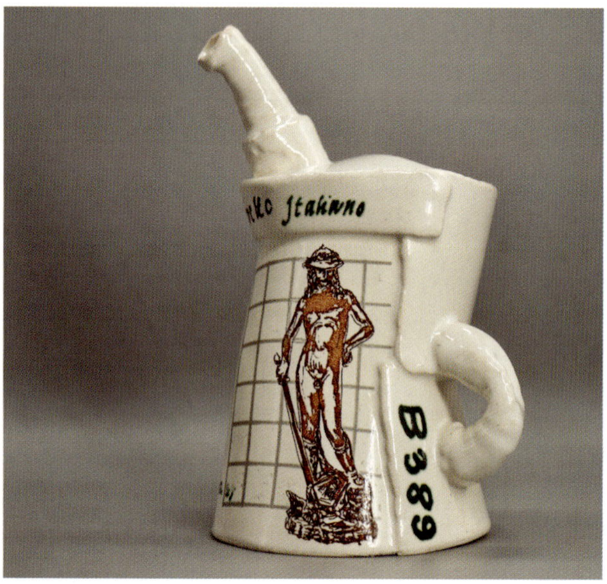

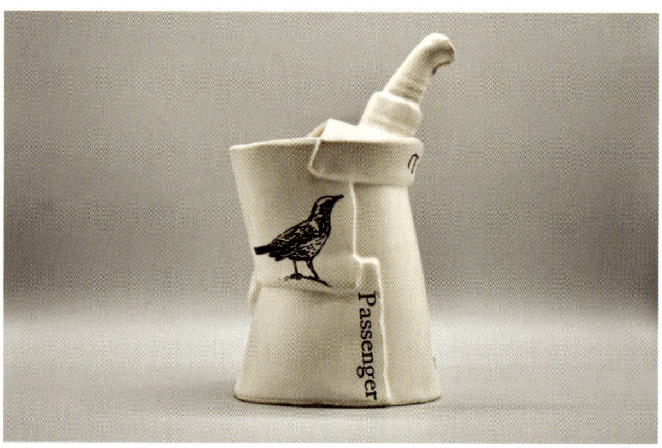

Ferretto Italiano (2022).

Frances Priest Neo-*modernisme*

In the Gràcia district of Barcelona, on the southern slope of Carmel Hill, north of Sagrada Familia, lies Parc Güell, a private park designed by the famed architect Antoni Gaudí (1852–1926). Originally conceived as a site for an exclusive housing estate by the entrepreneur Eusebi Güell (1846–1918), a lack of sales meant the park became a public space in 1926. Designated a UNESCO World Heritage Site in 1984, the park is a testament to Gaudí's vision of Catalan *modernisme*, a heady architectural mix of French Art Nouveau, the English Arts and Crafts Movement, and Middle Eastern and East Asian arts. Artists such as Gaudí could claim influence from global art and design motifs because European imperialism had rendered it accessible. As a student, for instance, Gaudí encountered the Victorian design bible *The Grammar of Ornament*, which was first published in 1856 by the Welsh architect and designer Owen Jones (1809–1874).[106] *The Grammar of Ornament* seems like a quasi-Darwinian attempt to categorise design motifs from around the globe, though the Victorian sense of superiority is acute. The book moves from a clearly defined sense of global 'Otherness' (the first chapter is titled 'Ornament of Savage Tribes'), towards a European sense of 'Self' related to classicism and an appreciation of nature (the last two chapters are titled 'Italian Ornament' and 'Leaves from Flowers and Nature').[107] Interestingly, the book also demands a unification of architecture and the decorative arts, something that Gaudí's Parc Güell offers in abundance.

One of the most striking features of the park is the serpentine bench located in the main terrace. Adorned by shards of ceramic tile, it is formed of a patchwork of abstracted shapes, which hint at mathematic precision, yet resist strict geometry. This sampling of cultural reference points highlights something of the eclectic nature of *modernisme*, which in its piecemeal of references, seems to pre-figure the late twentieth century postmodernist approach of quotation and recontextualisation.

I begin this analysis of the work of Frances Priest with Gaudí because there is a revealing, if indirect,

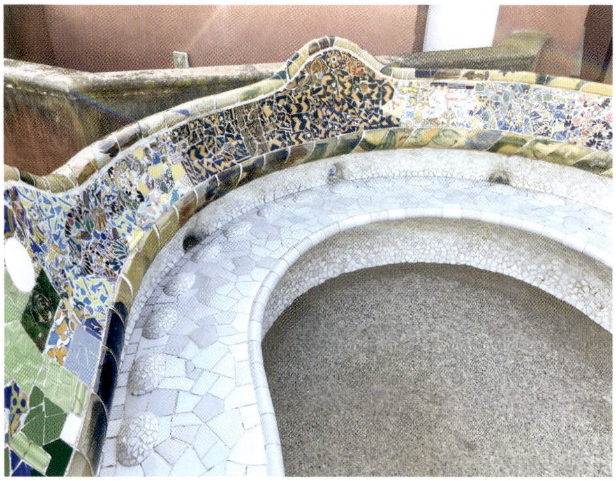

A section of the Serpentine Bench by Antoni Gaudí in Parc Güell, Barcelona.

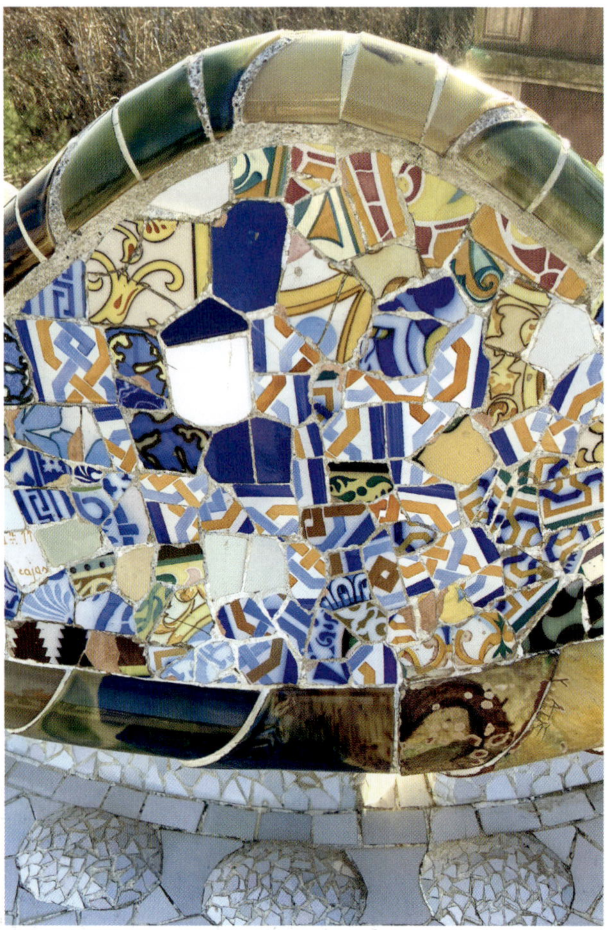

A detail from the Serpentine Bench in Parc Güell, Barcelona.

relationship between the two. Priest, like Gaudí, has long been preoccupied with the interpolation of architectural form and decoration. Both encountered Jones' *The Grammar of Ornament* during their formative years, even if the book was to have a more profound significance upon Priest. Nevertheless, as Jones proposed, 'the Decorative Arts arise from, and should properly be attendant upon, Architecture', and, as a consequence, 'Architecture is the material expression of the wants, the faculties, and the sentiments, of the age in which it is created.'[108] Priest's outputs are more modest in ambition than Gaudí's grandiose architecture, yet, like Gaudí, she is a great synthesiser of visual languages. Her work represents an amalgamation of the (ostensibly male) architectural strand of contemporary British ceramics with the legacy of Victorian design.

In the contemporary British urban landscape, the Victorian era seems to be abundant: in municipal buildings and town halls, railways stations, churches, and clock towers. It is so ubiquitous that, amidst the day-to-day bustle of the town and city, it risks being overlooked. Priest, however, explores this heritage – with all its possibilities and problems – head on. The work she produces is both international yet decidedly British: a product of Victorian sensibilities and colonialism, yet fully aware of the meaning of this legacy in a post-colonial, multicultural age. To understand how Priest occupies such nuanced territory, it is important to consider her work as a totality, as a series of developments linked by a causal thread. In the loosely chronological analysis that follows, I seek to explore how Priest takes colonial grand narratives, fragments them, and reassembles them into contemporary objects that might articulate a post-colonial politic. Her method progresses from visual analysis, into critical deconstruction and fragmentation, and resurfaces as rearticulation; a process I have sought to mirror in the structure of this chapter.

The first decade of Priest's career was devoted to deconstructing the vessel to consider how the contour of shape affects perceptions of space, akin to how an architect considers the flow of space through a building. The trajectory of these investigations aligns her work with Martin Smith and Ken Eastman,[109] as well as Nicholas Rena (included in this volume). Like these artists, Priest explores how deftly crafted line, form, and surface can make an architectural statement in space through the constraint and release of volume. *Broken Ellipse Series I* (2003), for instance, offers rhythmic counterpoint between mass and space; the volume of the deconstructed vessel cloaked by two exterior sections straining for an impossible embrace. Fine inlaid lines, describing either circles or stripes, extend this sense of containment and release across the surface of the work, adding a visual metaphor that evokes the sentiments of holding on and letting go. A piece from a later series, *Balanced Blue* (2005), introduced pattern more overtly and utilised strong colour to guide the eye into registering different layers of architectural space. The blue plane, for instance, modulates from internal to external

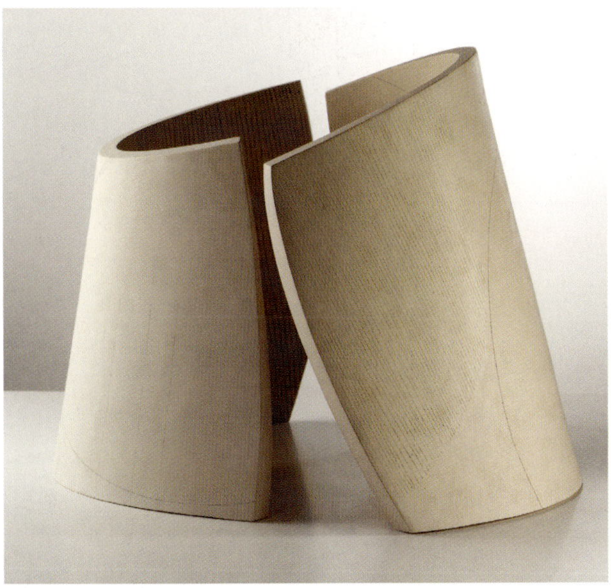

■ *Broken Ellipse Series I* (2003).

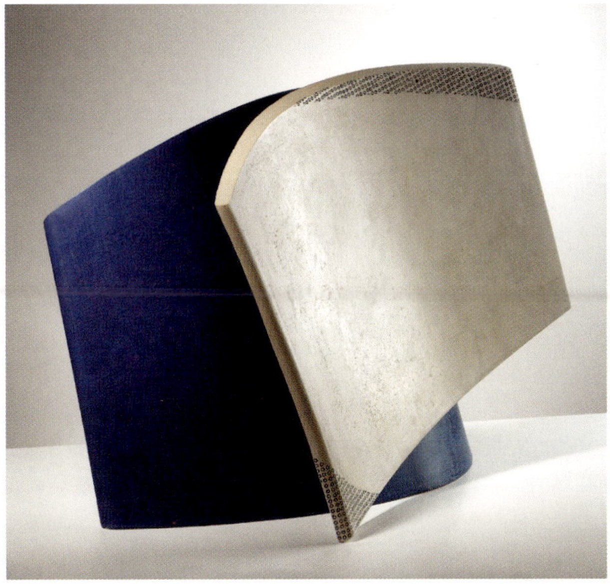

■ *Balanced Blue* (2005).

space via its proximity to the other section, highlighting how architecture is constituted by a series of contextualised relationships. This form also evokes a reading related to emotion: the white section, with its repeated pattern of blue inlaid circles, is connected to the blue plane, but it also resists absorption into it by remaining white. This seems to symbolise how one party is supported by, but remains independent from, the other. In a similar vein to Richard Serra's *Torqued Ellipse* series of works, *Balanced Blue* obtains its expressive power by being both balanced and imbalanced; the applied decoration stabilising a form that otherwise risks awkwardness.

Balanced Blue was, perhaps, a pivotal work for Priest, for it clearly articulated not only how architectural form and decoration could become co-dependent, but also the role of the spectator in making objects meaningful. In the same way that architectural space is fully activated by people occupying or moving through it, so ceramic objects are realised by spectator response. *Balanced Blue* can be considered as expressive of reactionary modes of perception between the artist and audience via the

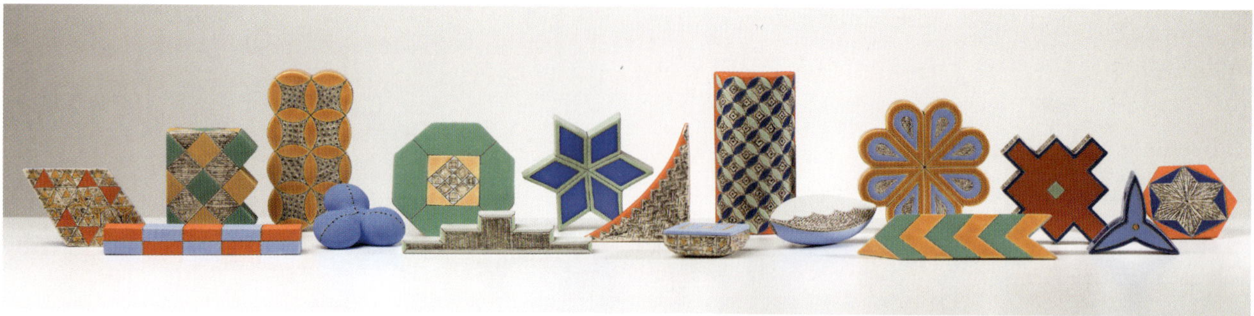

Collection | Grammar of Ornament, Byzantine I (2020).

object (this is in addition to balance in the aesthetic composition of form). For me, this piece balances the demands of the creator with the consumer.

In 2009, Priest created a series of different sculptural objects – initially cylinders, rhomboids, and various kinds of convex form (some redolent of Chinese spinning toys) – that featured more complex surface designs. Patterns were arranged to work with or against contours, producing varied visual effects for each piece. When placed together as an installation, the interplay between these forms created a visual rhythm as the eye moved between individual elements and the whole composition. Yet, there was no 'final' composition; the objects could be placed in any arrangement. This empowers the spectator to become curator, to touch the installation and fundamentally alter its form. The installation has developed into an important strand of Priest's practice (such as the more recent *Collection | Grammar of Ornament, Byzantine I*, 2020). In this sense, fragmentation and rearticulation have become central to her methodology.

***

Gathering Place | Grammar of Ornament, India, iii (2017) is a product of divergent histories, geographies, and visual identities. It is both complete as a work, and yet internally fragmented. Patterns composed of smaller elements in darker hues are registered by

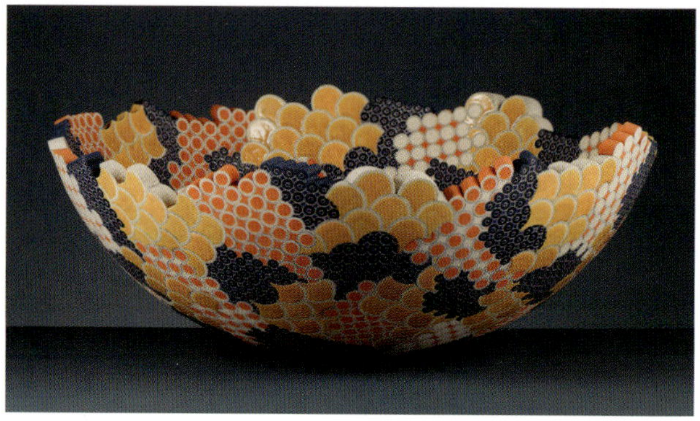

Gathering Place | Grammar of Ornament, India, iii (2017).

the eye more quickly, affording them a faster sense of visual pace that is offset by the larger and more complex geometric constructions in bright yellows and oranges. Even works that are designed by Priest to standalone nevertheless conjure a sense of curated installation.

***

Depending on the project, ideas might be sought from the motifs on specific pages of Jones' *The Grammar of Ornament*, her own life drawings (for example, plants on the Scottish Isle of Raasay), or tile factory pattern books. Through a combination of drawing out ideas and digitally manipulating motifs in Photoshop, Priest arrives at raw design patterns. These patterns are then layered until satisfying compositions are found. The compositions are then drawn out and coloured, producing taut painterly studies that evoke the best of British constructivist art (Kenneth Martin, 1905–1984, particularly comes to mind).

Priest achieves architectural presence in her work by utilising a relatively limited range of forms:

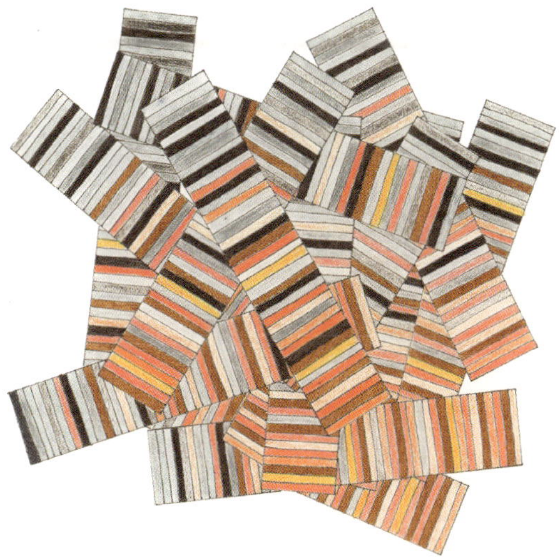

Objet d'Emotion *Stripe* Sketch [1] (2019). (Scan of a drawing by Frances Priest)

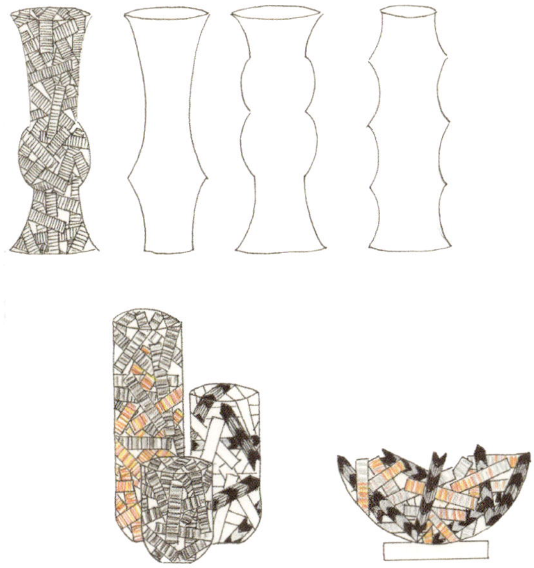

Objet d'Emotion *Chevron* Sketch [2] (2019). (Scan of a drawing by Frances Priest)

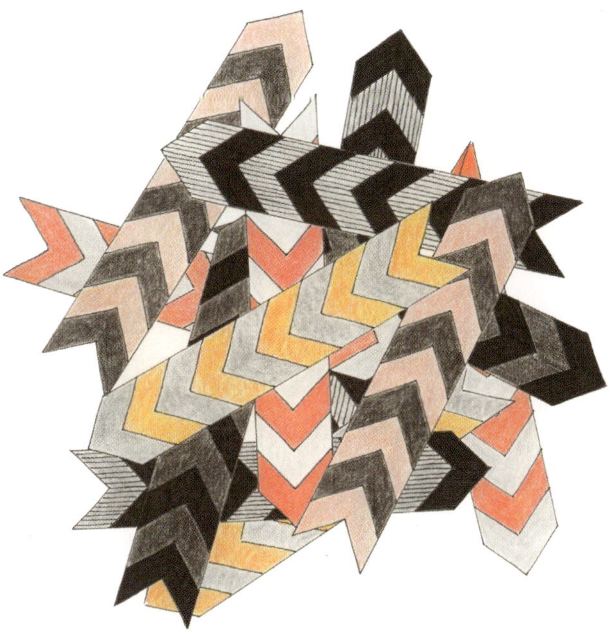

Objet d'Emotion *Chevron* Sketch [4] (2019). (Scan of a drawing by Frances Priest)

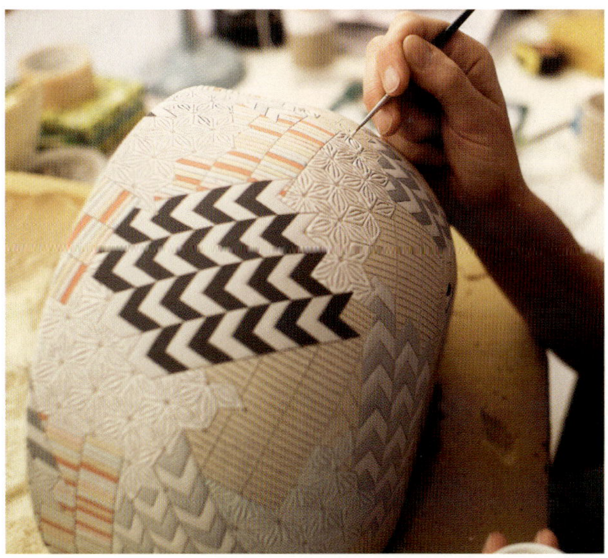

Priest working on *Chevron, Stripe and Asanoha* (2019).

the cylinder, bowl, box, or plinth. Her choice of form is directed by how she considers pattern will augment, or even disintegrate, as it is repeated across a surface. Further drawings will be made to establish how pattern will behave, to observe the shift between regular and irregular rhythms in producing sensations. Only once this lengthy process of preparation has been completed will the form be made, the pattern incised into the clay surface, and the coloured glazes applied.

***

The *Chevron, Stripe and Asanoha* series (2019) comprises enclosed vessel forms. These forms maximise the available space for applied pattern, turning each work into a kind of spatial drawing, whilst the concave tops are vaguely redolent of the bowl. The series was produced as a collection for the jewellery specialist Valery Demure at gallery Objet d'Emotion. Forged in conversation with Demure, the works stand as a record of their collaboration, Priest's own assessment of Demure as a person, and the wider world of fine jewellery and couture fashion which she inhabits. As a kind of portraiture, the geometric designs suggest divergence, complication, busyness, and dynamism. Chevrons direct the eye like arrows to points of connection, which may lead to further chevrons, or to sections of stripes which have a vertical rather than horizontal rhythm. These works exhibit an ordered quotation, the careful layering of experiences, perhaps alluding to the necessary interconnections between different modes of artistic practice.

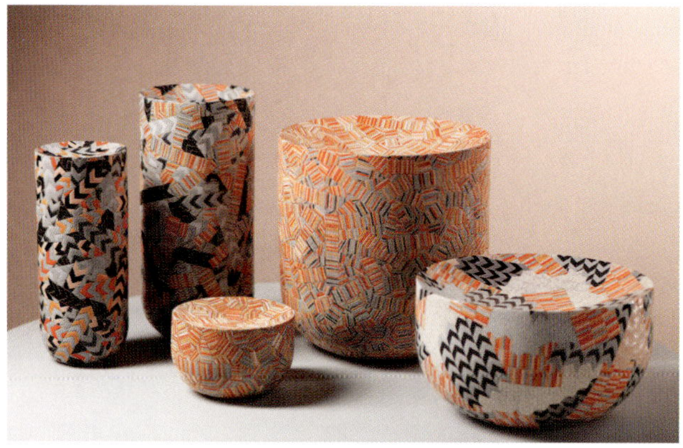

Chevron, Stripe and Asanoha series (2019).

***

The *Vessel & Plinth | Grammar of Ornament – India* series (2019) comprises small bowls placed on grounds. The thick rim of each bowl enables both form and decoration to participate in the sculpting of space. The base of each bowl is rounded rather than flattened, meaning that the weight of each bowl determines how it will rest on the plinth. Accents of darker colours repeated in sympathy with, or against,

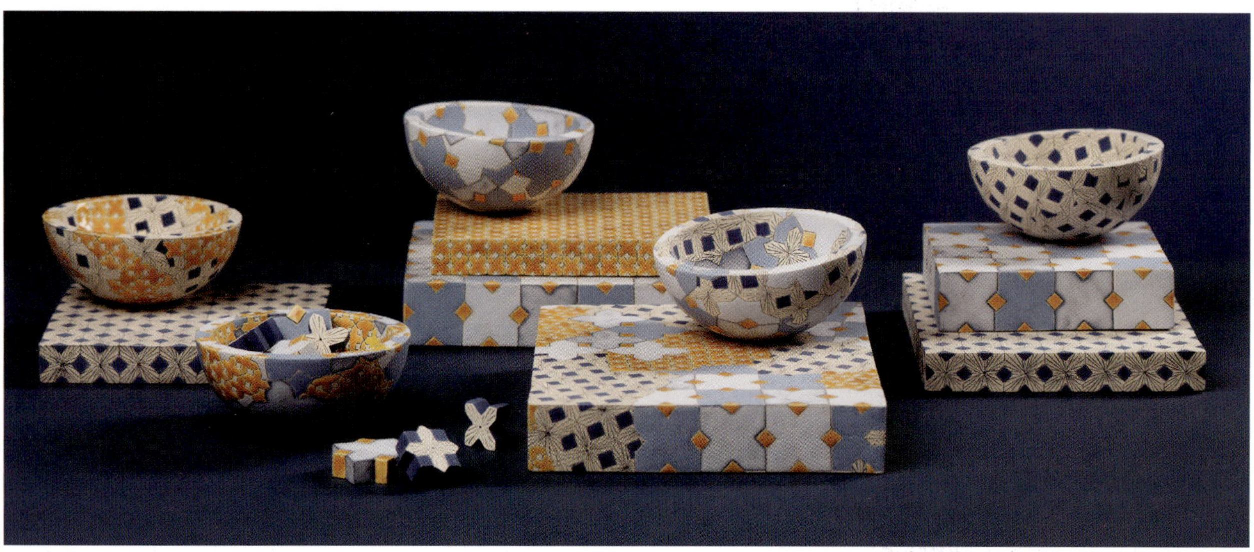

Vessel & Plinth | Grammar of Ornament – India series (2019).

the contours of the form affect its sense of poise, and this disrupts or augments shape or colour as it modulates across different forms. Like the sculpture installations, the work can be moved to create countless new compositions, the sense of impermanence intensified by the bowls as they teeter on their plinths.

***

Whilst the visual effects produced in Priest's work are visually compelling, is it possible to critique the invocation of 'India' in *Vessel & Plinth | Grammar of Ornament – India* as a product of colonialism? Or is Priest's work ostensibly concerned with British design histories? What critical space might her work occupy?

***

> [To mention] the English weather is to invoke, at once, the most changeable and immanent signs of national difference. It encourages memories of the 'deep' nation crafted in chalk and limestone; the quilted downs; the moors menaced by the wind; the quiet cathedral towns; that corner of a foreign field that is forever England. The English weather also revives memories of its daemonic double: the heat and dust of India; the dark emptiness of Africa; the tropical chaos that was deemed despotic and ungovernable and therefore worthy of the civilising mission. These imaginative geographies that spanned countries and empires are changing, those imagined communities that played on the unisonant boundaries of the nation are singing with different voices.[110]
>
> *(Homi Bhabha)*

***

> Appropriation is a complex discussion within the use of ornament. *The Grammar of Ornament* was created during a period within design history when individuals like Owen Jones were lecturing on the principles of good design and how it could improve people's lives. As this was broadcast mainly by privileged European men, we cannot shy away from the fact that their classifications were biased towards a Western ideal. Additionally, much of the material they referenced when providing examples from other cultures was acquired for British museums and galleries, predominantly as the result of colonial occupation, exploitation and pillaging. [...] And though Priest is acutely aware that her reverence for decorative design from this period in British history is intertwined with issues around colonialism, we could argue that Priest's own practice does not look to appropriate the work of others.[111]
>
> *(Sara Rothwell)*

***

To understand how Priest's work might bypass accusations of neocolonialism, and access a more critical neo-*modernisme*, it is helpful to consider the post-colonial theories of Homi Bhabha. Bhabha's work on nationalism is centred upon the relationships between ourselves and others. When we think of ourselves, at the most fundamental level, we are also thinking of others. This might sound rather strange, but if we had never met another human being, we would never need to use the words 'I' and 'you'. Instead, we would just 'be'. Yet, when we encounter another person, and we recognise the limitations of ourselves, we notice difference. Suddenly, I can see that 'I' am not 'you'... I become aware of the existence of an/other. Homi Bhabha contends that the self and the other are thus intertwined. This is especially important when considering the concepts of nation and nationalism, that is, how a nation describes its identity to itself. If one nation did not meet another one, there would be no need to communicate difference. Despite the idea of 'nationalism' seeming about 'us', Bhabha suggests it is wholly connected to 'them': 'us' and 'them' are co-dependent.

Having ascertained that a nation is only possible through its relationships to others, Bhabha then explores how the nationalist sense of self is always historical; it is only by looking back that we can see how 'people' acted on behalf of the nation, perhaps for the purposes of self-defence or shared belief. As Bhabha suggests, 'the linear equivalence of event and idea that historicism proposes, most commonly signifies a people, a nation, or a national culture as an empirical sociological category or a holistic cultural entity.'[112] Indeed, Owen Jones produces a linear historicism in *The Grammar of Ornament*, where each chapter is dedicated to a specific nation or geographical region, attributing stylistic essentialisms to the design of each locale (and from a European point of view, as noted in the introduction). By looking back, we supposedly have a stronger sense of 'who we are' and 'who we are not'.

Yet, despite the ordered chronology of such national histories, Bhabha contends that nationhood in the contemporary is a leap of imagination, for people can never agree on the facets of national belonging that are supposed to connect them. To reconcile the apparent certainty of the past with the slipperiness of the present, Bhabha suggests that the nation is produced through an uneasy mapping of history (what he calls 'the pedagogical') onto the contemporary (what he calls 'the performative'). He conceives of nationhood as a kind of performance, where particular views of history are commemorated to perform the historical national sense of self in the contemporary (these might include, for instance, support of a particular 'national' team, or collective acts of remembrance). However, by unmasking nationhood as an ideologically constructed performance, the true plurality that lies beneath is exposed. It is only through this diversity, Bhabha concludes, that nationhood can be truly recognised.[113]

Whilst Priest's utilisation of *The Grammar of Ornament* may risk reproducing colonial tropes, it also draws attention to the imbrication of the self and the other, the coloniser and the colonised, thereby breaking down the essentialism of an imagined sense of colonial racial homogeneity. In this sense, her work actively acknowledges the pluralism of nationhood. In fact, the deconstruction and rearticulation of *The Grammar of Ornament* in Priest's work is contingent upon an acknowledgement of Britain as a product of diverse histories, a salient point for a contemporary artist based in Edinburgh. For, as Bhabha suggests 'in the West, and increasingly elsewhere, it is the city which provides the space in which emergent identifications and new social movements of the people are played out.'[114]

The significance of social movement and the city in the post-colonial construction of the nation brings us back to space, and indeed, to architecture. In 2016, Priest was commissioned to design tiles for a corridor at the Royal Edinburgh Hospital, an NHS hospital focusing on mental health, with a view to brightening the space and improving user experience of the building. Over the next two years, Priest worked on a design that acknowledged the legacy of the Victorian era (by no means coincidentally, the period in which psychoanalysis developed) by drawing upon Victorian tile pattern books. Yet, the design was resolutely contemporary in its composition and colour scheme. The public space of a hospital corridor was an apt commission for Priest. Rooms, as containers, might be classified as a kind of scaled-up vessel, making an interior design tiling project a natural extension of her practice. Yet, it also enabled her to critically investigate Victorian design, and to utilise geometry and colour in the service of a more inclusive national narrative.

Priest's work is certainly a development of *modernisme*; perhaps it may be regarded as neo-*modernisme*

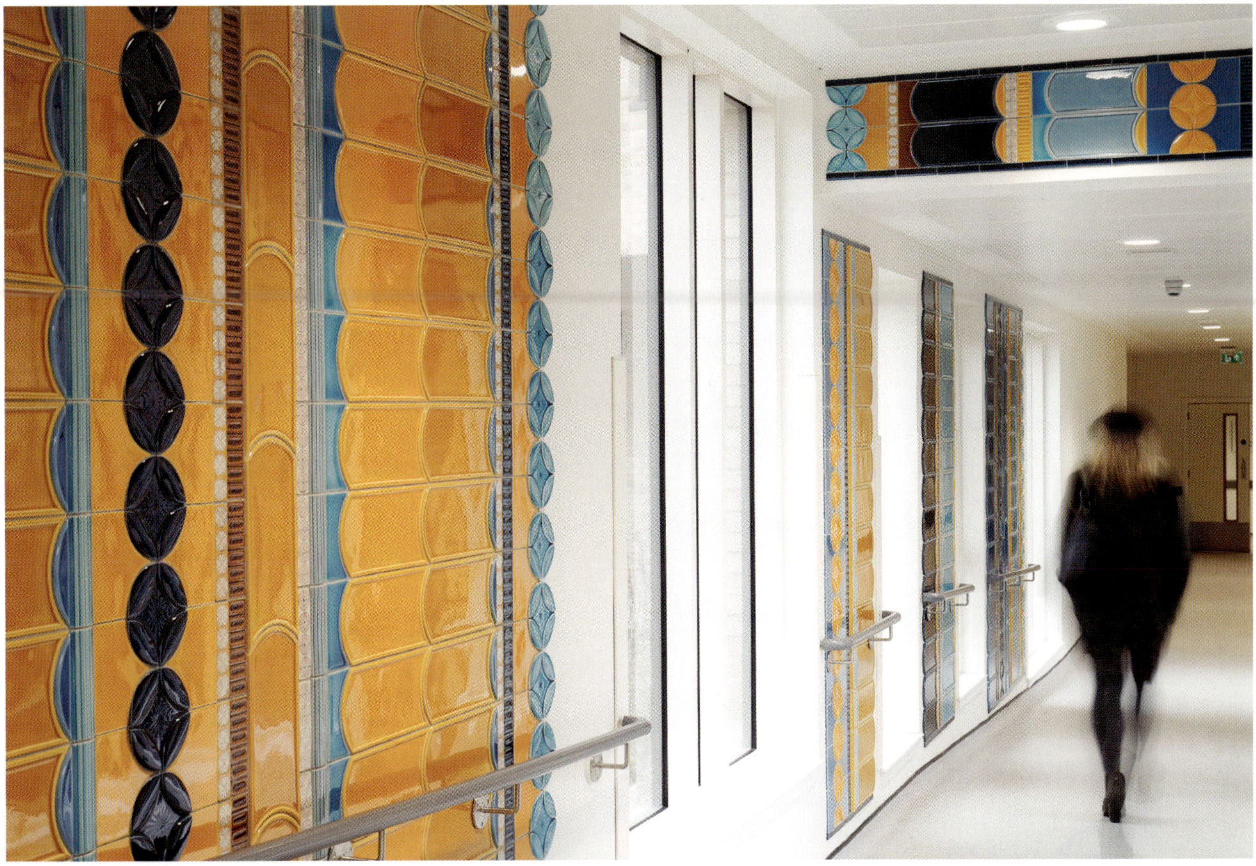

Tiled Corridor in the Royal Edinburgh Hospital (2019).

(a kind of postmodern *modernisme*), where the collaging of different graphic styles is a more condensed and self-conscious form of quotation. Indeed, unlike her predecessors perhaps, Priest is acutely aware of the colonial politics of recontextualising visual languages from around the globe. Her work is a product of colonial history, but it is not automatically an endorsement of it. Its patchwork of design references speaks to contemporary metropolitan multiculturalism, the hallmark of British approaches to diversity which seeks to hold identifiable cultural difference in suspension. In this sense, as Bhabha suggests, such hybridised work (regardless of who makes it) can offer a unique vantage point from which to articulate new pluralised national perspectives.

Priest documents connections, not only between Britain and elsewhere, but between Britain and its own sense of self. Her works – bowls, sculptures, and the interior of rooms – catch and hold a myriad of reference points, interweaving divergent perspectives into one contemporary statement. It is this critical element that, for me, makes the neo-*modernisme* of Priest different from *modernisme*, and from the narrative collapse of postmodernism. The power of Priest's neo-*modernisme* lies in the fact that it seems to bring us together to critically consider who we really are.

Nico Conti Ceramic Surgeon

'It is the great aim of machinery to make skill or strength on the part of the workman valueless,' wrote the surgeon Peter Gaskell in 1836, 'and to reduce him [*sic*] to a mere watcher of, and waiter upon, *automata*.'[115] In his monograph, *Artisans and Machinery: The Moral and Physical Condition of the Manufacturing Population*, Gaskell argued that mechanisation was causing the 'declension of the most numerous class of artisans in Great Britain, from comfort, morality, independence, and loyalty, to misery, demoralization, dependence, and discontent [...].[116] Not only did he fear that intangible craft skills would vanish in the face of rampant mechanisation, but also that artists would lose 'all free agency, and will be as much a part of the machines around him as the wheel or cranks which communicate motion.'[117] Some 140 years later, in 1976, a remarkably similar sentiment was expressed by Bernard Leach, who considered that:

> the machine is always on the cool side of man. It is the difference between machine-made silver spoons and the ones that have been hammered by hand. I think it is the precise quality of the machine, the nonhuman quality, that is driving hundreds of thousands of people back to clay. They want to enjoy themselves. They want to use and stretch their imaginations. They want to give expression to their feelings about life.[118]

Firm in his belief that even the most repetitive of production pottery work facilitated unrepeatability because it was handmade, Leach deemed machine-made work to be too calculated. Indeed, the hand shaping clay on a wheel is the metonym for studio pottery.

Yet, as with any tool, if work lacks expressivity, one could argue it is because nobody put it there. As early as 1902, the architect and design theorist Hermann Muthesius (1861–1927) suggested that:

> Regardless whether man's products emerge from a machine or from our hands, they will inevitably be artistic, so long as they are done properly. The machine is nothing but a more perfect instrument.[119]

Technology did not prevent expression; it simply had to be used expressively. This belief was expanded upon by the German philosopher Walter Benjamin (1892–1940), who argued in his 1936 essay 'The Work of Art in the Age of Its Technological Reproducibility' that technology enabled the production of art that lay out of reach of the human body. He observed, for instance, how the lens of a camera could see the world in more detail than the naked eye and record an image faster than the hand could draw. Focusing most of his essay on film, Benjamin believed that technology reframed questions of authenticity and reproducibility for the mechanised age. In what stands as a rather apposite response to the pessimism of the surgeon Peter Gaskell, Benjamin uses the metaphor of a surgeon (read: user of machines) and a magician (read: pre-industrial methods) to demonstrate the effectiveness of technology:

> The surgeon represents the polar opposite of the magician. The attitude of the magician, who heals a sick person by a laying-on of hands, differs from that of the surgeon, who makes an intervention in the patient. The magician maintains the natural distance between himself and the person treated; more precisely, he reduces it slightly by laying on his hands, but increases it greatly by his authority. The surgeon does exactly the reverse: he greatly diminishes the distance from the patient by penetrating the patient's body, and increases it only slightly by the caution with which his hand moves among the organs. In short: unlike the magician (traces of whom are still found in the medical practitioner), the surgeon abstains at the decisive moment from confronting his patient person to person; instead, he penetrates the patient by operating. – Magician is to surgeon as painter is to cinematographer. The painter maintains in his work a natural distance from reality, whereas the cinematographer penetrates deeply into its tissue. The images obtained by each differ enormously. The painter's is a total image, whereas that of the cinematographer is piecemeal, its manifold parts being assembled according to a new law.[120]

For Benjamin, the appeal of film lay in its ability to utilise technology as a means to penetrate deeper into reality, to assemble from fragments something that could not otherwise be realised. To transplant such analysis onto ceramics is to propose that artists who use machinery (such as 3D printing) can interrogate material in new ways that respond to the technological age in which we live.

Of course, technologies of some sort are used by all contemporary ceramicists, from pre-prepared clays and glazes to automated kilns that regulate firing temperatures. Of all the technologies at their disposal, however, 3D printing remains controversial. To print rather than throw a vessel is to expose the long-running anxieties about the loss of the artisan and the dulling effect of mechanisation described above. Indeed, as Bernard Leach was a key figure in the development of British studio ceramics over the last century, his vehement insistence on

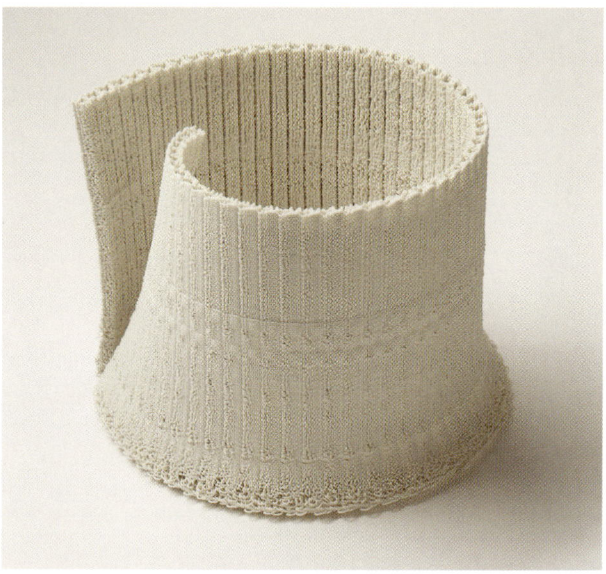

■ *Of Lace and Porcelain* (2019).

the handmade has remained seductive. One might even propose that the emergence of 3D printing in ceramics is a direct assault on his philosophy. That said, even though the technology is still in its relative infancy, some 3D printed forms could possibly still be produced by more traditional methods, such as hand-building or moulding. It is, as a consequence, tempting to construe 3D printing as nothing more than a dumbing down of studio skill and technique.

A convincing and robust challenge to this point of view can be found in the work of Nico Conti. Born in Malta, Conti spent two years (2017–2019) at the Royal College of Art in London developing techniques to print in 3D using porcelain. This meant not only becoming conversant with the technology, but also pushing it to its limits, altering the viscosity of the porcelain slip to create forms that teetered on the edge of what was possible to print. Drawing upon different formal vocabularies – Wedgwood, traditions of Maltese lacemaking, and religious architecture – Conti makes vessels that, quite simply, cannot be produced in any other way. Although they utilise vocabularies derived from pots, they do not have a base, meaning that these works are developed from the tubular contour of the vessel. His works sit in the grey area between the pot and the vessel, utilising aspects of both to explore the contingency of interior and exterior space.

Early pieces, such as *Of Lace and Porcelain* (2019), were characterised by textured surfaces resembling the structure of Maltese lace (*Bizzilla 'ta Malta*). Lacemaking took hold in Malta in the seventeenth century when examples were imported from Italy, France, and Spain. Although by the eighteenth-century silk was being spun domestically rather than imported from Sicily, thread had long been used, and flax was used again in the nineteenth century during a period of deep and lasting recession. After being shown at *The Great Exhibition of the Works of Industry of All Nations* in London in 1851, Maltese lace became extremely popular in Britain.[121] Conti evokes this Maltese export by using the 3D printer

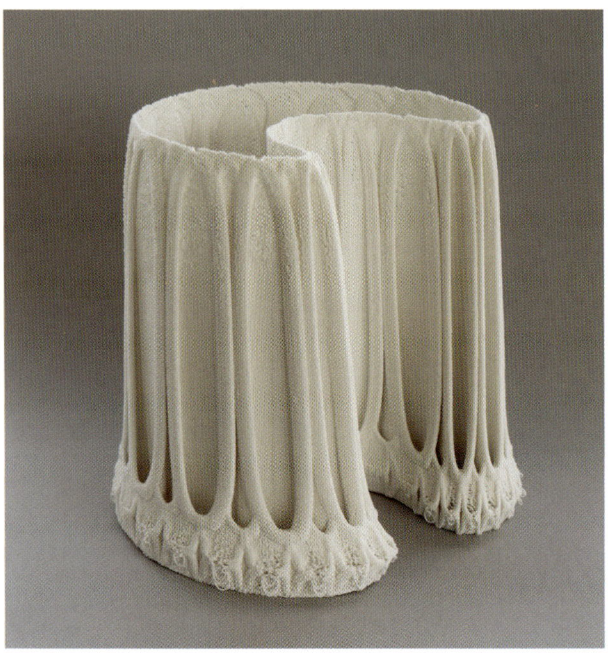

■ *Of Lace and Porcelain* (2021).

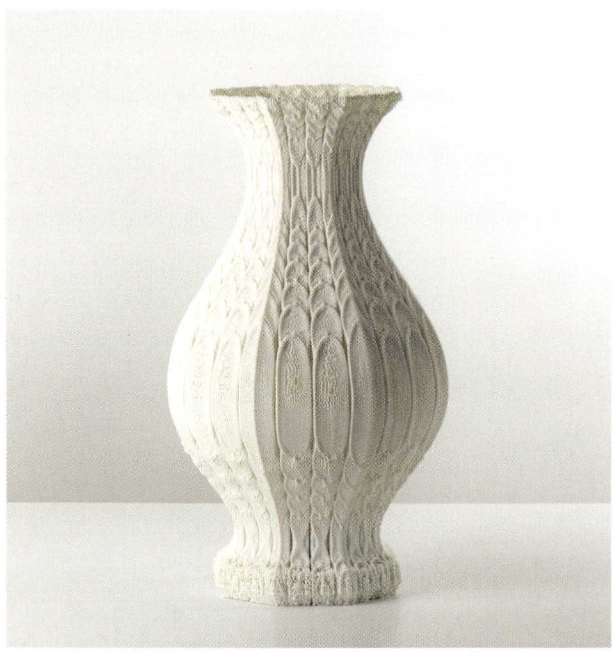

■ *Scalloped Vessel* (2021).

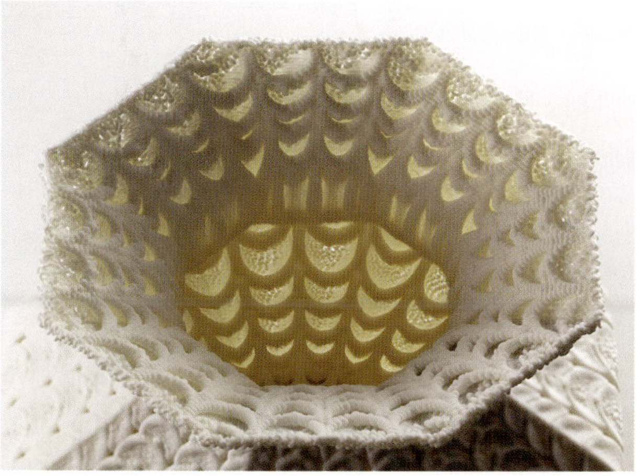

Interior of *Scalloped Vessel* (2021).

to weave his vessels into form, the lines of unglazed porcelain evoking the white and soft yellows of the thread used for lace. The spiral contour *Of Lace and Porcelain* (2019) allowed for consideration of how far walls could be manipulated and what structural load the printed porcelain could bear in its unfired state. Indeed, the work unfurls like a reel of film or a bolt of cloth, one edge falling inwards, the other beginning to collapse outwards. It has a lyrical quality, a facet that some might find surprising in a 3D printed vessel.

The move towards more architectural forms enabled Conti to explore the translucency of porcelain, how light could become integral to the composition of a vessel. A later form from the *Of Lace and Porcelain* series (2021) evinces a more sculptural edifice. Here, the ornate base section opens out into a series of vertical elliptical shapes that elongate the vessel, similar in effect to lancet windows in a church. *Scalloped Vessel* (2021) utilises translucency to stunning effect; the exterior appearing solid, but light revealing a net-like patchwork of shapes to the interior. The patterning seems to collapse lacemaking with architecture, a reminder that the plasticity of lace enabled it to add textural sculpting to clothes (on sleeves or as neckerchiefs, for instance). Yet the firing of porcelain fixes the structure, as though the lace had been soaked in liquid starch. The shape of this vessel is developed from nineteenth-century Wedgwood bulb vases, the period in which Maltese lace became fashionable in Britain. This situates the vase as a reflexive comment upon the nineteenth-century aristocracy, who were able to use their fortunes to bind together new combinations of luxury goods from across Europe. It also enables Conti to bypass Leach and align his work with the Wedgwood factory, where technical experiments in the late eighteenth century led to the development of dry-body (unglazed) stoneware and the famous jasperware and caneware ranges, as well as creamware

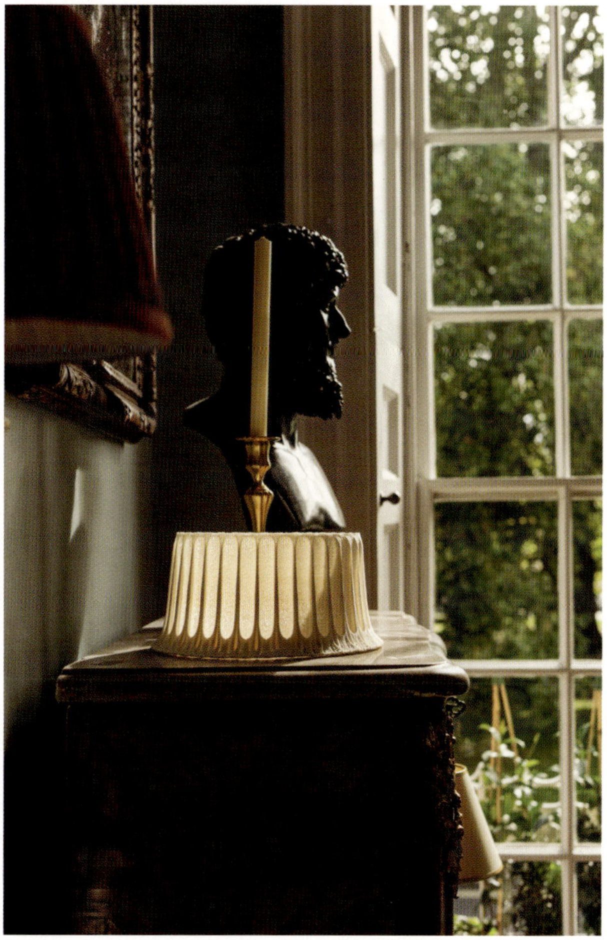

Filigree of Light Cathedral I (2020).

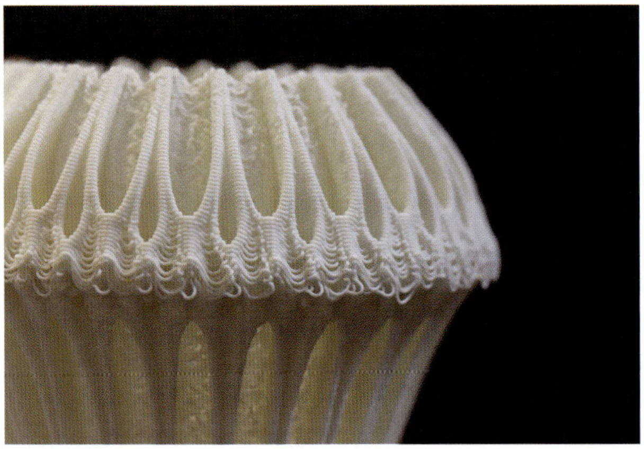

Filigree of Light (2020).

basket forms. Conti thus implies that his unglazed 3D printed porcelain forms are simply the latest iteration in a long line of technical developments in ceramic production.

Architecture became a key consideration in the *Filigree of Light* series. *Filigree of Light Cathedral I* (2020) utilises translucency magnificently as a central compositional concern. Light contours across the form according to the thickness of the surface, the lancet window-like shapes affording the work a strong architectural presence. A significant development occurred when Conti began to construct his vessels with two independent (double) walls. Treating each wall as an independent plane, he layered additional complexity into the composition, utilising the translucency of porcelain in ever more inventive ways. *Filigree of Light* (2020), for example, manipulates the density of the vessel walls in the upper mid-section, allowing light to show through the lower and uppermost sections of the work. Natural light shining on the form appears to illuminate it from within, as though it were a lamp without a bulb. The presence of the lines of printed clay around sections of the vessel again evoke the fragility of lace. Such details could not be produced by throwing or moulding.

Filigree of Light: Laced Urchin (2021) is a small vessel that demonstrates Conti's ingenuity in creating different visual rhythms across surfaces. The external body of the vessel has a horizontal patterning caused by the printing, which gently undulates. This is in stark contrast to the vertical lines of the interior, where porcelain is layered to produce columns that rise up to the rim of the vessel. The central section of the base evokes the rose windows of a cathedral, the twelve points of the pattern providing a visual focus for the columns that emanate from it. Despite its diminutive size (8cm high by 10cm wide/3in by 4in), the detail inside the vessel and finding such detail is quite breathtaking; the work offers the same kind of visual impact as walking into the massive chambers of an ornate cathedral. Capturing this sense of awe and astonishment in such a small vessel is a significant achievement in the computation of form.

Conti's approach to the double walled vessel has become extraordinarily complex in a relatively short period of time. For instance, from the outside, *Gentle*

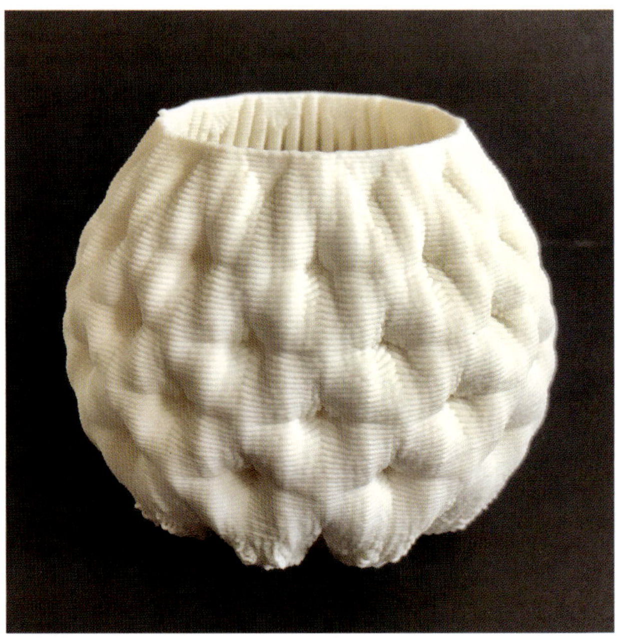

Filigree of Light: Laced Urchin (2021).

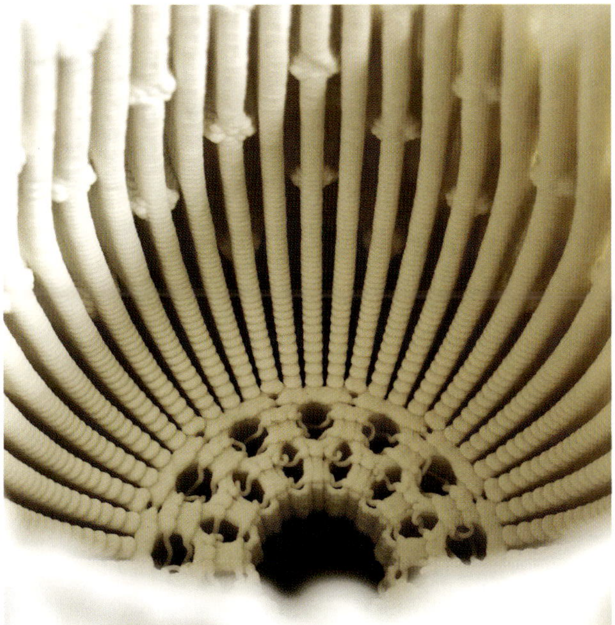

Interior of *Filigree of Light: Laced Urchin* (2021).

Embrace (2021) appears to consist of two separate vases, one cuddling up to the body of the other. The interior, however, reveals that both forms are interconnected: the top of the taller form leads down towards the bottom of the smaller one in a diagonal movement. *Gentle Embrace* reveals what an embrace might actually symbolise, the union of two people who are so close that they operate as one unit. In its evocation of a harmonious and loving relationship, this is an especially moving work.

Since at least the start of the Industrial Revolution, critics have decried the stultifying effects of technology. Machines are incapable of creating work with any expression of feeling, they claimed; their calculated precision is too cold. Yet, if Muthesius suggested machinery is simply a kind of tool, questions of legitimacy are less about the means and more about the maker. Can, following Benjamin, 3D printing create work that the human body could never produce unaided? Conti's work suggests not only that it can, but it does. His approach sits at the most technical end of the contemporary technology underpinning ceramic practice, but his capacity for expression is as strong as any of the other artists included in this book. Like Benjamin's surgeon, Conti delves into the body of the vessel, seeking out expressive potential in the deepest recesses of form. In so doing, his work also reflects the digital reality of the twenty-first century. Of course, in the same way that the painter still uses oil to summon an individual imagining of the world, the potter's wheel will always spin its magic. Yet, as Benjamin asserted, 'it has always been one of the primary tasks of art to create a demand whose hour of full satisfaction has not yet come.'[122] Conti's career is in its earliest stages; there is much yet to be discovered.

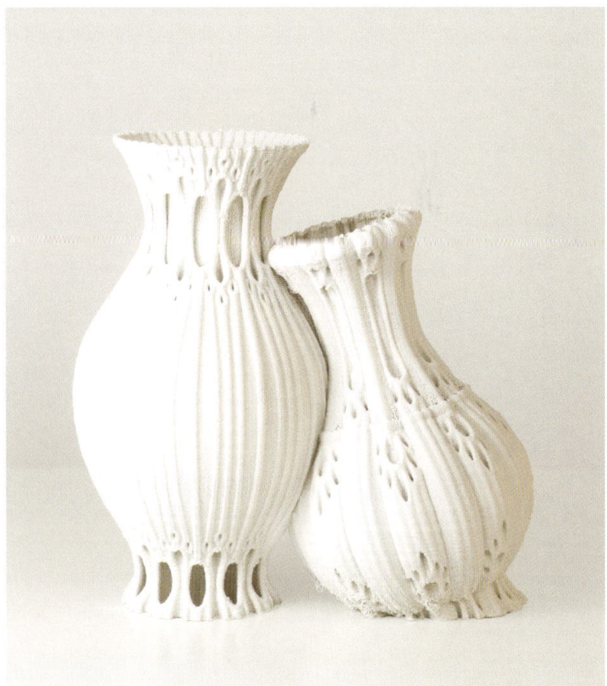

Gentle Embrace (2021).

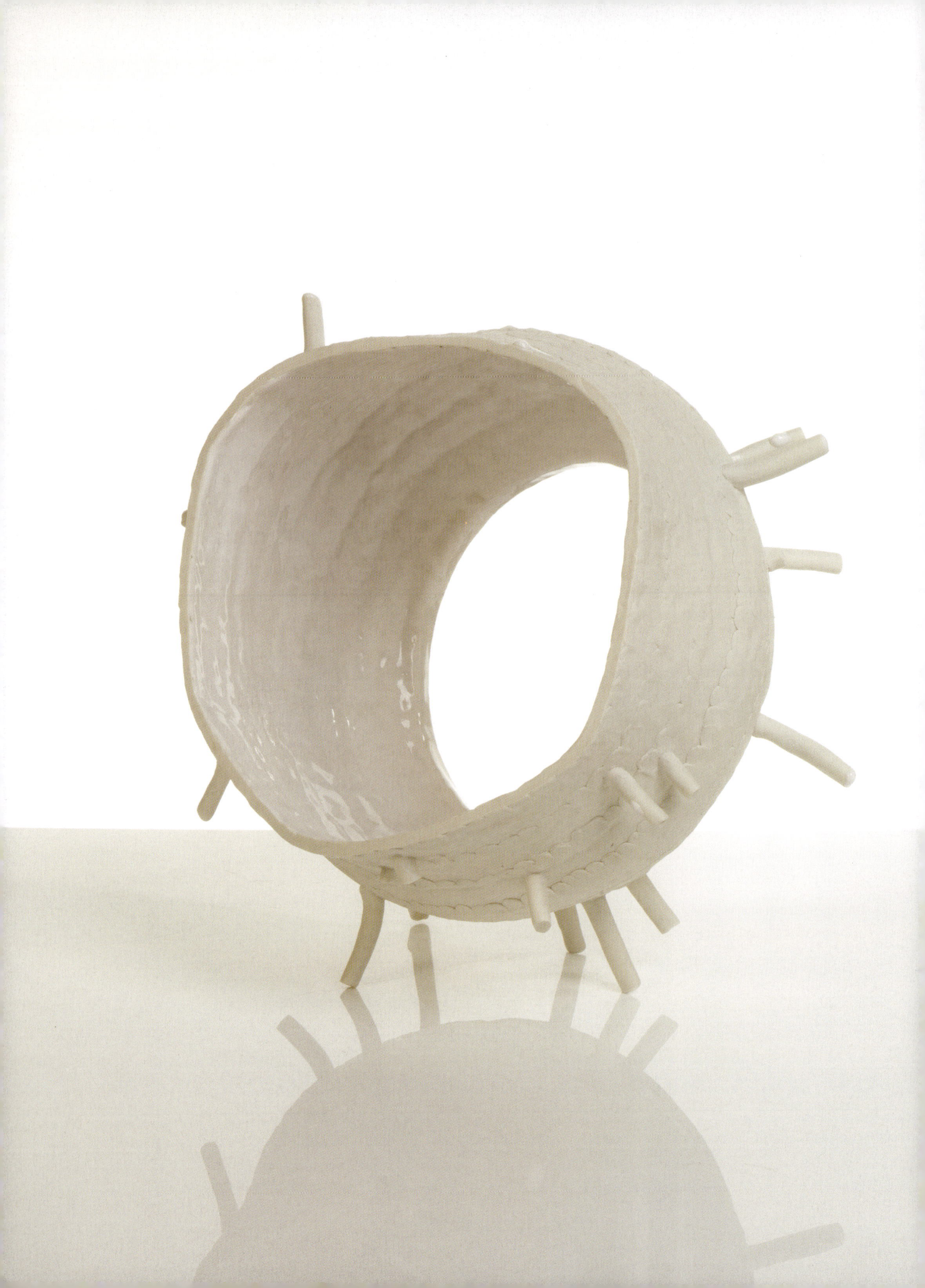

The Tangible

Toni De Jesus
Points of Contact

Touch:

(verb) to bring something, such as a hand, into contact, usually lightly, with something else; to have dealings with, be associated with or be a party to something; to concern or affect; to deal with (a matter, subject, etc.).

(noun) an act of touching or the sensation of being touched; a small amount, quantity, distance, etc., a trace or a hint; an artist's individual style or approach.

(*Chambers Dictionary*)

Don't keep pretending, as they do, don't make believe, stop acting as if you wanted to make us believe that there is something one could call touch, an understood thing itself about which we could pretend to agree, and say something new, in the very place where, in touching upon the untouchable, this thing remains untouchable. Touch is finitude. Period. Stop at this point. Haven't you yourself said 'there is no "the" sense of touch'?[123]

(*Jacques Derrida*)

Touch is integral to ceramics. To touch clay is to engage in the act of making through its manipulation on the wheel, as a slab, or into a coil. The artist, touched by inspiration to create, leaves the trace of their own touch in the work. This trace, once fired and released into the world, offers pleasure to the hands of others. Touch is transformed into something touching, affecting, even emotive; something that extends beyond the time and space of its original creation. Indeed, to touch the work of a deceased artist is to reach out and grasp now absent fingers. Ceramic objects are subject to numerous kinds of 'touch'.

In the quotation above, the French philosopher Jacques Derrida (1930–2004) argued that 'there is no "the" sense of touch'.[124] Instead, he conceived touch as being multiple, as *touches*. This idea is developed from Derrida's wider project of deconstruction which emerged from his analysis of language. For Derrida, words have no intrinsic meaning within themselves. They become meaningful only because of their differentiation from other words. For example, 'young' and 'old'; if there were no physical differences between human beings as they aged, there would be no reason to assign them into categories, and the words 'young' and 'old' would not exist. To make sense, the words 'young' and 'old' are dependent upon difference. This, Derrida argued, reveals how we categorise the world: not through meaning as an end in itself, but through *differences* in meaning.

How does difference relate to touch? Our psyche is formed through language from the earliest stages of our lives. As soon as we begin to speak, we begin to exist in the world: we can express our need to eat, drink, or be held. As we become older, and our world magnifies, so our vocabulary expands. Yet, for Derrida, the introduction of an exterior language from the moment we are born paradoxically separates us from ourselves. This separation is most clearly expressed in the word we most commonly use: 'I'. As Derrida argues, 'at the very moment when 'I' makes its entrance… it signs the possibility or the need for the 'I' (as soon as it touches itself) to address itself, to speak to itself, to treat itself (in a soliloquy interrupted in advance) *as an other*.'[125] For Derrida, the word 'I' functions to refer to ourselves as though we were someone else, splitting our psyche into multiple parts. One way to consider what he means is through the fact that the word 'I' is not a natural sound; it is simply one sound in an exterior inherited language that we are taught from birth. That the sound 'I' is not natural is confirmed by its expression as 'je' in French, 'ich' in German, 'wo' (我) in Chinese, and 'watashi' (私) in Japanese. 'I' is a linguistic formulation in English that has been taught to those who speak it; it is not a natural occurrence. This means that, strangely enough, and despite its meaning, 'I' is not an individual; 'I' is always communal. For Derrida, this shared aspect of language serves to make us multiple within ourselves: there is the physical person, and then there is the communal 'I', which uses language to refer back to itself. Each psyche is thus irrevocably split into two.

This is important because touch is expressed through language. If, for example, I were to put my hand in a fire and then say, 'I hurt myself', I have used language to explain my sensations of pain. Yet this language is not from me: the words 'I hurt myself' are collective, and they must be collective otherwise no one else could understand them. I invoke the exterior 'I' of a shared language to communicate to you how 'I', 'hurt', 'myself'. Even words such as 'ouch', 'ow', or the sucking in of air through teeth to express pain, are taught responses that have entered our inner consciousness from the outside. If language has divided us from ourselves, then our touch is also multiple because it is always expressed through a communally shared mode of communication, that is, through language. We cannot help but think about ourselves, and even how we process the physical responses of our senses, without language. As J. Hillis-Miller observes, ‘touch is always mediated, distanced, divided, parted, translated, transplanted, translated, prosthetic…’.[126] Thus, Derrida concludes that there is not *the* sense of touch: the relationship between language and our own sense of ourselves is necessarily multiple.

I begin this analysis of the work of Toni De Jesus with a lengthy introduction to Derrida’s ideas because, for me, his approach implicitly acknowledges how touch is multiple and external. One of the striking aspects of De Jesus’s aesthetic is his use of coiling. In most of his works, coils are compressed together by the artist pressing downwards with his fingers. This process of manufacture is not disguised but highlighted; his imprint is left exposed to become integral to the form and surface. This turns his work into a personal statement, almost a kind of diary, where the private reasons for making are enmeshed into the structure of the work. Although these ideas are not obviously expressed, and his work is not perceptibly autobiographical, in form and substance they nevertheless capture something of the prospects and pressures of contemporary life. Each piece seems to extract time from time, the present from history, and public from private.

This is caught in some of the forms De Jesus chooses to make. For example, the pot is a symbol of civilisation. Shards of ceramic pots are the staple of archaeological digs and museum displays. For De Jesus, the pot is tied to the domestic sphere, but only to offer a kind of veiled social commentary. The imposing stature of his *Ginger Jars* (2018), for instance, alludes to the significance of the pot as a cultural carrier through time and space, bound up with the colonial imagery of Portugal’s role in the expansion of the fifteenth century spice trade. De Jesus may nod to his identity as British-Portuguese here, but his work is not romantic about form or its associations. He does not, for example, offer platitudes about human civilisation or the perfect domestic environment. Rather, his work explores taught complexity and potential dysfunctionality.

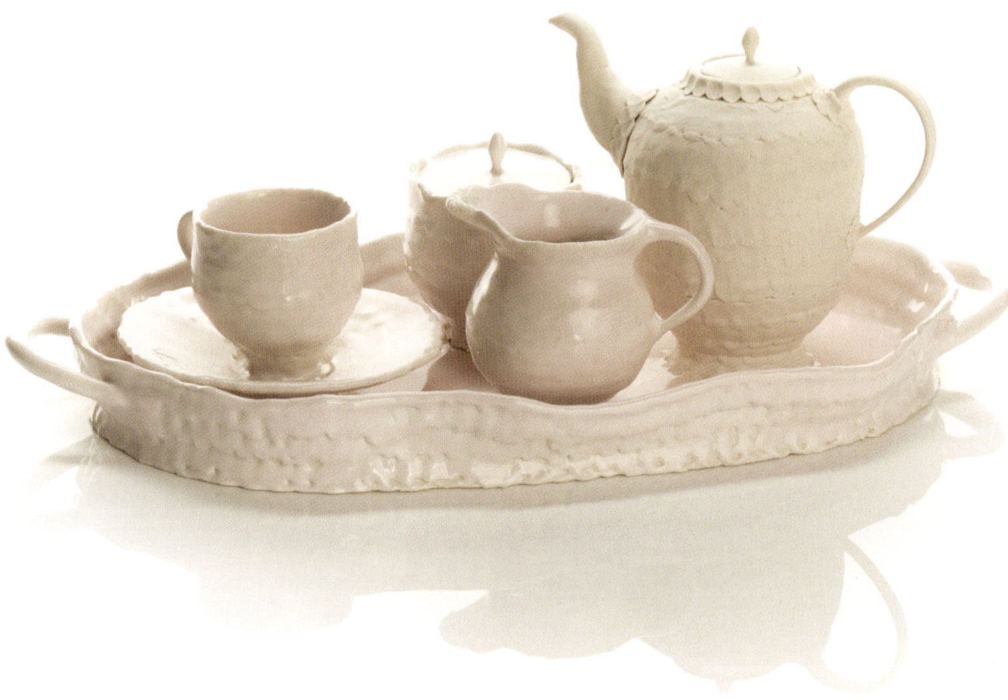

Tea Set for One (2019).

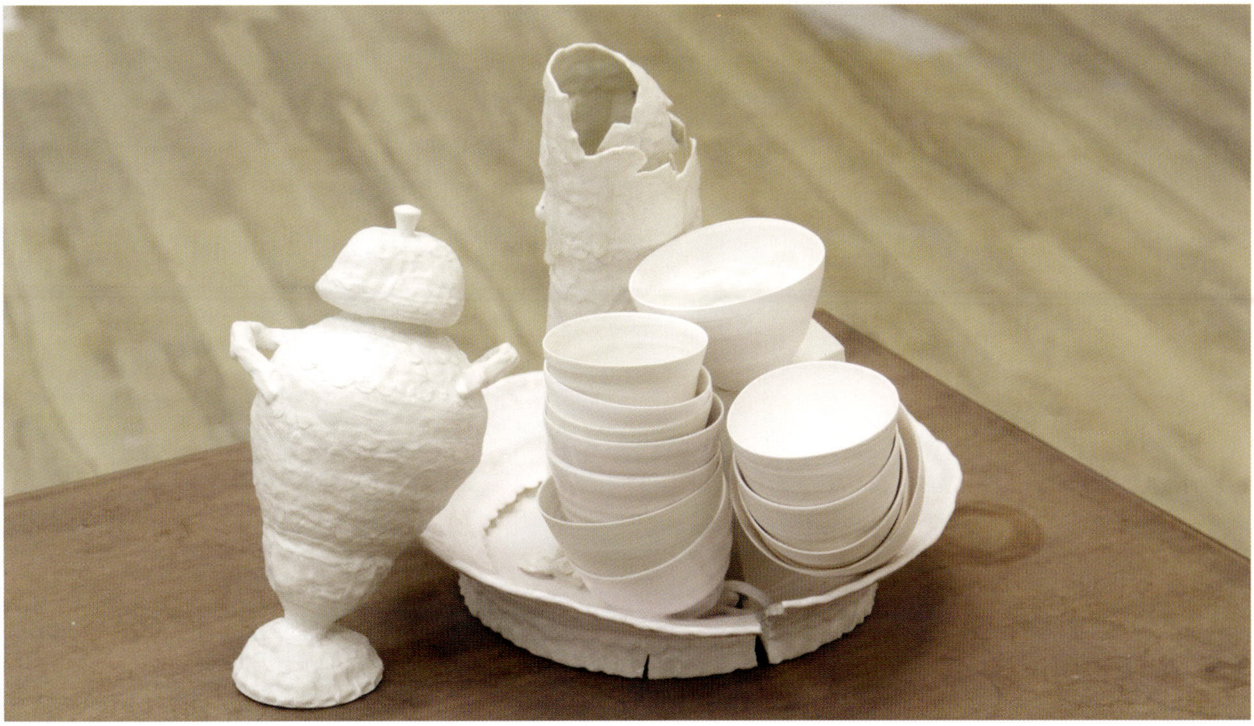

Natura Morta. They Also Get Tired (2021).

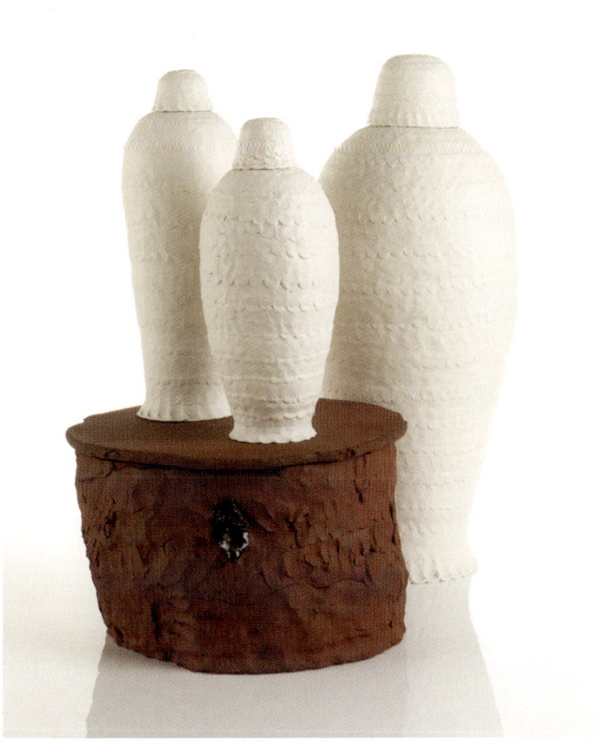

Ginger Jars (2018).

For instance, at first sight, *Tea Set for One* (2019) appears to be a perfectly functional tea service. Upon closer inspection, however, it becomes apparent that the teacups will not lift from the tray, and whilst some pots can be held, the lids are sealed on, rendering them useless. Encountering this work is predicated upon discovering which parts can be moved and which are fixed, what can be utilised and what cannot. Through its domestic associations, the tea service touches on the complexity of negotiating family life: how does a family remain 'functional'? When a family member closes themselves off, how can they be made to open up again? *Natura Morta. They Also Get Tired* (2021) also speaks of familial relations, the integral forms of the tea bowls at odds with the leaning the coffee pot, cracked vase and plate. Taken as a whole, the work symbolises the exuberance of youth and the wearying effects of age.

Vessels become metaphorical of their own form, inviting speculation about what is at the heart of each work. Some pieces, such as *Implode* (2019) and *The Passage of Enormity* (2020–21), can be displayed on different planes, which in turn affects the meanings they conjure up. *Implode*, for instance, is an open-ended vessel that can be positioned on different axes, enabling the interior space to be understood in different ways. When positioned on a horizontal axis, the soft compression of the side of the vessel gives the piece strength (its undulations resembling a table), but when placed inversely, it evokes the softness of a pillow as the undulation recedes into the form. When displayed on a vertical axis there is a strong sense of internal spatial compression, evoking the title of the piece, *Implode*.

The Passage of Enormity occupies similar sculptural territory, underscoring the playfulness that is important to De Jesus's work. When positioned with the lower rim on a surface, the piece presents itself almost like a pot. Yet, it cannot be functional because it has no base. Conversely, when laid on its side, supported by the twig-like spikes that emanate from its body, the piece becomes more sculptural and less pot-like. Yet, paradoxically, the glazed interior curvature of the work now has the capacity to hold liquid. Ingeniously, by making the vessel more sculptural it becomes more functional.

The fact that this work, like *Implode*, is glazed to the interior inverts expectations as to the most significant surface. The shiny interior draws attention to the undulations of the artist's fingerprints, his trace somehow more present on the internal surface. The outside of the work, left unglazed, is the part most likely to be touched by the spectator, especially as the work is repositioned in various orientations for display. As such, the interior might come to represent the artist himself, whilst the exterior, exposed to the world, represents, and facilitates, the touch of the spectator. Such a reading activates these works into portals – the 'passage' in *The Passage of Enormity* – that expand across time and space. The ceramic body is altered into a literal meeting point between the touch of the artist and the touch of the spectator. Touch thus becomes multiple.

Whilst the titles are suggestive, the lack of autobiographical detail leaves room for the viewer to explore their own domestic predicament and/or state of mind in relation to each work. Cylindrical forms such as *Transposition*, *Verruca*, and *Seeking Imperial Yellow* (all 2021), are akin to containers of experience; their smooth interiors standing as a visual and textural counterpoint to their augmented exteriors. These vessels are connected by the fact that material – glaze or porcelain elements – have been added to the exterior surface of the pot body. The reason for these additions is only hinted at by the title. *Transposition* appears to graft new elements onto the porcelain body, like cuttings from a tree. Is this the expression of cultural acculturation, of moving between locales and adapting to new cultural contexts? The viral infection of *Verruca* seems to have left sores across the skin of the work. Is this a response to the Covid-19 pandemic, of personal infection, or of a metaphorical infection in terms of a person, an emotion, or a state of mind? *Seeking Imperial Yellow* could be a technical quest to obtain the

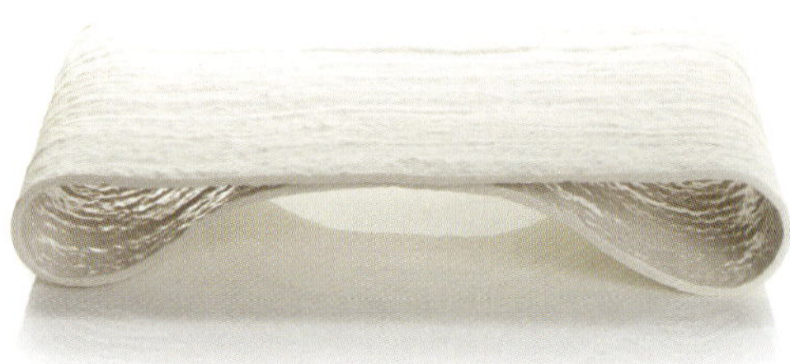

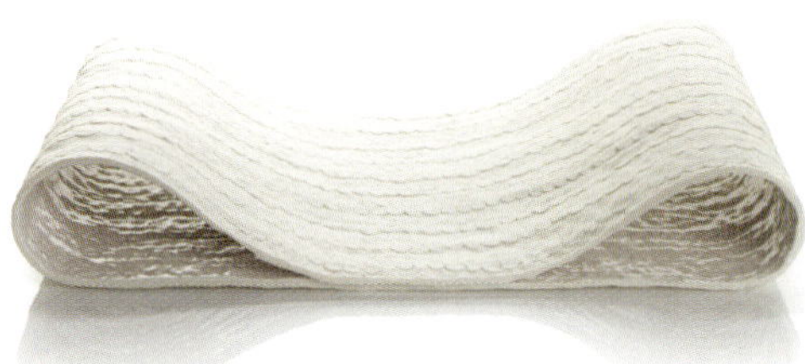

Implode (2019).

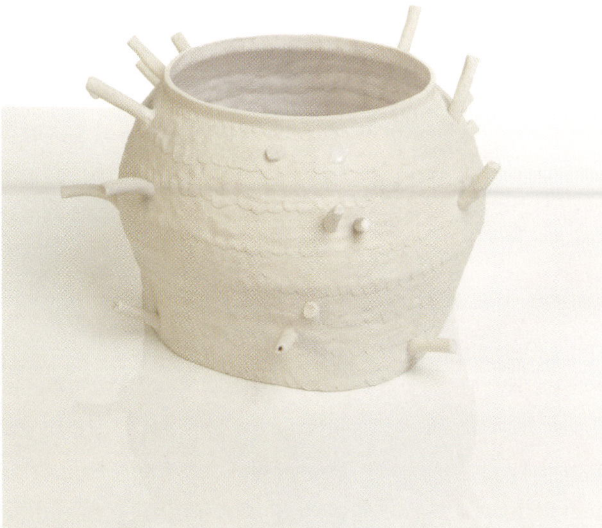

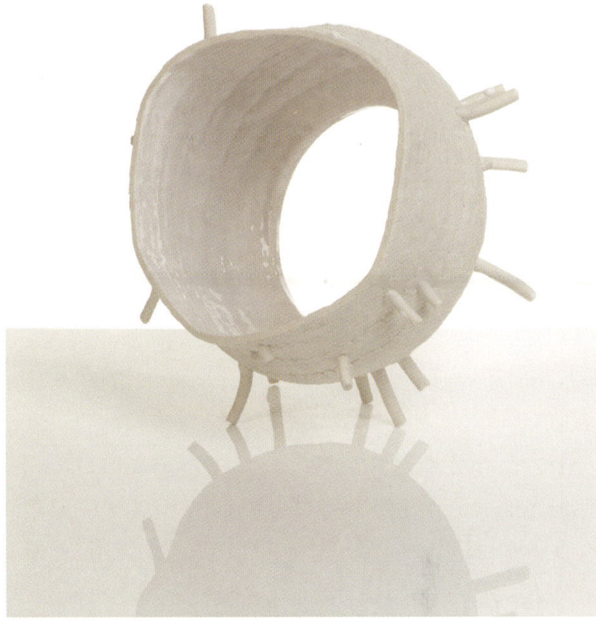

The Passage of Enormity (2021).

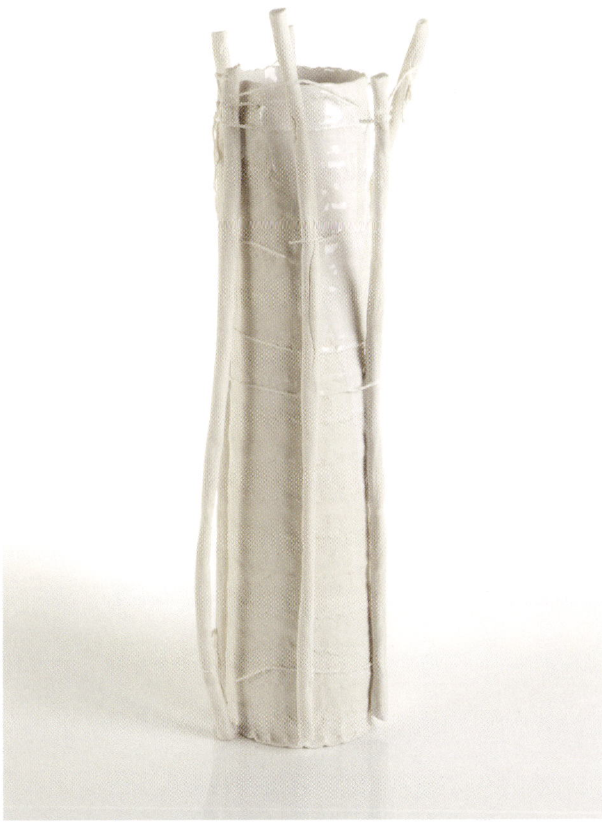

Transposition (2021).

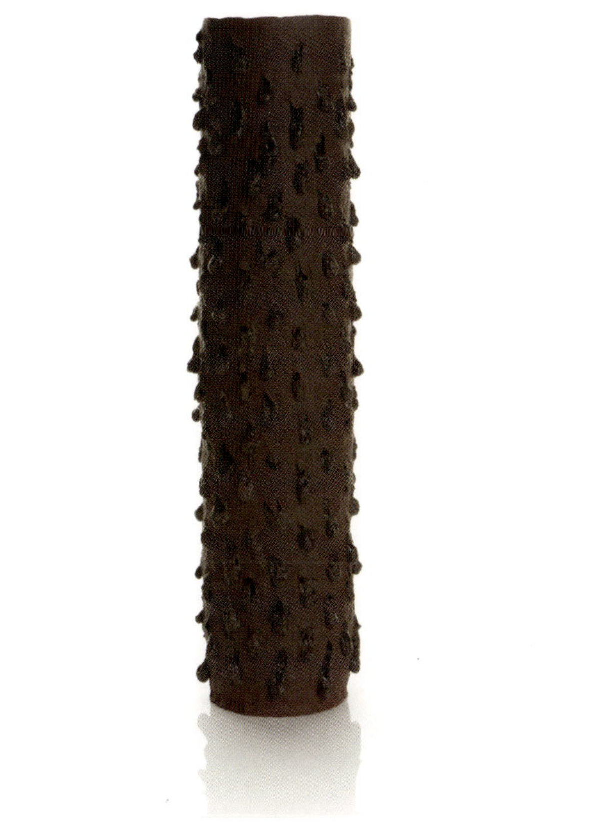

Verruca (2021).

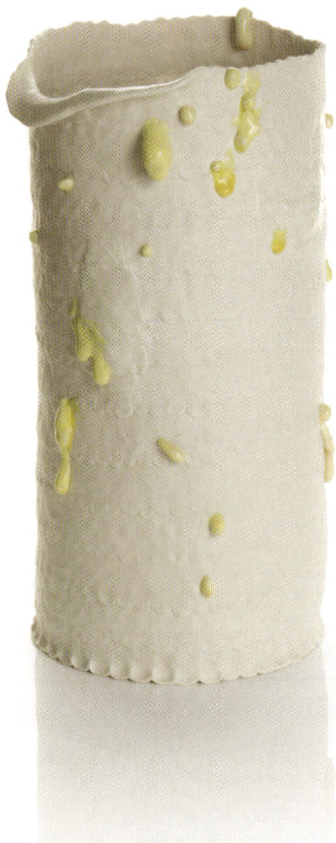

Seeking Imperial Yellow (2019).

right glaze colour, but it could also express a search for something better, an aesthetic, an environment, or trajectory for life. The barnacle-like marks act as stimulation for, and a reflection upon, the meanings the works might accrue after their release into the world. As such, they are beacons of touch, points of contact between the audience and the imprint of the artist. This connection potentially establishes a shared sense of community; we may not share individual circumstances, but the ups and downs of life are common to us all. Indeed, *Encher o Saco* (2022) is based upon a pun, the title literally translating from Portuguese as 'to fill the bag' but which carries the meaning of expressing annoyance. The work is a compressed bag-like form with spongey pink additions. These additions seem to feed off the form, like germs attacking a cell. Interaction is not always convivial.

Whilst he produces individual coiled pieces that hint at, but do not easily facilitate, utility, De Jesus also throws beakers on the wheel that are intended to be functional. Although they offer an aesthetic counterpoint to his coiled work, these beakers stem from

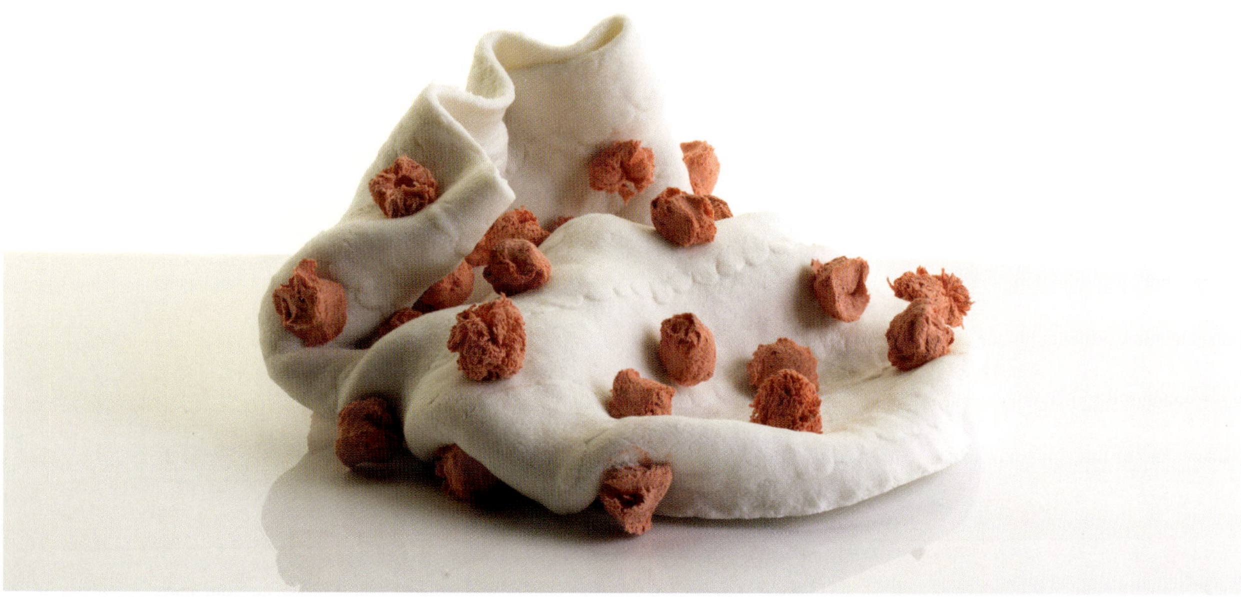

Encher o Saco (2022).

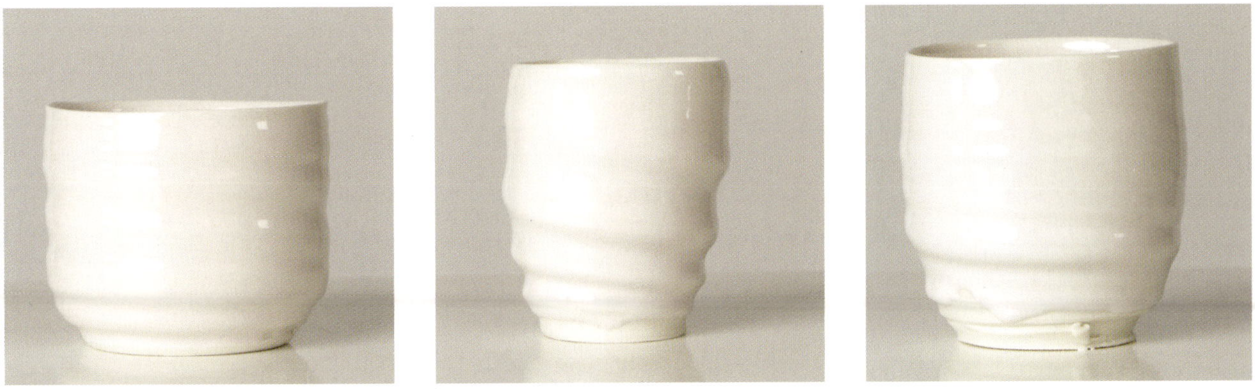

Porcelain Beakers (2022).

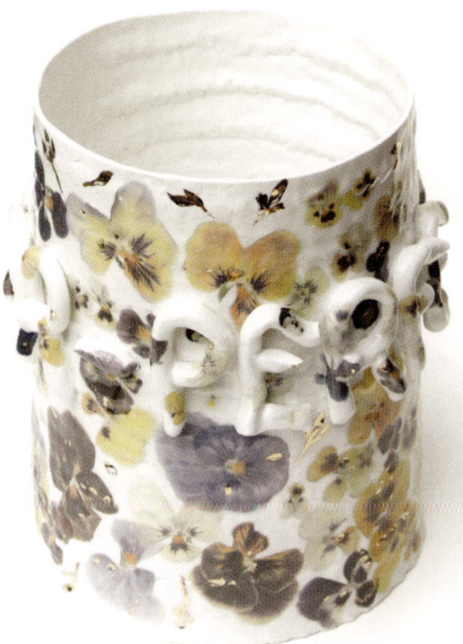

Amor Perfeito (2022).

the same creative impulse. The imprint of the hand from throwing each piece on the wheel is retained in the final form. This provides each beaker with its own distinct identity even as it becomes part of a coherent group of work. The marks swirl upwards across the body of each beaker, as if it were being thrown in front of us. Thus, as with the coiled work, the imprint of the maker remains acutely visible as part of his aesthetic of tactility. To hold a De Jesus beaker is to metaphorically shake hands with the artist.

De Jesus's work constitutes a reminder that ceramics, beyond the visual, is also a language of touch. Touch does not only mean the physical manipulation of clay. As the dictionary definition describes, it also signals the touch of emotion, of personal subjects or socio-political matters that inspire the artist to make, as well as the distinctive approach that an artist might take. *Amor Perfeito* (2022), literally writes feelings into words, the gold lustre and transfer prints of petals supporting the words 'amor perfeito' ('perfect love'), that have been written out in clay. The work expresses the joy of all kinds of love whilst evidencing how ceramics has a tactile as well as a visual language. Drawing upon Derrida's analysis of words, the work of De Jesus demonstrates that this tactile language of ceramic is similarly multiple. Clay, like words, multiplies touch through its inevitable externalisation. To pick up and hold any vessel, pot, or sculpture, is to invest in the multiplicity of touch that constitutes ceramics as a practice. De Jesus's work is a reminder that works in ceramic are a point of contact, an invitation to utilise an object to form a tactile bond. This bond is not only communal. Perhaps by traversing words, it moves us towards a closer relationship with ourselves.

Gareth Mason Tripartites

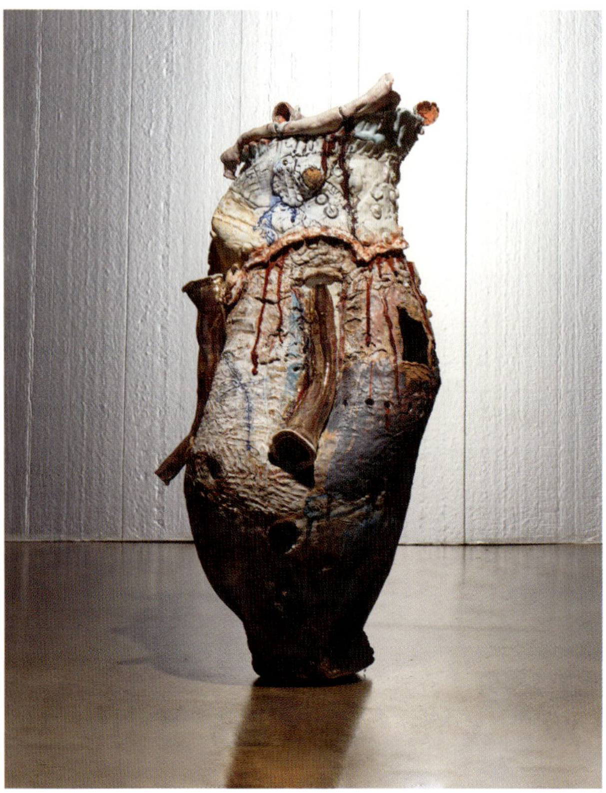

Where the Duende Wounds (2019).

Writing about ceramics, for me at least, is rooted in the detailed observation of work. These observations are then developed into ideas, which I discuss with the artist for the purposes of ratification, augmentation, or rejection. Writing is therefore constituted by collaboration and trust. In the extensive conversation that follows, this otherwise hidden process is made manifest through a series of email exchanges with the potter Gareth Mason (himself a capable writer). I have chosen this structure because it gives focus to what I perceive to be an important concern of his: conversation. Mason aptly describes the reception of his work as a 'love triangle' involving maker, object, and audience. Here, the 'triangle' is expressed through images of his work, and words from both Mason and myself. This reflexive structure also seeks to capture something of the balance between experience and spontaneity, important to Mason's processes of production, but also to my own approach when writing.

21 February 2022

Ashley Thorpe: *Your work exhibits a kind of tautness. I am reminded of the tightrope walker Phillipe Petit crossing the World Trade Centre in New York in the 1970s, with a pole and no safety net. And without permission.*

What do I mean by tautness? I mean balance between construction and deconstruction; of closing off and opening out. These works seem architecturally monumental, but also domestic and utilitarian. I am a resolute critic of the art/craft divide; if ever there was a discipline that required both art (expressivity) and craft (skill and competency), ceramics would seem to be it. The sense of sturdiness and vulnerability in your work is centrally important. They suggest the collapse of binary oppositions: the point of any artist's work? Overturning preconceptions, exposing boundaries as constructs. Showing that systems are by their very nature predicated on the existence of the unsystematic (if there was no 'chaos', why would 'order' have been invented?). There is a sense of mutual dependency in the aesthetics of your work. With construction comes deconstruction, order with chaos, life with death.

And so: the tightrope walker must learn to be instinctive, reactive, but planned, controlled, and calm. One knows what is required, but one cannot know how to respond until the moment comes to pass. To pre-empt is to fall. To be slow to react means failure. There is a similar alertness in your work. It might sound verbose to suggest that you make as though your life depended on it, but there is an urgency, vigour, vitality, a struggle, survival, a kind of triumph, a spirit. It's a visceral thing. Rough emotion; like the rugged textural surfaces on some of your pots. Perhaps this reminds us of the base elemental struggle that the niceties of civilisation shield us from. If the pot is a totem of civilisation, its collapse stands for human vulnerability.

Vulnerability is not automatically the same as weakness, of course. There is, after all, strength in allowing oneself to be vulnerable. Perhaps the collapse of male and female stereotypical characteristics is what I am alluding to here. For the tightrope walker is also vulnerable. And unbelievably strong. It's the agility of these two things together that seem to me to construct any worthwhile art.

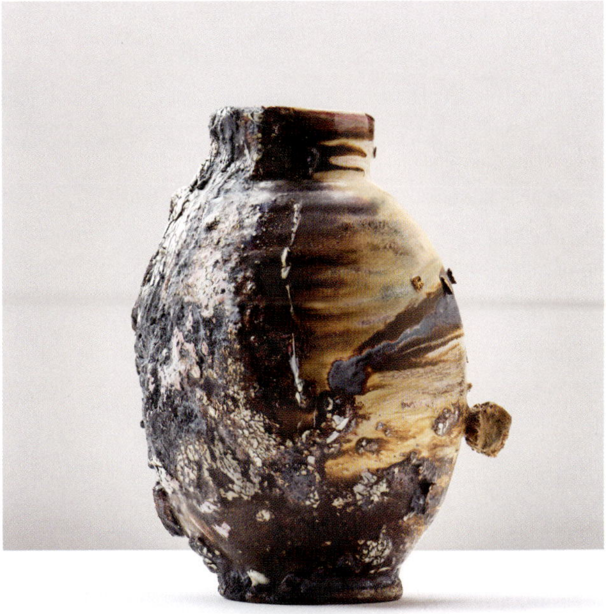

■ *Pressure Ridge* (2007–2012).

3–9 March 2022

Gareth Mason: It may sound rather torturous but a sense of tension — *tautness* as you put it — is important in what I do. My things often end up appearing to be somewhat… imperilled. I have called this quality dissonance in the past, a device for the disruption of harmonic flow, as might be deployed in poetic or literary form or in the deliberate use of discord or cacophony in musical composition. How is this tension manifest in my work? It is a literal, material tension, and also, as it were, an experiential one. 'Material' tension becomes apparent when matter is placed under visible stress: my aesthetic offering can be starkly physical, and I leave a vivid evidence trail. I contend that tension is central to any penetrative aesthetic encounter. The creative tension you highlight can leave us bemused as observers or upend our precious suppositions leaving us breathless in a new reality. We can resist it or embrace it, but it is difficult to be indifferent to it. All art, indeed, everything we perceive, manifests internally, bodily: we transform the world into emotion by means of the senses and the poetic imagination. This ability has nothing whatsoever to do with connoisseurship and I love that.

There's something in your choice of the words 'without permission' that speaks to the conforming pressure of received norms and polite behaviour. Also, to being a bit of a daredevil, or a 'risk junkie' (as I have described myself in the past). Put it this way: I 'get' what extreme sports people do. I am a mischief maker; it must be said. The playful and haphazard — sometimes reckless and absurd — aspects of my muddy adventures are as important as the mindful and painstaking ones. I dislike the hackneyed phrase 'subverting expectations' because who am I to make assumptions about the hopes my fellow beings may hold for art? However, to contradict that statement, the fact that I co-opt items with an ostensibly mild-mannered and settled cultural identity (pots) and give them something of a primal makeover can upset the odd apple cart. My aesthetic ambitions have a certain temerity, even now, more than a fifth of the way into the twenty-first century. 'Authoritative' and lay voices alike still decry pottery's ability to elicit thoughtful response and emotion as, say, poems or symphonies do. I embrace the effrontery. It's a bit punk.

Whilst exhibiting at Ceramic Art London some years ago I was approached by a well-to-do gentleman whose opening gambit to me was, 'I suppose you're *deconstructing*, are you?' He was secure in his knowledge that the crafted item ought to have an objective 'correctness', akin to the idea of 'honest work' explored by *Crafts* writer Peter Dormer: that crafts people's integrity should hinge upon their conspicuous fealty to 'the rules'.[127] My work, in this gent's eyes, knew no such allegiance. His good-natured disdain disguised waspish barbs. As opposed to active 'deconstruction', which strikes me as a clinical, intellectual exercise, I am engaged in something altogether earthier; a kind of 'reverie of the hands', to misquote Gaston Bachelard. 'The hands dream'[128], he said, and he spoke truly, because mine do. They dream in material. I am absorbed in the unfolding mystery of matter. Ceramics is an arena of endeavour that offers a daunting vista of dreams. In the hand-dream space, just as in the subconscious mind, a lot of free-association occurs and I listen, in as unfettered a way as I can. But dreams have a habit of receding before our grasp. It is an emotive thing. This path is not for everyone. It has taken a lot of quiet despair, resurgent faith. Cast-iron convictions about 'rightness', such as those my cynical gent espoused, utterly preclude any space for unfolding experience and mystery. I have never known such certainty and I hope I never do.

Mastery equates to control in popular belief, yet virtuosity does not solely depend on skill. I firmly believe that intuition is fed by experience. Consequently, it should follow that the greater the expertise, the richer the capacity for spontaneity. It interests me that this is clearly not the case. When people remark sometimes that my work appears 'free', as though not inhibited by over-reliance on skill, I am quick to affirm skill as a tremendously liberating force. That is not to say that it doesn't benefit from the occasional firework up its backside. I esteem skills of all kinds and hold my abilities dear, but they are not my warder. Hence my reluctance to accede to predetermined ideas of what skill 'ought' to deliver. Meaningful improvisation takes as much discipline and practice as any skill: it is equally active and alert, but with added jeopardy. My transgressions from the pottery norm were not undertaken lightly, nor have they been easy. Emergent experience reinvigorates the 'tried and trusted'; its little grenades of alchemy penetrate more deeply into the nebulae of the poetic imagination. This talk of skill bears upon your mention of balance. It is probably fair to say that I operate largely on the fulcrum between knowing and not-knowing, between the controlling hand and the dreaming hand.

It is a multi-layered business but at root it is straightforward and universal: the processes I am hung up on are common to all of us because we permit the physical world to intrude upon us every minute of the day. There's no great mystery. Aesthetic experience is entirely commensurate with quotidian life. The enduring wonder to me is how the senses, emotions and intellect subconsciously commingle in response to arousal, or in the *creation* of arousal. I am in the business of arousal.

You talk of 'overturning preconceptions, exposing boundaries as constructs. Showing that systems are by their very nature predicated on the existence of the unsystematic...'. This speaks to the idea of bridging, blurring, or puncturing the artificial delineations that human reasoning has imposed upon the world and that really appeals to me. But what a grandiose enterprise for such a minor sphere of aesthetic operations as mine! I appeal to '...the body's silent conversation with things...'[129] as much as to the intellect. I hope my offerings are sufficiently meaningful as to reward sustained — or superficial! — engagement; intuitive or analytical attention. Ah, but where does meaning reside? I contend, more in others' responses than in my intentions, therefore what I'm doing is setting up the conditions for association. Nowadays art denies societal consensus around meaning in the main; a fact exhilarating for some, bemusing for many. I am grateful that you approach my work with an eye to decoding my 'conditions for association'. The transmission of meaning between things and people is a boundlessly intriguing process to me.

But isn't it just a freak show? A rogues' gallery? Am I not just dealing in undisciplined wackiness? I simply testify that in clay and words the things I make proceed from me truthfully. What do I mean by that? In both a flippant and a profound way, mine is a 'warts and all' endeavour.

A few closing thoughts on vulnerability and strength. I want to set aside the obvious generality that pots encompass both deep-time resilience and fragility simultaneously. Fired clay's propensity to awe-inspiring longevity is indeed magical but this is personal. Nothing is resolved for me. I have made an ally of my doubt. This doubt is rich and impassioned and I would absolutely not be without it. My work is nothing if not a faithful representation of fallible, human becoming. In the name of what? Communication, ultimately. The instances of communication (artistic or otherwise) that move me tend to involve disclosure of some kind, a 'reaching in' to some tender place and realising it in the world, so that it becomes an offering of fealty and respect. In art I see this as a kind of aestheticised sincerity.

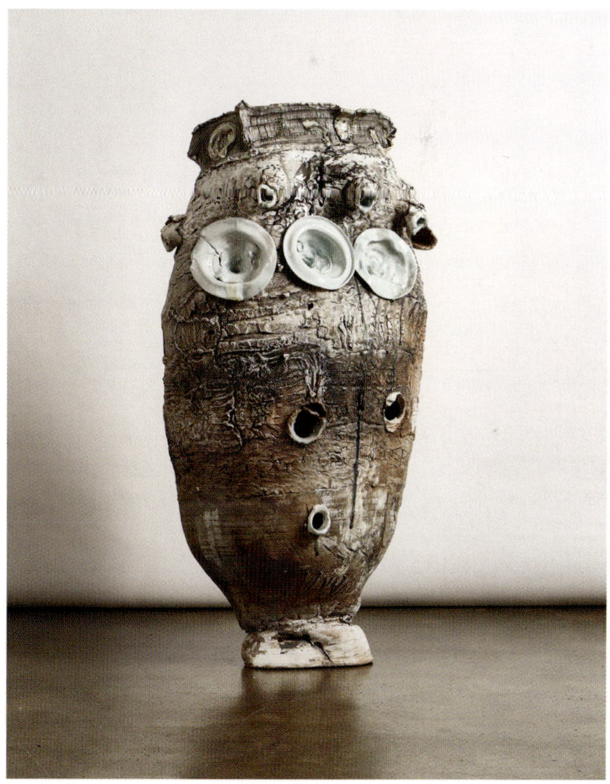

■ *Manatee* (2019).

The sense that something more substantial, more consequential, (dare I say it) more meaningful than mere formula has been committed to and realised. And what do we experience when we encounter such moments, such works? For me it's relief; a reassuring sense of fellowship; validation: the personal can be universal; quietly renewed resolve. My pots are just mute accretions of igneous flotsam adrift in the unfathomable void that awaits us all until they are exposed to other beings, other senses, other minds. That moment of exposure is a tender one for me, each piece of work being a summation of my cumulative uncertainty, proffered in good faith. If this esoteric and modest act amounts to a strength then it is a minority strength in today's world, but perhaps it is a strength that we need more of.

10 March 2022

AT: *I wonder, then, why do you make pots? The pot is the most archetypal ceramic form, yet the twentieth century bore witness to an opening out of possibilities, especially in the US (a place where I sense your work is perhaps better understood). You may balk at this, but the idea of allowing the personal to access the universal strikes me as a rather 'Bernard Leach' view of ceramics in the world. Yet, you take this aspiration and talk of 'mischief' and 'grenades', of being 'flippant', even 'shocked'. I doubt Leach would approve. So, do you use the pot because the reverence accorded to it allows for maximum ambivalence? Do you simply like to provoke? Did Phillipe Petit walk across the World Trade Centre just because he wanted a crowd to look at him? And yet, I don't sense that you make your work out of, or for, attention-seeking circus theatricality. You sincerely mean what you say. And that sincerity extends to wanting to test limitations; of the pot, of ceramics, and of yourself? I am curious to know why you speak in and through the forms that you do. Is the pot simply a product of ceramic training, as Alison Britton once said? Or is it one of the languages of the discipline, that kind of thing that Ewen Henderson argued was fundamental for any kind of meaningful visual communication?*

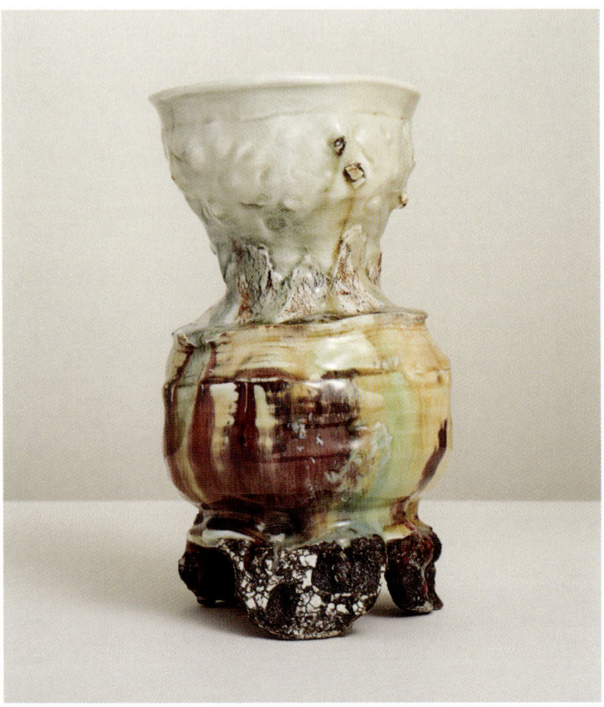

Neckline (2016–2017).

And in the interim of our correspondence, Russia has invaded Ukraine, and war has once again returned to Europe. Of course, war never went away (the twenty-first century had already seen Afghanistan, Syria, Sudan, Ethiopia, Congo, the Maghreb, Libya, and countless other countries engage in bloody battles). Perhaps it is only when it falls on your doorstep that people take full and proper notice. My earlier comment – 'the base elemental struggle that the niceties of civilisation shield us from' – now has a different context to inhabit as millions migrate and hospitals are bombed. Certainly, it makes me look again at your work. Can pots be political? Are yours?

13 March 2022

GM: I was in the British Museum on Friday and your reasonable question hung in my mind: why make pots? I have been asked it before and never really felt

I have given a satisfactory answer. 'Do you use the pot because the reverence accorded to it allows for maximum ambivalence?' You're right in that the pot has a strong identity in the popular imagination, but I don't believe that this identity accords with your word 'reverence'. I think it fair to assume that the dominant conception of the pot is one of a certain homely utility that doesn't warrant substantial contemplation. Ours is, to say the least, a 'niche' concern after all. Perhaps the *indifference* afforded the pot makes it a ripe target to spotlight its contemporary ambivalence. Or the reverence I afford it seeks to shift it from relative anonymity to a potential subject of ambivalence.

You mention Leach and much as Leachean mythologising – his own and others' – sought to instil 'truth' (to material, and so on) I can never put out of my mind the feeling that his project was a conceit built on a kind of earnest craft moralising between the son of a British colonial lawyer (the man himself) and a Japanese colonial aesthete philosopher (Yanagi).[130] It is compelling and seductive and all of that, but it is also cultish and somewhat despotic. Much as I owe the 'Leach Tradition' a respectful nod for my very existence and will never deny its importance, I remain a sceptic. I doubt Bernard would deign to acknowledge that pots can convey the 'personal-as-universal' in the sense I mean it. Yanagi would indict my work for harbouring 'the seeds of perversion'.[131] No, Leach would definitely not countenance my advocacy of messy, awkward 'disclosure' as a means for human connection in pots. His was a loftier intellectual promontory framed in Edwardian emotional inaccessibility.

It's more nuanced than simply stating I'm not out to provoke. My somewhat warped version of honesty has to include the 'mischief' and 'grenades' ... being 'flippant', even 'shocked', indeed the whole gamut of potential response – or more precisely *experience* – because these are the very things that I am interested in investing pots with. It is about the sublime, in short, because that is what I believe pots can be. If that is provocative, then so be it. And, returning to your question, 'why pots?', I make them because I think that they are vehicles as capable of conveying the sublime as any other medium in the pantheon of human endeavour. Leach would probably disagree with that too. I think he cordoned himself with his dogma. I am wary of dogma, gurus, and the like. I doubt everything, even my icons. Clearly, I don't know my place.

'Sublime', incidentally, is not a word you will likely find on the lips of any of today's gatekeepers of the art world. Like 'beauty'. These are terms I am actively repossessing.

I don't subscribe to either Britton or Henderson's views as you state them. My engagement is distinctly earthy, like so many of the pots I admire from ceramic history. It is the sheer breadth of their cultural and symbolic possibility that I am interested in, rooted in their centrality to human progress, not only their ubiquity but their capacity for myth and storytelling, their proximity to ritual and power, their ability to carry echoes, vibrations of human experience, and all their meanings diluted by time. Walking through the museum yesterday, this is what I was seeing somehow in the objects, be they of the humblest origin, like an earthen Minoan cup I love, or the most rarefied of Song Dynasty porcelains, as in the Percival David collection, or Bernard and Lucie's old Moon Jar[132], now seen as the epitome of neo-Confucian restraint (which, of course it was when it was made, as a product of the Joseon Royal Kilns in Yeoju). Pots have readily allied themselves to endeavour and belief throughout history and existed as 'carriers' of so much more than the miscellaneous commodities they were ostensibly designed to 'contain'. Their forms are laced with complex lineages and interlinked mysteriously across continents and cultures. There is something in the pot that is intrinsically human and 'close to the

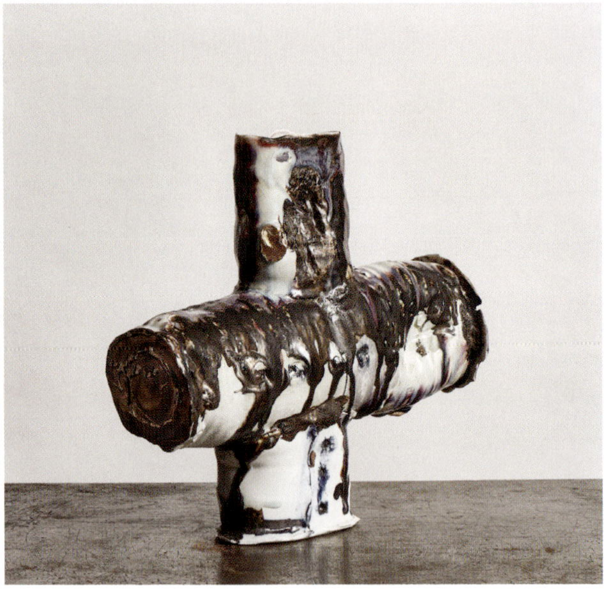

Tàpies (2012).

body', which runs under the radar of any fashionable ideology or theory. Just look at an ancient Japanese Jomon 'flame' pot, for example, and deny its eerie evocations.

What do pots say about our 'now', in all its miscellany and insecurity? I am a product of my own time and in clay I want to be so fully. Isn't everything punctured, fractured, doubtful; isn't any notion of 'authenticity' now questionable in an era of fake news and misinformation at a level so invidious as to delight Mephistopheles himself? Are not previously accepted canons of right and wrong now irrelevant? What is today's version of Leach's much-vaunted 'Head, Heart and Hand'? – 'Like and Subscribe'? His vision of authenticity was itself a construct, a pastiche. Against this dizzying backdrop, how can I in anything like good conscience be other than the practitioner I am? I jerry-rig myself with each body of work, each piece of writing. I keep working the problem.

Petit crossed the Twin Towers on a high wire because they were there and he wanted to pit his human skill, ingenuity, his very being against brute phenomena. It is the same with practitioners of any 'high stakes' enterprise and there is certainly room for such hazard in art. The Spanish have a good word for it: '*duende*' – an aesthetic jeopardy wherein skill yields to the power of raw being. Resplendent. Fiery. Spine-tingling. Here at the edge, scope for exploration will never be exhausted because the *duende* does not fall within the fickle ambit of fashion: it knows no cordons. Here the unknown remains a potent force, asserting the importance of incomplete, emergent experience.

I have always eschewed overt narrative exposition in what I do, favouring instead the more ambiguous regions of suggestion and allusion through physical means. Still, if we witness a gaping, bloodied fracture in the 'skin' of a pot our bodily intelligence recoils. Just as it does from a bomb crater outside a shattered maternity hospital, to turn to your stark reminder of recent events. I have seen first-hand the ruins of shrapnel-pocked bombed-out buildings and looked at historical and contemporary conflict-damaged armaments. Aftermath is eloquent in all its forms, sometimes brutally so, and needs no curatorial expertise to make its mark on the engaged observer. Pots are no strangers to this. They are survivors of the privations of the Silk Road, containers of death, objects of avarice and subjugation; they have prevailed through conflict and wreck of all kinds as they accompany the bitterest of humanity's misadventures. Clay is an indiscriminate recipient of the physical human imprint, and I want its sighs and screams in equal measure. Much as 'the niceties of civilisation' tend to deny, mute, suppress its screams they are eloquent, and I will not exclude any part of its spectrum of expression.

So, revisiting your suggestion of the word 'provoke', I must concede that provocation is a legitimate means of eliciting response. It must be out of my horror of complacency, but I am invariably the first in line to experience clay's provocation. For me, opening the kiln is one of life's loaded moments. I need to jolt myself into presence, I need to 'go there' first. I do not do to anyone else anything I am not prepared to do to myself first. So, if my muddy adventures make me uncomfortable then it follows that the same may be true for others when they witness my output. Aesthetic discomfort has proven very useful to me. However, other beings must and will always be masters of their own responses. Aesthetic experience is beautifully internal, particular, mysterious; I encourage others to fully inhabit their own and reserve the right to use all the means at my disposal to explore the machinations of mine. Pots, for now, are the perfect vehicle.

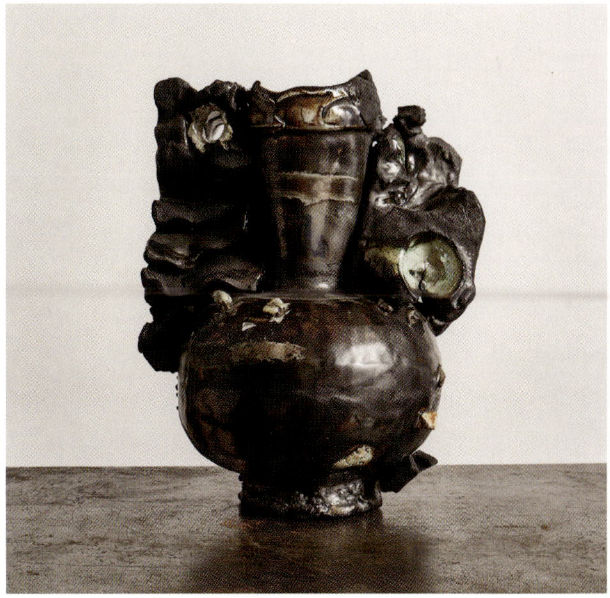

Cannon (2009–2016).

18 March 2022

AT: *I have just returned from a visit to your studio, which not only afforded the opportunity to see some of your work up close and personal – even touch it – but also the opportunity to talk about your practice. I took an early work of yours with me – probably made in the mid-nineties, you said – a dark blue vase with light crystallisation on the surface. Being slightly mischievous, I suppose I brought it with me partly to see how you would respond to an encounter with an earlier piece. Some artists are very ambivalent about the history of their processes of discovery and are left feeling that they allowed work into the world that should have been destroyed. I was struck by how pleased you were to see it. This was not because you had any sentimental attachment to this piece per se, but simply because you seemed affected by the circulation of your work, of an object being produced by you and crossing your path over a quarter of a century later. The transient nature of this re-encounter was arresting, and perhaps this mapped on to my own experience of spending a couple of hours alongside new work in your studio. In such instances we are confronted by the ephemeral nature of all our experiences with material objects. Pots existed before us and will exist after us. The pots you make will outlive you, the pots I have collected will end up who knows where… Pots thus carry experiences as metaphors; they are repeatedly emptied out and filled with new meanings. When we spoke, this is what I meant by my attraction to artists who leave room for the spectator; to not overburden work with intention to the point that it is like reading a page from someone else's diary. Instead, some work allows for a meeting between artist and audience that is out of time and out of space. Perhaps this is why a Minoan cup can still capture our attention? Perhaps this is why you have sought to render the pot as an object capable of psychological and visceral expression?*

I was also struck by the slight undulations on the lip of this earlier vase. It is not a perfect ellipse but has shifts that craft a sculptural line with a strong sense of movement. There is beauty in perfection of course, but there is also beauty in dissonance and asymmetry. In this sense, the culmination of your practice feels like an affirmation of what the hand can do, a celebration of strength and fragility. This brings me back to tension, but specifically the muscles of the body; the tendons exerting control in different combinations for different effects, just like Petit's body. Your work is thus as much about an embodied process of making as anything else. Feeling with the mind's fingertips. Does this ring true for you? If so, has it always done? Is this why you are drawn to clay as a material?

21–22 March 2022

GM: What, I wonder, makes an experience memorable at all? What inclines some experiences to linger in the consciousness longer and with a more intense poignancy than others? Aesthetic experiences, I should say. We dwelt a while in conversation upon the nature of 'triggers' and you, as a drama practitioner, educator, performer (I am a purveyor of drama too) know that some moments vibrate with their own sense of potential and possibility. It is the job of the performer to alight upon them, bring them to being with such fidelity as to render them 'real' for others, in order to make that 'love triangle' we spoke about (between art work, artist and viewer) fertile; in order to bypass other beings' filters, or in order to enable other beings to colour the experience (of the work) with their own, to recognise its kinship or antipathy. That, or to encourage the empathic leap of faith that attends all acts of powerful communication. Hence my reliance on 'bodily intelligence': what counts for my body applies to others. This is equally true of negative experiences as it is to alluring ones, hence the role that horror or violence have in drama. Am I saying that some of the qualities I deploy in ceramic form – some of my violations against the pot – should have the same penetrative punch as a gunshot to the face in a Martin Scorsese movie? Yes, I think I am. Should this be dismissed as mere 'shock value'? – a quality much derided in critical terms? Shock is actually a powerful means of gaining attention, and by shock I am referring to a disruption in the perceptual field, a break in the commonplace. But repeated shock can be desensitising or chase people away. I want to reward the souls who linger after the initial 'double-take'. Hence my search for the means '...to render the pot as an object capable of psychological and visceral expression'. Belief feeds the search.

Our experience is by no means solely ephemeral in relation to objects; it is pretty scant in relation to all we behold, and the longevity of ceramic objects can highlight this quite starkly. This is, as we discussed, an evocative component of ceramic experience, of the pot/vessel, because in their great age historic survivors, like the Minoan cup I mentioned, whisper of their past human associations, each at their own wavelength. It takes a bit of tuning-in sometimes, to imaginatively enter the object's sphere of being, but the archaeologist's thrill at unearthing is not simply that of uncovering spoils. There are other channels of communication, other ways in. This is all to do with the elaborate interplay of stimulus and emotion, and a reminder of human temporality can be an emotive trigger. I am engaged in a search for material qualities that have latent emotional affiliations. The selection and organisation of such material is a dark art, the circuit that only the perceiving eye can complete as it brings to the experience its own associations. Emotion is not what is expressed. Emotion is entirely a conjuring of the viewer's own personhood. I am attracted to the idea that a given artwork is in fact an 'open circuit' like this, waiting in potent readiness to complete some latent personal association in the viewer and linger subsequently in the imagination. Or, indeed, to create some entirely new association which becomes an open circuit carried by the viewer, awaiting consummation in future like experiences, to their consequent inner enrichment.

This links to your idea, which appeals to me, of the artwork being a means for artist and audience to meet 'out of time and out of space'. An evocative thought. The quality of this meeting is coloured by the extent to which the artist has 'created space':

the work is a window on the mind and body that created it, though an artwork needs no discernible evidence of bodily intervention to call to the body. James Turrell is a master of creating such space: his light works, in their immersive nature, are undoubtedly informed by innate embodied intelligence, his own and everyone else's. Turrell trusts this and fosters autonomous aesthetic experience in the process. I am doing the same, though my 'triggers' are grubbily physical when compared to Turrell's ethereality. The pot's apparent familiarity makes it a lovely trojan horse for these shenanigans. I want pots to cause stirrings in places that polite aesthetic precedent would insist are inaccessible to them. So, it is not just a case of meeting the audience 'out of time and space' but also out of context: my things have no right to behave the way they do (so pot orthodoxy goes). Perhaps their sheer impudence can be a spur to new experience. That's fine by me.

All art is evocation, and clay has a wanton propensity to evoke. Its capacity to 'accept' and record bodily intervention is positively rude. What a playground it is. Battleground, sometimes. 'Feeling with the mind's fingertips' indeed! I rely upon 'the mind's fingertips' to trace where my fingers have been. Much has been made over the last decade and more in neuroscience of the discovery of 'Mirror Neurons'. Their precise role is disputed but I find the idea of a neurological basis for empathy – emotive and physical – compelling. Irrespective of the mechanism by which it works, we undoubtedly reach out empathically to the world around us, largely subconsciously. To imagine physical empathy, just witness someone yawn and suppress the desire to do so yourself; we recoil from a thorn, yearn for the skin of a lover, are both attracted to and repelled by fire.... It follows that all of my scratchings and smearings in clay are sensorially directed in the hope of calling to the appropriate receptors in my fellow beings; in order to stir them in ways they may not be able to immediately articulate. It is not for nothing that we are embodied. Our embodiedness informs our every interaction with the environing world. It can be communicated with directly, in ways that circumvent the rationalising influence of language. In my world, the physical trumps words.

23 March 2022

AT: *And, of course, this is the biggest challenge when* writing *about ceramics. Perhaps this is why there are significantly more books on ceramic technique than the work that is actually created; it is much easier to describe process than allude to its sensory potential. Indeed, using words to describe sensation is like trying to signpost strangers through a village shrouded in mist. All criticism is subjective, and I have always sought to openly acknowledge that there is no 'one' way of interpreting a pot. If readers disagree with me (and they are very welcome to) I hope the words bring*

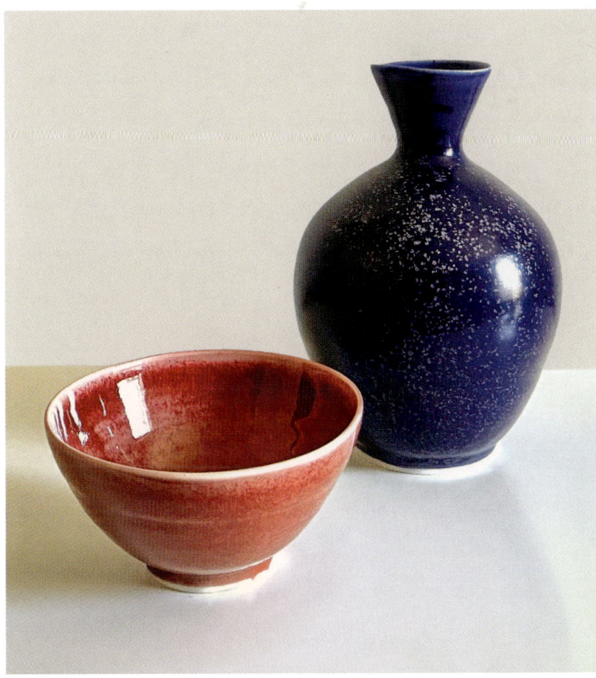

Cobalt Blue Glazed Vase, Copper Red Glazed Bowl (c.1996).

more into the conversation about the power of ceramics, across all its approaches. I am, as you can tell, an optimist.

You said that 'the pot's apparent familiarity makes it a lovely trojan horse', *and in many ways I think this is what Ewen Henderson was alluding to when he spoke about the vocabulary of ceramics. The pot is not a means to fix a definite (philosophical) form à la Bernard Leach, but a vocabulary to facilitate personal expression and communication. It is a means to an end. I think everyone included in this book uses the sliding scale between pot–vessel–sculpture for their own expressive purposes. This book stands as a record, and as a response, to this.*

To accompany the exchange between us, I have selected images of some of your works for reproduction. Looking at photos of pots rather than the real thing is about as accurate as using words to describe experience, so perhaps they are well suited. In the paragraphs that follow, I offer my own interpretation of some of these works. You are welcome to comment on these thoughts as much or as little as you wish.

One of the striking things about your work is the relationship between glaze and form. Sometimes it speeds across plains. Yet it can also swirl around recesses with a heavy viscosity, or be rough, volcanic, distinctly 'earthy'. The points where different kinds of glaze meet might draw attention to significant intersections in form. Sometimes there is balance, other times there is a kind of awkwardness. Sometimes there is stasis, other times there is a strong sense of ongoing movement, as though the form might still melt, or the glaze might still run. It is all of this, taken together, that provokes response. In Pressure Ridge (2007–2012), *for example, half of the pot is covered in amazing textural crustacea, which collides with a runny glaze from the other half of the pot (a product of firing the glaze with the work on its side). This evokes all kinds of sensations – from stormy weather fronts to a desire to contain antithetical emotion. Here, containment becomes a metaphor that rationalises the form. The shape of the pot, its interiority and exterior surface, become primed for psychological projection.*

Similarly, Manatee (2019) *documents how you explore the skin of the pot; of opening lesions, closing wounds, scoring, scarring, and embedding barnacle-like flotsam and jetsam. The size of the work (some 130cm/51in high) and leathery appearance evoke its namesake, whose skin is frequently cut by the propeller blades of boats.* Manatee *is not necessarily, or not only, a mimetic description of an animal in clay, however. To me, the work is more broadly concerned with the battle-scarring of life events on the skin – that pliable organ that shields the bodily interior from the exterior world it must navigate. The playing out of these interior and exterior forces causes scarring and rupture, but also beauty and strength; in other words, tension. In this sense, the pot speaks of survival, and not just of humanity.*

The body of the pot as a metaphor for the human body more specifically is apparent in works such as Neckline (2016–2017). *Here the foot, body, and neck of the vase stand as embodiments demarcated by different uses of glaze and material. The lip of the pot is akin to an opening of the mouth: the viewer looks down the throat of the pot with all its visceral connotations. This seems to be a pot about physical exposure, the blood and guts of the body ripped open in a gruesome act of ceramic surgery.*

Other works seem more benign in comparison. Tàpies (2012) *carries a mirror of its own form. Whether the combination of the vertical and horizontal forms reads as a parent lovingly carrying their child, or a literal cross to bear (or perhaps both) is very much in the eye of the beholder. This is not a particularly intricate form and yet it evokes narrative, emotional, and psychological complexity. It might suggest that we choose to carry others or that others in our lives demand to be carried. People, or indeed any concept you might conceive of, might be saved from the metaphorical fire or equally stolen away with little resistance. Is there a selfless offering being made, or is there a desire to hold on to something that seeks to escape? This powerful work asks us fundamental questions about the nature of our existence. And it is still very obviously a pot.*

The title of Cannon (2009–2015) *is interesting to consider in relation to the 'potness' of its form. You said that* 'I want pots to cause stirrings in places that polite aesthetic precedent would insist are inaccessible to them'. *The dark coppery tones of* Cannon *could turn it into a kind of cannon ball pot, which is fired into the world of ceramics to smash preconceptions. Yet, in the addition of wings to the side, there is a sense of acculturation, of bringing in wider spheres of influence to render the pot as a fully expressive object. The implied violence is not iconoclasm but the creation of new opportunities for self-expression.*

In contrast, the wings of Shadow Chaser (2010–2013) *appear to be more concerned with the internal rather than external. The central column seems to be compressed by the exterior, and yet this is not necessarily an oppressive condition. The wonderful mix of colours across the central column suggest that compression creates a flowering of beauty, creation, and survival. With the bad comes the good, with despair comes hope, with death comes life.*

And so, the final work I have chosen, Mammon, Tarnished, Black Rock Series (2010), *stands as an open-ended expression of what your pots might communicate. The word 'mammon' appears in* The New Testament *to mean wealth, the desire for which is stated in* The Sermon on the Mount *as being incompatible with faith ('You cannot serve both God and mammon': Matthew 6:24). This pot asks us to consider what is of value and what is corrupting? Is material wealth the key to fulfilment? From this stems a wider existential questioning of the nature of civilisation, its constructed fragility, the wounds of inequality, the opening of potential, even the baring of the soul. The reflective gold lustre invites us into the work by bringing in our reflection. But it also repels us by shielding the sections of the pot it covers from our prying eyes. Is all as it seems?* Mammon, Tarnished, Black Rock Series *offers an invitation to meet you, the artist, through the object, and to commune on the big questions. Just what is this – existence – all about?*

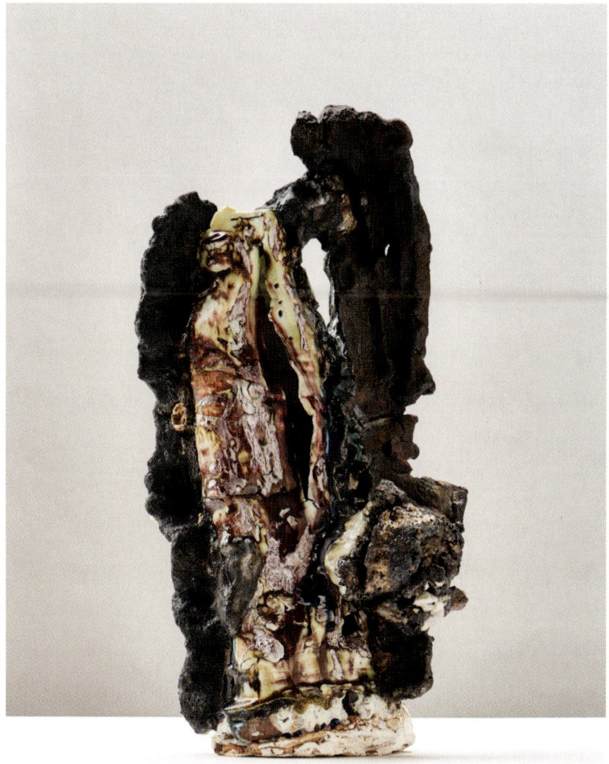

■ *Shadow Chaser* (2010–2013).

26–29 March 2022

GM: 'The shape of the pot, its interiority and exterior surface, become primed for psychological projection.'

I am not going to reflect on your thoughts and impressions of specific pots, because those are wholly and rightly your own. I do, however, want to develop some thoughts on your mention of 'shape', 'interiority' and the nature of 'priming' because these are central to ceramic experience as I live it.

My most obvious agent of 'priming' is clearly form, in the sense of shape, or even (perhaps especially) silhouette. To return briefly to your excellent question, 'why pots?', form is a 'way in'. The expectation that if a thing is shaped like a pot, then it should surely be a pot is a reasonable one. It is partly for this reason I am attached to recognisable 'pot-hood' in spite of my avowed eschewal of all things narrative. Nevertheless, representation still leaves room for play. It's a bit of a tease. Familiarity is a spectrum, and my things are familial in the sense that, say, exotic sea creatures are. Though they share bodily attributes with us – their eyes are recognisably eyes (but what eyes!), their limbs are clearly limbs (but such limbs!) – their true nature is pretty alien. I overlay the 'knowable' with less obviously 'relatable' qualities, which require a bit more 'audience participation'. We spoke of perceptual dissonance previously. The place where the knowable and the unfamiliar meet catalyses new and hopefully enriching experience.

An object's ability to be 'primed for psychological projection' is moot until that moment of perceptual alchemy wherein viewer response is aroused. This arousal is a mélange of intellectual and emotional qualities, formed in the crucible of each individual's accumulated experience of relations with the beings and objects of the world. We all navigate by such an internal 'map'. I like to think the creative ambiguity of my things invites 'audience participation' vis-à-vis meaning. I don't take this for granted, beyond the positive assumption that everyone constantly draws upon their 'inner map' as I do.

I am fond of a quote attributed to the great Catalan artist Antoni Tàpies in which he states that if the viewer is incapable of generating their own 'inner images' they will see nothing at all in his work.[133] In truth, however, the viewer's interest is always focused according to his or her proclivities. My appeal to the human animal's ability to project (psychologically, empathically, sensorially) hinges on my ability to compose a perceptually diverse source of stimulation and thereby present multiple points of access; I want to maximise the opportunity for engagement. This is the process of 'priming' that you highlight, and, in my case, it can be rather protracted. The lengths I go to in order to realise my vision of ceramic experience are absurd. The key thing for me is that the work should have the capacity to provide some reward irrespective of the viewer's attunement to 'inner images'. The same organs of arousal are at work for us all, regardless of our perceptual privilege or poverty. Their inner effect requires no great insight: its beauty is its autonomy. Once it has left my hands, however, my work is subject to the kindness of strangers.

The matter of 'interiority' is something we all know through homeostasis, that remarkable inner equilibrium of unasked bodily processes. The pot's 'body-ness' is congenial to our own in this way and, pertinently and consequentially, it invites contemplation of what's-going-on-inside. It follows that my penchant for 'piercing the skin' of the pot may well imply some shocking display of viscera; that's a valid simile, albeit a tad morbid. I hope it also betrays my fascination with the human 'inscape' in all its multiplicity. I am interested in 'being', as substance and subject: in our physicality, the very 'matter' of us and also that other mode of 'being', the alert, sensing 'self' of inner experience, which is equally biological in origin for all its seeming intangibility.

I indulge in the intrigue around interiority, in ceramic terms. When we encounter an opening, we are confronting a mystery, which arouses instinctual curiosity. The urge to take a peek is almost irresistible. Ceramic experience offers me an analogue of this, which I live quite vividly. I call it a peep show. The larger work especially offers a chink on inner worlds. Indeed, speculation as to interior nature being an age-old concern, as our Cro-Magnon forebears hesitantly ventured into openings in the primordial vessel itself – the earth – so I intrude, trespass. Sometimes with trepidation. The 'belly' of the earth was once venerated as a site of womb-like gestation, its orifices likened to bodily ones; the act of ingress

Mammon, Tarnished, Black Rock Series (2010).

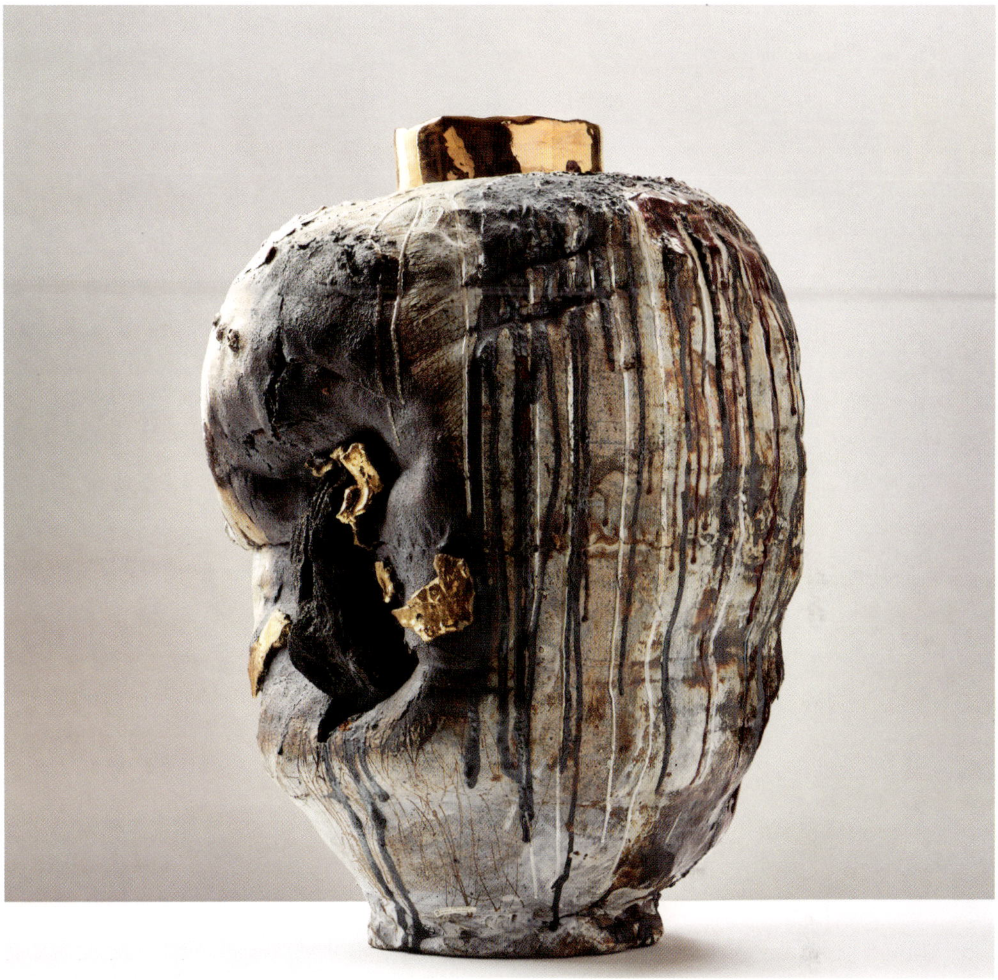

and egress ceremonialised, sexualised, rendered both human and otherworldly. It is not for nothing that the cave has long been a locus of ritual and mystery. Since the earliest conquest of the material world – and the nascent stirrings of the 'spiritual' one – subterranean ores and pigments have been loaded with potency, ripe for transformation into visionary things. I have sympathy for the idea that chthonic mythology still whispers in the industrialised consciousness. Such body-and-world rites were early proofs of our species' susceptibility to material bedazzlement. Pots, too, have visionary properties: they are threshold spaces, agents of metamorphosis, thus 'primed' for liminality. The historian of religion and philosopher Mercia Eliade rightly claimed, 'such primitive intuitions die hard'.[134] I go out of my way to keep their ember glowing.

Sarah Purvey Streams of Consciousness

There is a raw power to the work of Sarah Purvey; a directness. Her ceramic vessels and paintings on canvas or paper are not separate elements that are 'worked on' intellectually; rather, they are immediate expressions of her perceptions and feelings in a moment. In the same way that the wall of a vessel creates both an interior and exterior space, so her work represents a meeting point between the exterior perspective of the spectator and the interior emotions of the artist. She and her work are thus totally conjoined: each piece stands as a diary of unfiltered feelings, produced through a stream of consciousness.

Trying to capture this immediacy as a writer is a challenge. Purvey does not plan out her work but responds to the compositional challenge of the moment in the very process of making. In trying to reflect this here, I have decided to take the unusual step of dictating my thoughts out loud, without fully planning what I am going to write, and presenting the results with minimal editing. Immediately I feel confronted by the need to listen to my own thoughts as they enter my head, to somehow be more precisely attuned to what I sense in her work. Trying to organise these thoughts into a fluid and lucid flow as I go is immensely challenging. I want to allow ideas to come through without stuttering, overthinking, or filtering. Perhaps I reveal my anxieties around the act of writing here. In any case, the fact that this is proving so difficult only serves to attune me to the achievements of Purvey. To achieve a fluency of mark-making on both vessel and paper in this way requires acts of faith, self-belief, and a confidence in intuition. It seems fraught with danger: to allow a flow from mind to hand when you are acutely aware it will enter the public domain brings immense pressure, and a sense of vulnerable exposure. As I muse upon my own thoughts just as they come out of my mouth to be captured by the computer, I cannot help but venerate the mind-hand relationship that Purvey has so powerfully developed across her career.

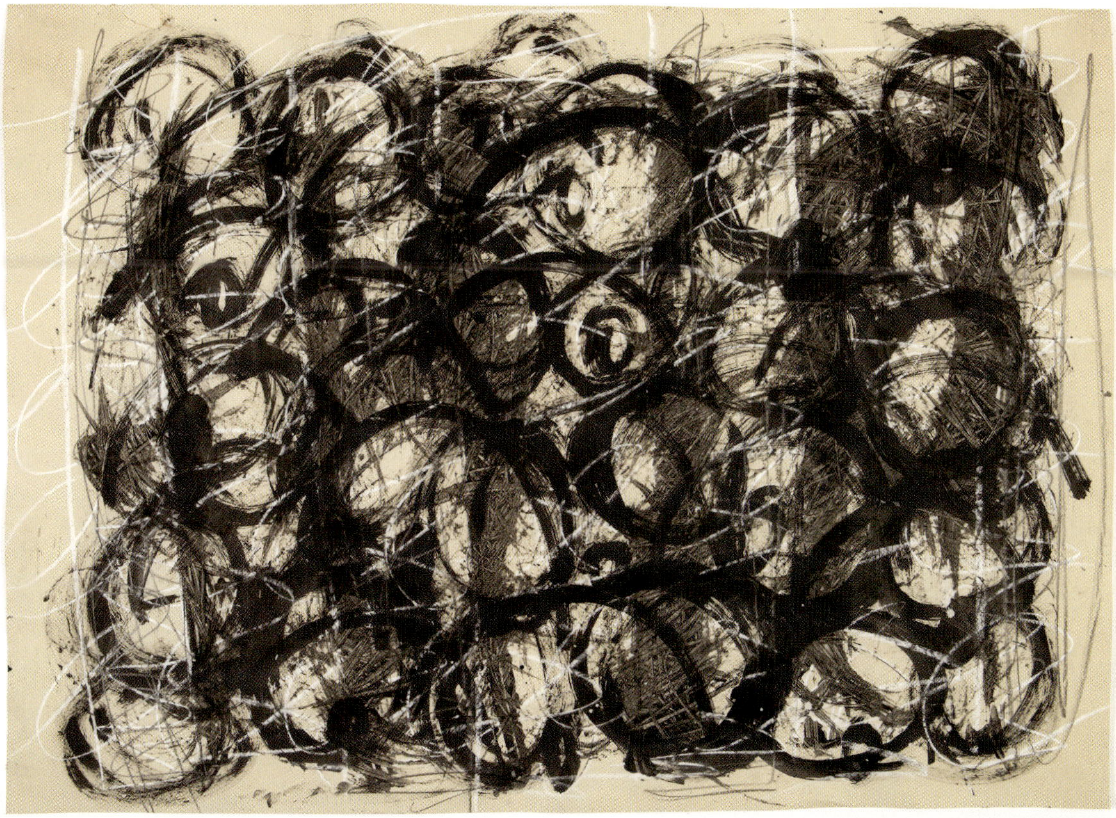

Untitled (2014).
(Courtesy of Swindon Museum & Art Gallery)

Purvey's work has mutated a great deal since she first began to exhibit in 2009. In these earlier years, the relationship between her ceramic and drawing practices seemed less clear, even though they are derived from the same impulse. In all her work, Purvey seeks to document her feelings at speed. At first glance, her aesthetic appears to be derived from Abstract Expressionism. This is particularly the case with some of her drawings, such as *Untitled* (2014), where the swells of Indian ink, chalk and pencil are evocative of artists such as Jackson Pollock (1912–1956) or Cy Twombly (1928–2011). However, a direct comparison with these artists is a little unfair. Purvey's images are a product of her own desire to express herself on paper at great speed, and this necessitates a kind of action

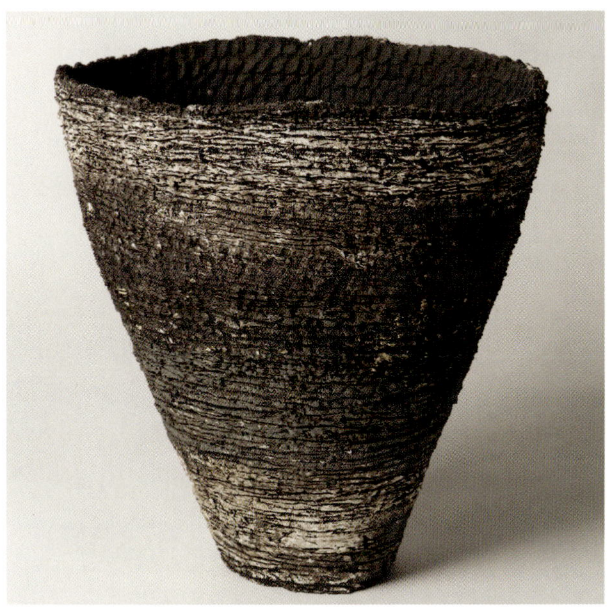

Landscape Series Ochre (2012).

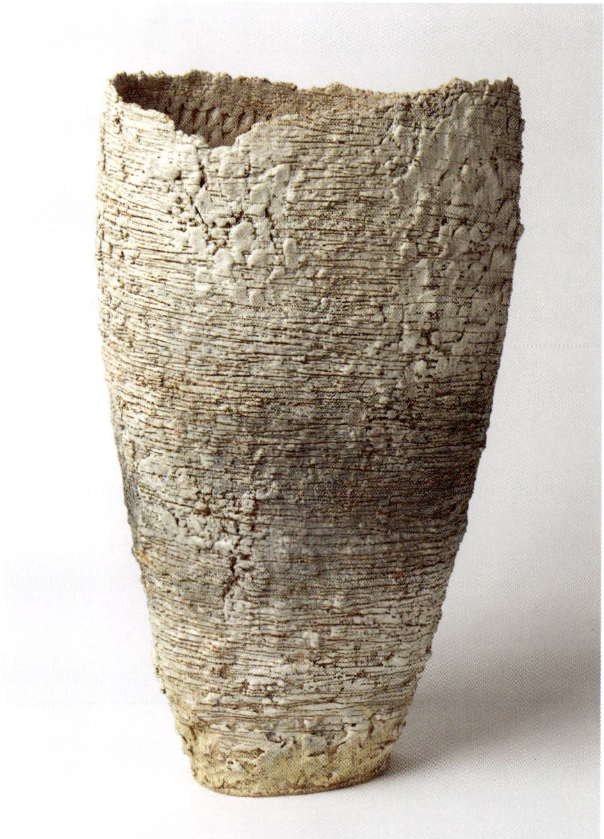

Transcend (2014).

painting. It is not the composition of these painters that she emulates; rather it is their aesthetic of speed and movement. Rapidity of execution is a key component of each drawing; the layering of marks, as well as the overall composition, have a strong sense of movement that offers a satisfying dynamism.

In comparison, her earlier ceramic vessels, such as *Landscape Series Ochre* (2012) and *Transcend* (2014), seem restrained, slowly considered, and self-consciously realised. Is this because of the demands of the medium of clay – of having to create, then fire, each piece? Perhaps. Yet, the making of the form is an integral part of the expression; the vessel itself is fundamental, not superfluous, to the statement she makes. Whilst it may seem that her ceramic vessels are the product of a much slower process, this is only partially true. The vessels are made from the coiling and pinching of clay until the form is tall enough to act as a base canvas. This coiling is undertaken at speed, assisted by using a heat gun to help the sections dry quickly enough to support the upper layers. The fingerprints that create the interior texture of each vessel stand as a record of their making; they offer tacit recognition that each vessel is a product of the movement from her mind to her hand. These pieces are personal; her fingerprints highlight how each piece is, in an abstracted emotional sense, an autobiographical act of making. Further marks are then made to the exterior through the application of more clay (usually the same as the body), which is vigorously worked into the surface and scored to create texture. These incisions provide the vessel with a sense of velocity, even spinning. In this sense, the surfaces of her clay works are treated as vigorously as those made of paper. And it is because they have equivalence with her ceramic practice that the drawings are reproduced here.

Despite the features of speed that are apparent across her output, at this stage, there is nevertheless a sense of aesthetic separation between her two-dimensional works, and her vessels which present as more benign. The latter seem akin to representations of geological landscapes: of rock or stone, the jagged teeth-like marks left in a quarry, or even an abstracted Frank Auerbach-like landscape in oil, complete with foreground, horizon, and sky. There is a tautness to these vessels; a rough and weathered exterior shields a vulnerable interior bearing the artist's own fingerprints. It is as if Purvey has not yet reconciled with the task she has set herself. This is not to suggest that these earlier works are unsuccessful: they strike me as a kind of powerful abstract drawing in clay. As such, they carve out an inventive visual language for the vessel, one which has served her as a point of artistic departure. Nevertheless, her work in two and three dimensions was not yet resolved.

A decade later, the two- and three-dimensional aspects of her practice had become more closely aligned. The mark-making on her vessels became significantly freer and less self-conscious. On *Witnessed* (2016), the looser application of clay to the surface has made the vessel more painterly, gestural, and expressive of emotion. The use of a semi-circle shape to form a repeated pattern divides the vessel surface into a discrete number of frames that oscillate across and around the surface, evoking the *Infinity Net* paintings of the Japanese artist Yayoi Kusama. These frames act as compartments for texture, delineating the background surface into discrete moments of experience, and which build cumulatively around the vessel to express how a state of mind is produced from a range of complex emotional provocations. Here, Purvey captures the complexity of what it is to feel, exposing the tension between opposing emotions, teasing us with clues about the possible intentions behind the work, but never confirming them.

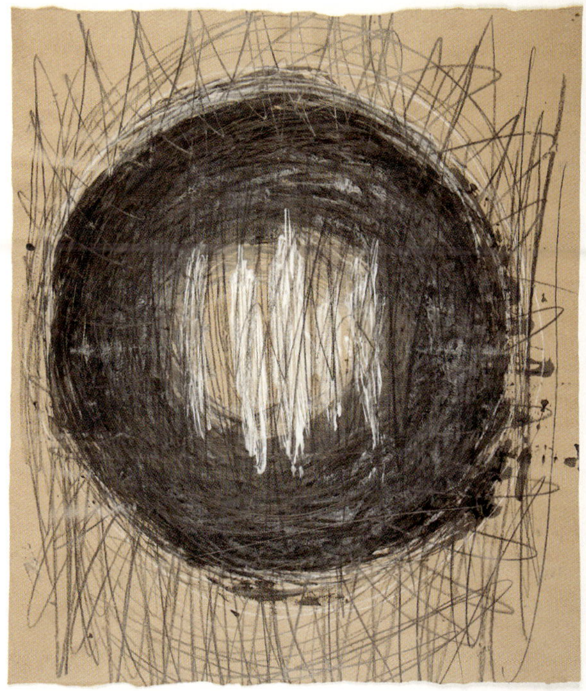

Pace (2015).
(Courtesy of Chippenham Museum)

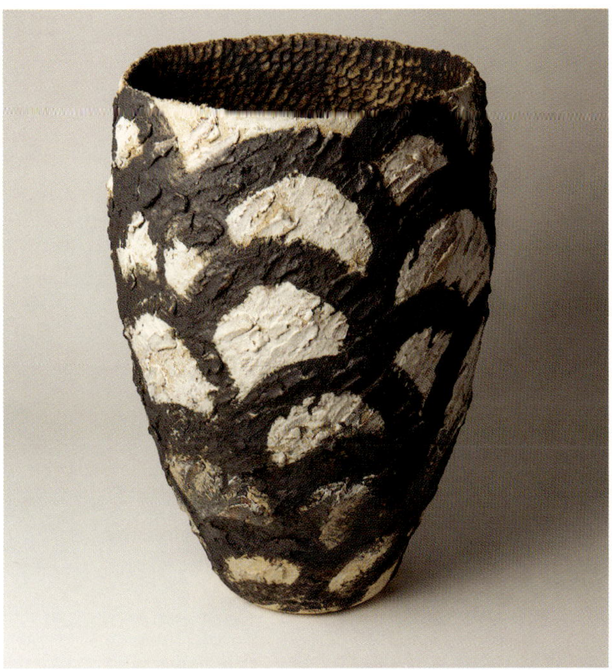

Witnessed (2016).
(Courtesy of Swindon Museum & Art Gallery)

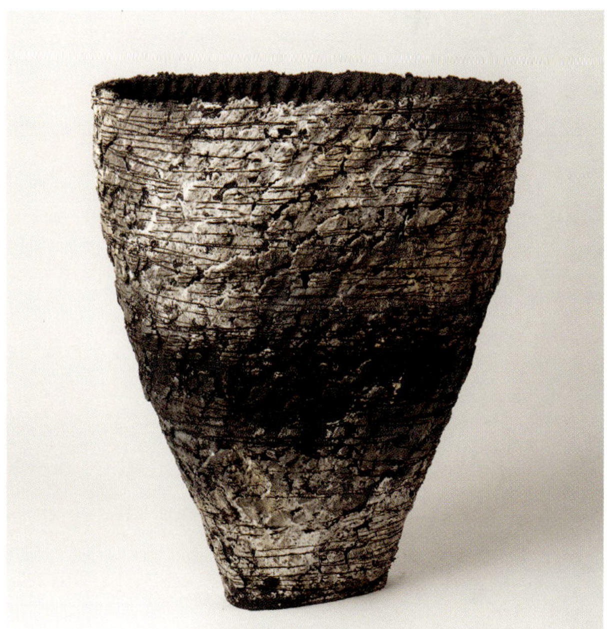

Capped (2017).

In other examples, the incised lines of *Capped* (2017), have become more fluid, confident, and lyrical. The feeling of weathered rock is still present, but it is less constricted, as though the incised lines now represent the passing of air across the vessel surface. It is as if the psychological shield observed in earlier work has started to soften. Interestingly, the background of the drawing *Pace* (2015) has the same fluency as the incised lines of *Capped*. The circular motif that constitutes the main form is reminiscent of the circularity of the vessel, whilst the white lines might symbolise the emotion that Purvey has placed inside each vessel. The title of the drawing alludes to speed, and perhaps thus represents the expressive energy of the artist bursting forth whilst she is at work. But each viewer should seek their own conclusions about the drawing and make it meaningful for themselves.

In her most recent body of work, two and three dimensions exist in equivocality. The application of acrylic, ink, and oil gives each two-dimensional work a sense of texture, whilst the freer approach to ceramic surface has rendered her vessels more painterly. Shapes that might appear in a drawing to contain space on paper become three-dimensional protrusions on her vessels (such as with *Untitled*, 2020). Here, there is a greater confidence and dexterity, and a stronger sense of immediacy between mind and hand. Such fluency can only be arrived at through experience over time; it reminds me of how the rapid mark-making by masters, such as Shōji Hamada (1894–1978), belied a lifetime of daily practice.

Purvey herself also seems more at ease with the public revelation of her own interior world. Whilst I have no doubt she will destroy, or continue to work upon, pieces that she does not find satisfactory, there is an increasing looseness and space to her compositions. This enables the effects of layering – now fundamental to her work – to be more lucidly revealed. *Burst* (2021) has a wonderful golden-yellow at the centre, echoing *Pace* (2016), but modifying into a less perfected, and thus more expressive, composition. The semi-circles of *Witnessed* (2016) have been expanded in *Boundary* (2021), facilitating a clearer differentiation of background tone. This results in a stronger evocation of emotional turmoil which, through the process of making, is resolved into a single composition, and thus a single state of mind.

In her recent drawings, we are also able to discern the intensity of layering. The composition of each picture has a greater sense of space, enabling the comprehension of different sgraffito-like effects. The more open the composition that Purvey makes, the more room the viewer is given to absorb the instinctive decisions she has made, enabling them to better appreciate her skill. The same palettes of yellow, black, white, and grey, that are at the core of her vessels are also now in her drawings, further cementing the two spheres of her artistic activity into one. Whilst some of her pictures are based upon the interweaving of different layers of patterned marks – an abstracted rendering of frames of mind – others seem more directly mimetic, as portraits of individual figures, body parts, or heads. It is as though Purvey's work has become more thematic; she has the confidence to explore the same impulse through a range of abstracted languages.

This leads us to two fundamental questions: why make vessels when drawing is also a viable outlet, and why use the same narrow palette of colours over such a long period? The answer to the first question, I believe, lies in the fact that three-dimensional objects are more confrontational. A picture on a wall can be observed without a need for spatial negotiation: the same movement through space can occur regardless of whether the spectator chooses to look at the picture on the wall or not. Three-dimensional objects are different. They jut out; we must comprehend

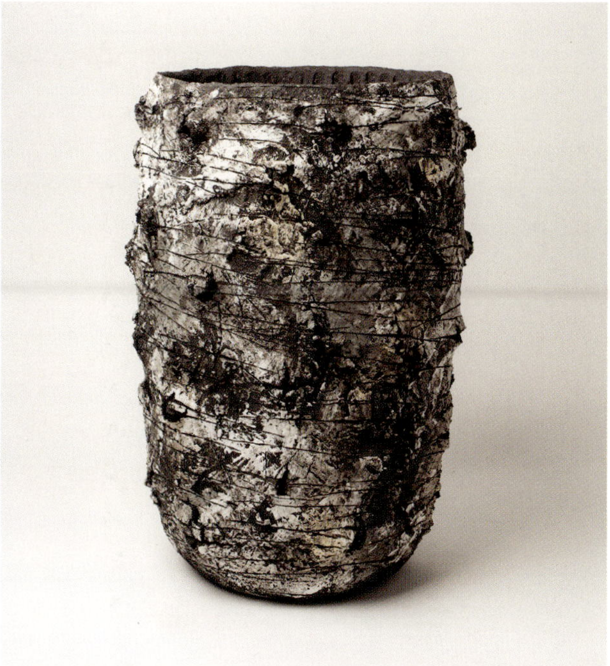

Untitled (2020).

them to be able to traverse around them. Given Purvey's very personal approach to their making, each vessel might be regarded as an emotional capsule of her own experience. Her vessels are figurative in an abstract sense; the finger-printed interior might represent the artist herself, whilst the exterior expresses how she perceives the world, or how she wants the world to perceive her. Thus, the ceramic pieces are an assertion of her place in the world; that as a person she has the right to exist on her own terms, expressed in the literal occupation of space by her vessels.

Within this framework, her choice of colour is undoubtedly psychologically revealing. It would, however, be wrong to offer a pseudo-psycho analysis of her work here, not least because to fix what it might mean would be to diminish its expressive capability. Certainly, there is a darkness to them, but this does not automatically mean that the artist is in an ongoing state of anxiety or depression. After all, the opening out of space in her compositions has enabled the layering of colour to become clearer. Thus, if

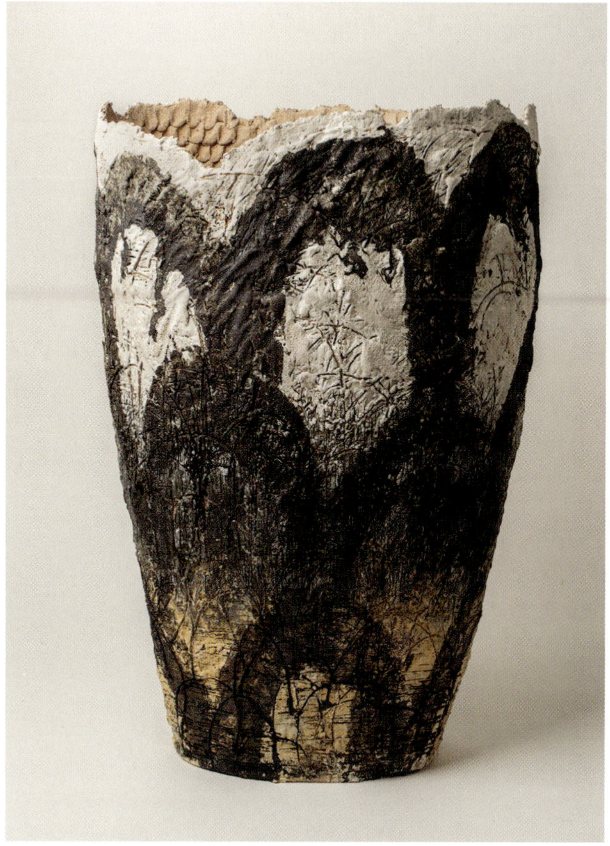

Boundary (2021).

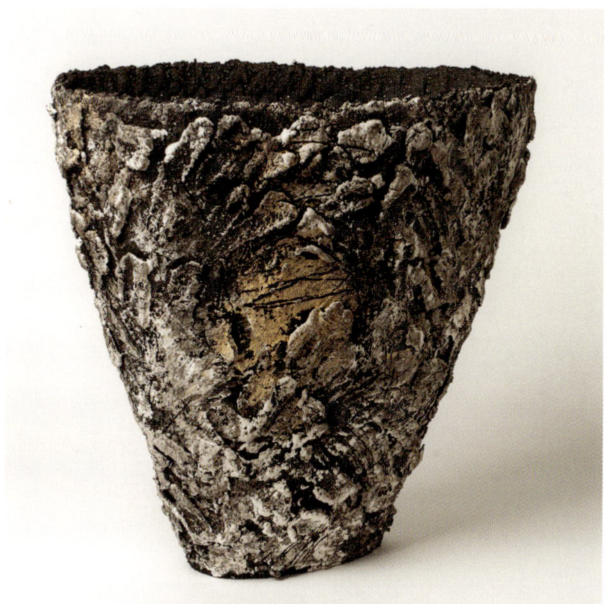

Burst (2021).

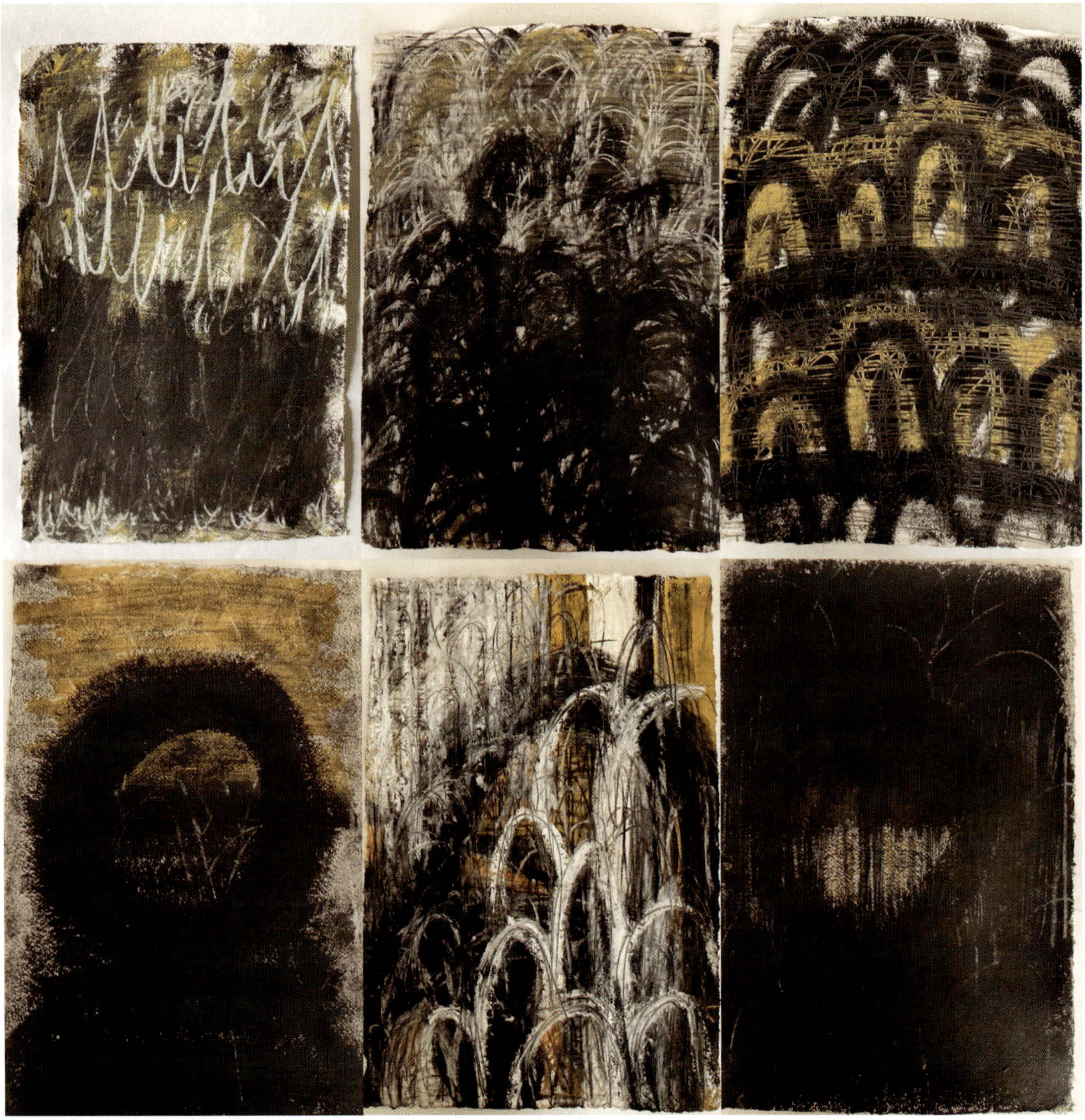

Drawings on paper (2021).

the foreground emphasises blacks and greys, these colours are offset by the exuberance of yellows and whites in the middle and background. The emotional states conveyed are thus complex: not simple angst, nor overwhelming cheerfulness, but the interweaving of the two. This is, after all, the very stuff of life.

Purvey's output stands as a diary of more than a decade of stream of consciousness productivity. Whilst her pieces are dependent upon a very personal process of creation, importantly, their reception is dependent upon a response that is equally as personal. When confronted by her work, the

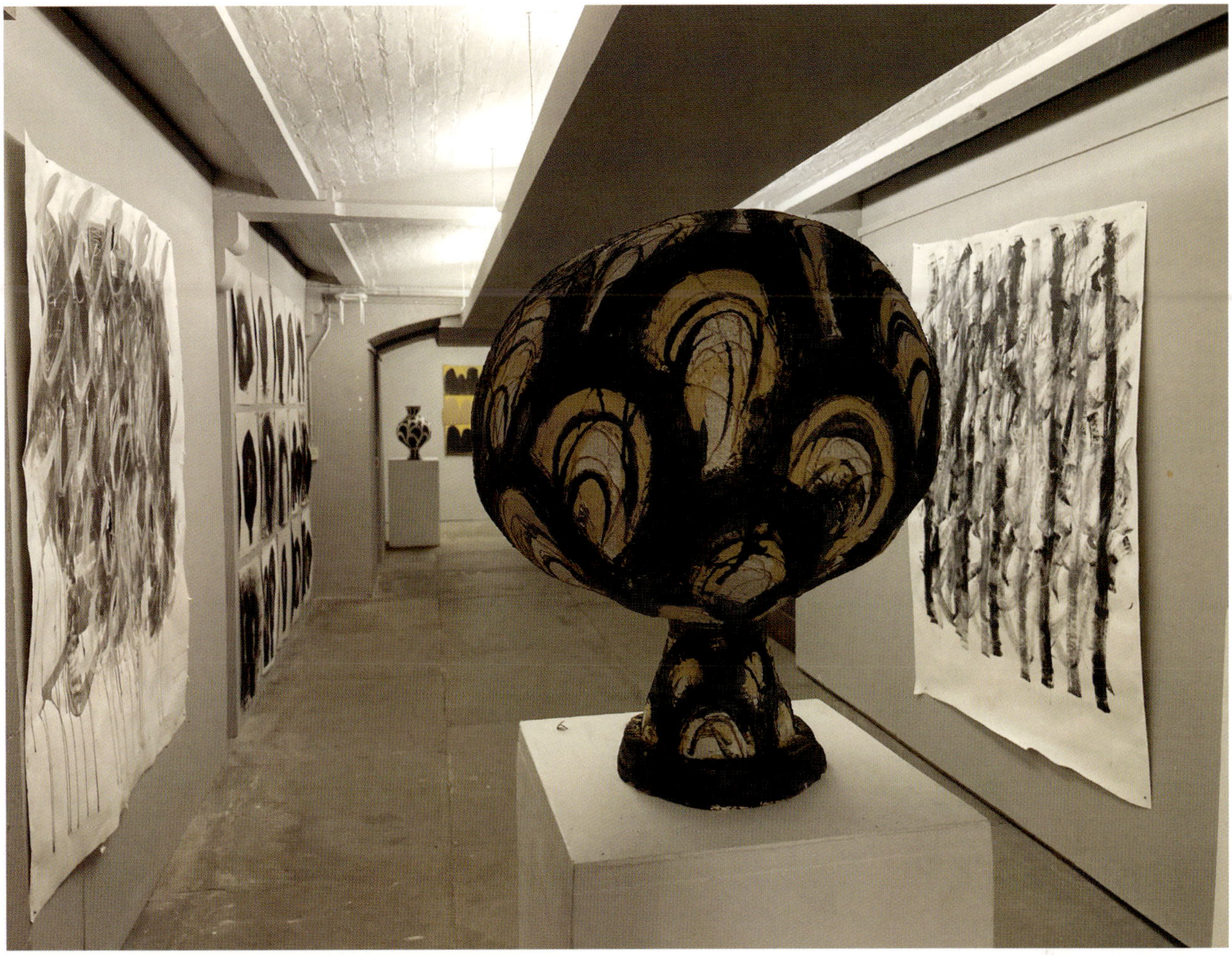

Gallery Corsham Court Residency (2021).

spectator is asked to associate their own experience, to perhaps engage in their own stream of consciousness narrative as a mode of self-analysis. Purvey's vessels are a product of, and demand, instinctive and reactive thought. For me, this is encapsulated in one of her latest works, a pot-like vessel, which is turned upside down. Here, the vessel seems to become a head, expanded to bursting point with thoughts and emotions that urgently need to come out. This could be read as a self-portrait of the artist, or it could be a portrait of myself; a writer, a thinker, someone who has many things to say and a limited amount of time to say them. The strength of Purvey's work lies in the fact that it reveals something fundamental about her, about me, but ultimately, about all of us.

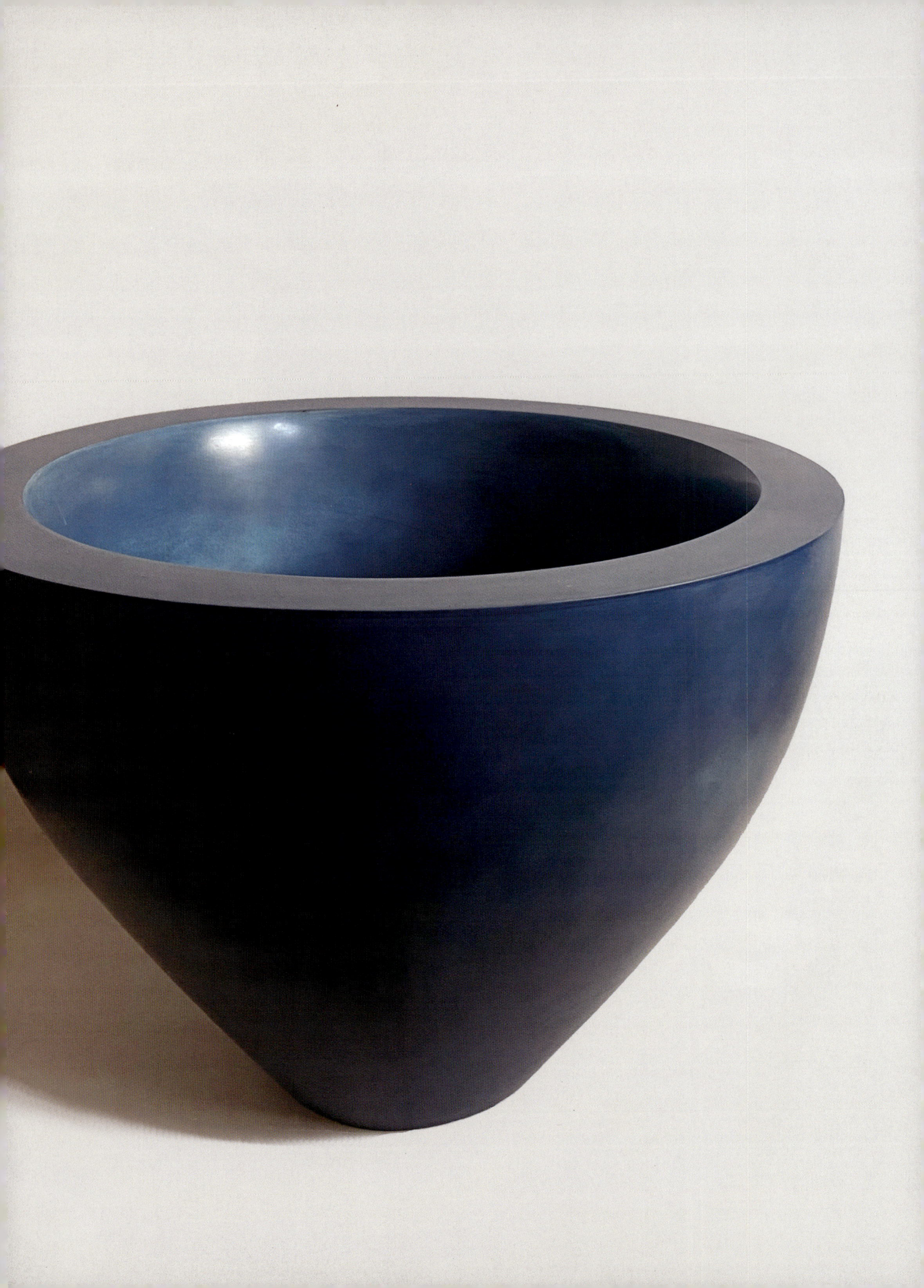

The Intangible

Chun Liao Palimpsests

> *Palimpsest* (noun): a parchment or other ancient writing surface re-used after the original content has been erased.
>
> (*Chambers Dictionary*)

I first met Chun Liao in Spring 2022, in the China and South Asia room at the British Museum where her work, *Flaming June* (2014), was on display.[135] This installation of nestling pots is a response to Sir Frederic Leighton's 1895 painting of the same name held in the collections of the Museo de Arte de Ponce in Puerto Rico.[136] The painting depicts a young female figure in a bright orange flowing dress, curled up and peacefully asleep on a Mediterranean balcony. Liao's work draws upon Leighton's palate of colours to abstract his composition, the arrangement of pots evoking the Pointillist painting techniques of Georges Seurat (1859–1891) and Paul Signac (1863–1931). Indeed, neo-impressionism seems an appropriate point of reference, given its scientific approach to optics. After all, finding the right glaze recipes and firing temperatures to enable a porcelain pot to match the colours of a painting demands a rigorous and methodical approach to testing. The result is an effervescent ceramic installation that shimmers with sensation, an impression of *Flaming June* rather than its literal representation.

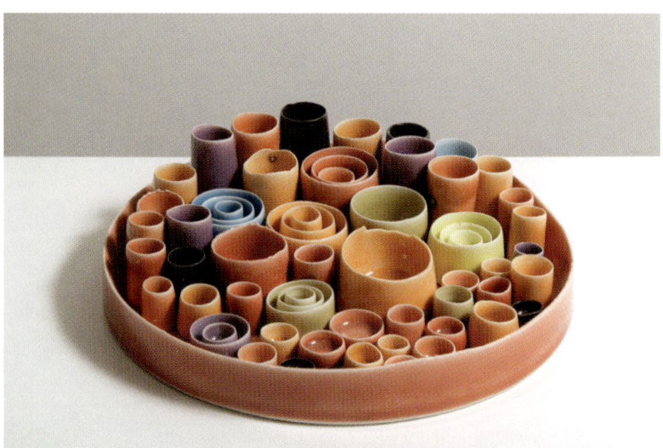

■ *Flaming June* (2014).

Surrounded by excitedly chattering tour groups, we moved from the exhibition rooms to sit outside the front of the museum and talk. She explained that there is always a contemplative and emotional impulse behind her making (indeed, the British Museum website records that Liao donated *Flaming June* to their collections in memory of her daughter). I show her a small example of her work that I have in my possession, and she vividly recalls the feeling she had when she made it but reveals little detail. Such discretion might disappoint those who feel that the artist's intention is the most accurate barometer for determining the 'truth' behind a work. Yet it is also clear that Liao wants her audience to make their own discoveries.

As we talked more, it became clear that her pots and installations stand as a kind of diary, but one that seeks greater immediacy and complexity than the linearity of language allows. Her work captures the transience of life, its joys and its sorrows, but in a way that leaves as much room as possible for audience response. As we talked about the happy accidents that had affected both of our lives – how both of us had fallen into ceramics by serendipity – I suddenly thought of the sociological term 'habitus', which describes the forces and motivations that influence how we behave. As Karl Maton explains:

> *Habitus* focuses on our ways of acting, feeling, thinking and being. It captures how we carry within us our history, how we bring this history into our present circumstances, and how we then make choices to act in certain ways and not others. This is an ongoing and active process – we are engaged in a continuous process of making history, but not under conditions entirely of our own making. Where we are in life at any one moment is the result of numberless events in the past that have shaped our path. We are faced at any moment with a variety of possible forks in that path, or choices of actions and beliefs. This range of choices depends on our current context (the position we occupy in a particular social field), but at the same time which of these choices are visible to us and which we do not see as possible are the result of our past journey, for our experiences have helped shape our vision.[137]

Liao's works are an expression of her own habitus. Her pots cohere around the past, the present, and the future. They are a means to interrogate and document how her past shapes her present emotions, and how, in turn, such emotions demand new developments in approach to her work. In this sense, whilst Liao's output has varied considerably in form, it is possible to consider it all as a single continuous expression of habitus. Threads of emotional association are spun between her works like a web across time and space. But only the artist herself can see them. Once a pot leaves the studio, it has to embark upon its own journey. If her pots are diaries of habitus, they are primed to be overwritten with new experiences. These pots are palimpsests.

When I spoke with Liao, she went to great pains to explain technique to me. At first, I thought this was a kind of defence mechanism against the prying eyes of strangers; a means to focus on how work was made rather than the impetus behind its creation. Yet, as I sit down to write, I wonder if placing any

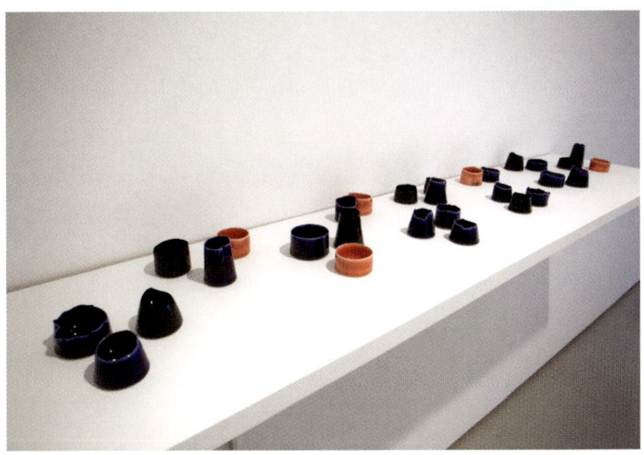

Blue February (2012).

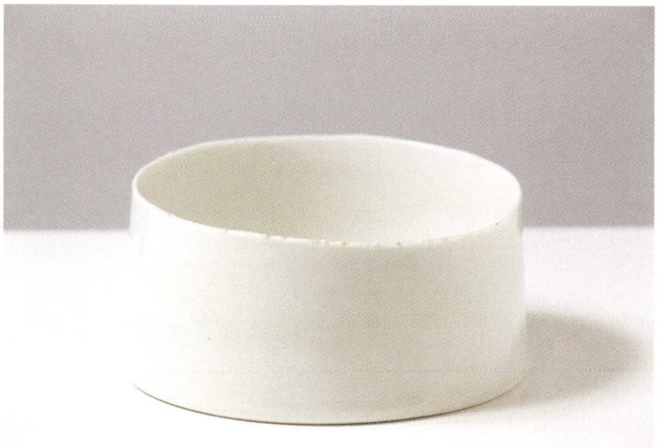

White Vessel (2012).

written interpretation on her work is a little fatuous. I always try to write from my own perspective in the hope that readers will critically engage, even disagree, with my thinking. Certainly, to offer any kind of categorical interpretation of Liao's pots would be detrimental to their communicative power. There is, therefore, a need to proceed carefully. Liao's work challenges us with questions about our own lives: our hopes, dreams, tragedies, and despairs. To explore elemental aspects of her form and technique is, at least, to emphasise the vocabulary through which Liao asks her questions. This seems a good place to start.

As we sat outside in the spring London sunshine, Liao explained how she had spent many years searching the archives to piece together the raw glazing techniques of Lucie Rie (1902–1995). Most potters throw a pot, and after allowing it to dry, bisque fire it to make it durable. It is then glazed and fired a second time. Rie developed a technique that allowed her to throw the pot, glaze it when leather hard, and fire it only once. When Liao arrived at the Royal College of Art in 1996, Rie had just passed away. Thus, in 1998, Liao pursued an MPhil in raw glaze research, amassing notes from scraps of information to piece together Rie's method. Liao has always worked in porcelain, its smoothness suiting her throwing method and approach. Yet it is a thorny material; its tendency to shrink in the kiln can lead to deformation and a higher loss rate than would be experienced with other clays. Thus, the problem for Liao was to rediscover how to glaze porcelain in its unfired state and still achieve strong results.

After much trial and error, Liao succeeded. The outcome was the development of surfaces that have a strong sense of movement. Glaze moves down the form as it is fired, usually revealing the porcelain rim, and giving bowls a completely smooth, satisfyingly weighty, base. Indeed, to apply glaze to a bisque fired piece would mean that the undulations of the porcelain form underneath would show through. By firing only once, the glaze and the porcelain fuse together producing a sensuously smooth form. The application of specks of jeweller's alloy to the rims of her pots enable vibrant streaks of colour to emerge. As Liao later wrote in correspondence with me:

> I like these seemingly random and uncontrollable effects; when you put metal, porcelain and glaze together and throw them into the heat. Something happened inside the kilns, not just on the surfaces, the personality of pots changed. They speak for the emotions within, when words failed.[138]

There is a strong sense of movement across the surface, but in some works, also of repair. In *White Vessel with Staple* (2012) for instance, a metal alloy seals a cut to the side of the pot, like a surgical staple across a wound. In *Installation of Twelve Pots* (2004), a green streak running down the side of two pots is caught in the glaze of another. These three pots share a connection that separates them out from the others, suggesting a narrative that might be about group or family dynamics. The choice of gas or electric kiln, the use of metal alloys and its cumulative build up in the kiln, and the presence of alloys in the clay itself, all create different possibilities. Liao's ability to deduce in advance what the impact of these variables might be is a testament to her skill. Yet, as is always the case, it is the opening of the kiln door that reveals the extent of assumed transformation.

Some pieces are more straightforwardly narrative, however. The four installations named after

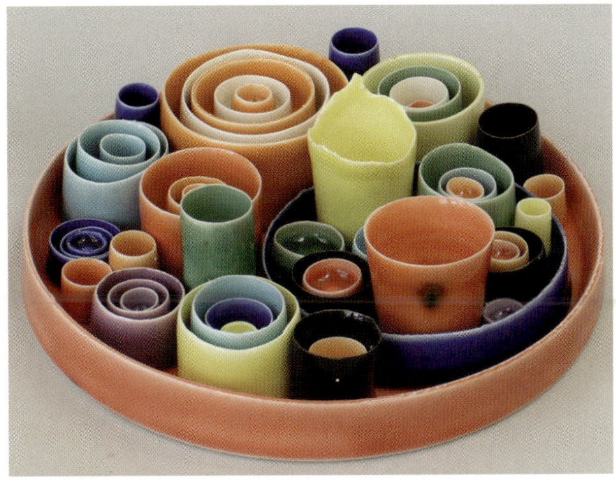

Autumn (2012).

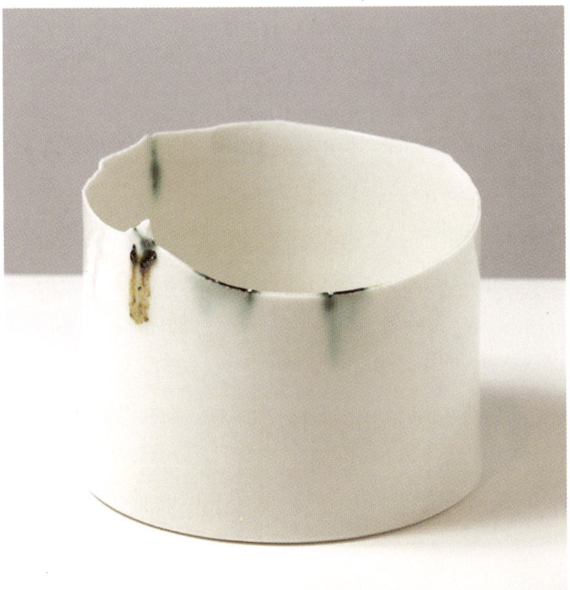

White Vessel with Staple (2012).

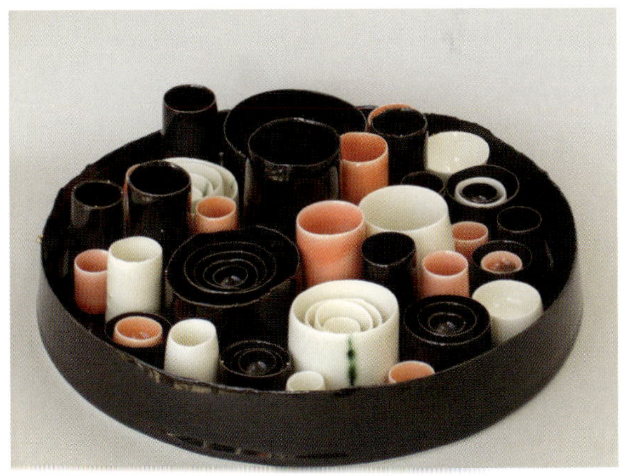

Winter (2012).

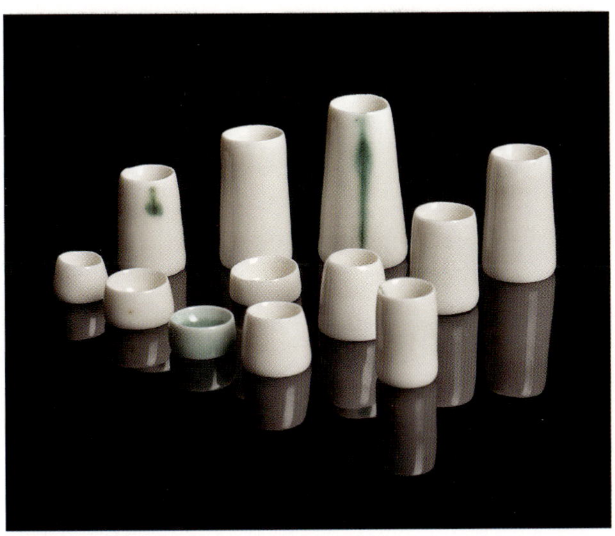

Installation of Twelve Pots (2004).

the seasons of the year are derived from the artist observing changes in her own garden. *Autumn* (2012), for instance, is full of late summer colour, the preponderance of yellows and oranges evoking the russet of autumn leaves. *Winter* (2012) is considerably bleaker, the black tones call to mind hibernation and death, with the white evoking frost, and the orange recalling the remnants of leaves rotting on the ground. The dish that encircles each installation is a reminder that seasons are cyclical. Birth and death, decay and renewal, are ongoing, even as they are captured in the most enduring of material: ceramic.

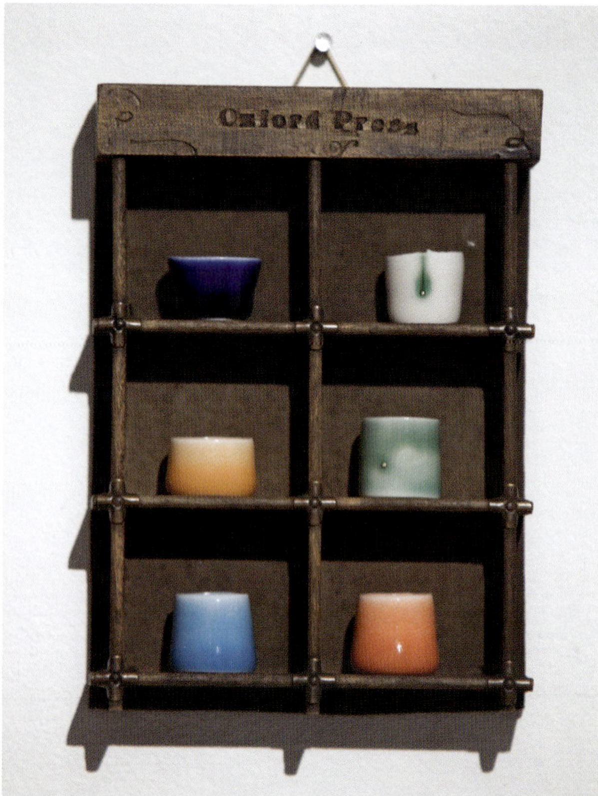

Small Is Beautiful (2011).

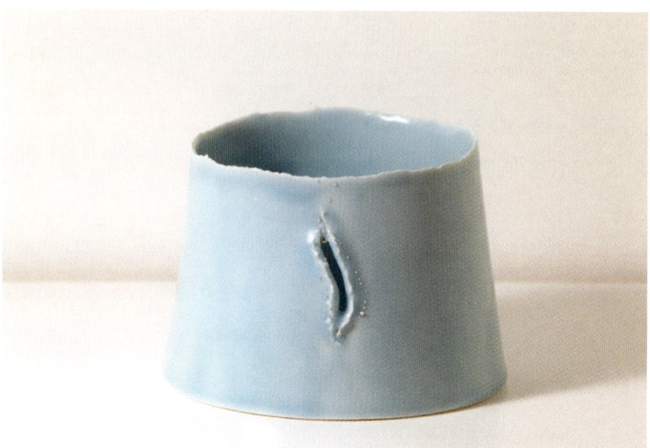

Long Winter III (2017).

One of the strengths of Liao's approach lies in her ability to evince individuality from even the smallest of pots. The series *Small Is Beautiful* consisted of tiny thimble-like porcelain pots that were placed into letter press trays that the artist purchased from an antiques seller on Portobello Road in London. Bemused by the ever-expanding size of contemporary ceramic forms, Liao decided to move in the opposite direction by creating the smallest works she could. Astonishingly, Liao utilised the raw glazing technique even on these delicate pots, ensuring that her trademark – the pulling of glaze down the pot to expose the white porcelain around the rim – was still in evidence. Such concern reveals her determination that all pieces, even when at their smallest, must powerfully communicate something on their own terms. Indeed, as a point of comparison, *Long Winter III* (2017) is a much larger work; its cool blue suggestive of winter, its undulating rim and gashed side populated with dots of frost-like silver alloy. It is a stark, lonely, and beautiful piece of work, one that expresses acceptance of solitude, if not a yearning for the light of spring.

The titles of Liao's works are always carefully considered, directing audiences towards what is potentially at stake in each piece. The use of pottery as a means to express emotional complexity produces abstraction, but one that only increases communicative power. For me, *Lament* (2012) suggests waves of grief, the eye registering the small colourful pots at the right extremity of the installation at a faster tempo than the larger white and green pots in the centre. To lament is to become consumed by grief, where time slows down, and feelings are most acute. Then, as my eye travels down the left side of the installation, the colours are darker, the lament casting a shadow even as life moves on. Eventually, colour returns, and life begins again, even though the two orange pots at the outer extremities connect, suggesting a circular path.

This, of course, is my reading of *Lament*. It is imbued with my own experiences of grief and loss. My experiences are different to yours, as they are different from Liao's. This is the power of pottery: to direct without dictating, to achieve the lyrical and poetic without recourse to words. To relay my own

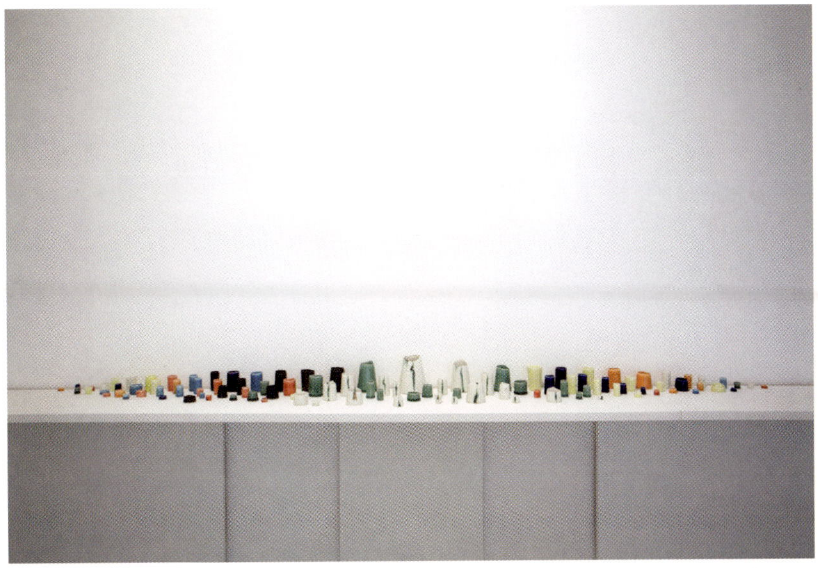

Lament (2012).

thoughts about Liao's work in writing still seems like an act of gross irreverence. But this essay should be regarded as palimpsest-like; nothing more than the projection of writing over forms produced by Liao's own self-erasure. And so, to my surprise, I find myself ending by echoing Liao; to ask the reader to forget these words, to wipe the slate clean, tabula rasa, and to look again for themselves.

Nicholas Rena
Matter That Matters

Ceramic works 'work'. In what sense? Of course, pots are a product of 'work': the artist's technical understanding, decisions about style and form, and the hours of labour required to make a pot. Yet, besides labour, 'work' can also mean effectiveness. Effectiveness in pottery could refer to utility; for example, the 'work' of a jug in containing liquid. However, utility is not the only concern. The way a pot looks and feels, the sensations it provokes, the memories it brings, and the philosophies it describes are also significant to its working as a meaningful object. Pottery can be regarded, therefore, as pertaining to 'work' in different ways.

This understanding of 'work' – as referring to labour and effectiveness – has led the philosopher Andrew Benjamin to consider art and architecture as intertwined practices. In the rather dense quotation that follows, Benjamin argues that both artworks and buildings 'work' long after they have been created or built:

> intrinsic to art works is their capacity to work. In place of the static and the substantive centrality is given to what can be described as the object's workful nature and thus to its active or dynamic quality. As a consequence what insists is the question of the way the work works. What needs to be noted in this context is threefold. In the first instance, it is the move from the substantive to the dynamic. In the second, there is the necessity to replace completion with a productive sense of work and finally the necessity to rethink art's material presence as itself involving process. Occasioned by the last element is the need to reposition a concern with materiality. Instead of the simple evocation of matter, once it is rethought in terms of the continuity of process – production and materiality as always connected – matter will become 'mattering'.[139]

Put differently, an architect works (labours) on the design of a building and oversees its construction, but when this process is complete, the work (effectiveness) of a building has only just begun. A building must function for its users and adapt over time to meet the demand of new requirements. Similarly, Benjamin proposes, an artist works (labours) on the creation of art. Yet, even when this labour is complete, the artwork continues to work (be effective) by generating meaning for its audience. Indeed, if an artwork is really 'working', its significance will continue to be debated and revised for years, decades, perhaps even centuries. This is what Benjamin means by matter becoming 'mattering'; an object has importance – it matters – to the world. Thus, artworks 'work' (are effective) in perpetuity in the same way that buildings are. In turning Benjamin's argument towards architecture and pottery specifically, it can be suggested that buildings, as containers, share some of the same 'work' concerns as studio pottery. Utility, aesthetics, and the production of meaningful experience are important to both.

Nowhere is this connection more readily apparent than in the work of Nicholas Rena. Trained as an architect before moving into studio ceramics, his monumental works harness the architecture of bowls and jugs for the purposes of aesthetic and spiritual contemplation. By alluding to the ritual significance of these forms, Rena's work poses questions that are both material and transcendental. Like architecture, his forms dynamically shape space, like mini chapels for personal prayers. Yet, they also draw attention to the way in which form inhabits and animates space. For example, *This Endless Baptism of Air* (2012) uses colour to draw attention to the interior of the bowl, the azure blue suggestive of water against the flesh-like pinky-red of the exterior. This colour combination maps on to our experience of the work; the spectator is on the outside looking in, whilst the interior convex implies the holding of some kind of holy water that is alluded to but never seen. The interplay between the material and the transcendent, the actual and the implied, produces a feeling of ethereal transience, that the ritual has happened before, will happen again, and as a consequence, we are but momentary witnesses.

Such symbolism also alludes to the significance of iconography to religion, the need to manifest divinity through material objects to afford a physical manifestation of an unseen presence. *Annunciation Jug and Vase* (2008) utilises the notion of flow to expose communication from the divine to the earthly. There is no literal connection between the jug and the vase; the pouring is implied through the spatial relationship between the lips of the two forms – a term that also alludes to the mouth and thus communication. Consequently, the Annunciation – the announcement by the Angel Gabriel that the Virgin Mary would conceive a son – is here symbolised through the pouring of invisible liquid from one mouth to another. The connection between the material forms of the jug and the bowl allude to immaterial divinity.

Obviously, three-dimensional sculptures and two-dimensional images have long been used to

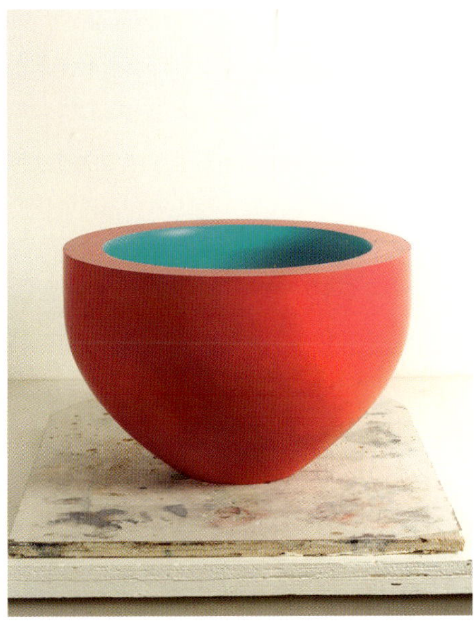

This Endless Baptism of Air (2012).

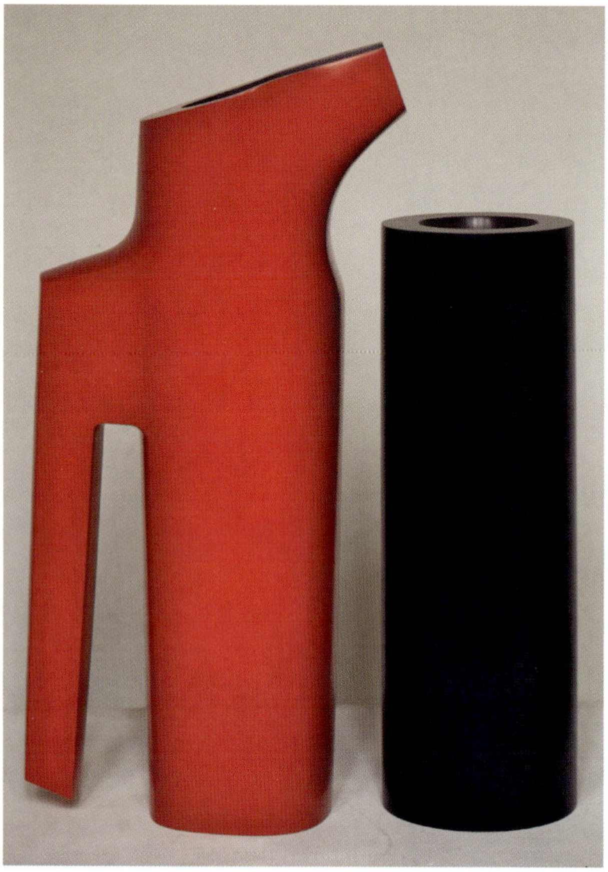

Annunciation Jug and Vase (2008).

express religious piety, but Rena's work draws upon both iterations, abstracting historical references into contemporary sculptural statements. For example, *The Supper at Emmaus (after Caravaggio)* (2014) is based upon the famous 1601 painting of the same name by Michelangelo Merisi de Caravaggio (1571–1610), held in the collections of The National Gallery in London.[140] The painting depicts the appearance of Jesus to two of his disciples three days after his crucifixion, who finally recognise him when he breaks bread with them at supper. Rena emphasises the domestic imagery of the supper to create three forms that abstract Caravaggio's composition. The colour of the central vase reflects the red tunic worn by Jesus as he blesses the bread. The same colour appears to the interior of the other

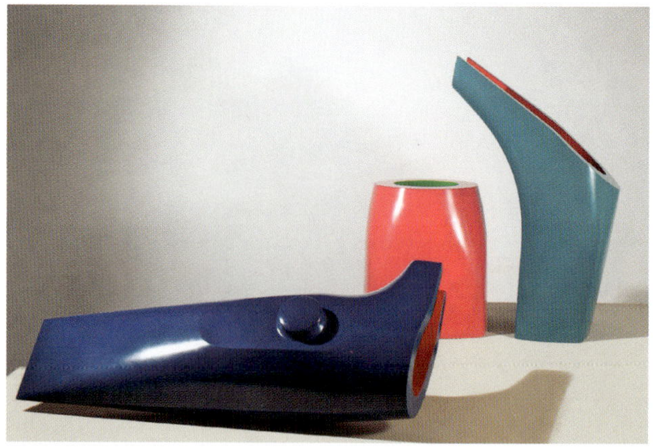

The Supper at Emmaus (after Caravaggio) (2014).

two forms, suggesting the interiority of the disciple's belief, and the efficacy of Jesus' blessing of the bread, which is then consumed (interiorised). The dark blue sculptural jug has no flat base so it must always lie prone. This reflects the prominence of the table that runs horizontally along the lower quarter of the Caravaggio painting. Yet, Rena's composition also alludes to the resurrection, the prone blue sculptural jug moving through the divinity of the red vase into the upright green jug form. Rena's remarkable precision in composition enables him to produce work that both abstracts and yet crystalises symbolic aspects of the painting.

Relationships between material and space – what is stationary and what is activated by the dynamic movement of spectators – is central to architecture, but also to architectural art. As the American sculptor Richard Serra, whose large-scale works are often architectural in ambition and realisation, has observed:

> Architecture is made up of connections, of tissues between spaces, which sculpture can forgo. That suspension happens at the interval. It's not a joint because it's spatial; it's a break that connects. In architecture you're directed through connections that are predicated on function.[141]

For Serra, the 'interval' is the point in a work where the spectator has multiple options for access, choosing to experience elements in an order and from a perspective that suits their own preference. This means that the space running around and through architectural art is not empty. In fact, it becomes central: space is a dynamic site full of potential.

Rena's installation *The Ecstasy of St Teresa (After Bernini)*, held in the Jerwood Space, London in 2008, demonstrated an acute understanding of this. An abstracted response to the marble sculptures of the same name in the Cornaro Chapel in Rome by the Italian sculptor and architect Gian Lorenzo Bernini (1598–1680), Rena's installation consisted of four islands upon which jugs, bowls, and urns were placed. The central island (see Detail of *The Ecstasy of St Teresa*, 2008) consisted of a dark purple jug and bowl, the latter with a red interior. These two forms could almost be abstracted representations of the two central figures in the Bernini sculpture; the handle of the jug evoking the wings of the angel who pierces Teresa of Avila (1515–1582) with a spear in her ecstatic vision. As with *The Supper at Emmaus (after Caravaggio)*, the colour red is used to denote the Biblical symbolism of blood, death, life, flesh, penitence, and martyrdom. Rena's use of yellow seems to echo the spiritual light that emanates from the top of Bernini's sculpture, the golden rays activating the other forms into their red colour, and thus a state of piety. The opening out of the installation into islands enabled audiences to move between and amongst the different elements – an impossible act when contemplating Bernini's sculpture in the Cornaro Chapel. Spectators are thus invited to place themselves within the sculpture, to immerse themselves in the ecstatic vision of Teresa of Avila rather than regard it from afar. Because the ways in which the spectator activates the space around and in the installation is always different, each person has an individual vision of the work. Moving through this work is a private encounter, but one that is also communicable and experienceable by others. In this sense, Rena's *The Ecstasy of St Teresa* does not merely depict the vision of Teresa of Avila; it emulates it at the level of aesthetic (ecstatic) experience.

Rena's innate understanding of architecture as a series of dynamic spaces was further evidenced when he participated in the 2013 group show *Marking the Line: Ceramics and Architecture* at the Sir John Soane Museum in London. A leading architect of his generation, Sir John Soane (1753–1837) turned his house into an educational museum in perpetuity, a decision endorsed in his lifetime by an Act

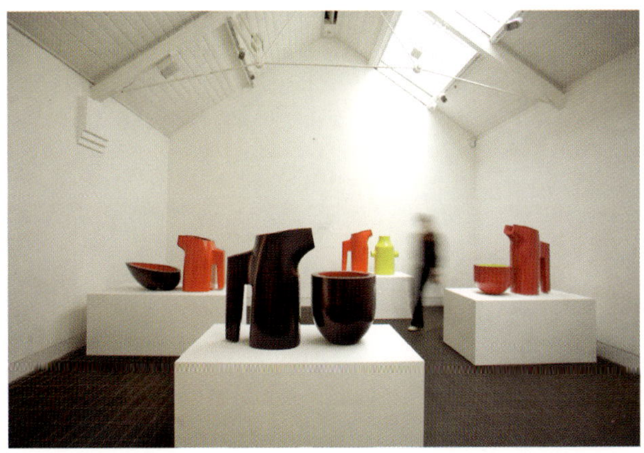

The Ecstasy of St Teresa (After Bernini), Jerwood Space, London (2008).

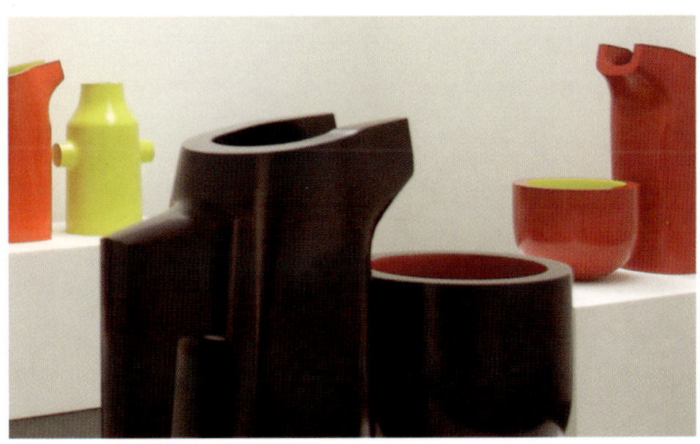

Detail of *The Ecstasy of St Teresa* (2008).

of Parliament in 1833. Alongside pieces by Christie Brown, Carina Ciscato, and Clare Twomey, Rena's works were carefully placed around the museum to facilitate dialogue between the historical collections of the museum and the contemporary period of the exhibition. For instance, *Persephone* (2013) was placed in front of a glazed pedestal bookcase upon which stands an angel figure.[142] The two parts of Rena's work echo both the two doors of the bookcase and the wings of the angel. In addition, the title of the work speaks to the classicism of much of Soane's own collection, as well as his macabre collection of plaster death masks, which is caught in the title *Persephone*, the Goddess of the Underworld and thus Queen of the Dead. In contrast, *Green Remembrance* (2013) was located in the shadow of a plaster rosette, the four petals pulling the eye in like the dark void at the centre of Rena's vase. Shadow elongates the form of the vase into a silhouette, resonating with the dimly lit contours of the rosette. The colour green evokes growth, rebirth, and resurrection; the erstwhile made anew. By placing the present in careful dialogue with the past, Rena highlighted how the experience of historical architecture is always contemporaneous. Impressions of space, just as much as objects, shift through time, acquiring new resonances in the very moment of experience.

Indeed, in his philosophical analysis, Benjamin stressed how memory remains significant to the appreciation of art and architecture:

> Both architecture and art can be sites of memory. Modes of remembering, and therefore, the way the work of memory occurs will in each case be different. Nonetheless, in certain instances works situated in the present remember. Remembering need be neither complacent nor nostalgic. Daniel Libeskind's The Jewish Museum Berlin (1999) is a perfect instance of a project that maintains its architectural integrity and yet which also allows for what can be called *present remembrance*. The latter being the form of memory demanded by the concerns of the present.[143]

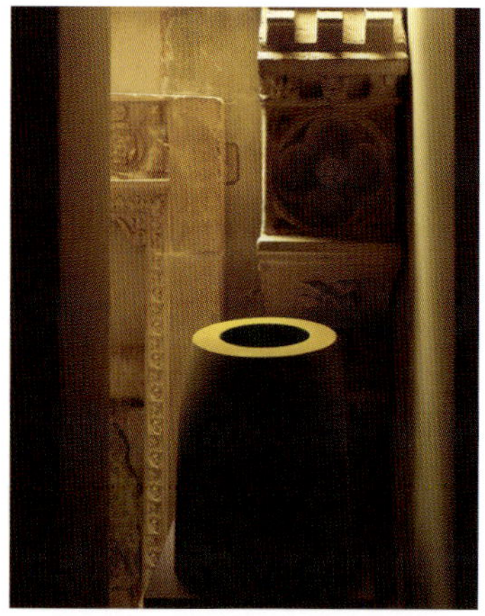

Green Remembrance (2013).

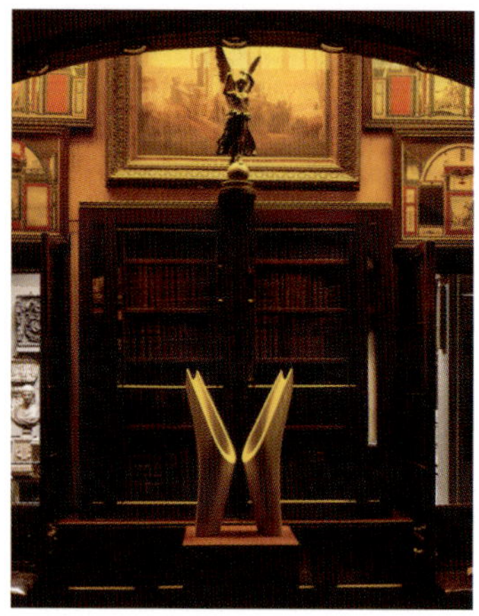

Persephone, displayed in the Sir John Soane Museum, London (2013).

The notion that memory is recalled through the demands of the present is at the heart of the arresting bowl *The Harmony of the Year* (2013).

Although the date of production suggests that this work is concerned with a specific year, the date does not form part of the title. The year in question could be any year, whilst the nature of harmonisation – expressed in the relational hues of purple and blue – is left unsaid. The spectator interprets for themselves the nature of remembrance; the specific circumstances that stand out as convivial and efficacious are individual. In *The Harmony of the Year*, memory is both shared and personal, a communal heaping of exclusive recollections that are collected in the interior of the bowl. In this sense, Rena's works are architectural palimpsests designed to be written over and over again in successive encounters. Indeed, this is made explicit in *Oracle* (2017), a quite radical departure from the smooth aesthetic for which Rena is known, yet emblematic of the power of his work to elicit re-inscription. The bodies of these stoneware forms are marked by time, as though they had been unearthed from an archaeological site as evidence of an ancient pictographic language.

Rena's jugs and bowls are produced to be refilled with associations. Like architecture, these objects move through space and time and are in a continual process of coming into meaning. If such movements demonstrate the 'working of the work' of architecture, Rena's works participate in similar acts of 'present remembrance'. His ceramic forms are concerned with reimagination, recontextualisation, and re-citation, of the ritual connotations of the bowl and the jug, but also of containment and release. Rena's works continue to work once they have left the studio: matter relentlessly matters.

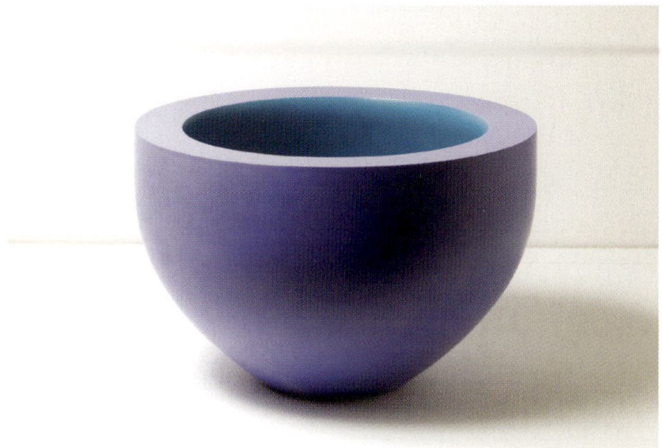

The Harmony of the Year (2013).

Oracle (2017).

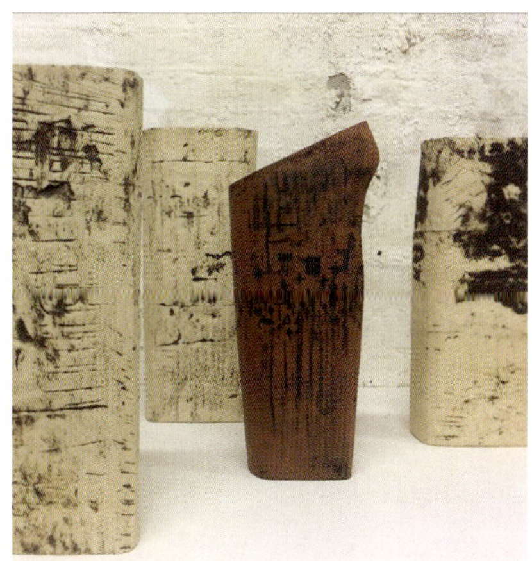

Lawson Oyekan
A Unified Theorem

Creation myths, religious texts, and scientific analysis have all sought to answer one question that has consistently vexed humanity: how was the universe created? Developments in physics, mathematics, and technology, many arising in the twentieth century, have provided us with new understandings of the forces that govern the universe. For example, Albert Einstein's (1879–1955) theory of general relativity offered a mathematical calculation that accounted for how gravity is a product of four-dimensional spacetime (the three dimensions of space, with the added dimension of time). Yet, he was acutely aware that not all forces were produced through gravity; some were the product of forces described by quantum mechanics – the positive, negative, and neutral charges behind atomic structure that create strong and weak nuclear forces, as well as electromagnetic force. Einstein devoted the last years of his life to reconciling gravitational force with quantum mechanics, but died without realising his Grand Unified Theory.

In 1999, the Nigerian mathematician and physicist Gabriel A. Oyibo offered a mathematical solution to Einstein's conundrum, which he titled *God Almighty's Grand Unified Theorem* (GAGUT). Oyibo observed that in different times and cultures, 'waves' were believed to be centrally important to the creation of the universe.[144] The Christian Bible (John 1:1), for instance, suggested that in the beginning was the word of God, which, as language, Oyibo observed, are sound waves. The Big Bang theory constructed the universe as energy waves emanating from a compressed state of high density. Meanwhile, Ancient Egyptian creation myths suggested that the universe was created from the stormy waves of Nun, an ocean from which the pyramid (the most precise of all geometric structures) of the universe emerged. By emphasising the wave, Oyibo demonstrated how these myths and scriptures correspond with contemporary mathematical conceptualisations of the universe. Indeed, Oyibo highlighted how everything can be understood in terms of geometry.

Even written language – from the hieroglyphs of the Ancient Egyptians to the roman alphabet you are reading now – is formed from geometric shapes that are spaced between co-ordinates.

Out of this geometric understanding, Oyibo observed that the one thing connecting all matter is its perpetual motion. This led Oyibo to conclude that all matter exists as a concentration of force. Oyibo was thus able to contend that gravity (Einstein's general theory of relativity) is entirely compatible with the attraction/repulsion of quantum mechanics: both are forces. His findings (expressed in the equation $G_{ij,j}=O$) were subsequently reviewed as mathematically viable, but, at the time of writing, remain scientifically unproven by physicists.[145] Some claim that GAGUT reveals nothing new about the structure of the universe, whilst others have been taken aback by the lack of interest in Oyibo's calculations. Indeed, the dispute over the validity of this model has led to heated debates about the willingness of physics – a discipline dominated by white European and American mathematicians and scientists – to accept scholarship from black Africans.

The work of Oyibo was brought to my attention by the ceramic and stone sculptor Lawson Oyekan when I visited his studio in the Vosges region of eastern France. The son of a high court judge, Oyekan was born in London and raised in Nigeria, spending much of his childhood engaged in artistic activity. He demonstrated an early aptitude for drawing and painting, but also for carving, where he would produce small sculptures in granite as he sat beside female labourers, whose task was to split enormous boulders by woodfire. At school, he excelled in mathematics and applied chemistry, becoming engrossed in calculus, geometry, and the molecular structure of elements. However, his irrepressible creative streak led him on to an art foundation course in 1983 at East Ham in London, where he developed an affinity with clay. He subsequently studied at the Central School of Art and Design (1985–1988) specialising in ceramics, and then the Royal College of Art (1988–1990). As Oyekan later admitted:

> The use of clay, particularly to me, was inspired by something a bit more scientific: how to realise the mysterious capacity of clay and understand it as condensed information. Clay has all of the physical remains of the past, human, trees and everything else. I use clay to understand what is already inside, to explore the energies that appear mysterious.[146]

From this, it is clear that Oyekan's interest in clay lies in its ability to evince narratives that reach to the

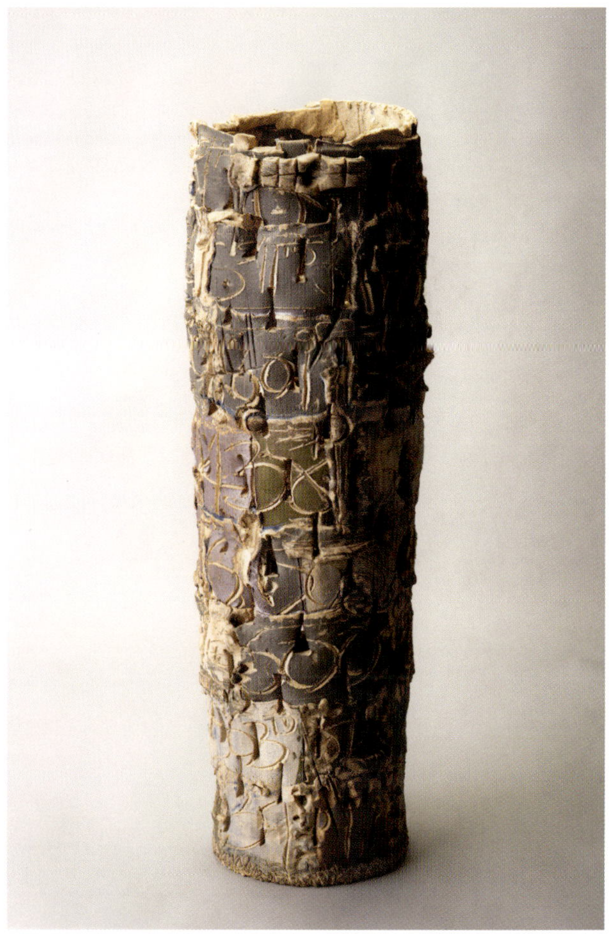

Ero Minneapolis (2006) from the *Solstice Lip Series*.

heart of who we are, where we have come from, and how we are tied to the forces that govern the universe. He establishes connections between the cerebral and aesthetic, the visceral and the scientific. In sympathy with Oyibo's GAGUT, Oyekan's orthogonal forms exhibit a kind of ceramic unified theorem, where matter is submitted to force (the potter's wheel) and the energy of mass (the heat of the kiln) to create forms that surpass the empirical.

Such unification is pursued by Oyekan in numerous ways. In his *Solstice Lip* (2006) series, works are comprised of different clays that have been rolled into slabs and collaged together, across which numbers and algebraic letters have been scored. One rather obvious reading of these works would be that they attest to Oyekan's love of mathematics. This is true, but the works are symbolic of more than this: they allude to the significance of mathematics in ancient African cultures, where a geometric understanding of the universe via the pyramid was clearly in evidence. The Pythagorean theorem – named after its apparent inventor, Pythagoras of Samos (c.570–c.495BC) – was already being utilised in ancient Egypt, where trigonometry enabled the construction of the first recorded pyramid at Saqqara in c.2630BC. Indeed, Oyibo has argued that the Nun creation myth, where a pyramid rises from the stormy waves, proves how the ancient Egyptians recognised the centrality of geometry to the comprehension of the universe.[147] Oyekan's works connect these different threads together. His sculptures assert how mathematics pre-existed Western European understanding: as with the ancient pyramids, he uses material mined from the earth for the construction of geometric monuments that allude to the contemporary mathematical modelling of the universe.

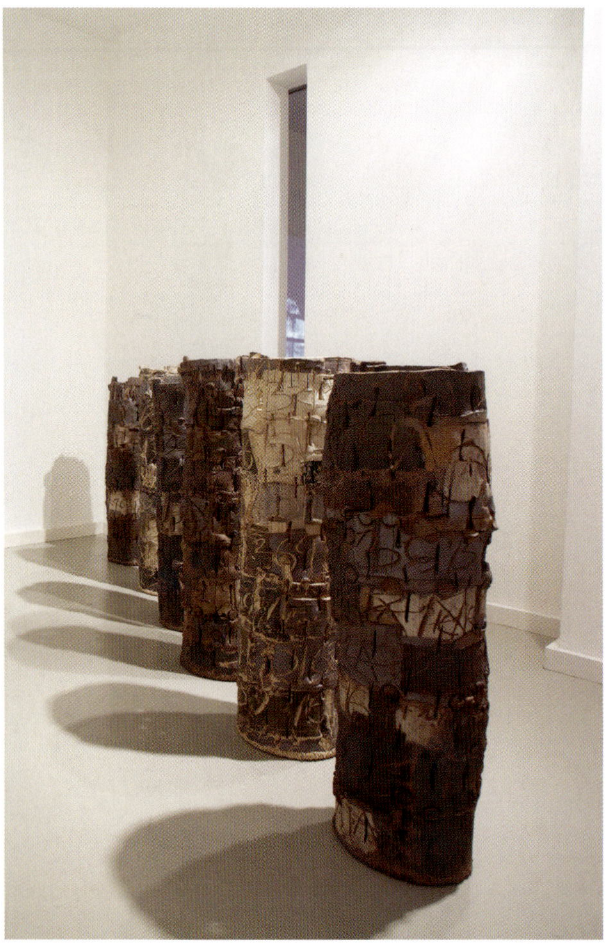

■ *Solstice Lip Series* (2006).

A compelling dynamic in Oyekan's practice is his utilisation of ceramic processes as reflexive of the idea being investigated. The centrifugal force of the wheel, for instance, connects pottery to gravitational force – the attraction that keeps us rooted to the ground in which clay is formed. Throwing on the wheel, where left and right hands must move together, is a symbol of synthesis. In *A Handful of Stratum Ore 1* (2019), as with many of Oyekan's works, the thrown clay body is punctured. This could be interpreted as symbolic of the ways in which humans puncture the ground to extract minerals. Yet, the connection between the interior of the pot and the exterior produced by its puncturing is more emblematic of elemental movement and synthesis: of light photons as they travel across surfaces, air as it weaves itself through holes, and of water as it pours through the base. In all these instances, there is the reunification of material after its passing through a ceramic membrane. Indeed, raised into the interior of the form, the base evokes an ant hill, a reminder that the ground not only disposes of the carcasses of life but is also a thriving home for life itself. The circularity of the pot thus alludes to the circle of life – death and renewal – which is conducted through the very material from which ceramics are made: the earth.

Inevitably, the symbolic meaning of these gashes is dependent on the form and tone of each work. Some pieces, such as *Coming Up For Air* (2001), present like saplings, where sudden growth is implied by a narrow base giving way to a thickening of the trunk. Yet, its height – more than six feet tall – affords the sculpture an anthropomorphic quality. Holes become membranous pores in a leathery skin, which defends a psychological interior from prying eyes. Thus, the work both asserts itself into space and shrinks away from

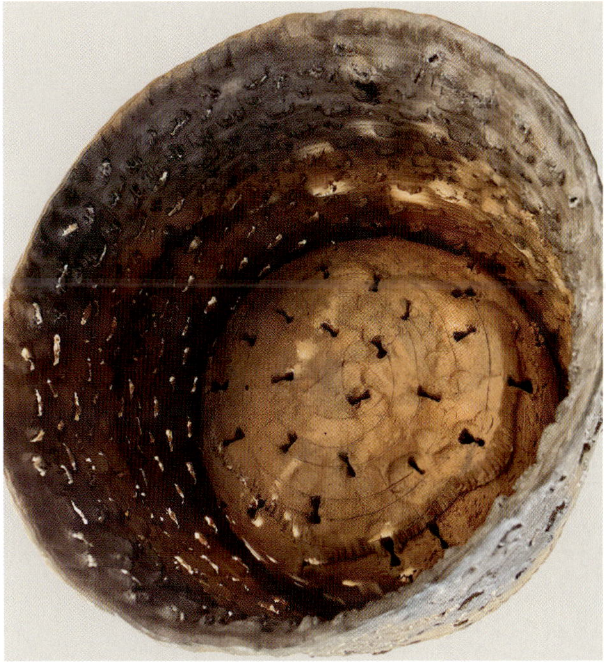

Interior of *A Handful of Stratum Ore 1* (2019).

the world, a contradictory narrative that is dependent on light, which Oyekan has knowingly deployed for expressive effect. The earthy terracotta of the sculpture reflects light, but the economical spacing of holes means that the darkened interior absorbs it. This interplay produces a feeling of interior privacy, leaving us to make assumptions about the meaning of the work based upon its title and our perception of its relevance. In this sense, the work challenges us with ourselves. It asks us to consider what we see and how, in response, we formulate value judgments. Is the artist describing the contradictory feelings of exhibiting work, of only giving us the part of himself that he wants us to see? Or is this a critical comment on the demand for psychological self-exposure in contemporary art? Oyekan's work is, like an archaeological dig, rich in narrative layers. What we read into his work reveals as much about ourselves as it does the artist. The inscription and re-inscription of meaning is a part of the expressive power of his work, a fact alluded to by his etching of shapes and letters into the surfaces of his sculptures.

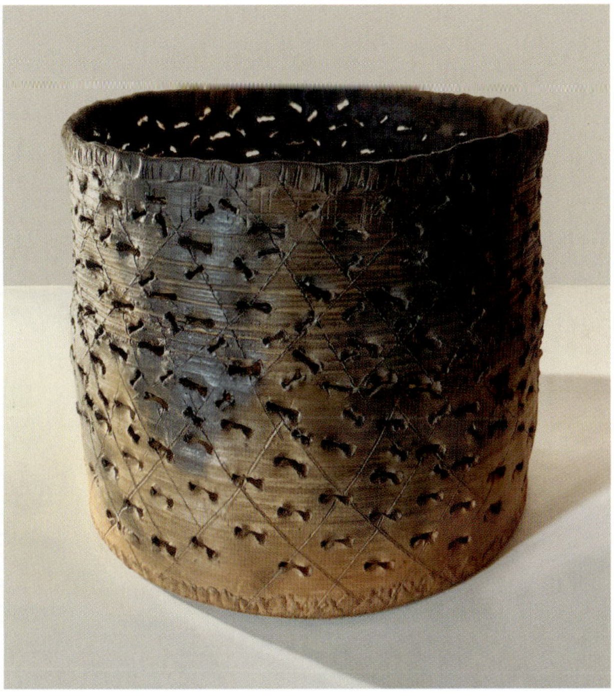

A Handful of Stratum Ore 1 (2019).

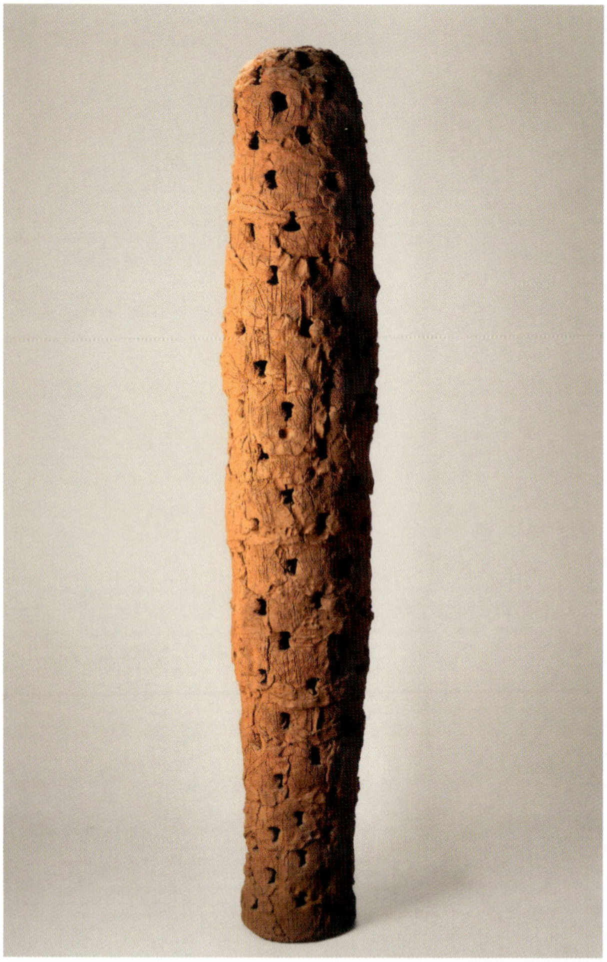

Coming Up For Air (2001).

In fact, many of Oyekan's works feature writing. In some instances, such as *Fort Ore 1* (2016), the writing is fragmentary, with only a few words legible. Here, writing signifies the patching together of multiple moments in time. Treasured memories, personal histories, passionate relationships, the zealousness of the good times, and the frustration of the bad, coalesce to be written to the exterior, and even the interior, of the work. The punctures to the body are larger and more forceful, symbolic perhaps of past injustices – individual and personal, collective and racial – that constitute the stabs of life, and the jabs of imperialism and insidious white systemic superiority. *Fort Ore 1* is concerned with defensive shielding but nevertheless reveals how we are shaped – inside and out – by our experiences. Meanwhile, *Body Undivided* (2014) features the repetition of words, many in vertical lists, such as 'collaborations', 'instinct', and 'piracy'. Perhaps these words relate to the contradictory feelings associated with acts of creation, especially the desire to collaborate, which is concomitant with a need to follow instinct even as it risks diminishing collectivism. Taken together, these words evince a strong sense of self; the need to honour one's own impulses in all situations. Indeed, the lines that divide the lists of words could be emblematic of lines in the sand that cannot be crossed.

Many of Oyekan's works are expressions of personal experience, but the exact circumstances behind the creation of each piece is not fully disclosed in the work itself. *Bonnie Charlie* (2015), for instance, may relate to the Scottish poem of the same name by Carolina Oliphant (1766–1845), in which the last Stuart heir to the English throne, Bonnie Prince Charlie,

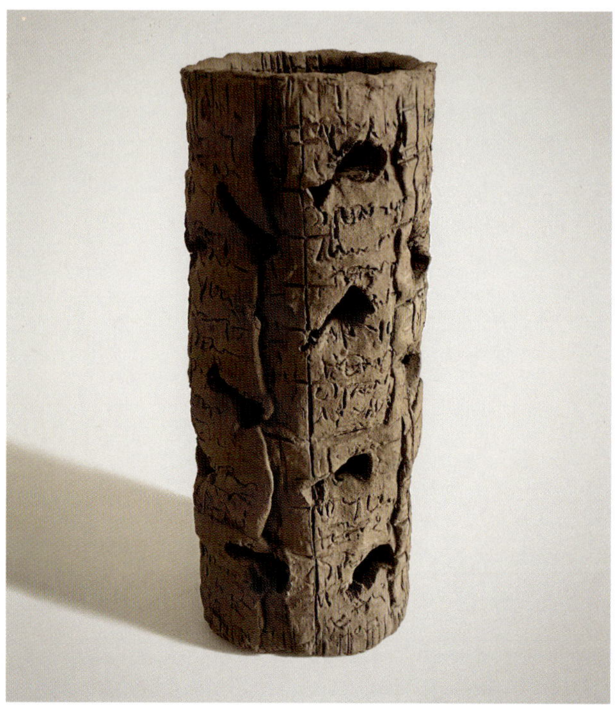

Fort Ore 1 (2016).

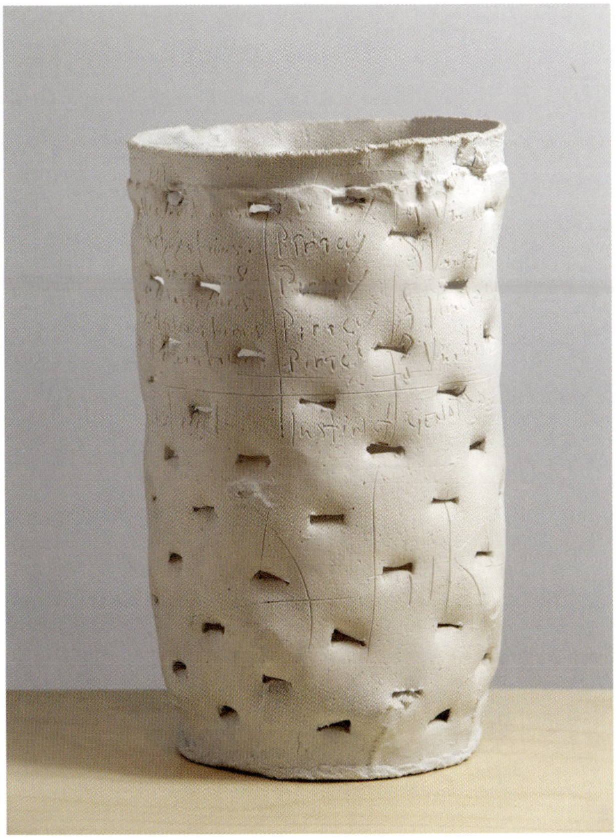

Body Undivided (2014).

flees to France from Scotland following his defeat at the Battle of Culloden in 1746. The relationship between the work and poem is at first unclear; it seems unlikely that *Bonnie Charlie* is a testimony to historical events. Perhaps the work refers to the poem via the line 'Will ye no' come back again?', which is repeated several times in the poem, though it does not appear on the work itself. The two small sculptural pots then symbolise the uncertain finality of a separation. Will one ever be reconciled with the other, who is intent on emigration to France?

When we met, Oyekan told me of a serious illness he had experienced, where a benign tumour eventually required the removal of his kidney and a large part of his intestinal tract. Yet, as a result of careful diet management, Oyekan returned to full health; his intestines regenerated, and his body adapted to functioning with one kidney. *Eda: Abu-di, Ore: (Ideure-Indestructible Stomach) 1* (2014) appears to relate to this difficult time. The pot is both 'complete' and 'incomplete', the gashes redolent of the artist's compromised health, but the solidity of the base capturing his desire to continue with his work; his 'indestructability'. Of course, as pots are concerned with the consumption of food, the form is reflexive of its subject matter. Indeed, the roundedness of the pot has a geometric affinity with the tubular construction of the stomach. Such a reading transforms the holes into metaphors of damaged intestines, whilst compressed inlets in the clay wall are evocative of both the belly button and the intrusive slicing of the surgeon's knife and the surgical stapling of skin. Oyekan's ingenuity as a sculptor means that the same expressive elements can be read in numerous coalescing ways.

Whilst some of Oyekan's works are developed from the form of the pot, others are enclosed vessel forms that are entirely reliant on the interplay

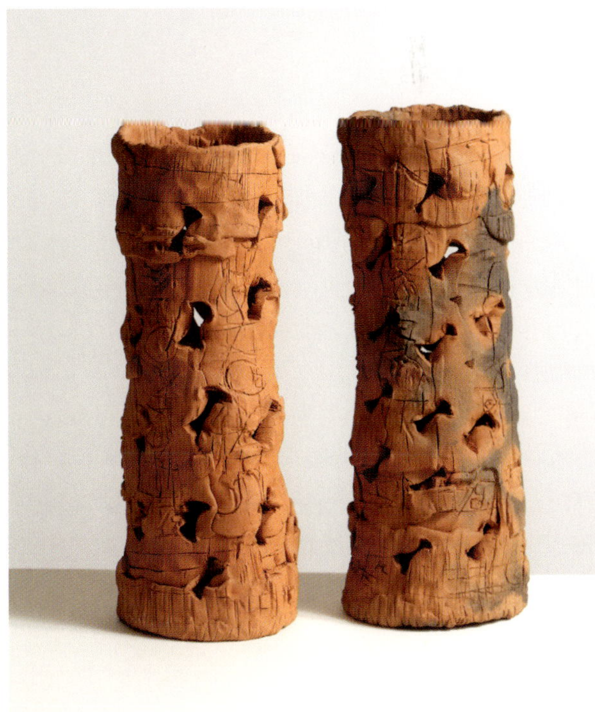

Bonnie Charlie (2015).

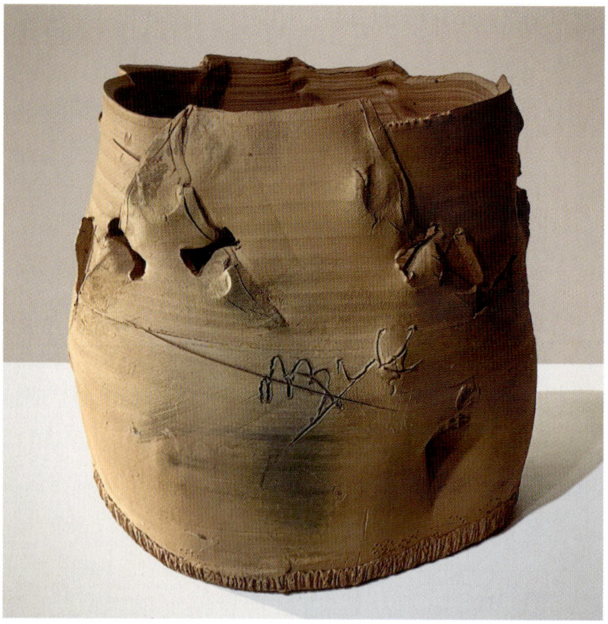

Eda: Abu-di, Ore: (Ideure-Indestructible Stomach) 1 (2014).

between interior and exterior space for expression. *Da' Pupa* from the *Autonomous Resonator Series* (2005), for example, was inspired by the shifting textures and colours of a large crowd which Oyekan observed from a high platform whilst waiting for a TV interview. For me, these forms also evoke seed pods or insect hives, the ceramic wall of the vessel once again a defence from prying intruders. Given the title, the pairing of forms invites speculation as to their resonance. Resonance refers to sound, the ceramic enclosure serving to amplify any sound waves produce to the interior. How do these forms then speak to each other? Both are produced from a collaging of different clays: the marks left by the pressure of the artist's own hand in pummelling the form together offers a textural counterpoint to the scored lines that run across, down, and in circular formations across each plane. In this way, the vessels echo each other. Yet, each has its own proportions. The height of each vessel affects the incline of the curve of the body, which in turn affects the roundedness of the upper section. These vessels are geometrically engineered but individualised in expression. They stand as metaphors for understanding and misunderstanding; our ability to make connections (resonances) across barriers, but also our clumsiness in reconciling difference.

Oyekan's desire to harness the different properties of clay has led to a rich body of work that celebrates the intrinsic properties of his chosen material. His work in stone and in clay may seem divergent, but as he pointed out to me when we met, both are produced by geological force. His forms allow the beauty of matter to speak, whether it be the expansive planes of a sculpture created from one material, or the arresting patchworks produced by a conglomeration of clays. As *Battlefield Ore, BDSVWWI Superstrata Amalgam 1* (2017) demonstrates, Oyekan reveals the innate splendour of all kinds of earth by

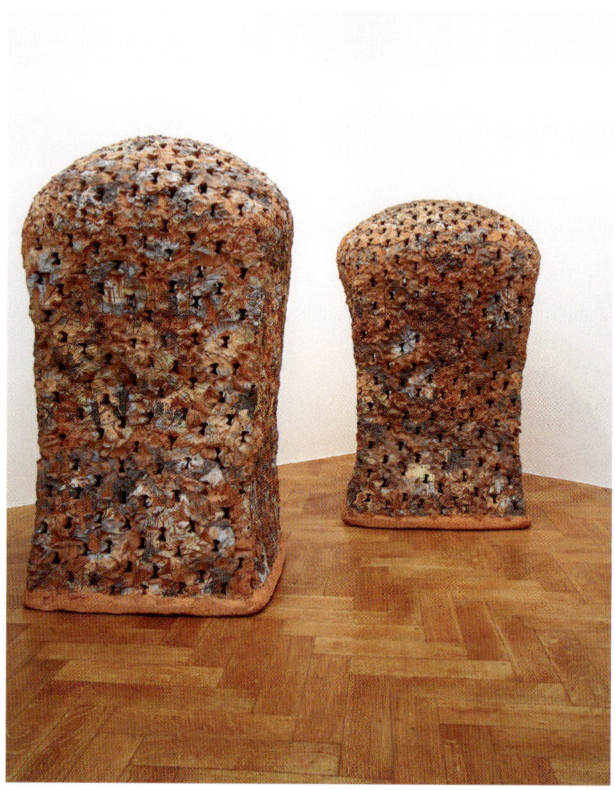

Da' Pupa from the *Autonomous Resonator Series* (2005).

submitting it to pressure (the hand on clay) and heat (the effect of the kiln). The production of ceramics by Oyekan can thus be regarded as an extension of the natural geological processes that produce clay itself, whilst the centrifugal force of the potter's wheel is simply one iteration of Oyibo's unifying principle: that all matter moves. Oyekan's work convincingly situates ceramics amidst this general unified theorem.

The circle as a geometric totem of oscillation and movement is also one of cyclical interconnection. Oyekan's works unify the material with the immaterial, the permanent with the transitory, acts of memorialisation with the immediacy of the visceral, process with completion, and life with death. From this, Oyekan's sculptures assert the need for humanity to express itself on a more equal footing. To do so, we must remember and account for past injustice – mark the scars – to move towards a new, more equitable, future. Indeed, before we went to his studio, Oyekan drove me to La Nécorpole Nationale de La Fontenelle, a First World War cemetery in Ban de Sapt, just a few miles from the German border. Containing the remains of nearly 1,100 soldiers, it is a beautiful hilltop cemetery, situated amidst a landscape scarred by trenches that have recently become maintained as an informal part of the memorial. The stone centrepiece, by the sculptor Émile-Just Bachelet (1892–1981), stands as a monument 'aux vaillants défenseurs du sol vosgien' – 'to the valiant defenders of the Vosgien soil'. Oyekan explained that he often went to the cemetery 'to feel'. He did not say what he felt, and I did not think it appropriate to ask. What did I feel? Of course, one is confronted by death, murder, and loss, but also solace, solitude, and peace. The trees moving in the wind were a reminder of the transience of life; the gentle rustling of leaves

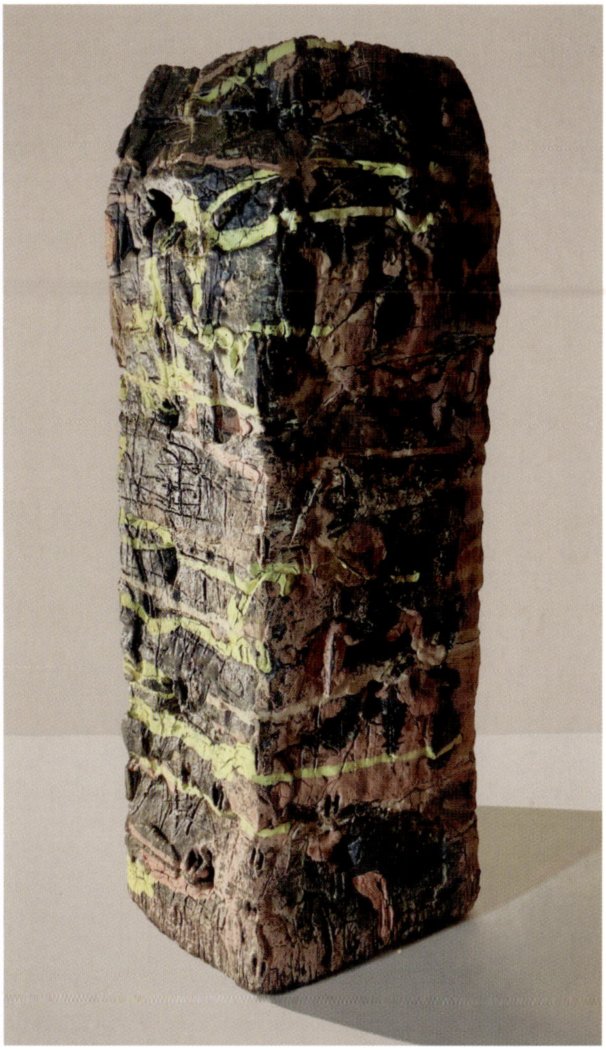

Battlefield Ore, BDSVWWI Superstrata Amalgam 1 (2017).

a stark contrast to the stillness of the stone crosses, those interminable Christian symbols of remembrance and physical decay. For me, La Fontenelle unified the past with the present, the dead with the living, the forgotten with the remembered, and stillness with movement. Looking again at *Battlefield Ore, BDSVWWI Superstrata Amalgam 1*, I cannot help but think that such interconnectedness also lies at the heart of Oyekan's powerful work.

Akiko Hirai
Nothing Comes from Nothing

みな人のひかりをあうぐ空の月のどかに照せ雲がくれせで
O moon in the sky whose light is sought by one and all:
shine gently and do not hide behind the clouds[148]

Historically, the moon holds an important place in Japanese culture. According to Shintō belief, the moon was deemed a male 'god' (*kami*, 神) and named Tsukuyomi-no-mikoto (月読命), shortened in old Japanese to '*tsuku*', and which has since evolved into the modern Japanese word for the moon: *tsuki* (月). The Tsukimi (月見) 'moon viewing' festival is still celebrated each full autumn moon, which, derived from autumn festivals for abundant harvests, is marked by decorative displays of pampas grass, the reading of poetry, and the consumption of special foods. In Shingon Buddhism (真言宗), a form of esoteric Buddhism that arrived in Japan in the Early Heian Period (794–950), the full moon is often cited in poetry as

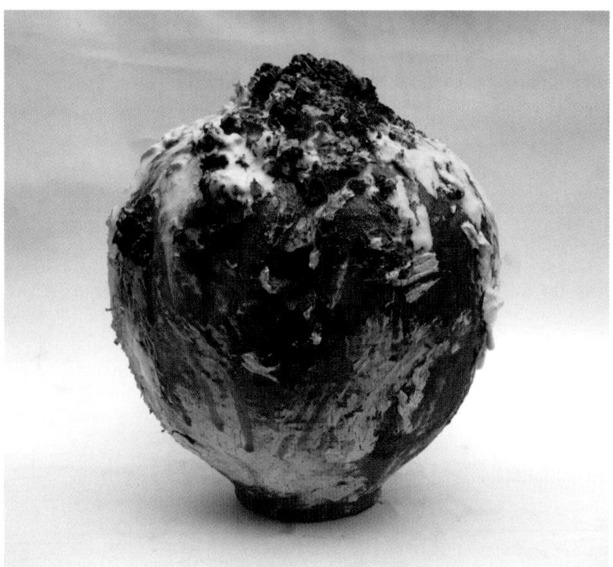

The Moon (2012).

a symbol of enlightenment.[149] Indeed, the opening lines of this chapter come from a poem written by The Great Kamo Priestess Senshi (大斎院, 964–1035), in which the moon, construed as a Buddha, is entreated to shine for all eternity.[150]

Akiko Hirai is best known for her instantly recognisable moon jar forms. This series of work was initially inspired by her encounter with the 'Leach-Rie' Joseon Dynasty moon jar held in the collections of the British Museum.[151] In conversation with the author, Hirai expressed admiration for the imperfections of this work, the particles of ash that had become attached to the jar in the kiln, the cracking of the glaze, and the small chip to the rim. These aspects, Hirai told me, meant the pot now bore the scars of its own experience; it was honest about the nature of its creation, the scratches and chips to the surface recording its journey through time. Indeed, ceramic is often considered to be one of the most enduring materials, as evidenced by the seemingly endless exhumation of pottery shards from archaeological sites. Yet, as Susan Buys and Victoria Oakley have highlighted, this 'state of *permanence* requires some qualifying: the permanence only applies to the material itself and not the object it forms.'[152] Pots are not a stable form; they are vulnerable to breakage, shock, discolouration, and wear.

Some of the earlier moon jars made by Hirai were discarded because she considered them too perfect. She felt that their cleanliness and perfection lacked resonance, affording the work no sense of identity. As her exploration of the form continued, applied 'imperfections' became more emphatic, developing into a range of expressive tonalities. In the most notable examples, the moon jar is no longer recognisable in its smooth classical shape; the form has become little more than a base for the sculptural application of material and glaze. But for what purpose?

To better understand the significance of Hirai's approach, not only to the moon jar but to her general philosophy, it is worth exploring some of the fundamentals ascribed to Japanese culture. Animism – the existence of unseen spirits alongside those living in the mortal world – remains important to Japanese spiritual thought. As Fabio Rambelli notes, 'to many Japanese, their country has a split ontological outlook: on the one hand, there is Japan as the concrete place of their everyday lives; on the other, an invisible realm populated by all kinds of presences: ghosts, spirits, ancestors, gods...'.[153] Although animism is often popularly tied to the Shintō belief that all natural phenomena are inhabited by spirits (*kami*), recent research has demonstrated that animism took hold in the Japanese consciousness only in the Tokugawa Period (1600–1868), as popular belief in spirits entering Buddhist nirvana began to wane.[154] It was also at this time that the important social ideologies of *mura* (村) 'community', and *ie* (家) 'family', were commonly adopted. As Annette Marfording has observed, nationalist Japanese scholars:

> often represent two aspects of Japanese society during the Tokugawa period as prototypes of modern Japanese society: the village community (*mura*) and the family system (*ie*). In the village community, rice cultivation and irrigation necessitated a high degree of cooperation and loyalty to the group. The argument is that present cultural values such as harmony, consensus, and loyalty to the group originate from the *mura*. Under the family system, the head of the household had supreme authority and control over the members of his household. Their individual interests were sacrificed in the interests of the family as a whole. *Ie* is represented as the origin of cultural values such as social hierarchy, group-orientation, benevolent paternalism, and familism in Japanese labor relations.[155]

Although Marfording subsequently challenges the romantic orthodoxy of this account by arguing that

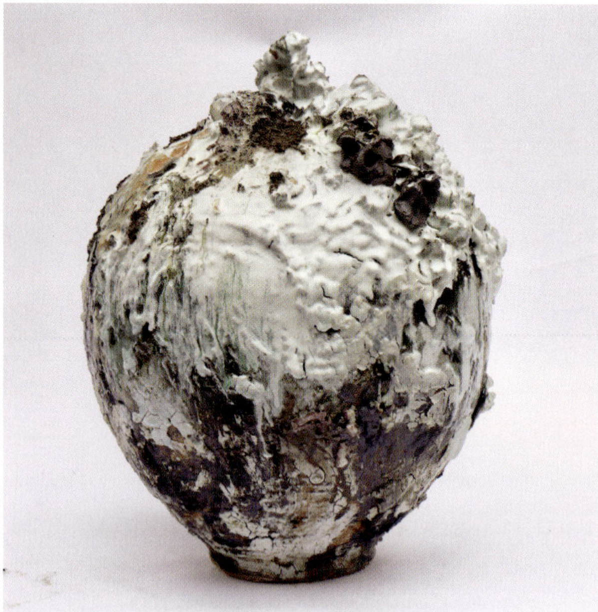

The Moon Jar (2016).

the ruling Tokugawa shogunate were in fact implementing neo-Confucian ideas to maintain social order,[156] 'community' and 'family' have nevertheless remained significant to the fabric of contemporary Japanese society.

These underlying philosophies are also captured in Hirai's work. During a visit to her studio, the artist explained to me how she considered her moon jars to be representative of the human body, its emotions, psychologies, senescence, resilience, and fragility. When we are born, we are free of burden and responsibility. As we grow older, we become marked by our experiences and weighed down by the baggage we must carry. There is, therefore, a sense of animism to each jar; like the poem quoted at the opening of this chapter, the moon jar represents the unseen elements of a human emotional psyche, perhaps even the soul. Hirai works hard to make each moon jar distinctive. In some, the glaze is runnier, leaving a strong sense of rapid movement down the side of the jar. In others, the glaze has more viscosity, leading to greater accumulation of material. Material might be assembled around the rim, or it could be strategically placed around the sides, necessitating the propping up of the pot in the kiln. Some jars are shiny, others are matt. This differentiated approach empowers each jar to express specific traits, from the stoic to the nervous, the methodical to the panic-stricken (the reading is very much in the eye of the beholder). Observing the jars as part of a series brings out these similarities and differences more readily. Indeed, they are particularly effective when viewed as a group – as a 'family' or 'community' if you will – of works, each using shared aesthetic vocabularies to present different emotional and psychological states. Perhaps this explains why collectors are so hungry to purchase numerous examples.

Although Hirai told me that she makes moon jars as expressive of human experience, I also consider them to be self-portraits that capture the thoughts and feelings of the artist herself at a given moment in time. Of course, all works of art are in some sense autobiographical, for experience is always behind the impulse to create. Yet, as a potter who was born in Japan but has nevertheless lived in London since graduating from her ceramics course in 2003, there is a sense of acculturation in these works. In the social sciences, acculturation can mean 'the cultural and psychological changes that result from the contact between cultural groups, including the attitudes and behaviours that are generated.'[157] To change between cultural contexts is to amass new experiences, modes of being, and to shift, mutate, and hybridise identities. The layering of material on the moon jars suggests that surface accumulation might symbolise Hirai's own acculturation, a process that has enriched rather than diminished aesthetic expression.

Whilst I was at her studio, I asked Hirai, quite bluntly, whether she minds being called 'a Japanese potter'? She paused and looked a little awkward. 'It's a label that I work with', she admitted gauchely. Perhaps such ambivalence stems from her desire to find her own artistic voice, something that was unlikely to happen had she been apprenticed to a potter in Japan. In such apprenticeships, the master is followed unquestioningly, and the pupil must figure out the philosophy behind the master's actions based upon their own observations. Explanations are rarely forthcoming. Such modes of teaching relate back to the philosophy of *ie*, 'family', described above, where the individual's needs are supressed to the supreme authority of the master. Hirai's formative experiences in the Japanese education system left her feeling that an alternative means of accessing ceramic training was the only way for her to develop the confidence to practice. Thus, in her mid-twenties, Hirai came to Britain, and after a period back in Japan, returned to London to undertake her ceramic training when she was almost thirty.

Hirai's ambivalent relationship with Japanese ceramic tradition might lie in the fact that she works in a style known as *getemono* (下手物), which translates as 'low-quality product', a 'strange thing', or a 'strange combination'. As Hirai once wrote:

> Soetsu Yanagi, the founder of the Arts and Crafts movement [in Japan], recategorized everyday utensils and unrefined handmade objects from *Getemono* (meaning 'second rate' object) to *Mingei* (meaning 'Folk Art') in order to remove any negative connotation from such things. (I personally like the word *Getemono*, and prefer to call my pots *Getemono* instead of *wabi-sabi*). Even among Japanese people there is a negative connotation in these objects. It is a reductionist idea, as in opposition to refined objects, all unrefined things are bad.[158]

By embracing the term *getemono* as defiantly as she does, one senses something of a rebellion against Japanese aesthetic hierarchies. Certainly, the success she has achieved in Europe would have been

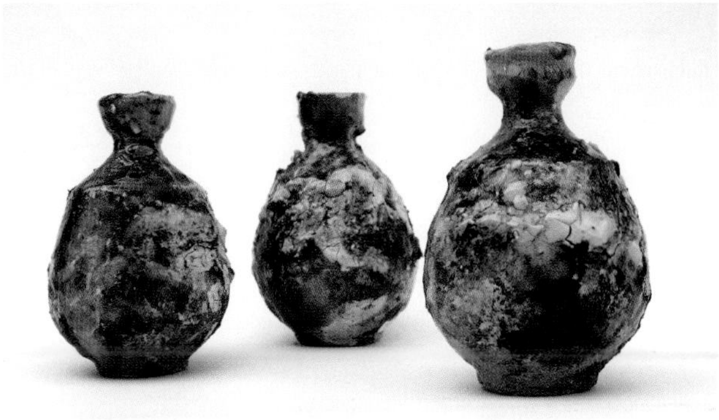

Sake Bottles (2009).

far harder to accomplish had she stayed in Japan. Although this success is important (not least in enabling her to be financially sustained by her practice), it was by no means guaranteed. As she later wrote, 'I was, and maybe am, naive, gullible and clumsy, so I have acquired a lot of 'marks' in my life, like my pots.'[159] Self-expression was the primary determinant in studying ceramics in the UK, and then setting up her studio in London, even if such an undertaking was financially risky. She is, perhaps, a Japanese potter only in the sense that she spent the first twenty or so years of her life in Japan. It is inevitable that aspects of her practice will emerge from the culture she was surrounded by as a child. Yet, to label her as 'a Japanese potter' in a rather fatuous way is to gloss over the complexity of her life and of her practice. Her approach is more individual, more hybridic, than such pejorative labels allow.

To this end, much of her work is inspired by European rather than Japanese aesthetics. Her *Still Life* series of bottles, for instance, respond to the work of Giorgio Morandi (1890–1964), whose oil paintings depicted thoughtful groupings of pots. Yet, the real impulse behind Hirai's *Still Life* bottles stems from the location of her London studio, which is nestled in the particularly multicultural neighbourhood of Dalston. Each bottle represents a person of different gender or race. When they are

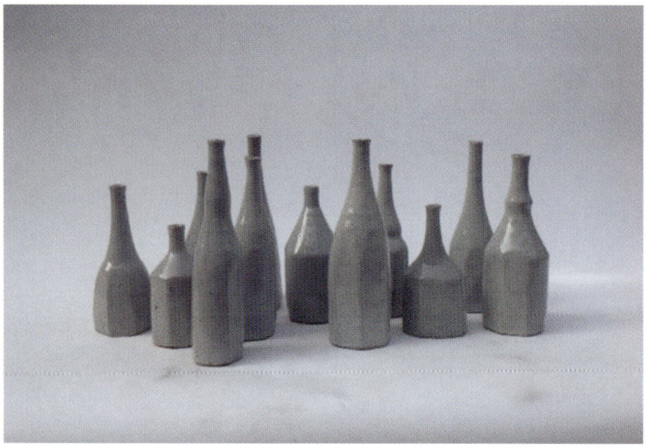

Still Life Bottles (2012).

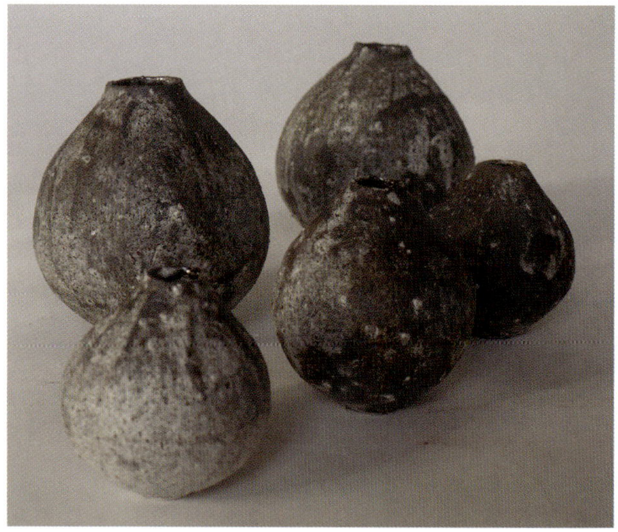

Bulb Vases (2013).

placed together, these entities co-exist as a celebration of the multicultural urban city. These works might, in some sense, be a product of the Japanese notion of *mura* 'community', but it is the multiculturalism of twenty-first century London, rather than Tōkyō, that is the primary stimulus. In this sense, the *Still Life* bottles are a reconfiguration of the Japanese aesthetic emphasis on capturing the physical environment in art. Hirai captures not the blossom of a cherry tree or the breaking of a wave, but passers-by on a busy metropolitan street.

This is not to suggest that Hirai has turned her back on nature. Far from it. Some forms are inspired by plant life, such as the shape of poppy seeds or plant bulbs (the latter evidenced in the series of *Bulb Vases* reproduced here). Surface textures reference natural phenomenon, such as tree bark, or more ephemeral experiences, such as spring morning dew, or small pools of rainwater. That this aesthetic is caught in a myriad of beautiful utilitarian forms – vases, tea bowls, and plates – suggests tacit recognition that functional pottery can be poetic and life-affirming. Food and water are essential to all forms of life. Hirai's pots are a reminder of how the transient experience of taste connects humanity to the rest of the natural world as perceived in fleeting sensations.

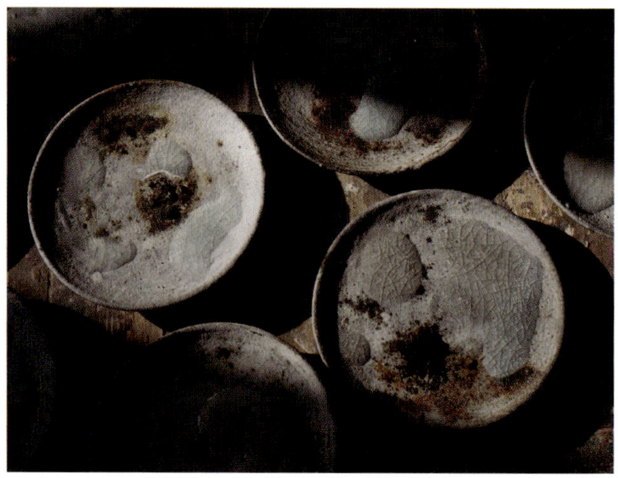

Rain Drop Plates (2010).

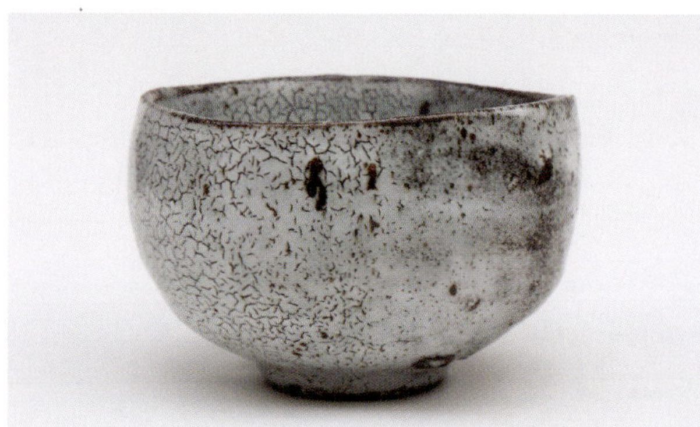

Teabowl (2021).

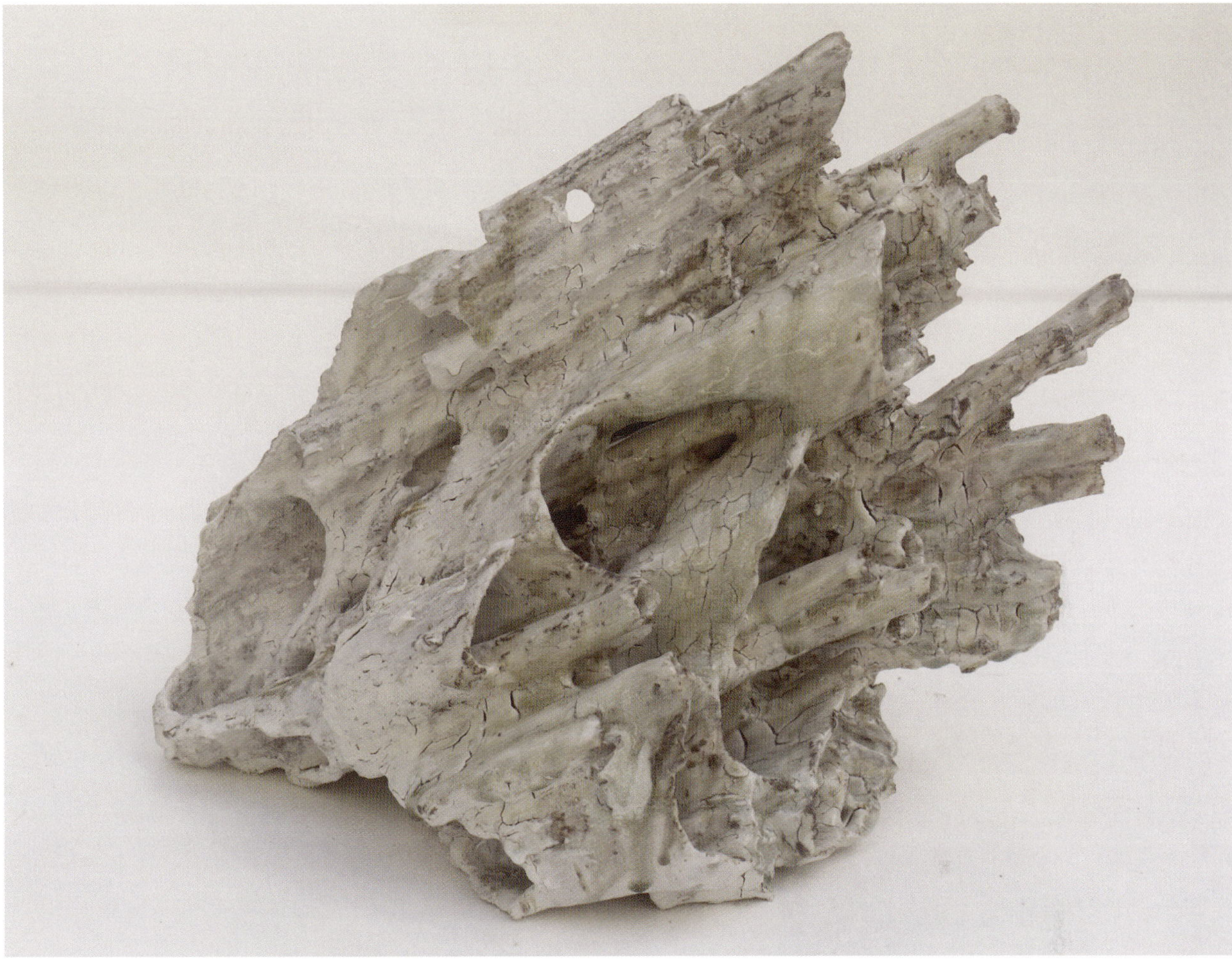

■ *Abandoned Mulberry Wood* (2019).

Yet, Hirai's exploration of the natural work has also produced a series of highly innovative sculptures. *Abandoned Mulberry Wood No Leaves* (2019) is a ceramic evocation of the same subject. The abundance of life that is the substance of her more functional forms is here replaced by a lifeless husk. These sculptures capture the inevitability of death and thus the transience of life. The contemplation of death is an important aspect of Buddhism, as evidenced in the existence of the *Kusōzu* (九相図) tradition of art in Japan, which has existed since at least the late thirteenth century. *Kusōzu*, or 'Pictures of the Nine Stages [of a Decaying Corpse]', detailed the different stages of the body in death – from recent death through putrefaction to skeletal remains – as a means to evidence the impurity of the mortal world.[160] Although Hirai's *Abandoned Mulberry Wood No Leaves* is nothing like the graphic depictions of a rotting corpse found in the *Kusōzu*, the purity of this skeletal sculpture suggests a purification of life after death. Despite the subject matter, these works are celebratory rather than morbid *memento mori*. Architectural complexity is explored as a thing of wonder; the skeletal remains are only present by virtue of extinguished life, a fact to be celebrated rather than mourned. In this sense, like her *Bulb Vases* and *Rain*

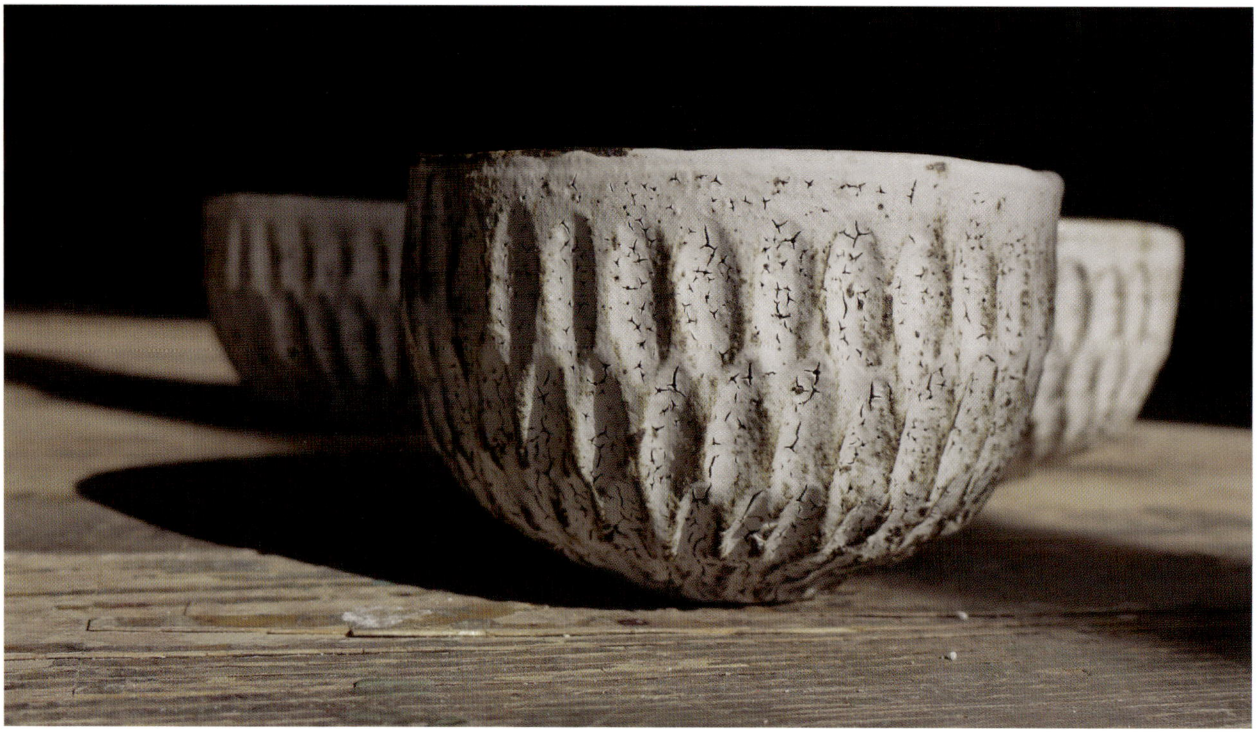

Kohiki Bowls (2012).

Drop Plates, this series of sculptures are observations of transience.

All of Hirai's work exhibit a lyricism, including her *Kohiki* standard ware. Imported into Japan from Korea in the sixteenth century, *Kohiki* is a technique where the clay body of a pot (usually rich in iron) is covered in white slip and then a translucent glaze. This style of pottery found favour with the warrior class (for whom tea was a status symbol) and became associated with the tea ceremony. Hirai's approach to this technique is, as would be expected, an individual one. She applies translucent glaze only to the interior, leaving exposed the white (or grey) glaze to the exterior. This produces a slightly rough, coarse texture that accentuates the sense of touch, and which contrasts with the smoothness of the interior. This approach to *Kohiki* exhibits a perceptive consideration of utility, not only in terms of practicality but also sensation. Like the tea ceremony itself, they highlight tea drinking as a phenomenon of sight, taste, touch, and smell.

In many ways, Hirai's standard ware exemplifies her practice. It places emphasis on the transient moment – the experience of drinking tea has equivalence with the sensation of rain soaking the skin, of observing the decaying bark from a tree, or even fleetingly passing strangers on a busy street in London. To focus on such transience is, in fact, to contemplate the Buddhist conception of the emptiness of all things. For nothing will last. As the Heart Sutra (*Shin Gyō*, 心経), the best known of all the Buddhist sutras – including in Japan, espouses:

Matter is not different from emptiness. Emptiness is not different from matter.
Matter is emptiness. Emptiness is matter.
So too are sensation, recognition, volition, and consciousness.
色不異空。空異不色。
色即是空。空即是色。
受想行識。亦復如是。

Rather tellingly, Hirai created a series of ceramic heart sculptures, *Broken Heart Syndrome* (2022). Produced from a mould, each heart was individualised with different glazes. At first, these realistic sculptures seem at odds with the rest of her more poetic and allusive output. Yet, given the above, they occupy similarly allusive territory. More than the realistic depiction of the heart in the corporeal sense, these are symbols of the transience of life, and our obsession with the material world.

When I met the artist in her studio, we talked about the ways in which her work was a product of her experiences. 'Nothing comes from nothing,' she explained. Having lived in Japan for the majority of the first three decades of her life, Japanese social and religious codes have inevitably shaped her as an artist. This does not find expression in conventional traditions of Japanese pottery, however. Her training in British institutions – firstly by studying ceramics at Harrow, and then product design at Central St. Martins – has enabled her to explore her own sense of self without the restrictions of apprenticeship. Indeed, Hirai utilises both studio ceramics and product design in her practice. By creating particular treatments of form with certain constraints, she is able to produce highly individualised work in an economically sustainable way, and at price points that range from tens of pounds to many thousands. To achieve such success at a relatively late starting age, and in a country on the other side of the world from where she was born, is no mean feat. And just in case you thought that Hirai's maxim 'nothing comes from nothing' was evolved from a Buddhist sutra, well, appearances can be deceiving. It was Aristotle, in *Physics*, who observed that 'nothing can come out of what does not exist'.[161]

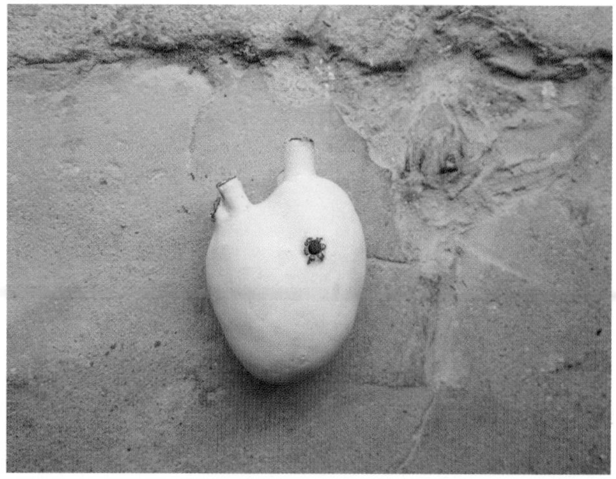

■ *Broken Heart Syndrome* (2022).

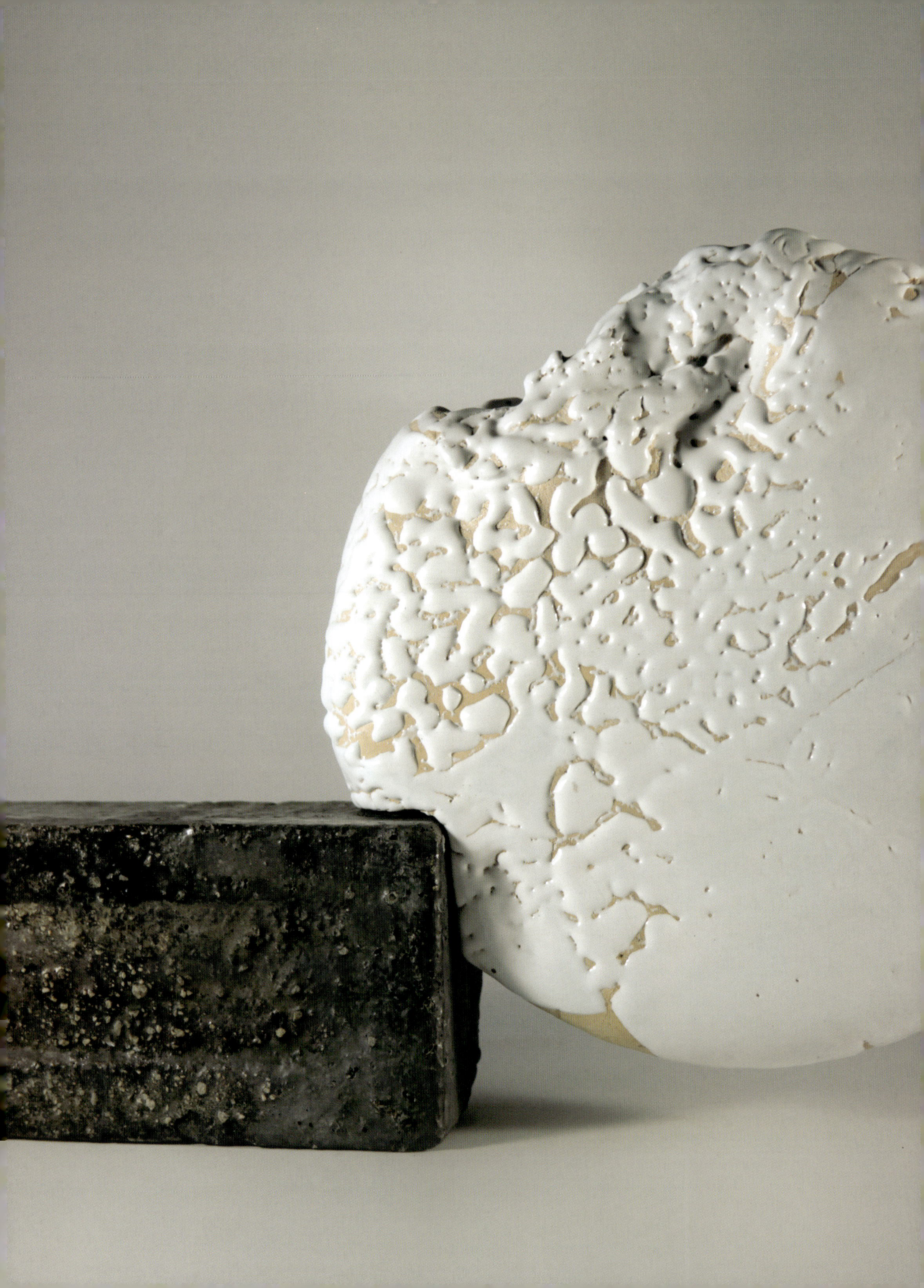

Colliding Worlds

Tim Copsey Tableau-ware

> Film, photography and installation art all share aspects of the temporal and the figural (those aspects related to form and representation). They are doubled arts in that sense, requiring a temporality of creation and a temporality of viewing which do not participate in the same framework.[162]

The moon undulates as clouds drive across at speed. Soft moonlight shines on a spray of white flowers, which sway gently in the breeze. A sea of leaves rustle, like rippling waves, as the wind brushes past them. A group of tiny white flowers peer from behind shielding fronds; even the moonlight seems to make these delicate blooms recoil. A shiny dark rock hilting with foliage comes into view. An arm reaches through the darkness to place a large frond into the arrangement. This rock – actually a vase – is rotated on a wheel. Another lighter vase, shielded by the first, is revealed. It is, in fact, this vase that contains the cuttings. In the final image, the vase seems to symbolise the moon itself, whilst the life and inevitable death of cuttings from nocturnal blooms speak to its waxing and waning.

The above is a description of a short film from a series entitled *Serving Suggestions* by ceramicist and filmmaker Tim Copsey. Although these two practices might appear antithetical, both are constituted by methods of production: the material of subject and form, shaping, editing, distributing, and showing. The series *Serving Suggestions*, playfully developed from illustrational directives on food packaging, draws connections between the landscape of the Peak District and Copsey's own pottery. Recalling something of the documentary style of Patrick Kieler, the tableau imagery in Copsey's films offer a poetic take on natural phenomena, and how it can be reflected, even housed, in the pots he makes. These films do more than assert a simple connection between Copsey's pots and his surrounding landscape, however. They

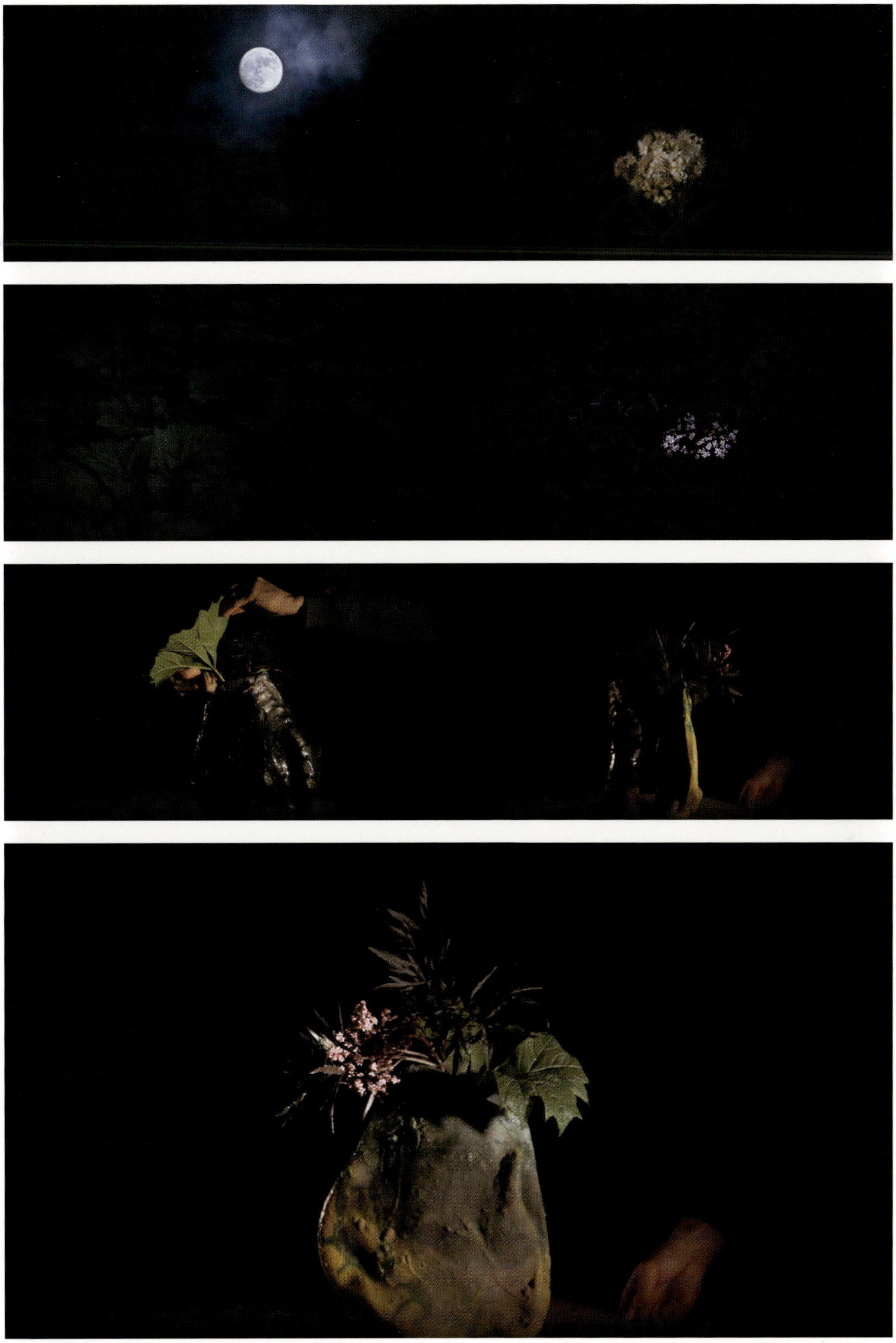

Stills from the short film *No.3 Serving Suggestion: Moon* (2020).

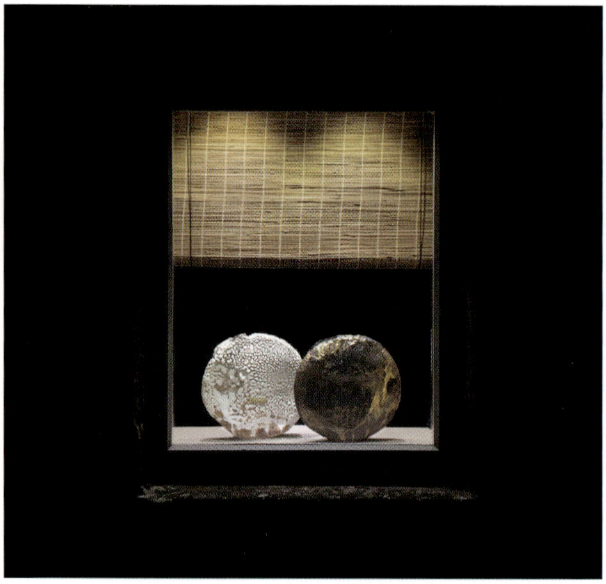

The Eclipse (2021).

also reveal how his pots are themselves visual metaphors for his own experience of the landscape.

Such imagery is most obviously discerned in Copsey's circular *Blossom Vases*, which are press-moulded to give them a uniform shape. The form is used as a base canvas to be altered as Copsey sees fit. Whilst this technique offers an economically viable process to produce work, it also facilitates the creation of groups where ideas mutate across forms. In discussion, Copsey described this approach as being in keeping with the maintenance of drystone walls in the Peak District. With so many walls requiring attention, Copsey observed a lack of preciousness about the cutting and fitting of capstones by stonemasons. Despite this unfussy method, when observed as a series, the capstones have strong aesthetic appeal. Their arrangement in sequence enables a stronger appreciation of formal similarity and difference.

Interestingly, a series of scenes in a film is also described as a 'sequence', which creates meaning from the careful juxtaposition of images through editing. Indeed, the pioneer of film montage, the Soviet filmmaker Sergei Eisenstein (1898–1948), wrote of the significance of '*emotional* combinations, not only with the visible elements of the shots, but chiefly with chains of psychological associations. *Association montage*. As a means for pointing up a situation emotionally.'[163] Shots that might appear disparate, exploring divergent narrative themes or visual ideas, are edited into a sequence which the viewer rationalises into a coherent narrative. It is the juxtaposed relationship between shots, rather than the content of the shots per se, that produces a psychologically and emotionally charged sequence. Copsey's short *Serving Suggestions* films are dependent upon montage for the creation of meaning: the juxtaposition of the tableau-like shot of the moon in the sky with the white flowers in the darkened leaves draws a visual parallel, establishing causal associations between the two. It does not require much of a leap to apply these ideas to his *Blossom Vases* when they are arranged in a sequence. In the two works constituting *The Eclipse* (2021), there is a light and a dark vase; the 'moon', and its eclipse by 'the sun'. The spatial relationship between the two works suggests that the 'moon' is either rescinding or emerging from behind the darker 'sun', the light from the latter too bright to be seen by the naked eye. Like a tableau from a film, it is the relationship between these two pots that generates meaning.

Such juxtapositions are centrally important to Copsey's aesthetic. In *Levelling Up* (2022) and *Moon* (2021), the rounded forms are placed next to pieces of brick. In part, this could reflect Copsey's formative years, which were spent in the brick-working community of Hollins Green, near Warrington in Cheshire. The proximity of the Rixton Claypits meant clay was locally sourced, establishing a close local connection between clay as a natural resource and its use in constructing houses. These works express symbiosis, where the industrial and the natural, the urban and the rural, are intertwined, if uncomfortably. There is also, perhaps, something of the decline of manufacturing in Britain as it has gravitated towards a post-industrial economy. Nowhere is this clearer than in Stoke-on-Trent, where flora and fauna increasingly impede upon the fabric of abandoned potteries. Alternatively, perhaps these works serve as a reminder that the romantic idyll of the countryside all too often airbrushes out the existence of cities, towns, and villages, upon which the local economy depends. Indeed, the centre of Manchester is only thirty miles away from the Peak District National Park. Yet, the Rixton Claypits mentioned above are now in disuse and the local council has designated the area as a nature reserve. Land harvested for raw materials to make bricks has since been returned to nature. These works seem to encapsulate this awkward sense of human give and take with the natural world.

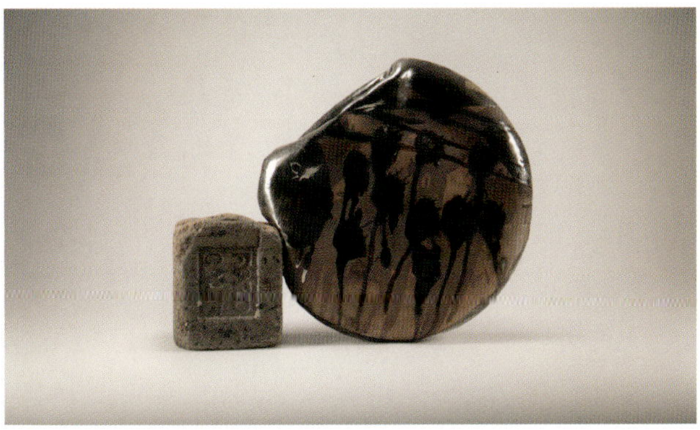

Levelling Up (2022).

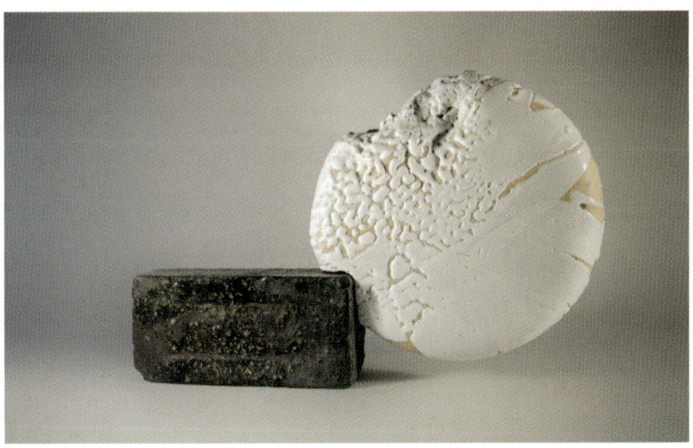

Moon (2021).

If *Levelling Up* and *Moon* convey a sense of the urban bleed into the rural, Copsey's *Tokkuri* bottles at first suggest the opposite, that the rural can be brought into the urban. The pot can be interpreted as a symbol of the man-made, making the attachment of what appears to be a rock emblematic of nature's willingness to cling to whatever humans throw at it, be it urban sprawls or the carving up of land for the purposes of farming. Yet, Copsey's work is more complex than this binary suggests. His *Tokkuri* – which, according to Japanese popular myth, were named after the glugging sound, akin to the word '*tokku*', they make when pouring – blur this divide, constructing the entire work as emblematic of an experience of the landscape. Landscapes may themselves be viewed as kinds of 'containers': our experience and aesthetic appreciation of landscape is almost always framed by man-made structures, whether they are stone walls, roads, paths, hedgerows, or gates. Decisions around the placement, material, and form of these man-made elements are informed by the very landscape its crosses – the peaks, rivers, shorelines, and forests. Copsey's work does not, therefore, pit the urban against the rural; rather, it documents co-dependency, of human activities informed by, rather than working against, the land. His pots are topographical sculptures that express journeying

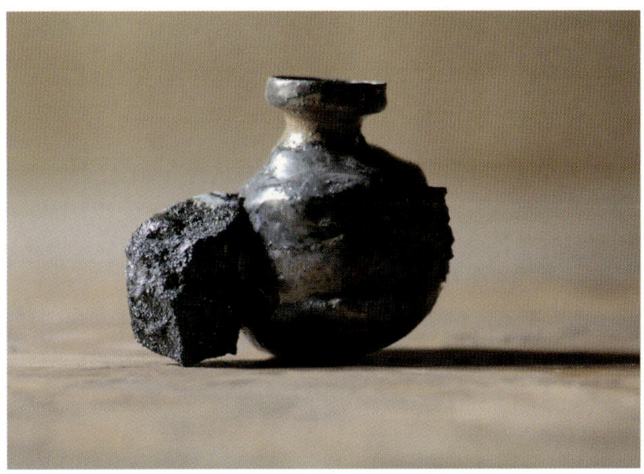

'Raw Waterfall' Tokkuri (2021).

through the landscape. The surfaces evoke snow, dew, dirt, lichen, moss, feldspar rocks, even the glistening of water as it lashes a pebble in a stream. These recollections are sculpted into pots, but they become fully present only when they are used. The '*tokku*' sound the *Tokkuri* make, for instance, serve as a reminder of water falling from rills into shallow pools.

Juxtaposition is also deployed tonally across the same pot, specifically in the relationship between interior and exterior surfaces. The pink interior of *'The Dropped Cornet' Guinomi* (2020), for instance, provides a strong contrast to the gold lustre of the exterior. The reflective lustre on the outside evinces the sensation of water, but its metallic shade could construe the vessel as a rather cold and forbidding form. The pink – proffering a sense of the fleshy – offers the pot warmth, as

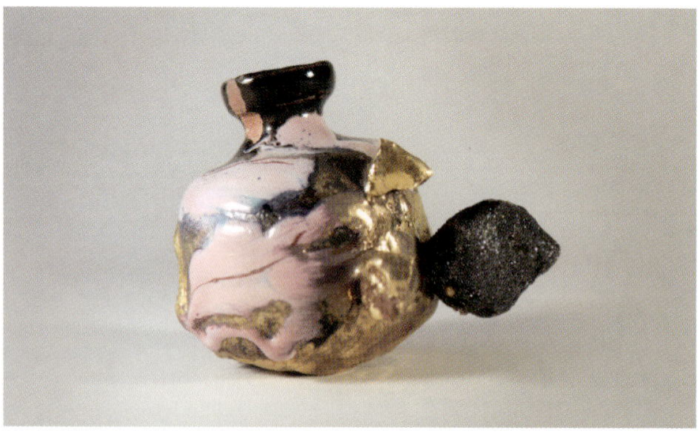

'Pink, Black, Blue, Gold and Glitter Waterfall' Tokkuri (2021).

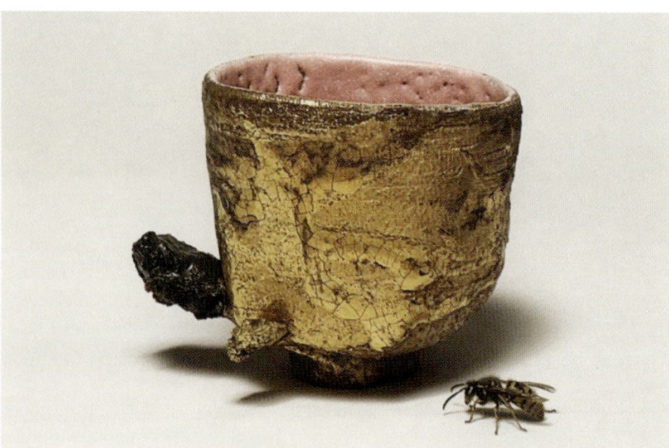

'The Dropped Cornet' Guinomi (2020).

though the liquid contents give sustenance. There is, in fact, something a little nest-like about this pot; the clay body defending the interior from outward assault. The rock-like protrusion is reminiscent of a handle, but more significantly it firmly locates the exterior of the pot in the evocation of the landscape, the gold evolving into a stream that flows around a rocky island. On *'Grumpy Panda' Jar* (2021), gold has been applied to the interior of pot, the exterior conveying a sense of ice-cold stone. Here, the arrangement of colours could signify a natural spring rising through layers of rock. Yet, it could also be understood as emblematic of a protective dwelling with a welcoming fire. Light shimmers and refracts through the liquid contents, animating the jar once the 'frosty' lid is removed. These are beautiful, quietly poetic pots, which invite contemplation, manifesting nature into our everyday actions.

The elevation of the everyday rituals of living via functional pottery, especially in Japan, was of course admired by Bernard Leach in both aesthetic and philosophical terms. His assessment of the validity of the Anglo-Japanese tradition looms large over British studio pottery, not least as a product of his own writings, but also from commentary written by others. As noted in the Introduction, the significance of other contemporaneous avant-garde makers, William Staite Murray in particular, were overshadowed by an accepting public seemingly at ease with uncontested endorsements of Leachian lore.[164] However, the orthodoxy of Leach's philosophy, especially in relation to form, has significantly lessened over time. Only a crude application of Leach would mean that any Anglo-Japanese pottery must be tied to his ideas from a century ago. Copsey's utilisation of Japanese form simply affords him the kind of expression he is looking for, specifically the capacity for pots to evoke natural phenomenon through form and surface. More distinctively, as noted above, Copsey's pots become fully present only when they are used. The placement of natural material

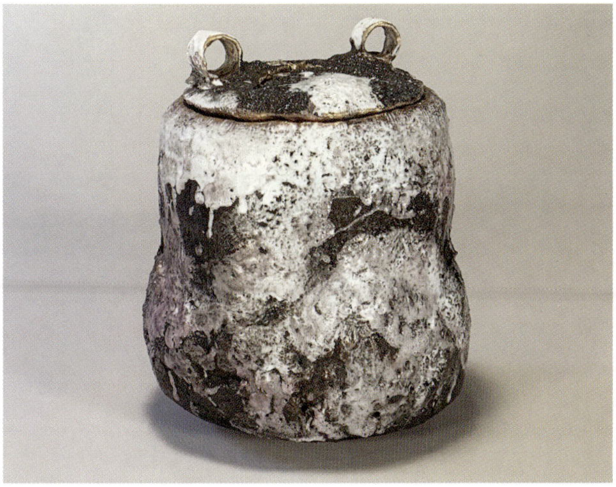

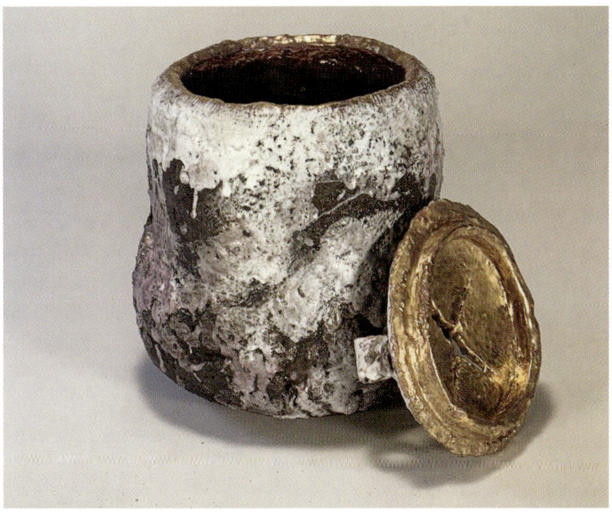

'Grumpy Panda' Jar (2021).

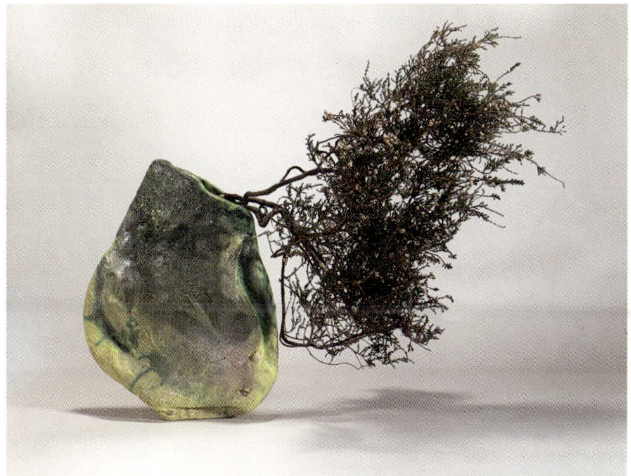

Green Moor Blossom vase (2020).

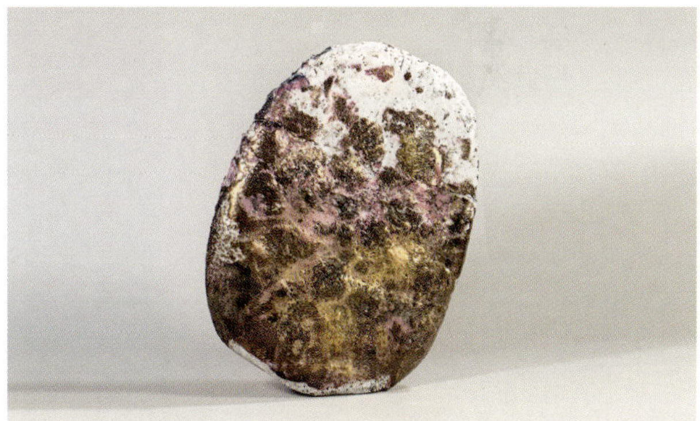

Langsett Moor Blossom vase (2020).

in his vase and pot forms – a nod towards the Japanese art of *ikebana* flower arrangement – augments the sense of nurture and nature in reciprocity that is at the heart of his practice.

Copsey's pots are not a glib celebration of the rural idyll. Instead, they are suggestive of a more nuanced human interaction with nature that is almost anthropological in its investigation. His forms express the taut relationship between man-made constructions – be they brick houses or capstone walls – and nature's complicated, often ambivalent, response to the human piercing of its crust. In this sense, Copsey's manipulation of clay speaks to the manipulation of the land, whilst his surfaces document sensory experiences of the Peak District landscape, the living matter that grows upon the surface of the clay earth. These documents of experience include not only nature's serene beauty, but also its uncompromising hostility. Copsey's work perches on the 'liminal outskirts of the town', between the safety of the hearth and the appeal of the wilderness. Refusing to side with the urban or the rural, Copsey's work conjoins the two in all its contradictions. These are, therefore, very modern pots. For if the twenty-first century has taught us anything, it is that our contemporary relationship with nature is, at best, mired in ambivalence.

Gabriele Koch Metaphorica

> The affinities of all the beings of the same class have sometimes been represented by a great tree. I believe this simile largely speaks the truth. The green and budding twigs may represent existing species; and those produced during former years may represent the long succession of extinct species. [...] From the first growth of a tree, many a limb and branch has decayed and dropped off; and these fallen branches of various sizes may represent whole orders, families, and genera which have no living representatives, and which are known to us only in a fossil state.[165]
>
> (*Charles Darwin*)

Gabriele Koch's work has undergone a dramatic evolution. She rose to prominence in the late 1980s with her coiled, smoke-fired, and finely burnished pots, such as *Textured Sphere* (2007) and *Pod Form* (2015). For the next thirty years or so, Koch exhibited internationally, demonstrating her mastery through a rich array of smoke-fired colours and forms, each with a stronger sense of formal focus and technical accomplishment. Her palette expanded to include smoky oranges, pinks, greys, blues, greens, and yellows, whilst her forms ranged from large and expansively rounded pots, through tall and stately vase-like forms and smooth platters, to smaller pots akin to tea bowls. Whilst her formal language draws from the idea of the pot as a container, her work explores the relationship between interior and exterior space, and this overlaps with the concept of the vessel. As Birks observed in 2000, 'a pot is a membrane between an inside space and an enclosing space. Gabriele's work can be seen in terms of the tension between the two…'.[166] In a catalogue from 1995, Sir David Attenborough summarised her work as 'elemental'; as a product of earth, air, fire, and water.[167] There is certainly a sense of wonder about the natural world: of smoke billowing from volcanoes, or clouds rumbling through the sky; of desert terrains viewed from the air, or a giant cliff face observed from below. Yet, such literal interpretations of her work are misleading. As Tony Birks remarked, 'although she is affected and perhaps inspired by nature and natural forms, never has she made a pot which is supposed to represent a living thing.'[168] Her work was and is not imitative, but reflective. Her forms encapsulate the subjective experience of nature – how it makes us feel – through a metaphorical language that could easily have its roots in abstract expressionism. Then suddenly, in 2012, there was a stark change in direction. The smoke firing and burnishing that had long been her trademark evaporated. Her new work was most often in combinations of black, white, or grey

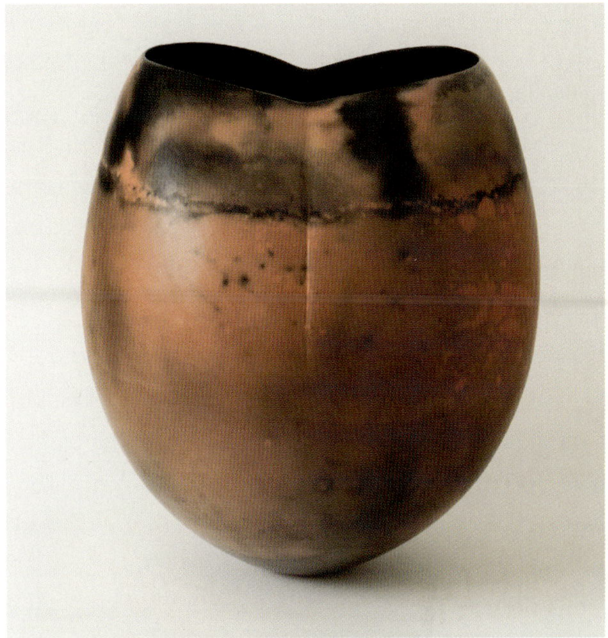

Pod Form (2015).

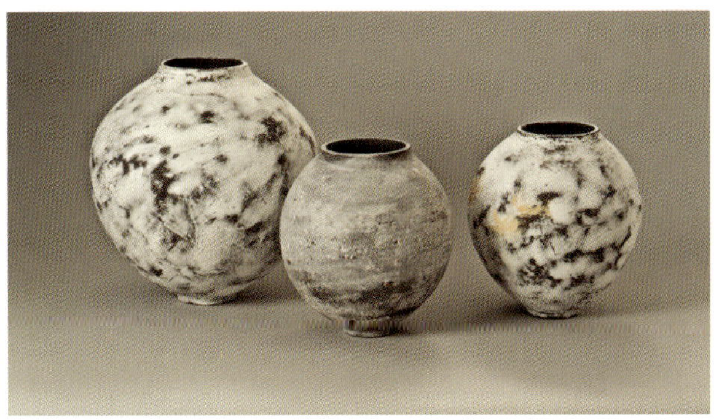

Moon Jars (2021).

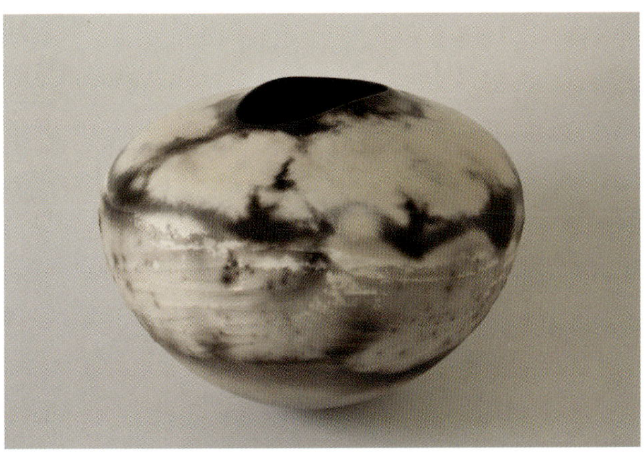

Textured Sphere (2007).

(sometimes with tints of orange), and featured porcelain smeared across, or beaten into, the surface. Such a dramatic shift in aesthetic seemed to announce a sharp break in her practice. Would her work now be divided into two phases: smoke-firing and its aftermath? As Charles Darwin observed, evolution always emerges from what came before, and Koch has deftly nurtured new growth from the same tree. There is continuity in her work, even if the smoke-fired pieces are now relics of an erstwhile process.

The moon jar shapes created by Koch in 2021 bear the closest formal relationship to the rounded smoke-fired pots for which she was arguably best known; the smearing of porcelain perhaps echoing the effect of smoke-firing. The more important connective between these two aspects of her work, however, lies in the fact that form and surface are indistinguishable. Depending on the effect Koch is searching for, surface is either created by additions to the clay body itself, or through the application of porcelain slip that still leaves the clay body visible, before firing. Thus, in terms of visual composition, the surface is multifunctional; it is both the decoration of the form and the form itself. This, in turn, demands synchronous acts of looking. If her smoke-fired forms sometimes encouraged the eye to move around the pot in a horizontal motion (leading some to imagine the more bulbous forms as representative of cosmology), here the eye is taken towards the outlines of the pot (one of the effects of using black material for the body is that it creates a flattened shape in space). The eye is then guided up the sides towards the rim, and then down into the vacuous mouth, into the interior. The mind's eye is asked to imagine this interior space, which, in turn, shapes how the eye perceives the three dimensions of the outside. A series of visual flows are created through the careful manipulation of the work's composition. By intuitive decision-making throughout the process of producing each piece, Koch skilfully maps out a visual composition that takes our eyes around, and even inside, form. This is one of the ways in which her work has remained totally consistent. Indeed, her use of form has remained relatively stable, and this focus on a particular vocabulary has enabled greater precision in compositional intuition. She is a master of making the body of a form succeed as both spatial container and chromatic decoration, whilst also manipulating our sense of interior and exterior space.

Although her work is not imitative of nature, it is very clearly attuned to it. She may be less concerned with literal documentation, but each piece stands as a clear analysis and articulation of our relationships with the natural world. This may seem at odds with her predicament as an urban potter: her studio is located on a major traffic artery that runs through north London. Yet, perhaps the centre of a metropolis is the most apt place to yearn for a connection with nature. Indeed, Koch's inspiration for making sometimes arises from viewing a particular cliff, or kind of stone, whilst out on a rural sojourn. However, the resulting work is a free and associative response to the memory of her encounter with nature. Each piece thus stands as an urban container of rural experience. They package up memories of nature and transport them back to the city as archives. Each piece is a metaphor for relationships between humanity and nature – our appreciation of its beauty, but also our culpability for its destruction.

Such awareness of ecological disaster is caught in the actual process of making. Koch uses a variety of grogged stoneware clays to coil a form, which is meticulously finessed until it is complete. Once the form has emerged clearly, Koch is able to consider how porcelain should be applied. However, the application of porcelain involves bashing it, quite violently, into the side of the coiled pot, effectively destroying the perfected form she has created. Before firing, the work must be reconstructed to resemble the original as much as possible. In this age of looming ecological disaster, and as time runs out for us to prevent catastrophic global warming, it is hard not to read Koch's process as symbolic of ecological damage. The construction of each piece is bound up with destruction; the literal pounding and battering of earth. The making of her work is thus akin to a metaphorical act of protest. Her process stands as a statement of frustration at the way we are destroying our own planet.

Of course, pottery, as the product of the handcrafting of natural material, perfectly encapsulates the nature/nurture duality. This is particularly apparent in the beautifully curvaceous black *Gated Vessel* (2020), which functions as the base for a series of uncharacteristic vertical stripes, curved rectangles, and semicircles in porcelain. The pattern is not a literal representation of anything, but it evokes a sense of uneasy order, off-kilter mathematics, the twist of modern architecture and thus, for me, the contemporary cityscape. This 'cityscape', which has again been beaten into the side of the body, crumples the form upon impact. Yet, as described above, Koch patiently remade the piece before firing it. It thus stands as a metaphor for a much-needed corrective relationship with nature; for our species to actively work to fix the damage we have inflicted. Koch's approach may be very subtle, but it is politically astute, and knowingly so.

In works such as *Snow Moon*, *Moon Jar*, *Orkney Stone* (all 2020), shiny burnished white surfaces have been chiselled with marks, and the battering effects on the pot have been purposefully retained. Highly textural, these incisions might evoke the texture of stone, or a chalky cliff, being hit by the sun. Yet, these marks also symbolise irreparable damage. Perhaps they imply that some environmental destruction cannot be undone. After all, the extraction of resources from the ground – through quarrying, mining, or the extraction of petroleum and gas – forever scar the landscape with the residue of human development and civilisation.

Koch has always been concerned with tactility as well as visual effect. The burnishing of her earlier smoke-fired work refracted light in unexpected ways, but it also afforded each piece a smooth and gently undulating surface. In her more recent work, undulations are created by the porcelain inlays. The placement of these lines around the centre of the exterior of each work, such as *Standing Forms* and *Giant Standing Form* (both 2016) is purposeful. The centre of the pot is where it is most likely to be held, and so our fingers are invited to feel the textural changes between material.

However, this decision also gives each piece a strong sense of centredness, poise, balance, and thus a pleasing compositional equilibrium. It is of no coincidence that the weight of the human body emanates from the centre; a fact recognised in movement practices such as Yoga and Tai Chi. I find, therefore, that Koch's forms have a sense of corporeality. They are not literal representations of human beings, but they do invoke body in terms of both pottery composition (the 'body' of a pot) and a person. With a refined symmetry, they remind us that, like pots, we too are

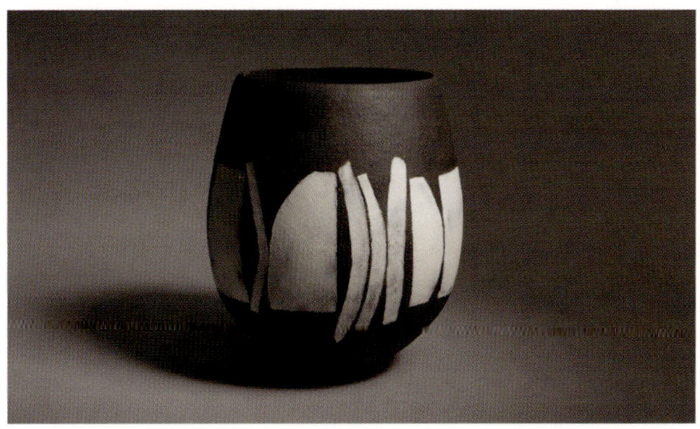

■ *Gated Vessel* (2020).

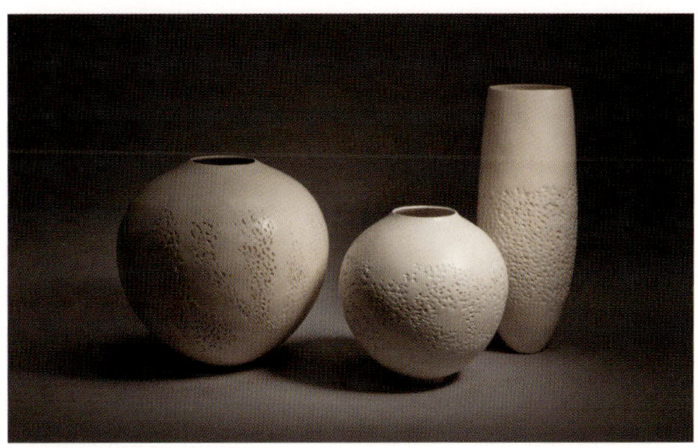

■ *Snow Moon, Moon Jar, Orkney Stone* (2020).

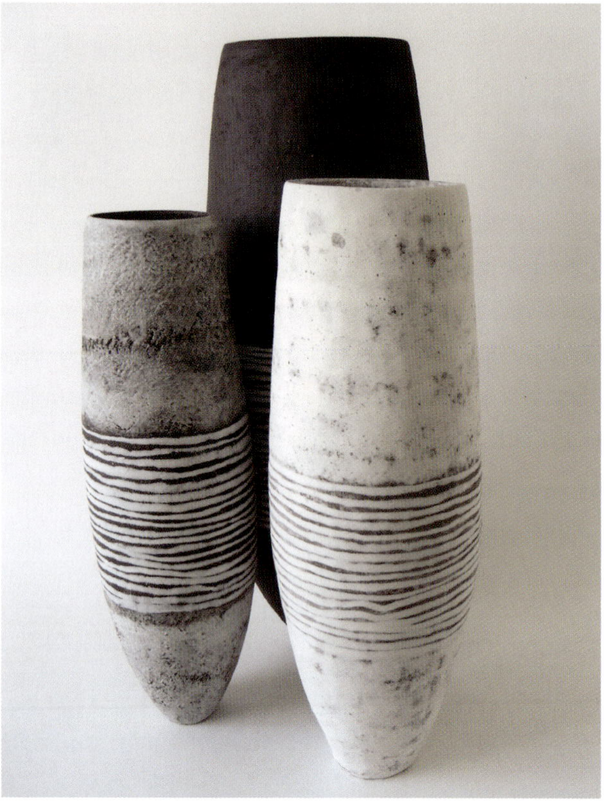

Standing Forms (2016).

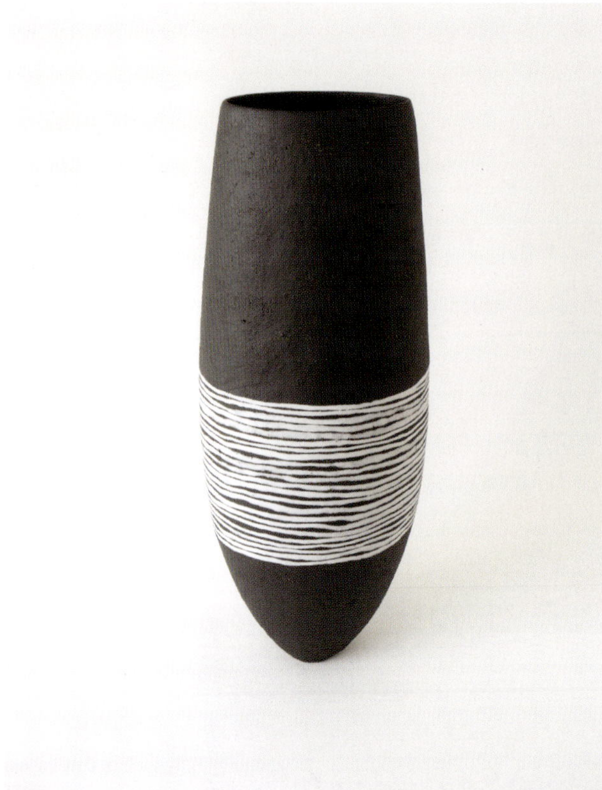

Giant Standing Form (2016).

water carriers (around sixty per cent of our bodies are made up of water). As the aesthetic of her work is calm and purposefully reflective, she seems to be inviting a quiet contemplation of the relationships between ourselves and nature. Koch's work is perhaps as spiritual as it is political.

Black and white are on opposing ends of the colour spectrum. Yet, as the well-known idiom reminds us, 'it's all there, in black and white'. The unification of these colours in Koch's work, including in the smoky grey of *Small Moon* and *Veiled Moon* (both 2021), communicates the stark reality of our current climate predicament. Koch resolves these colours into pleasing compositional forms, which have the stateliness of the best of Hans Coper, evoking spiritual serenity, as well as alarm at the pollution of our world. What makes Koch's work so powerful is its understatement: to express dismay through contemplation is a very skilful achievement. Yet, it also highlights how her work is not straightforwardly imitative of either life or nature. Koch is a master of the metaphor.

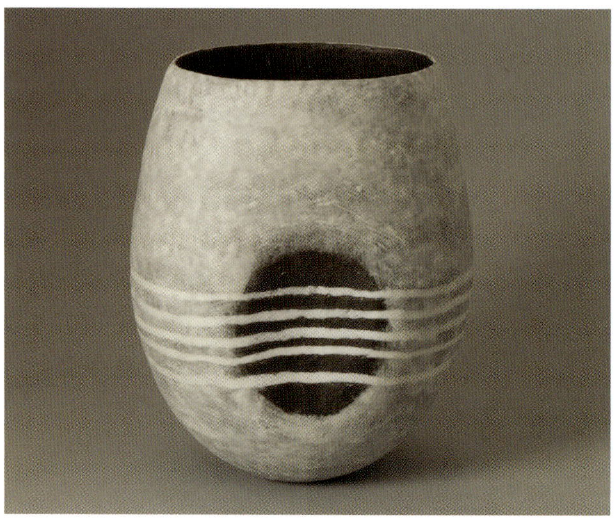

Small Moon (2021).

Veiled Moon (2021).

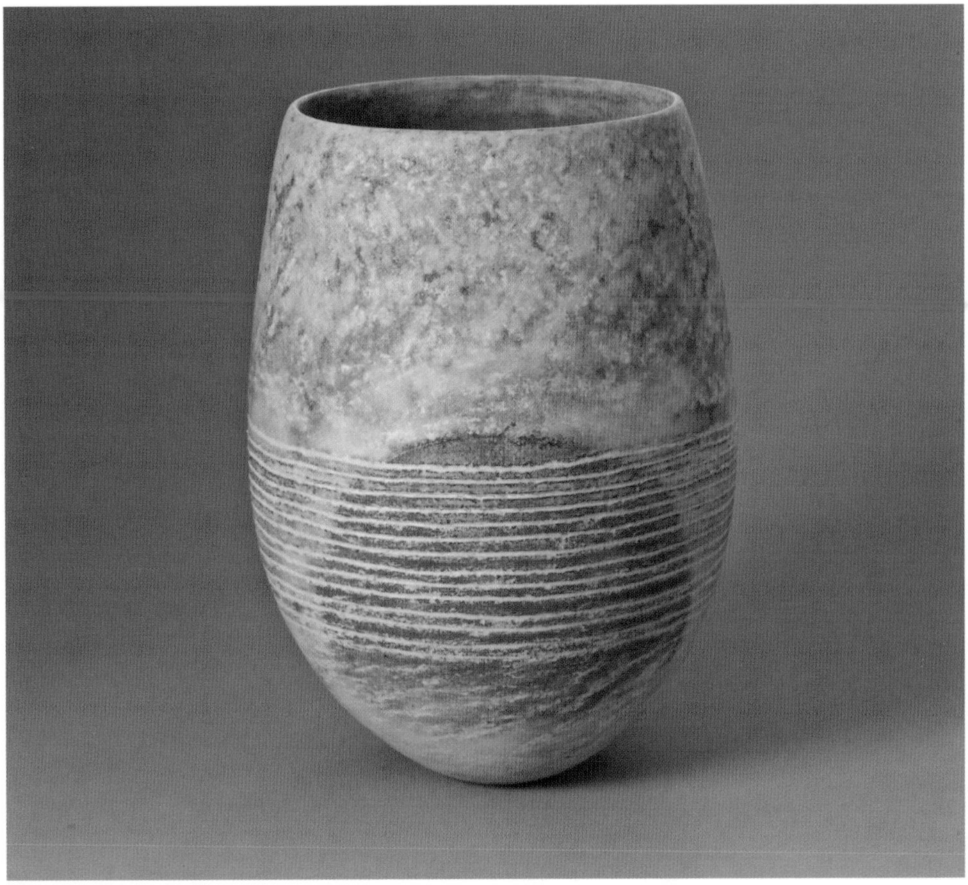

I opened this essay with what I considered to be an apt metaphor for Koch's evolution in style by quoting from Charles Darwin's seminal work *On the Origin of Species* (1873). I close with another quotation from Darwin, which, for me, captures the metaphorical force of Koch as artist 'creator'. It also proposes that her work, in its totality, is an unapologetic avowal of the righteous power of nature:

> It is interesting to contemplate a tangled bank, clothed with many plants of many kinds, with birds singing in the bushes, with various insects flitting about, and with worms crawling through the damp earth, and to reflect that these elaborately constructed forms, so different from each other, and dependent upon each other in so complex a manner, have all been produced by laws acting around us. [...] There is grandeur in this view of life, with its several powers, having been originally breathed by the Creator into a few forms or one; and that, whilst this planet has gone cycling on according to the fixed law of gravity, from so simple a beginning endless forms most beautiful and most wonderful have been, and are being evolved.[169]

Márek Líška
Here and Now

> Many have called Chernobyl the most costly environmental catastrophe in history.
>
> Sadly, this isn't true. Something else has been unfolding, everywhere, across the globe, barely noticeable from day to day for much of the last century. This too is happening as the result of bad planning and human error. Not one hapless accident, but a damaging lack of care and understanding that affects everything we do. It didn't begin with a single explosion. It started silently, before anyone realised it, as a result of causes that are multifarious, global and complex. Its fallout cannot be detected by a single instrument. It has taken hundreds of studies across the world to confirm that it is even happening. Its effects will be far more profound than the contamination of soils and waterways in a few unfortunate countries – it could ultimately lead to the destabilisation and collapse of everything we rely upon.[170]
>
> (*Sir David Attenborough*)

> People are suffering. People are dying. Entire ecosystems are collapsing. We are in the beginning of mass extinction, and all you can talk about is money and fairy tales of eternal economic growth. How dare you![171]
>
> (*Greta Thunberg*)

As a consequence of the unprecedented ecological crisis we face, sustainability in the production of studio ceramics has become an ever more pressing issue. By using electric rather than gas kilns, ditching toxic glazes, recycling studio waste, and sourcing local clays, ceramic artists have sought to lessen the environmental impact of their practice. Yet, the fragility of the environment is less commonly addressed in work as a subject in its own right. Whilst some artists, for example Kate Malone, draw upon nature for inspiration, it is often done through the aesthetics of abundance: the ripeness of fruit, the pineapple as a symbol of hospitality, and the pumpkin of fecundity. Connecting this aesthetic celebration of nature with environmental concerns is perhaps implied rather than asserted.

At the time of writing, it has barely been four years since Márek Líška graduated with a BA in Ceramics from the Cardiff School of Art and Design. This short period of history has borne witness to the Covid-19 pandemic, doubts that the 2016 Paris Agreement on climate change will be effective in keeping global warming below 1.5°C, and the desperate campaigning of Swedish activist Greta Thunberg in the face of apparent political indifference. Líška stands out as one of the few artists to confront the bleak reality of unfolding ecological disaster in the subject matter of their work; to overtly interrogate the unsustainable relationships between humanity and nature. Líška's practice does not agitate for a simple respect of nature. Rather, nature must be pragmatically and thoughtfully re-engaged with. We need to recognise ourselves as a species in a mutually dependent relationship with our planet, and that time is running out.

The significance of this co-dependency first surfaced in Líška's degree exhibition, *Raised Ground* (2018), which partly consisted of several sculptures depicting different kinds of vegetable. Some of the larger pieces, such as the oversized *Radish* (2018), comprised a sculpture mounted onto a wooden pedestal. This raised the work into the air and turned the vegetable represented into a kind of trophy. By reconfiguring the scale of vegetables, they were no longer small enough to sit inside the hand. Líška thus manipulated the audience into an insect-like relationship with the object, a reminder that we are but one of the many species dependent upon the life cycle of plants for survival. These works playfully repositioned the audience to consider the significance of nature to the continuity of our species. The roots of the *Radish* sculpture strained to re-enter the soil, as if some act of violence had pulled it out, the terracotta clay powerfully evoking both the skin of the vegetable and the soil from which it had been taken. The removal of the top section of *Carrot* (2018) spoke of a similar act of violence, its horizontal corpse at odds with its vertical growth. But how is the farming of vegetables – so crucial to our survival – an act of violence?

This was explained by *Bundle of Broken Asparagus* (2018), a piece also redolent of destruction, but more significantly, a critique of the consumer desire for perfectly formed vegetables. Despite attempts by supermarkets to push consumers into accepting misshapen produce, in 2013, a study found that forty per cent of all fruit and vegetables were discarded on cosmetic grounds.[172] Almost a decade later, in 2021, it was estimated that 4.5 million tons of edible food was disposed of unnecessarily in the UK alone.[173] Such wastage is unsustainable in the long term, not only because of the contribution it makes to greenhouse gasses as it decays, but also as the human population grows and climate change affects farmer's crop yields,

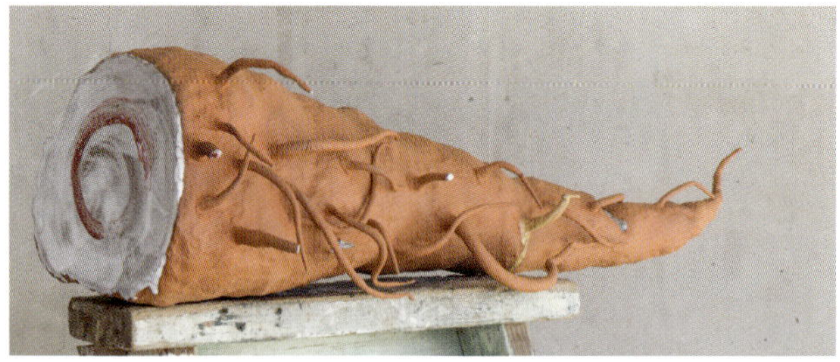

■ *Carrot* (2018).

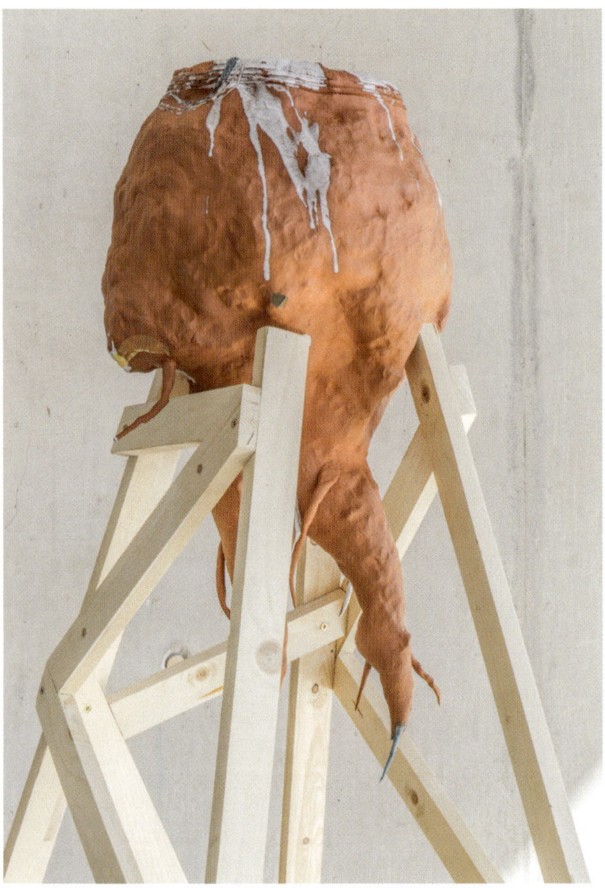

■ *Radish* (2018).

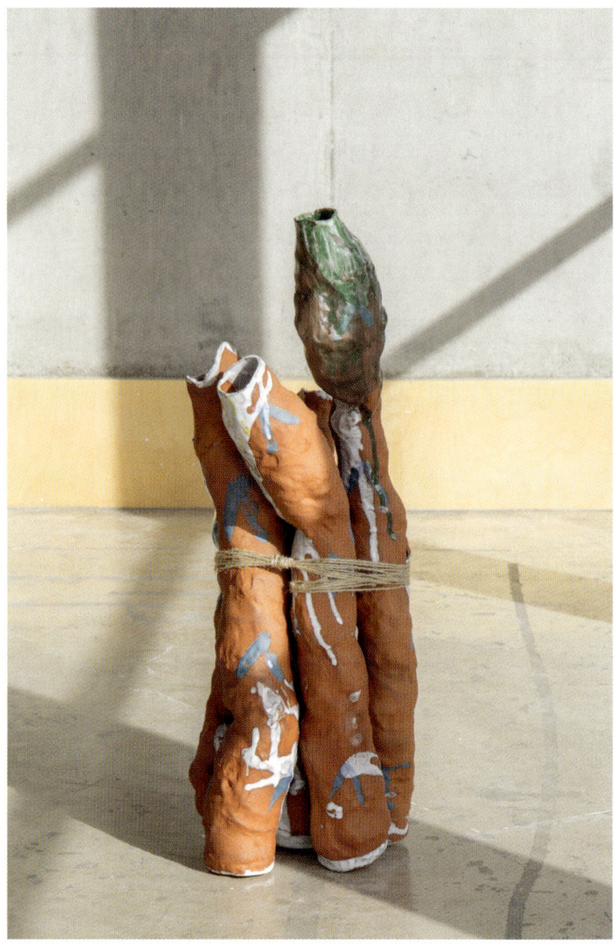

■ *Bundle of Broken Asparagus* (2018).

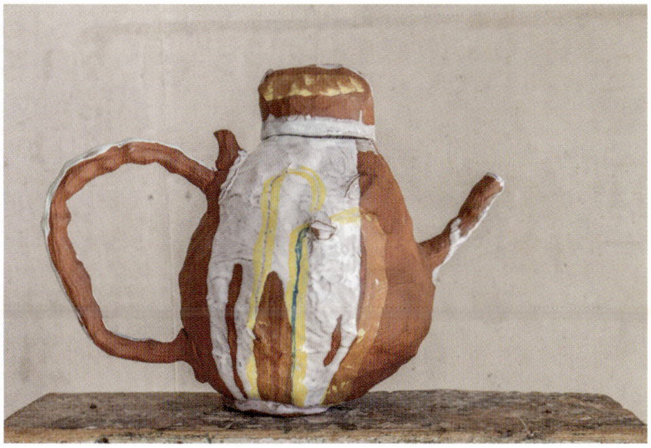

Pruned Teapot (2018).

supply chains may be threatened. *Raised Ground* was thus a challenge to the status quo, validating the imperfect vegetable as an inevitable outcome of production, but also critiquing the food industry – from supermarkets to consumers – for their culpability in damaging the environment through unnecessary food waste.

Whilst many of the works that formed *Raised Ground* were sculptures representing vegetables, others were pots with implied utility. *Pruned Teapot* (2018), for example, could be read as symbolic of the harnessing of nature for the purposes of mass production and consumption. The terracotta colour of the clay served as a reminder of how tea is grown from the soil, an obvious fact that is perhaps lost in the processing, refining, glossy packaging of the factory, and the bright lights of the supermarket. The wobbly coil that constitutes the handle and spout, meanwhile, evoked the spindly effect of cutting and pruning the branches of the plant to ensure maximum crop yield. Unusually for a contemporary teapot, perhaps, *Pruned Teapot* speaks to the actual process of growing tea.

Sculptural pots remained of interest to Líška in subsequent work, enabling the creation of reflexive pieces that comment on both ceramic production and the natural world. *Sprouting Split Pea Vase* and *Green Pea Vase* (both 2020) were concerned with natural growth, their playful form a product of planning, but also intuitive discovery. In creating each piece, Líška first makes rough drawings of different sculptural shapes – bulbous caskets, sweeping arcs, abstracted human figures – and explores these further in three dimensions by hand-building and coiling clay. It is only in the process of making that a form is satisfactorily achieved, the transition from two-dimensional drawing to three-dimensional object triggers further compositional decision-making. This approach is evidenced in the giant *Tall Split Pea Pod* (2020), a development of the earlier *Pea Vases*, and which was

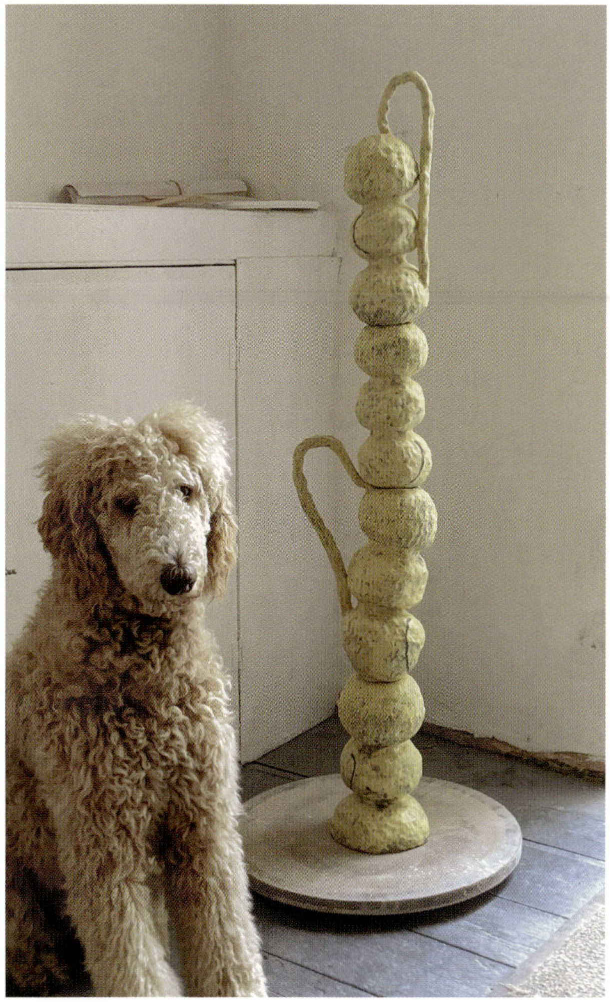

Tall Split Pea Pod, with the artist's dog, Cashew (2020).

necessarily fired in sections to achieve the required height, but also to facilitate easier transportation of the sculpture for exhibition. Taken as a group, these *Pea Vases* are nominally functional, evoking jugs as much as vases. Yet, they are also as organically composed as their grown referent. Split pea pods are, after all, a kind of vessel; their casings protect the pea seed crop suspended within. Interestingly, Líška decorated the vases with images of pests: snails, slugs, and caterpillars crawl across their surfaces. The presence of these pests, and the fact that the 'plants' have still sprouted, is a gentle but definite endorsement of organic farming.

The codependency of nature and humanity is perhaps most clearly expressed in Líška's other imaginative approaches to the vase form. *Pergola Vase* (2022), for instance, comprises two sections – one a bridge-like arch, the other a spherical pot. Read as one complete composition, however, the vase looks like a figure

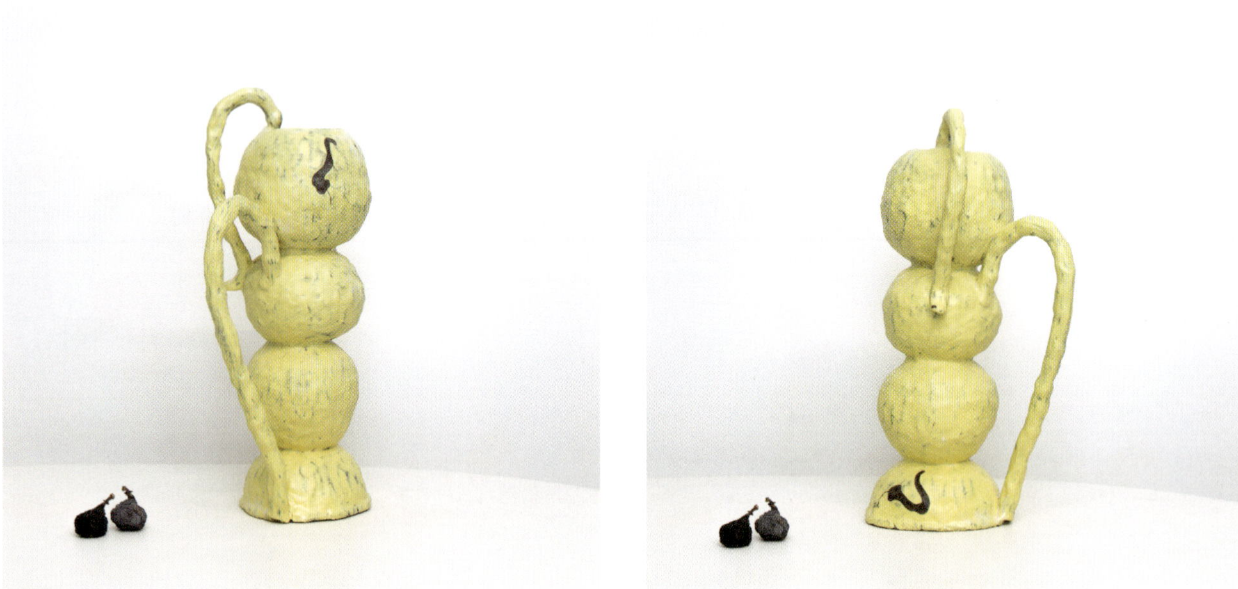

Two views of *Sprouting Split Pea Vase* (2020).

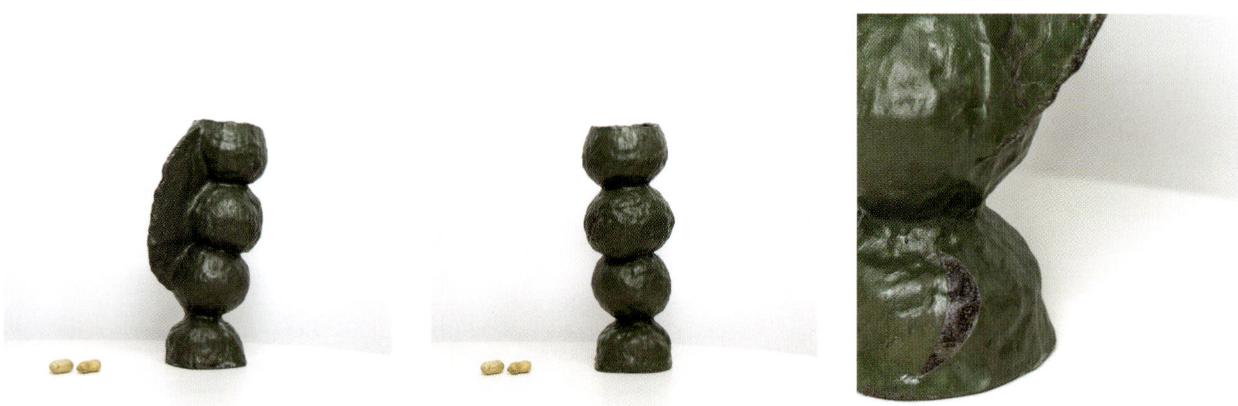

Three views of *Green Pea Vase* (2020).

holding itself in a gymnastic backbend position, its hips raised, and limbs outstretched in support. Plants grow from the 'head' and from the centre of the arch, what appears to be 'genitalia'. Such risqué playfulness is frequently found in Líška's work, but this is not superfluous; it is very much part of the point. *Pergola Vase* suggests that if we reattune our minds to live with nature (symbolised by the plant emerging from the 'head' pot), then our species will flourish (symbolised by the growth from the 'genitalia'). Yet, such a relationship demands a huge change in the way society operates, a metaphorical somersault in behaviour. Only through true integration with nature, that runs from the inside out, might disaster be averted.

In *Deconstructed Vase in Blue* (2019), Líška has sought to reduce the vase to its basic elements: base, support, and lip. In reducing the amount of clay needed to create a functioning vase (itself a decision with ecological implications), Líška has discovered the composition of a figure. The base, which includes a concave recess to hold water, also supports a Henry Moore-like abstracted torso, whose arms are held outwards to embrace the flowers, and whose head becomes a kind of full-stop to the vertical composition of the vase. The politics of this piece – the literal hugging of nature is obvious – yet there is also desperation and loneliness here. The solitary figure appears to cling to nature in desperation, but there is no recess for soil. Unless the plant is hydroponic, whatever natural matter is placed inside the embrace of the figure will eventually rot and die. The vase is thus emblematic of the powerlessness of the individual, whose love

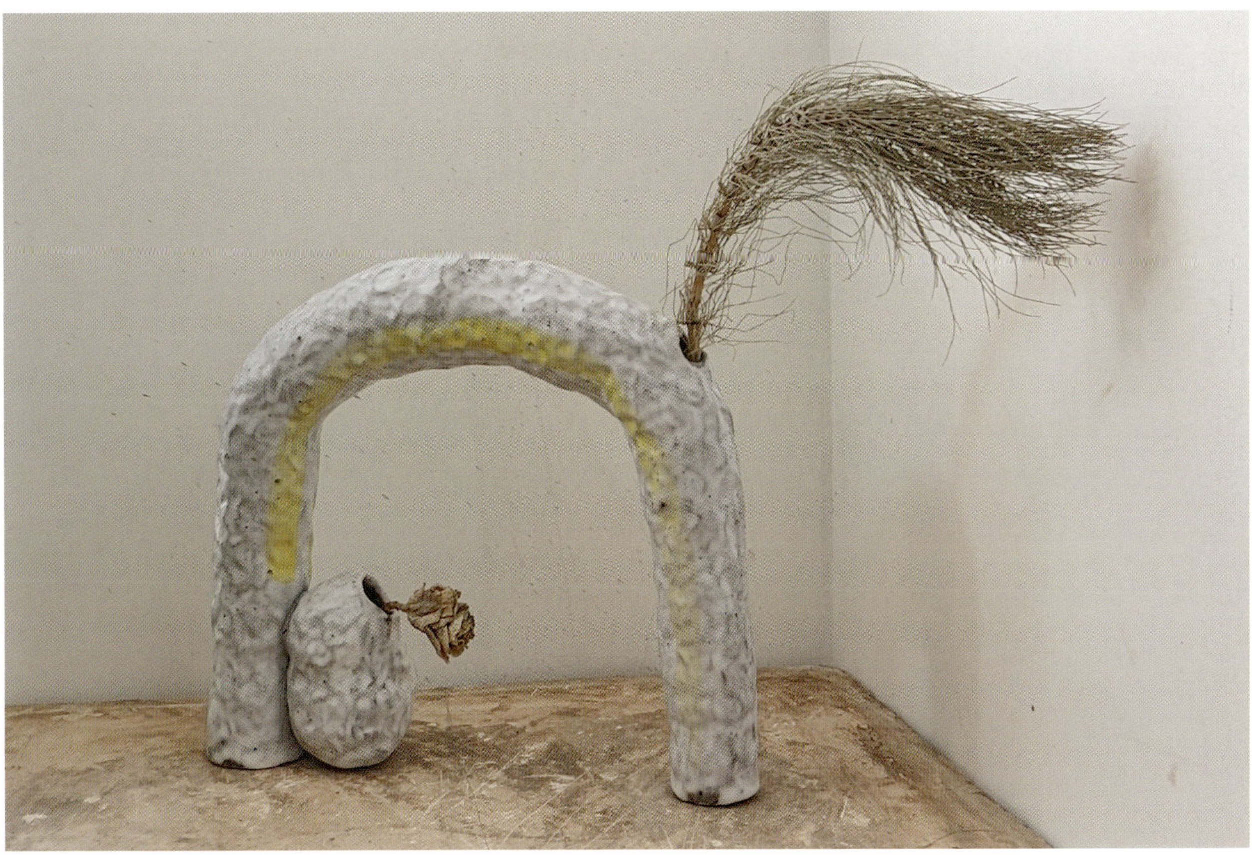

Pergola Vase (2022).

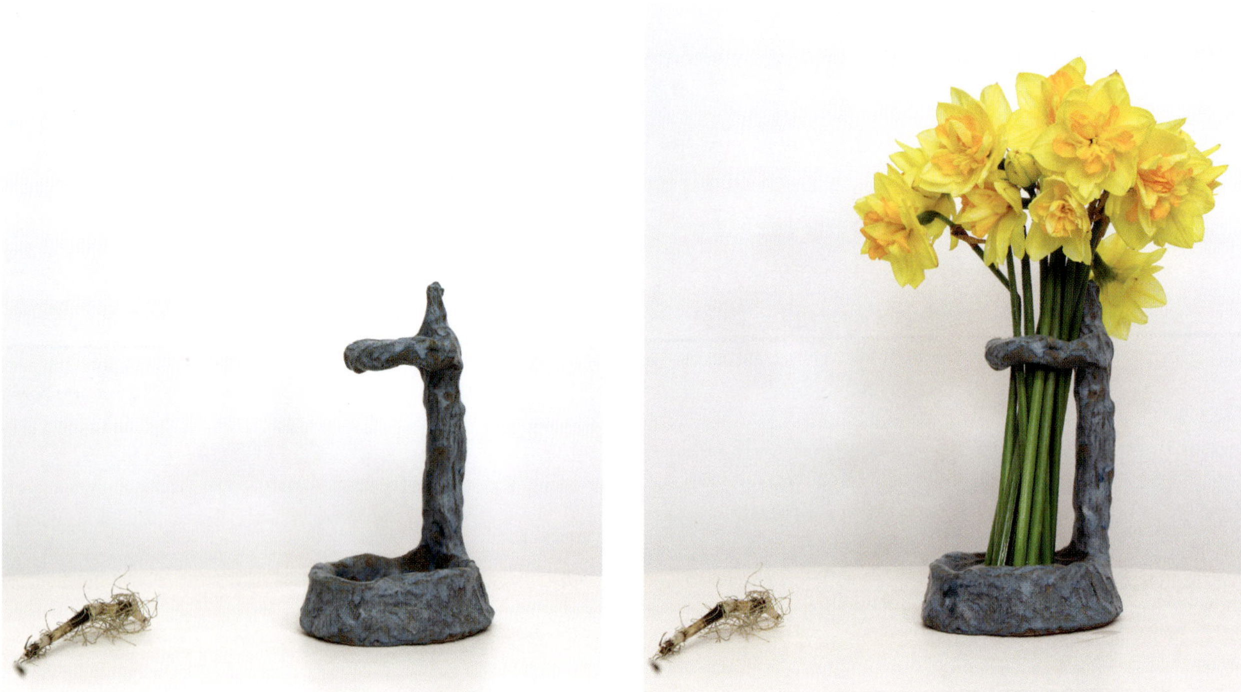

Deconstructed Vase in Blue (2019).

of nature comes to nothing as they are left immobilised by corporate irresponsibility and general apathy. Whilst some might critique Líška's work for being unrealistically romantic, there is recognition here that climate change is, as Sir David Attenborough asserted in the opening quotation for this chapter, 'multifarious, global and complex'.

The individual reaching out to be embraced by nature can also be observed in Líška's production of ceramic garments and necklaces, which are made by chaining together coils and following pattern block charts. Through its exploration of the relationship between internal and external space – between the body and the material shaping of the garment – ceramic clothing and jewellery constitutes an innovative kind of ceramic vessel, and an interesting augmentation of the vocabulary of studio ceramics. This development, however, has emerged from, and remains entirely consistent with, the other works described above. By clothing the body with ceramic, soil comes to protect humanity; we can immerse ourselves in the material of the planet. In this sense, Líška's ceramic garments represent an extension of *Deconstructed Vase in Blue*, except it is now nature that places its arms around humanity. Innovation is never sacrificed in the quest for ecological sustainability, nor political observation, in Líška's work.

This chapter was written at a time of great uncertainty and anxiety about the future. Here and now, there exists the possibility of salvation from environmental disaster, yet the required shift in policy and behaviour appears to be painfully slow and grudgingly undertaken. Economic strife and energy shortages threaten increased dependency on fossil fuels. Líška's work is realistic about the human capacity for change. There is a sense of despondency and a recognition

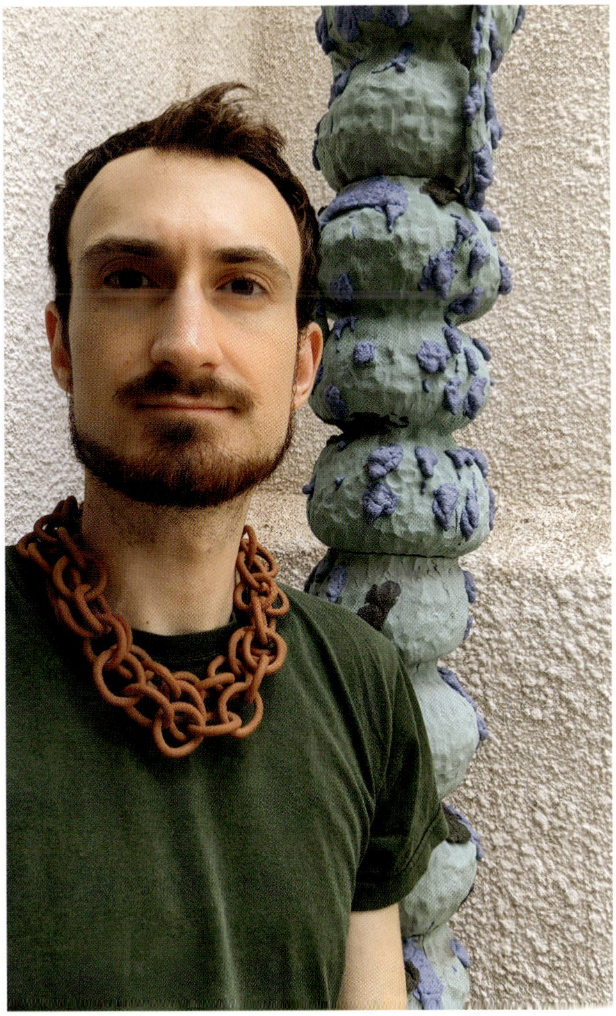

The Artist Wearing a Ceramic Chain Necklace.

that individuals can only do so much in the face of multinational corporate indifference, political unwillingness, and general disinterest. Yet, as Greta Thunberg stated in her speech to the UN Climate Action Summit in September 2019, also quoted at the outset of this chapter, 'the world is waking up. And change is coming whether you like it or not.'[174] The power of Líška's work lies in its understanding of how the nature of this change – the destruction or continuity of our planet in sustaining life – is almost entirely dependent upon action in the here, and in the now.

Afterword: Forms of Expression

The chapters of this book have evidenced how impassioned arguments about pots as being either art or craft are ultimately redundant. All potters, regardless of the work they create, demonstrate both craft (skill) and art (aesthetics). To utilise both is, in fact, a market necessity, for even the most unpretentious studio pottery mug will struggle to take on its industrially produced cousin unless it is comfortable to use and pleasing to the eye. Accepting that there remains much investment – ideological and economic – in the separate application of craft, and of art, to pottery, I nevertheless consider the debate to be a pointless cul-de-sac. Neither side will be victorious when both are necessarily intertwined. If there is an argument that needs to be fought, it is that critics, makers, craft shopkeepers, and gallery curators need to play their part in shifting the discourse so that pottery – indeed the field of ceramics as a whole – can be judged more widely as a discipline on its own terms.

At the same time, this requires a modification of the language used to analyse ceramic form. The interchangeable usage of words such as 'pot', 'vessel', and 'sculpture' – as observed in the introduction – are demonstrably problematic once they are unevenly applied to the work of different makers. Although I outlined some generalised definitions of these terms in the introduction, I also observed that, in contemporary practice, there was much crossing between them. I even went so far as to propose that 'theoretically at least, a work might exhibit qualities of the pot, the vessel, and sculpture as resolved elements in the same complex composition'. As it happens, this study includes one such work: *Deconstructed Vase in Blue* (2019) by Márek Líška. If a pot is rooted to the idea of domestic utilitarian form, then this vase is certainly a pot. Yet, the central body of the work resembles a human figure, which extends its arms to hug the flowers. This implies that the work should be classified as a sculpture. When these elements are observed in combination, they further produce a complex interplay between notions of interior and exterior space which speaks, if indirectly, to the qualities of the vessel. In particular, the developmental ratio between the base (the dish to hold water) and the lip (the outstretched arms of the figure) encourages us to imagine the intervening space as the interior of the vase. In other words, the work functions as a vase, but as a deconstructed form, it looks nothing like one. Líška's work demands we activate our imagination – bring our previous experience of the vase form to bear on the work – to complete it.

Deconstructed Vase in Blue (2019).

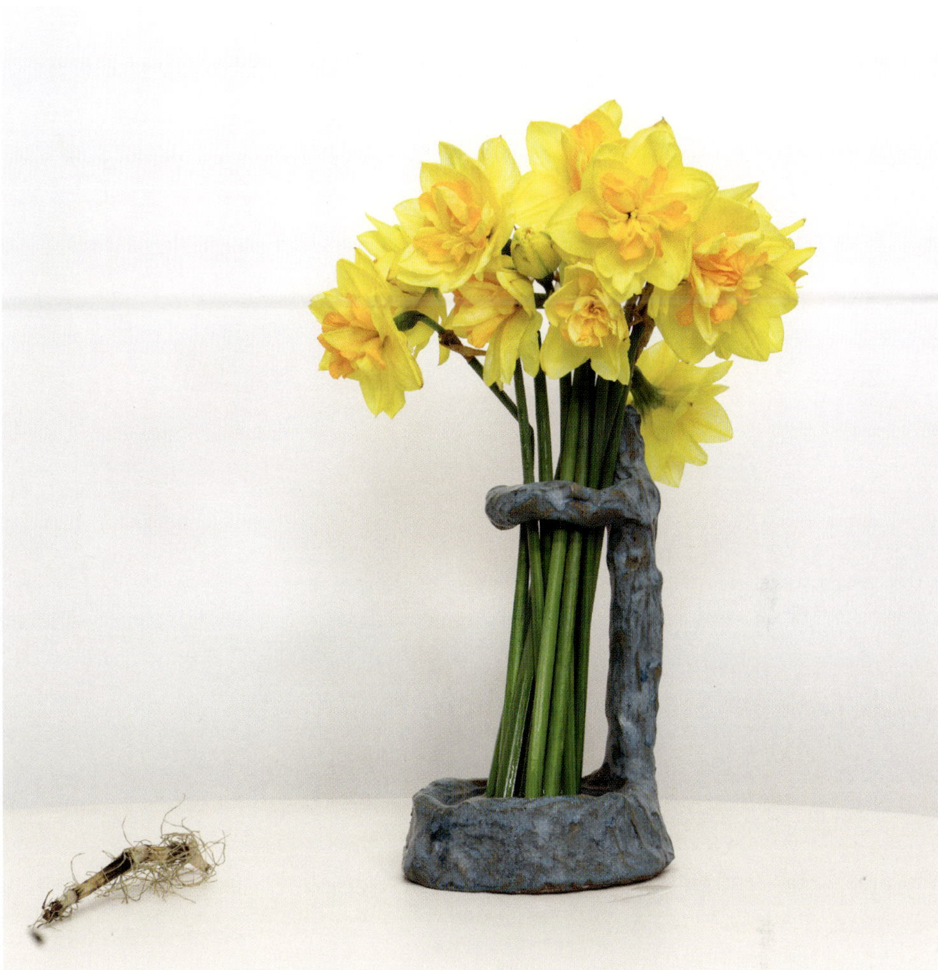

It is this intimation of interior and exterior space via our imagination, prompted by a sculptural form that is not self-evidently related to domesticity (and which is, in fact, dependent on the imaginary for our reading of it as a vase at all) that associates the work with qualities of the vessel. As a result, *Deconstructed Vase in Blue* innovatively draws together elements of the pot, the vessel, and sculpture in one reconciled statement. To describe the interweaving of formal vocabularies with some accuracy facilitates greater recognition of Líška's conceptual achievement, but more importantly, the possibility of its communication to others.

If anything has become clear to me in the writing of this volume, it is that pottery is a genuinely vital form of expression. It draws upon a myriad of vocabularies to express an ever-expanding range of perspectives. Pots can challenge the intellect whilst engaging all the senses. They might contest the politics governing our world, reveal the darkest recesses of our innermost psychologies, or revel in materiality to deliberate upon the largest of all questions: who are we, where have we come from, and where are we going? No wonder they have existed across all civilisations for thousands of years: pots are indeed astonishing forms of expression.

Artist Biographies

Nico Conti (b. 1992) is a Maltese artist working from both Malta and London. Following his BA (Honours) in Fine Arts at the Institute for the Creative Arts (2016) in Malta, he then moved to London to study ceramics at the Royal College of Art. During his time at the RCA, Conti was awarded various awards and was also invited to present his three-dimensional printed work to HRH, the Prince of Wales. Here Conti found new ways of subverting processes, drawing together his fondness of material and his inquisitive nature. His forms often represent nostalgic memories of nature and religious architecture. By embracing the tradition and heritage that surrounded his upbringing, Conti's work is autobiographical at its core. By pairing humble materials like clay with the latest technologies in 3D printing, Conti imbues his work with qualities of elegance, balance, luxury, and beauty. His unique pieces made out of the finest porcelain are designed to interact with light. With the continuous swift advancements in technology, art and craft are affected by modern tools and machinery. Conti now looks at clay and seeks to find new ways of working with it.

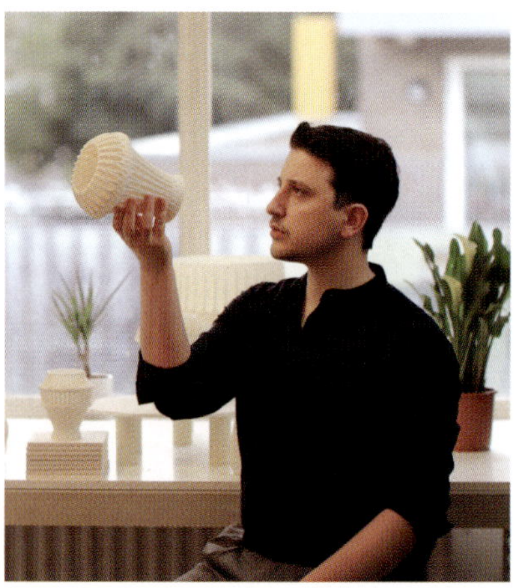

Nico Conti.

Tim Copsey (b. 1967, Lancashire, UK). The Peak District Pennine landscape and seasons are the backdrop to everything he makes: described as beautifully ugly or like space debris, he in essence makes bowls, bottles, cups and vases – although these are really just 'Serving Suggestions' – that inhabit the border between function and sculpture. He hopes that the work is playful, sometimes jarring but ultimately resonant of their materiality and the landscape from which they derive. Born into a small community where everything revolved around the local brickworks just 200 metres from his home, the built environment used these bricks, most neighbours worked there, and his father operated a dragline in the claypits. Before he was of school age he was digging and playing with that same bright red clay. As an undergraduate he fully intended to pursue ceramics, but while studying sculpture at Bretton Hall (now the Yorkshire Sculpture Park) he discovered working collaboratively with artists in other disciplines more fulfilling and ultimately built a career in multimedia, film, performance and installation art, which saw him working and showing internationally. His return to pottery in the early 2000s was immediate and visceral. Within a year he established a

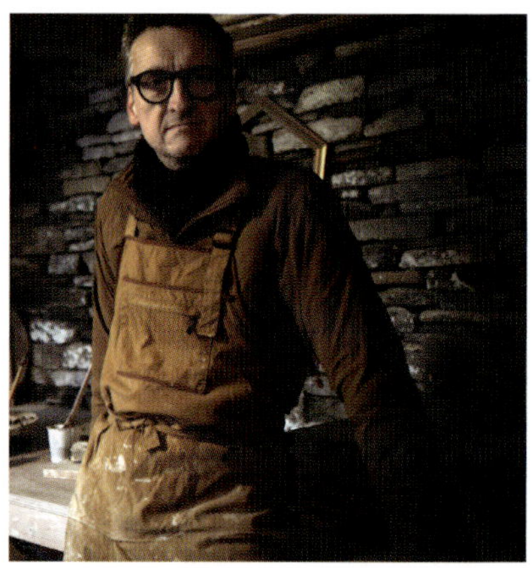

Tim Copsey.

studio and built a wood-fired kiln in the Peak District. Since then, his work has developed through an experimental and playful exploration of simple forms that offer continual adaption, whether that's through throwing, coiling or slab work. He is represented by a number of galleries and has work in many private and public collections.

Toni De Jesus was born in the UK in 1995. He grew up in Madeira, Portugal and in 2008 migrated once again to England. This is when he was introduced to ceramics and followed it through by studying a foundation course at City College Brighton and Hove (2013–14). He eventually studied at Cardiff School of Art & Design (2015–18), where he graduated and established his practice. Since graduating, De Jesus has been showcasing throughout the country, including FRESH at the British Ceramics Biennial (2019) where he was awarded the Guldagergaard International Residency (2021). Selected shows and exhibitions include COLLECT Art Fair with Ruthin Craft Centre (2021–22), Ceramic Art London (2022) and internationally at Galeria dos Prazeres, and 'Vaso de Altar' (2020), Portugal. De Jesus is currently based at Fireworks Clay Studios, Cardiff with a prolific collective of ceramicists. He is in the midst of producing a body of work towards his first solo show at MUDAS, Portugal.

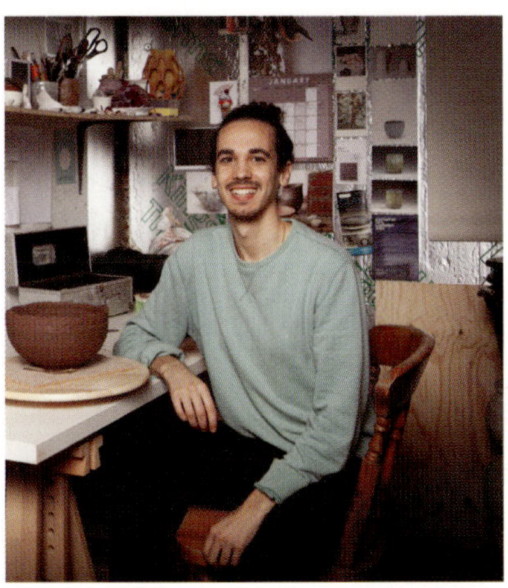

Toni De Jesus.

Stephen Dixon, since graduating from the RCA in 1986, has built an international reputation for figurative ceramics with a biting political and social satire. His work explores political narrative through a combination of ceramic form and printed surface, working in the British tradition of satirical artists like Hogarth and Gilray to question attitudes to the political, social and moral issues we face in our daily lives.

Dixon is Professor Emeritus of Contemporary Crafts at Manchester School of Art and lives and works in Manchester. His work is represented in major museums and collections in the UK and the USA and in 2009 he was the first artist-in-residence in the newly created ceramic residency studio at the Victoria and Albert Museum. In 2021 he won the prestigious British Ceramics Biennial AWARD for *Transient: the Ship of Dreams and Nightmares*, a collaborative project with refugees and asylum seekers.

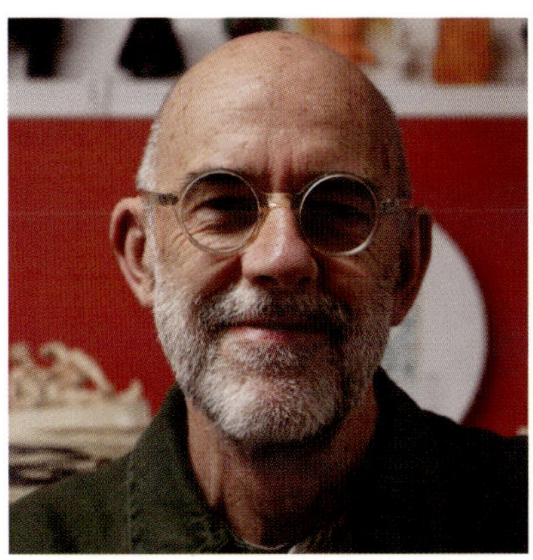

Steve Dixon.

Sara Flynn was born in Cork, Ireland in 1971, and trained at the Crawford College of Art & Design, Cork City, Ireland. Having begun her career in 1999 producing small-scale functional pots, as her skill has increased, she has moved entirely into making one-off sculptural decorative vessels. 'Closed' abstract forms are also explored through the production of limited-edition cast bronze objects. She is represented in London by Erskine, Hall & Coe, Mayfair, and has held six solo exhibitions with them since 2012. Her work is held in many major collections including The Victoria and Albert Museum London, England; The Devonshire Collection at Chatsworth House, England; The National Museum of Ireland; The Gardiner Museum, Toronto, Canada; The Fitzwilliam Museum, Cambridge, England, The Art Institute of Chicago, USA, and The Hepworth Gallery, England. She was shortlisted for the inaugural edition of the Loewe Foundation Craft Prize in 2017. She has been a

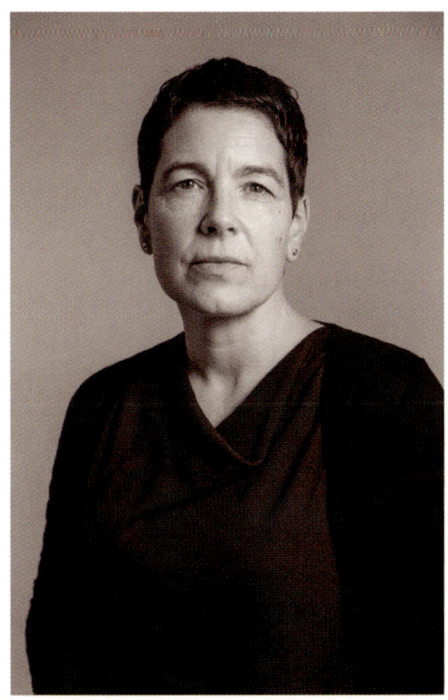

Sara Flynn.

member of the Experts Panel for the Loewe Craft Prize in 2018, 2019, 2020, 2022, and will be on the panel again in 2023.

Elizabeth Fritsch was born in 1940 in Whitchurch close to the Welsh border. She initially studied music at Birmingham School of Music and the harp and piano at the Royal Academy of Music from 1958 to 1964 before starting to make pots in 1966 whilst pregnant with her son. She experimented at home for two years before studying ceramics at the Royal College of Art, where David Queensbury was Head of Ceramics and her tutors included Hans Coper and Eduardo Paolozzi. At the Royal College she received the Herbert Read Memorial Prize silver medal for her thesis. After leaving College in 1971, she worked at the Bing and Gröndahl factory in Copenhagen. Her first solo exhibition was at Bing and Gröndahl Porcelain, where she was a major prize winner in the Royal Copenhagen Jubilee competition in 1972.

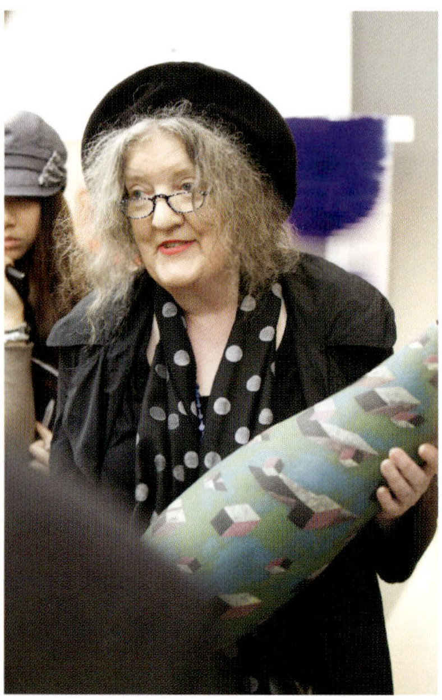

Elizabeth Fritsch.

Whilst at Digswell Arts Trust as a practising artist-in-residence she received the John Ruskin Bursary award for her Fictional Archaeology project in 1980. Her daughter was born that same year. In 1985 she set up her own studio in London, and in 1987 was chosen for the Bernard Leach Centenary Post Office Stamp issue with Hans Coper and Lucie Rie. Throughout her career Fritsch's work has been widely exhibited and collected. Her work is represented in public art museums, collections and galleries worldwide including museums across the United Kingdom. She was awarded the CBE in 1995 for services to the Arts and a Senior Fellowship from the Royal College the same year. She had a major retrospective of her life's work titled *Dynamic Structures: Painted Vessels* at the National Museum Cardiff in 2010–11.

Sam Hall was born in Shipley, West Yorkshire. After initially training at Harrogate College of Art, Hall graduated in ceramics from Loughborough College of Art in 1990. Now based in Cornwall he has a studio near St Ives. Having exhibited extensively nationally and internationally, he has gained a modest and appreciative audience over the last thirty years.

ON THE WALL IN [...] SAM HALL'S STUDIO IS A SINGLE WORD, SCORED INTO THE DUST COVERED PLASTER. 'FIGHT' IT SAYS. IT STRIKES ME AS A CALL TO ARMS, AN IMPERATIVE NOTE TO SELF THAT THOUGH LIFE MIGHT BE A STRUGGLE, SUCCESS CAN BE ACHIEVED THROUGH A WILLINGNESS TO ENGAGE AND DO BATTLE [...].

(Words by Alex Wade. Extracted from 'The Paradoxical Perfectionist,' *Cornwall Today*, August 2012.)

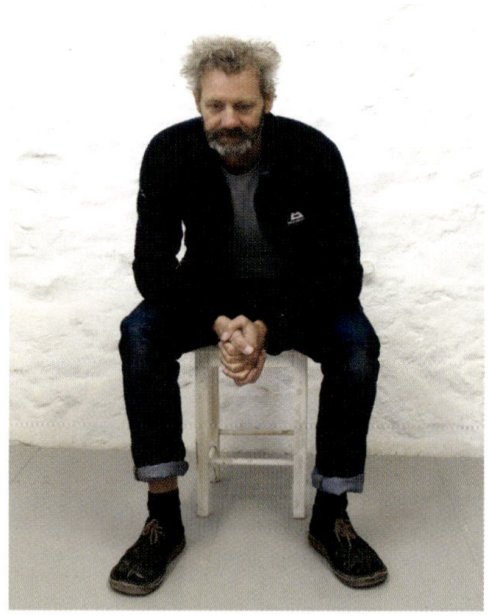

Sam Hall.

Akiko Hirai was born in 1970 in Japan. She initially studied cognitive psychology in Japan and obtained her degree in Bachelor of Letters before coming to England. During her first visit to study English, she was attracted by the English culture and complexity of multicultural society in London. It made her aware of her own cultural influence in her visual perception. These interests led to her second visit to England in 1999. She met many English potters and learned how to work with clay, soon after taking a degree

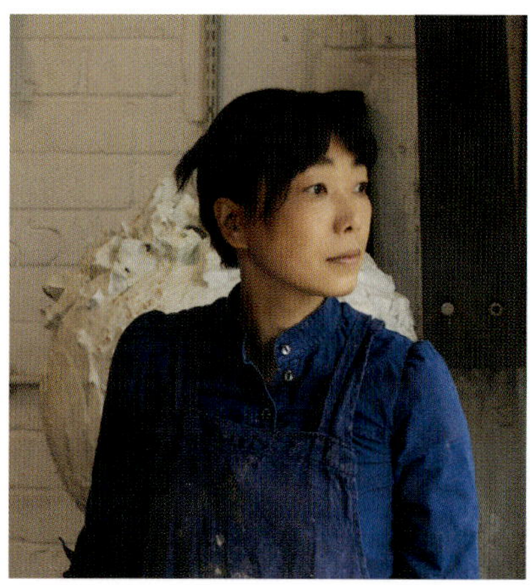

Akiko Hirai.

course in ceramics at the University of Westminster, then on to graduation from Central Saint Martins. After her graduation Akiko found her studio in The Chocolate Factory N16 in Stoke Newington, amongst other varying artists, where she now practises her ceramic work. Akiko makes practical ware using the Japanese tradition of allowing the clay to show how it wants to be fired itself. Her work also allows viewers to find out the language of the objects in their own ways. Her unique approach to ceramic work has had much high praise and her work is becoming more in demand from her commissions worldwide. Her work has also been acquired by some museums internationally. The list includes the V&A and Fitzwilliam Museum in the UK.

Dan Kelly was born in London and studied at Camberwell School of Arts and Crafts in the mid 1970s, where his tutors included Colin Pearson, Ewen Henderson and Ian Auld, as well as many other leading makers of that period. After Camberwell he went on to the Royal College of Art to extend his studies. During this time, he was able to experiment with all the making processes but concentrated on working on the wheel, where decisions are made in the moment and allow spontaneous, intuitive responses to the material. Over the years, Dan has pared down his working process, limiting the range of forms he works with and concentrating on a restricted palette of mostly black, white, and neutral tones. This allows him to challenge himself to subtly change details of the form and not overwork it with complicated glazes and surfaces. Dan continues to live and work in south London; he has exhibited widely in the UK and internationally, and his work is also represented in several museums.

Julian King-Salter was born in Oldham in the UK in 1954, and has led a rich and varied life in the British Isles and Eastern Australia, through which the making of pottery has been the longest running theme. Self-sufficiency, dance, healing self and others, and spending time in wild nature have been key themes throughout and, since 1990, parenthood. He sees creativity as a fundamental fruit of being human, and a cornerstone for life in a sustainable society, in which each and every person has enough resources to lead a fulfilling life. It feels as if both his life and work are at the same time, archaic, contemporary, and of the future.

Gabriele Koch grew up in Germany and trained in ceramics at Goldsmiths College. She established her studio as a professional ceramicist in 1982 with the help of a Crafts Council Setting-up Grant. She has exhibited widely in the UK, continental Europe, America and China, and her work is represented worldwide in private and public collections, notably the V&A, Fitzwilliam Museum, and Ashmolean Museum. She has lectured and demonstrated widely in the UK and internationally including Art Colleges in the UK and Israel. In 2011 she gave the Inaugural Rothschild Memorial Lecture in Gateshead. A monograph by Tony Birks introduced by Sir David Attenborough was published in 2009. She is a Fellow of the Craft Potters Association, a member of Contemporary Applied Arts and a member of the International Academy of Ceramics. Koch's interest in clay had first been kindled in Spain, an encounter with a sparse, desert-like landscape of strong earth colours, hints of Africa and early cultures,

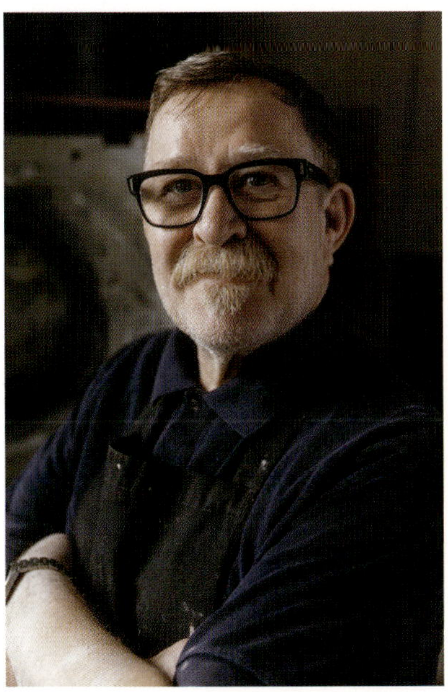

■ Dan Kelly.

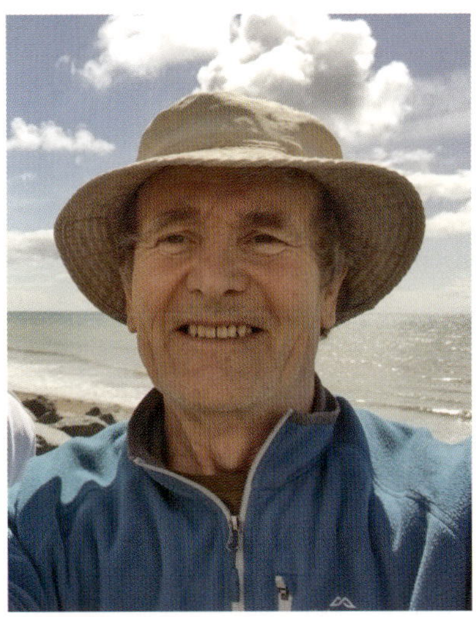

■ Julian King-Salter.

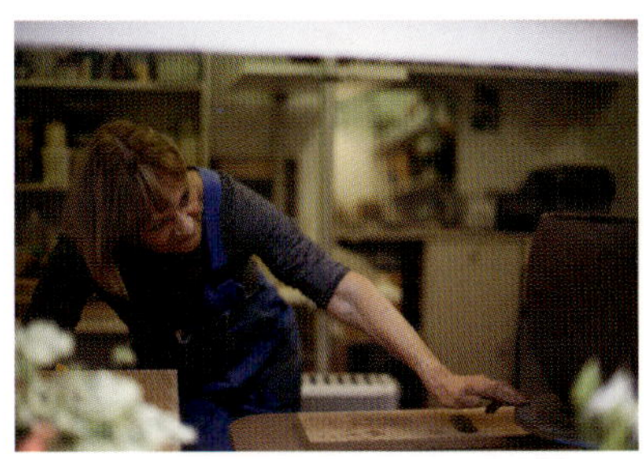

■ Gabriele Koch.

the contemporary work of Antoni Tàpies and Eduardo Chillida. Her interest in the elemental quality of ceramics led her to investigate the direct interaction between fire and earth, finding expression in her burnished, smoke-fired vessel forms. Today her work has developed a new language, combining a variety of stoneware clays with porcelain and slips at a higher temperature, still celebrating the beauty of the natural material. Concentrating on the vessel, her exploration of form, surface and texture is an ongoing process.

Chun Liao was born in Taichung, Taiwan and came to the UK to study in the 1990s. She holds an MA in Ceramics and Glass from the Royal College of Art, where she also undertook an MPhil research project in 1998. She now lives and works in London. Examples of Liao's work can be found in numerous notable international collections, including the Crafts Council Collection, Victoria and Albert Museum, The British Museum, and the Metropolitan Museum of Art and Design in New York.

Márek Líška is originally from Slovakia, an emigré with their parents to the UK in 2009 and attended Hereford College of

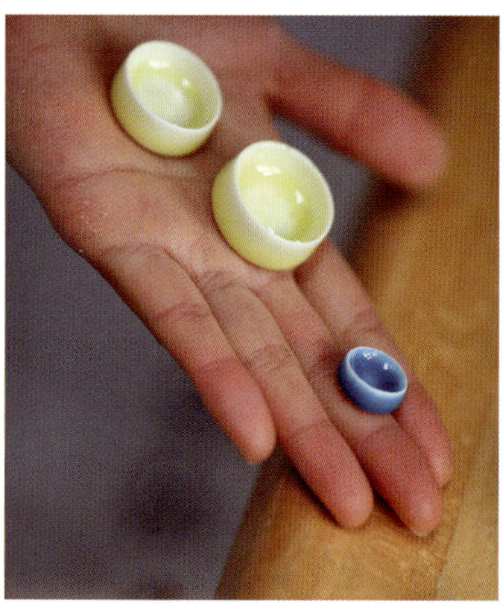

Chun Liao holding some of her pots.

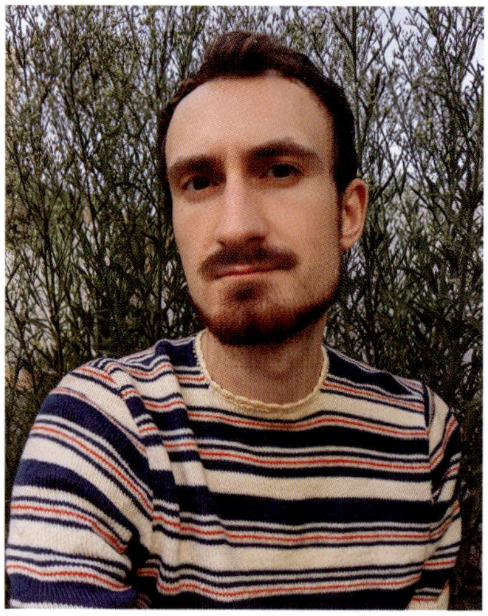

Márek Líška.

Arts soon after. As a graduate of the BA Ceramics course at Cardiff School of Art and Design 2018, Márek first adopted an ethos of a 'ceramic gardener' exploring ideas about our interaction with the world, and our role within nature. They look at growth that is fluid, protean, and transformative, capturing the transparencies of our physical and emotional worlds. Since graduating with First Class honours, Márek has been prolifically exhibiting and showing at trade shows, including the New Ashgate Gallery's Rising Stars 2019 selection; in 2020 at Galeria dos Prazeres, Madeira, Portugal; and was selected for the Young Welsh Artists of 2021, exhibiting at the Museum of Modern Art, Machynlleth. In 2022 Márek was commissioned to create work for the Glynn Vivien Art Gallery Swansea, responding to their collection and presenting it as a part of the *OYFC x GV: Queer Reflections* exhibition.

Gareth Mason is a potter of thirty-five years' standing and exhibits internationally. His first solo exhibition in America was in February 2011. Entitled *Other Forces*, it was held at Jason Jacques Gallery in Manhattan and began a long-standing professional relationship, continuing in the August 2022 solo exhibition, *Wild Clay*. Residencies include Syracuse University, USA (2019–20), the Jingdezhen International Studio, China (2016) and Long Beach State University, USA (2011). Speaking and 'masterclass' engagements include Everson Museum Syracuse (2019); Fitzwilliam Museum (2018); 'LabArtz', Taoxichuan, China (2016); International Ceramics Festival, Aberystwyth (2015); Greenwich House New York and The Clay Studio Philadelphia (2014); the American Museum of Ceramic Art, California (2013); SOFA Chicago Expo (2011); International Ceramics Studio, Kecskemet, Hungary (2010). A past columnist for *Ceramic Review* Magazine, London, he has also written for *Ceramics Monthly*, *Keramik Magazine Europa* and *Ceramics Art and Perception*, with the books, *A Decade In Cahoots* published online by Jason Jacques Press, and *More is More* by the same publisher, held in the Cfile online Library. Group exhibitions include *Shapes from Out of Nowhere* at the Metropolitan Museum New York; *Ceramics Biennale*, Hangzhou,

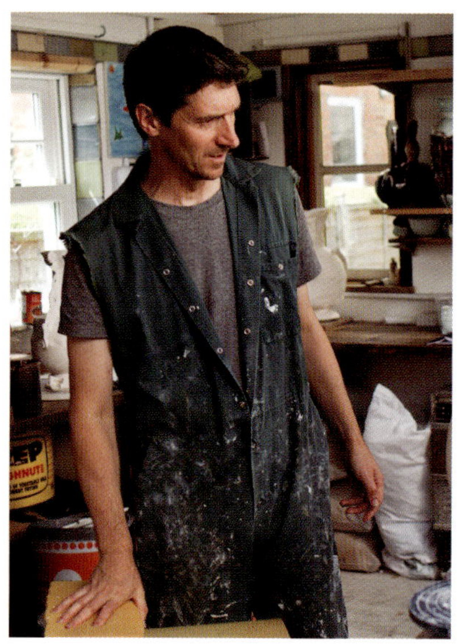

Gareth Mason.

China, Fitzwilliam Museum, Cambridge; Side Gallery, Barcelona; Centre Tignous, Paris; Yale Centre for British Art, Connecticut; Hiram Butler Gallery, Houston and Boca Raton Museum of Art, Florida. Collections include The Metropolitan Museum New York, Everson Museum, Syracuse, Mint Museum North Carolina and the Museum of Fine Arts, Houston, USA. Mason is a Fellow of the Craft Potters Association and Brother of the Art Workers Guild, London. He lives and works in Hampshire, England.

Magdalene Odundo was born and raised in Kenya, and began her career at an advertising agency in Nairobi as a trainee commercial layout artist before moving to the UK to attend a foundation course at Cambridge School of Art. Her BA Hons degree at Farnham (1973–1976), was in 3D Ceramics, Printmaking and Photography. A three-year museum education teaching post at the Commonwealth Institute, London (1976–1979), was followed with a postgraduate MA from the Royal College of Art (1979–1982). Now Emerita professor at the University for the Creative Arts, she taught at the university from 1997–2014. Magdalene Odundo has spent forty years in education as a maker, researcher, research supervisor, visiting lecturer, and external examiner, to various national and international universities. Magdalene has been a mentor to many young aspiring artists, encouraging many especially from Africa to take up ceramics as a profession.

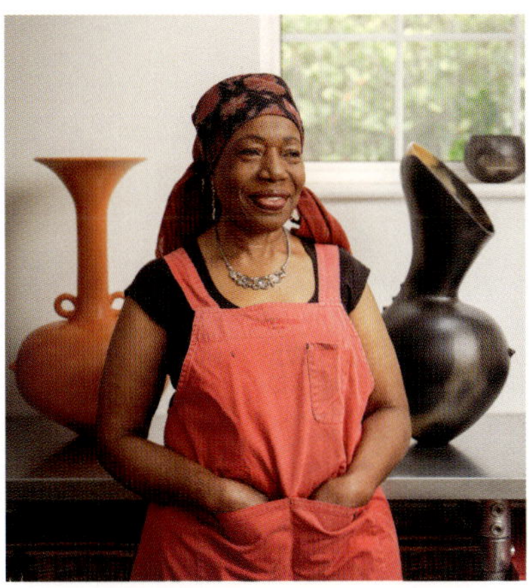

■ Magdalene Odundo.

Odundo was awarded the African Art Recognition Award by Detroit Art Institute in 2008, the African Heritage Outstanding Achievement in the Arts, Nairobi, Kenya in 2012 and a Lifetime Achievement Award from the International Ceramic Festival in 2019. She has honorary doctorates from the University of Florida, Gainesville, University of Arts, London, The Royal College of Art, London and Anglia Ruskin University, Cambridge. Magdalene Odundo is Patron & Trustee of the National Society for Education of Art & Design (NSEAD), UK, a Trustee of the Watts Gallery, Surrey and The Hepworth Wakefield, West Yorkshire and is a member of the National Museums of Kenya Nairobi's Contemporary Art Gallery project.

Odundo's work is represented in various public and private collections in several countries around the world. Odundo's recent exhibition, the groundbreaking *The Journey of Things* at the Hepworth Wakefield and the Sainsbury Centre for Visual Arts, Norwich, included installations in glass, bronze, print, drawing and photography. Odundo's work was also included in *The Milk of Dreams* at La Biennale di Venezia, Venice, 2022. Magdalene Odundo received a DBE from Queen Elizabeth II for her contribution to Art and Arts Education in the 2020 New Year's Honours.

Lawson Oyekan was born in south London and raised in Nigeria. In 2001 he won the Grand Price Award in the 1st World Ceramic Biennale, held in Korea. He had a solo exhibition at Canary Wharf in London in 2011. He has participated in residencies in the USA (the Northern Clay Centre in Minneapolis, Archie Bray Foundation in Helena, Montana, and the MICA in Baltimore), in the UK (Loughborough University, Oxford Museum of Modern Art, and Camden Art Centre, London) and Finland (South Karelia Museum in Lapeenraanta).

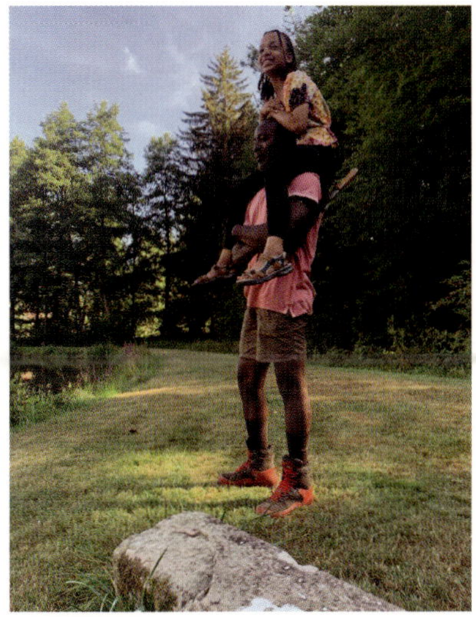

■ Lawson Oyekan, with Ella Oyekan.

Frances Priest is an Edinburgh-based artist and designer with a specialism in ceramics. Her work explores cultural histories of ornament and pattern. Central to the work is an interest in pattern books as a means of documenting and disseminating languages of ornament, reflecting upon the ever-changing interpretations of ornamental motifs as they move between drawing and material form. Over the past twenty years, Frances has developed an internationally recognised practice, represented in private collections across the globe and UK public collections including The Fitzwilliam Museum, The Victoria and Albert Museum and The National

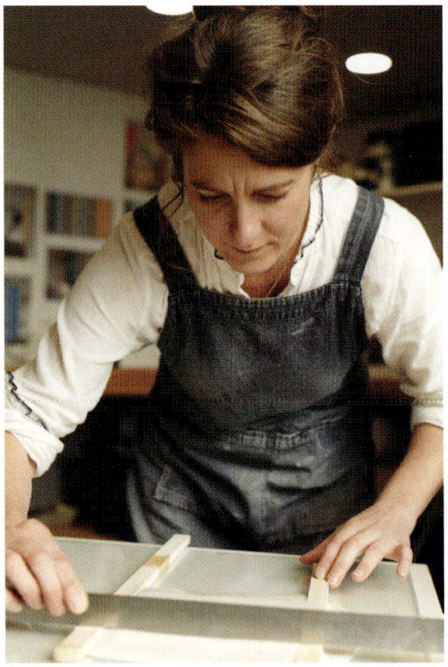

■ Frances Priest.

Museum of Scotland. Public commissions include *The Tiled Corridor* for Edinburgh & Lothians Health Foundation and *Patterns of Flora* for Atlas Arts. Her work has featured in biennials and awards including, European Ceramic Context, The Wesley Barrell Craft Award, The British Ceramics Biennale, Arts & Business Scotland Award, Homo Faber, and The John Smedley Craft Prize. Frances is a Homo Faber selected maker and a QEST Scholar.

Sara Purvey completed her master's degree in ceramics at Bath School of Art and Design, Bath Spa University in 2009, having completed her BA (Hons) in ceramics in 1991. Purvey is currently Artist in Residence at the Corsham Court Campus of Bath Spa University in Wiltshire. Purvey's solo exhibitions include galleries in St Ives, Amsterdam, Bath and Ludlow and she has shown widely in group exhibitions throughout the UK, USA, and Germany. Her works on paper and in ceramic have been acquired by public collections including Pallant House

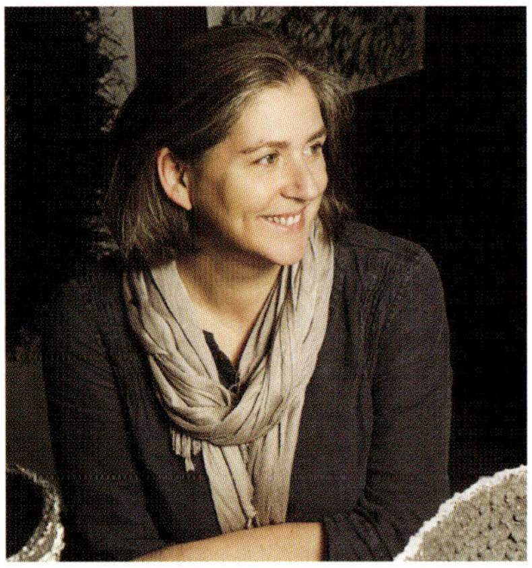

■ Sarah Purvey.

in Chichester, Swindon Museum and Art Gallery, Chippenham Museum Wiltshire, and the Bath Spa University Art Collection. Purvey's work is represented by galleries both nationally and internationally.

Nicholas Rena (b.1963) was educated at Eton College where he studied art under Gordon Baldwin. His postgraduate qualifications include an MA in Architecture from Cambridge University (1986) and MA in Ceramics and Glass at the

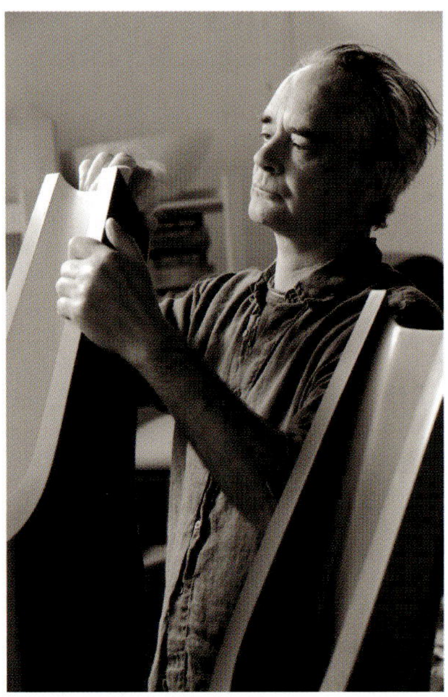

■ Nicholas Rena.

Royal College of Art (1995) where his tutors were Alison Britton and Martin Smith. He was selected for the Jerwood Prize twice, in 2001 and again in 2008, with *The Ecstasy of St Teresa*, a dynamic installation of typically oversized jugs and bowls in violently contrasting colours. His work is represented in the permanent public collections of the V&A Museum, the Louvre Paris and the Carnegie Institute, Pittsburgh, amongst others. Strong, thick-walled forms, press-moulded and carved, finished with painstakingly precise smooth surfaces layered with intense colour are the hallmarks of his art: 'Perhaps you might expect this of an ex-architect – a grander, deeper feeling for interior space and containing wall.' – Alison Britton.

Paul Scott is a Cumbria-based artist with a diverse practice and an international reputation. He is well known for research into printed vitreous surfaces, as well as his characteristic blue and white artworks in glazed ceramic. *Cumbrian Blue(s)* artworks can be found in public collections around the globe, including The National Museum of Art Architecture and Design Norway, V&A London, National Museums Liverpool; Birmingham, Boston, Brooklyn, Montgomery, Philadelphia & Pittsburgh Art Museums in the United States. Scott has held research fellowships in the Fine Art Department, University of Newcastle Upon Tyne (2000–2002), MIRIAD Manchester Metropolitan University, 2004–2007 (PhD) and 2012–2014 (Digital Research Fellow). He was Professor of Ceramics at Oslo National Academy of the Arts (KHiO) from 2011–2017. His most recent research project, *New American Scenery*, was enabled by an

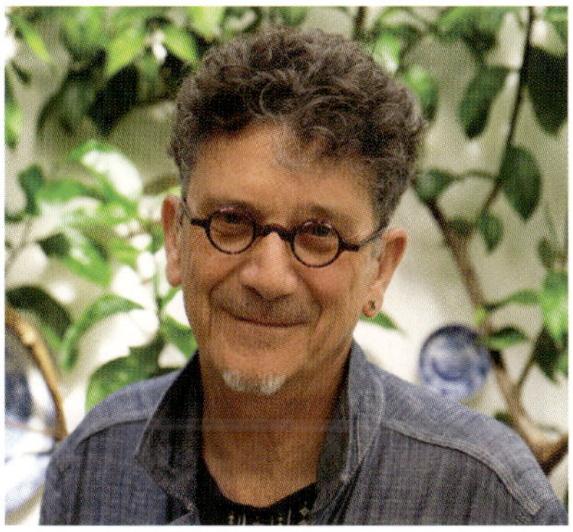

Paul Scott.

Alturas Foundation Artist Award, Ferrin Contemporary, and funding from Arts Council England.

Julian Stair is one of the UK's leading potters and writers on ceramics. He has exhibited internationally since 1986 and has work in over thirty public collections including the Victoria and Albert Museum, British Museum, Museum of Arts & Design, New York, Mashiko Museum of Ceramic Art, Japan, Museum Boijmans van Beuningen, Rotterdam and Kolumba Museum, Cologne. Regularly contributing to ceramic publications since the 1980s, Julian is an authority on the history of English studio ceramics (PhD, RCA, 2002). Recent solo exhibitions include *Equivalenze*, ICA Milan, Italy (2019), *Equivalence*, Corvi-Mora, London (2018), *Quotidian* (Corvi-Mora 2014) and *Quietus: The Vessel, Death and the Human Body* at Middlesbrough Institute of Modern Art, National Museum of Wales Cardiff, Winchester Cathedral, Somerset House, London and Manchester Cathedral (2012–2016). From rites of passage to the daily touch of a cup, Stair's work celebrates the dynamics of use and the way that pottery is integral to our social experience.

Jo Taylor studied ceramics at Bath Spa University, graduating from the Master's Degree with distinction in 2012, and was elected a member of the Royal Society of Sculptors in 2014. In 2019 she was commissioned by ITV to interpret their logo as sculpture, filmed for an ident as part of project *ITV Creates*. During lockdown in 2020 she was commissioned by the Crowood Press to write *Handbuilt Ceramics*, published in October 2021. Her techniques were featured in *Ceramic Review* magazine's 'Masterclass' article and accompanying film in September 2020. Exhibition highlights include *For Love of the Master, Dublin Castle 2022, Together We Rise, Chichester Cathedral 2022,* solo show *Convolutions in Clay* at the Young Gallery, Salisbury 2022; *COLLECT, Artefact* and *Crafting a Difference* with Vessel Gallery; *10th Gyeonggi International Ceramic Biennale* and *RWA Sculpture Open 2019*; *PlatFORM* at TATE Liverpool, 2018; Sweet 18, Kasteel D'Ursell 2015; solo show *Emergence*, Holburne Museum, Bath, 2012.

Tina Vlassopulos (b.1954, London, UK) received a BA (Hons) in Ceramics from Bristol Polytechnic in 1977 and moved back to London where she established her first studio at 401½ Workshops.

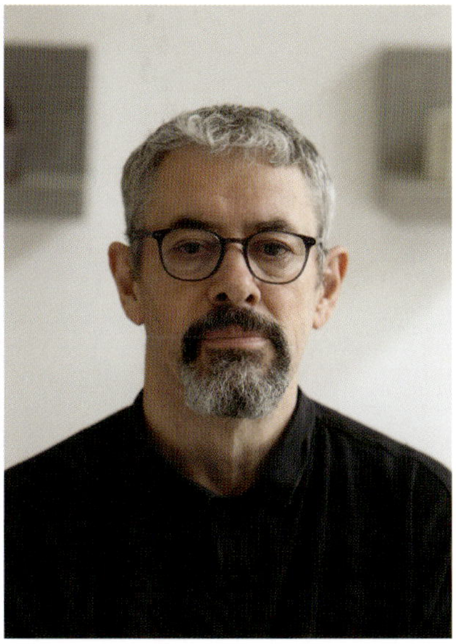

Julian Stair.

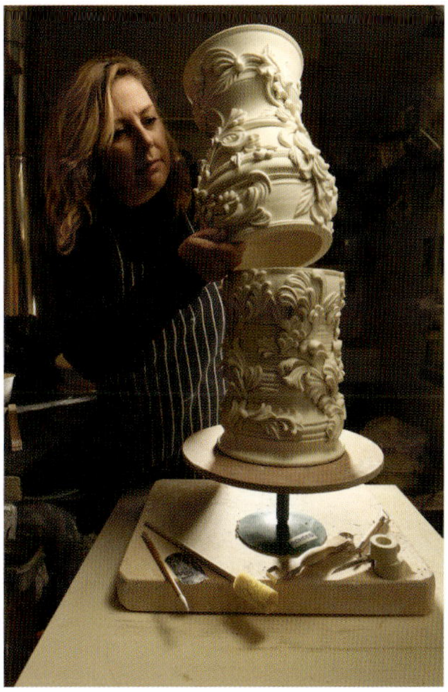

Jo Taylor.

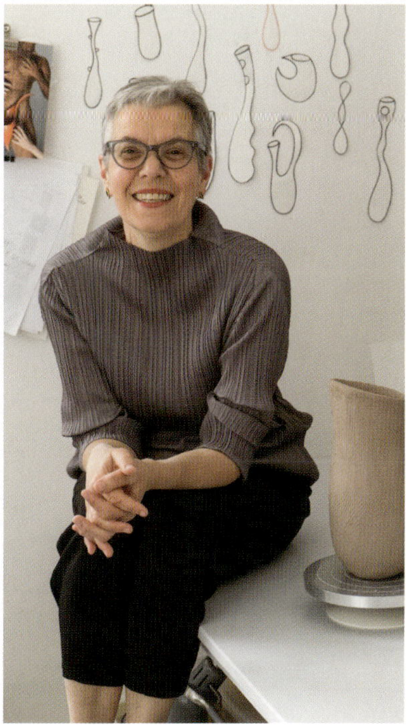

Tina Vlassopulos.

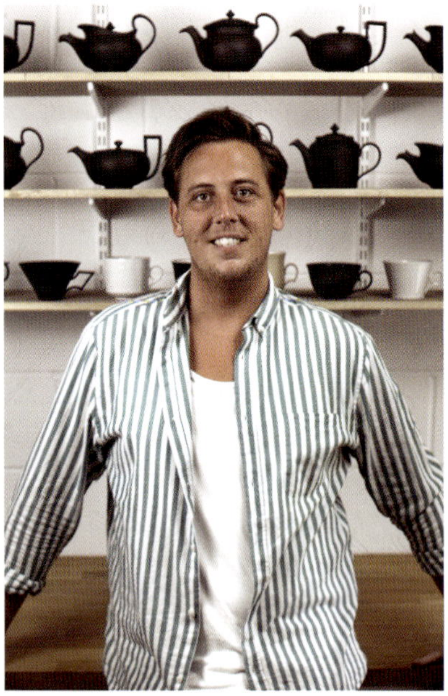

■ Matthew Warner.

She now works from a studio at home. Her work, which is in many public and private collections, has also won international awards, including The Sidney Myer Fund International Ceramic Award in 2006 and twice at The World Ceramic Biennale Korea in 2009 and 2021. Highlights include an installation called *Conversations with Friends*, which was shown at Collect Open at the Saatchi Gallery in London in 2019. In 2017 her work was shown at the Keramiekmuseum Princessehof in the Netherlands in an exhibition entitled *Sexy Ceramics*, and in 2014 her work was included in the exhibition *Vessels: The Spirit of Modern British Ceramics* at Mashiko Museum of Ceramic Art in Japan.

Matthew Warner (b.1989) began making at a very young age with his grandfather, who was a passionate supporter of Warner's work. Warner attended school in Chelmsford, Essex, where he was born, and later attended Colchester Institute to continue his art education. Upon completion of his Art Foundation he moved to London (2009), where he was one of the final cohort of students enrolled in Camberwell's prestigious ceramics course. After graduating in 2012, with the support of The Queen Elizabeth Scholarship Trust (QEST), Warner began an apprenticeship under Julian Stair and remained there for three years. In 2015 he established his studio at Cockpit Deptford, in southeast London, where he continues to work.

Notes

Introduction

[1] Laura Gray, *Contemporary British Ceramics and the Influence of Sculpture: Monuments, Multiples, Destruction and Display* (New York and Abingdon: Routledge, 2018), p.3.

[2] Ibid, pp.3–4.

[3] Alison Britton, *Seeing Things: Collected Writing on Art, Craft and Design,* 2nd edn. (London: Occasional Papers, 2022), pp.30–32.

[4] Katie Treggiden, *Urban Potters* (No pl.: Ludion, 2017), p.9; Emmanuel Cooper, *Contemporary Ceramics* (London: Thames & Hudson, 2009), pp.6–7.

[5] Grayson Perry, 'Climbing Everest Without Oxygen,' in *The Pre-Therapy Years*, ed. by Catrin Jones and Chris Stephens (London: Thames & Hudson, 2020), p.61.

[6] Ibid.

[7] Immanuel Kant, *Kant's Critique of Judgement*, trans. J. H. Bernard (London: Macmillan, 1914), p.184. Italics in this, and the quotations that follow, are in the original.

[8] Paul Greenhalgh, 'The history of craft,' in *The Culture of Craft*, ed. Peter Dormer (Manchester and New York: Manchester University Press, 1997), pp.25–35.

[9] William Morris, 'The Lesser Arts of Life,' in *Ceramic Art: Comment and Review, 1882–1977*, ed. Garth Clark (New York: E.P. Dutton, 1978), p.9.

[10] Ibid, p.31.

[11] Bernard Leach, 'Towards A Standard,' in *Ceramic Art: Comment and Review, 1882–1977*, ed. Garth Clark (New York: E.P. Dutton, 1978), p.78.

[12] Ibid, p.76.

[13] Julian Stair, 'From Precepts to Praxis: The Origins of British Studio Pottery,' in *Things of Beauty Growing: British Studio Pottery*, ed. by Glenn Adamson, Martin Droth and Simon Olding (New Haven: Yale University Press, 2017), pp.48–9.

[14] Ibid.

[15] Ibid, p.38.

[16] Peter Lane, *Ceramic Form: Design and Decoration (Revised Edition)* (London: A & C Black, 1998), p.28.

[17] Ibid, p.200.

[18] Rose Slivka, 'The New Ceramic Presence,' in *Ceramic Art: Comment and Review, 1882–1977*, ed. Garth Clark (New York: E.P. Dutton, 1978), pp.135–6.

[19] Alison Britton, 'Alison Britton', in Crafts Council, *The Maker's Eye* (London: Crafts Council, 1981), p.16.

[20] Ibid.

[21] Ibid.

[22] ICA, *Fast Forward: New Directions in British Ceramics* (London: ICA, 1985), p.27.

[23] Tanya Harrod, *The Crafts in Britain in the Twentieth Century* (Yale: Yale University Press, 1999), p.421.

[24] Edmund De Waal, *Bernard Leach* (London: Tate, 2014), p.75.

[25] The museum number for this jar is 1999,0302.1.

[26] See, for instance, Sainsbury's Centre for Visual Art, *Lucie Rie, Hans Coper, and their Pupils* (Norwich: SCVA, 1991).

[27] Martina Margetts, 'Metamorphosis: the Culture of Ceramics,' in Museum of Modern Art Oxford, *The Raw and the Cooked: New Work in Clay in Britain* (Oxford: Museum of Modern Art Oxford, 1993), p.15.

[28] Ibid, pp.13–4.

[29] Bruce Metcalf, 'Craft and art, culture and biology,' in *The Culture of Craft*, edited by Peter Dormer (Manchester and New York: Manchester University Press, 1997), p.81.

[30] Greenhalgh, 'The history of craft,' p.47.

[31] Harrod, *The Crafts*, p.10.

[32] Bernard Leach, *A Potter's Challenge*, edited by David Outerbridge (London: Souvenir Press, 1976), p.22.

[33] Ibid, p.26.

[34] Johanna Drucker, 'Affectivity and Entropy: Production Aesthetics in Contemporary Culture,' in *The Craft Reader*, ed. Glenn Adamson (Oxford and New York: Berg, 2010), p.593.
[35] Ibid.
[36] Peter Dormer, 'The status of craft,' in *The Culture of Craft*, ed. Peter Dormer (Manchester and New York: Manchester University Press, 1997), pp.18–9.
[37] Garth Clark, 'How Envy Killed the Crafts,' in *The Craft Reader*, ed. Glenn Adamson (Oxford and New York: Berg, 2010), p.446.
[38] Ibid, pp.446–47.
[39] Crafts Council, *Pandora's Box* (London: Crafts Council, 1995), p.5.
[40] John Houston, *The Abstract Vessel: Ceramics in Studio* (London: Bellew, 1991), p.12.
[41]Ibid.
[42] Ibid, p.13.
[43] Ibid, p.56.
[44] Alison Britton, 'Use, Beauty, Ugliness and Irony,' in *The Raw and the Cooked: New Work in Clay in Britain*, ed. Museum of Modern Art Oxford (Oxford: Museum of Modern Art Oxford, 1993), p.11.
[45] Gray, *Contemporary British Ceramics*, p.6.

Chapter One
[46] Magdalene Odundo et al., *Magdalene Odundo in Cambridge* (Cambridge: The Fitzwilliam Museum, 2021), p.62.
[47] Emmanuel Cooper, 'The Clay of Life: The Ceramic Vessels of Magdalene Odundo,' in *Magdalene Odundo*, ed. Anthony Slayter-Ralph (Aldershot: Lund Humphries, 2004), p.39.
[48] Ibid, pp.10–22.
[49] Ibid, p.15.
[50] Bernard Leach, *Drawings, Verse & Belief* (London: Jupiter, 1977), p.9.
[51] Ibid, p.5.
[52] Bernard Leach, *A Potter's Challenge*, p.48.
[53] Ibid, p.39.
[54] Magdalene Odundo et al., *Magdalene Odundo*, pp.6–7.
[55] Emmanuel Cooper, 'The Clay of Life', p.41.
[56] Ibid.
[57] Magdalene Odundo et al., *Magdalene Odundo*, p.9.

Chapter Two
[58] Victor Turner et al., *The Ritual Process: Structure and Anti-Structure* (London & New York: Routledge, 1969), p.69.
[59] Victor Turner, 'Liminal to Liminoid, in Play, Flow, and Ritual: an essay in comparative symbology,' *Rice Institute Pamphlet - Rice University Studies*, 60, no. 3 (1974), p.71.
[60] Richard Schechner and Sara Brady, *Performance Studies: An Introduction* (London & New York: Routledge, 2013), p.72.

Chapter Three
[61] Bernard Leach, *The Potter's Challenge*, pp.38–9.

Chapter Four
[62] Maurice Merleau-Ponty, *Phenomenology of Perception*, trans. Donald A. Landes (London and New York: Routledge, 2012), p.4.
[63] Ibid, p.145.
[64] For further analysis of this concept, and its applicability to ceramics, see Ashley Thorpe, 'Ken Eastman: Phenomena,' in *Contemporary British Ceramics: Beneath the Surface* (Marlborough: The Crowood Press, 2021), pp.147–54.
[65] Kent C. Bloomer and Charles W. Moore, *Body, Memory, and Architecture* (Yale: Yale University Press, 1977), p.37.

Chapter Five
[66] William C. Seitz, *The Responsive Eye* (New York: The Museum of Modern Art, 1965), p.9.
[67] Edward Lucie-Smith, *Elizabeth Fritsch: Vessels From Another World* (London: Bellew, 1993), pp.48–57.
[68] Seitz, *The Responsive Eye*, p.7.
[69] Ibid, p.18.
[70] Peter Dormer, *Elizabeth Fritsch in Studio* (London: Bellew, 1985), pp.18–22.
[71] Andrew Lambirth, *Elizabeth Fritsch* (London: The Fine Art Society in collaboration with Joanna Bird Pottery, 2008), p.12.

Chapter Six
[72] Cy Twombly, quoted in Kirk Varnedoe, *Cy Twombly: A Retrospective* (New York: Museum of Modern Art, 1995), p.27.
[73] Varnedoe, *Cy Twombly*, p.33.
[74] Jenny Sjöholm, 'The art studio as archive: tracing the geography of artistic potentiality, progress and production,' *Cultural Geographies*, vol. 21, no. 3 (July 2014): pp.513.
[75] Greer Crawley, 'The Archive,' in *Sediment*, ed. Mariele Neudecker (London: Anomie, 2021), p.99.
[76] William Shakespeare, *The Life of King Henry V*, ed. Barbara A. Mowat and Paul Werstine (New York: Washington Square Press, 1995), p.7.

Chapter Seven
[77] Hazlitt Holland-Hibbert, *Barbara Hepworth: Drawings from the 1940s* (London and New York: Hazlitt Holland-Hibbert, 2005), p.8.
[78] Louis Slobodkin, *Sculpture: Principles and Practice* (New York: Dover Publications, 1949), p.77.

Chapter Eight

[79] Brian Sparkes, *The Red and The Black: Studies in Greek Pottery* (London & New York: Routledge, 1996), p.2.

[80] Ibid, p.62.

[81] See Charles Sterling, *Still Life Painting: From Antiquity to the Twentieth* Century, 2nd edn. (New York: Harper and Row, 1981).

[82] Ben Nicholson, 'Extract from letter to Lilian Somerville, March 25/26 1954,' in Maurice de Sausmarez, *Ben Nicholson: A Studio International special* (London: Studio International, 1969), p.57.

[83] Alun Graves, 'Ben Nicholson's Designs for Foley China,' *The Burlington Magazine*, vol. 140, no. 1143 (June 1998), pp.386–90.

[84] Lucie Rie, quoted in Cyril Frankel, *Modern Pots: Hans Coper, Lucie Rie & their Contemporaries* (London: Thames & Hudson, 2000), p.67.

[85] Peter Aspden, 'Rules of Abstraction,' *FT Magazine*, 18–19 March 2006: p.34.

Chapter Nine

[86] Tamara Préaud et al., *The Sèvres Porcelain Manufactory: Alexandre Brongniart and the Triumph of Art and Industry, 1800–1847* (New York: Bard Graduate Center for Studies in the Decorative Arts, 1997), p.23.

[87] Ibid.

[88] Ibid.

Chapter Ten

[89] Howard Morphy, 'Art as a mode of action: Some problems with Gell's *Art and Agency*,' in *Museum Objects: Experiencing the Properties of Things*, ed. Sandra H. Dudley (London & New York: Routledge, 2012), p.351.

[90] Erving Goffman, 'Symbols of Class Status,' *The British Journal of Sociology*, vol. 2, no. 4 (December 1951): p.304.

[91] See Tristram Hunt, *The Radical Potter: Josiah Wedgwood and the Transformation of Britain* (London: Allen Lane, 2021).

Chapter Eleven

[92] Malcolm Andrews, *Landscape and Western Art* (Oxford: Oxford University Press, 1999), p.1.

[93] Ibid, pp.4–5.

[94] Gillian Rose, 'Looking at Landscape: The Uneasy Pleasures of Power, from *Feminism and Geography: The Limits of Geographical Knowledge*,' in *The Cultural Geography Reader*, edited by Timothy Oakes, and Patricia L. Price (London & New York: Routledge, 2008), p.172.

[95] James Walvin, *Sugar: The World Corrupted, from Slavery to Obesity* (London: Little, Brown Books, 2017).

[96] Sally Irwin, 'Forced Labour in Tea farming,' *The Freedom Hub*, https://thefreedomhub.org/blog/ending-modern-slavery/forced-labour-in-tea/. Date accessed: April 26, 2022.

[97] See also the chapters on Neil Brownsword and Connor Coulston in Thorpe, *Contemporary British Ceramics*.

Chapter Twelve

[98] B.L. Ullman, 'Satura and Satire', *Classical Philology*, vol. 8, no.2 (April 1913): p.186.

[99] Theodore D. Kharpertian, *The Menippean Satires of Thomas Pynchon* (Cranbury, London and Ontario: Associated University Presses, 1990), pp.25–27.

[100] David Mayer and Michael Gamer, '(Un)making a Monster: Melodrama, *The Satirist*, and the Cartoons of Sam De Wilde, *Nineteenth Century Theatre and Film*, vol. 48, no. 2 (2021): p.127.

[101] Frank M. Turner, 'Gladstone: A Political Not a Cultural Radical,' in *William Gladstone: New Studies and Perspectives*, ed. Roland Quinault et al., (London and New York: Routledge, 2016), pp.15–30.

[102] G.R. Searle, *Morality and the Market in Modern Britain* (Oxford: Clarendon Press, 1998), pp.1–47.

[103] Peter Brook, *The Melodramatic Imagination: Balzac, Henry James, Melodrama, and the Mode of Excess* (New Haven and London' Yale University Press, 1976), p.11.

[104] Ibid, pp.4–7.

[105] Ibid, p.1.

Chapter Thirteen

[106] Gijs Van Hensbergen, *Gaudí* (London: Harper Collins, 2001), p.76.

[107] Owen Jones, *The Grammar of Ornament* (London: Bernard Quaritch, 1868), pp.9–12.

[108] Ibid, p.5.

[109] For my analysis of the work of these two artists, see Ashley Thorpe, *Contemporary British Ceramics: Beneath the* Surface, pp.123–31; pp.147–54.

[110] Homi Bhabha, *The Location of Culture* (Abingdon: Routledge, 2004), p.243.

[111] Sarah Rothwell, 'Capturing Decorative Art – The Work of Frances Priest,' *The Decorative Arts Society Journal*, vol.45 (2021): p.19.

[112] Bhabha, *The Location of Culture*, p.201.

[113] Ibid, pp.211–3.

[114] Ibid, p.243.

Chapter Fourteen

[115] Peter Gaskell, *Artisans and Machinery: The Moral and Physical Condition of the Manufacturing Population* (London: John W. Parker, 1836), pp.357–58.

[116] Ibid, iii.

[117] Ibid, p.358.

[118] Bernard Leach, *The Potter's Challenge*, p.19.

[119] Hermann Muthesius, 'Art and the Machine,' in *The Craft Reader*, ed. Glenn Adamson (London & New York: Berg, 2010), p.114.
[120] Walter Benjamin, 'The Work of Art in the Age of its Technical Reproducibility (Second Version),' in *The Work of Art in the Age of its Technical Reproducibility, and Other Writings*, ed. Michael Jennings, Brigid Doherty, Thomas Y. Levin (Cambridge, Mass: Belknapp Press of Harvard University Press, 2008), p.35.
[121] Consiglia Azzopardi, 'Lacemaking in Malta,' *The Gozo Observer*, no. 16 (June 2007), pp.27–8.
[122] Benjamin, 'The Work of Art,' p.38.

Chapter Fifteen
[123] Jacques Derrida, *On Touching – Jean-Luc Nancy*, trans. Christine Irizarry (Stanford: Stanford University Press, 2005), p.138.
[124] Ibid.
[125] Ibid, p.34.
[126] J. Hillis Miller, 'Touching Derrida Touching Nancy; The Main Traits of Derrida's Hand,' *Derrida Today*, vol. 1, no. 2 (2008): p.159.

Chapter Sixteen
[127] Peter Dormer, 'The Language and Practical Philosophy of Craft', in *The Culture of Craft*, ed. Peter Dormer (Manchester: Manchester University Press, 1997), p.222.
[128] Gaston Bachelard, *The Poetics of Reverie: Childhood, Language, and the Cosmos* (Boston: Beacon Press 1971), p.72.
[129] David Abram, *The Spell of The Sensuous: Perception and Language in a More-Than-Human World* (New York: Vintage, 1996), p.49–53. '...this dynamic blend of receptivity and creativity by which every animate organism necessarily orients itself to the world...' (p.50)
[130] Sōetsu Yanagi (1889–1961), Japanese philosopher of crafts and founder of the *Mingei* (Japanese folk crafts) movement. Lifelong friend of Bernard Leach.
[131] Yanagi's seminal work, *The Unknown Craftsman,* (adapted by Leach) contains his famous essay on the Japanese National Treasure, the Kizaemon Edo Teabowl. Of it he says, 'It is not the product of nervous excitement, so it does not harbour the seeds of perversion.' Sōetsu Yanagi, *The Unknown Craftsman* (Tokyo: Kodansha International, 1976), p.192. (N.B. I am proud of my work's 'nervous excitement'.)
[132] Bernard Leach bought the jar whilst touring in Imperial Japanese occupied Korea with Sōetsu Yanagi in 1935. He gave it to the potter Lucie Rie in 1943 and it is now in the collections of the British Museum (see Note 25 for the Museum Number).
[133] Antoni Tàpies (1923–2012). Precise attribution unknown (probably an interview): 'The meaning of a work depends on the co-operation of the viewer. Those people who live without inner images, lacking imagination and the necessary sensitivity to generate their own set of mental associations, will see nothing at all.'
[134] Mercia Eliade, *The Forge and the Crucible* (Chicago: University of Chicago Press, 1978), p.41.

Chapter Seventeen
No notes.

Chapter Eighteen
[135] The British Museum Object Number: 2018,3014.1.1–63.
[136] Museo de Arte de Ponce Object Number: 63.0406.
[137] Karl Maton, 'Habitus,' in *Pierre Bourdieu: Key Concepts*, ed. Michael Grenfell (London: Routledge, 2012), p.51.
[138] Email to author, 28 May 2022.

Chapter Nineteen
[139] Andrew Benjamin, *Writing Art and Architecture* (Melbourne: re.press, 2010), p.98.
[140] Museum number: NG172.
[141] Richard Serra in Hal Foster, *The Art-Architecture Complex* (London: Verso, 2011), p.241.
[142] Museum number: XF377.
[143] Benjamin, *Writing Art and Architecture*, p.93.

Chapter Twenty
[144] The material that follows in this, and the subsequent, paragraph is summarised from a recorded lecture given by Oyibo explaining his theorem. See: Gabriel Oyibo, 'The Grand Unified Theorem (Full Lecture),' *YouTube*, https://www.youtube.com/watch?v=g_1-2Q5EI68. Date accessed: 28 September 2022, Last updated: March 1, 2014.
[145] For a review of the mathematical accuracy of GAGUT, see A. O. E. Animalu, *A Review of Oyibo's Grand Unified Theorum, With Realizations of a Hierarchy of Oyibo-Einstein Relativities*, http://www.math.buffalo.edu/mad/physics/Animalu_Alex_GAGUTreview1.pdf. Date accessed: 26 September 2022.
[146] Lawson Oyekan, 'Lawson Oyekan, Interview with Sarah Tanguy,' *axisweb.org*, https://www.axisweb.org/p/lawsonoyekan/. Date accessed: 29 September 2020, Last updated: 23 March 2007.
[147] Oyibo, 'The Grand Unified Theorem (Full Lecture)'.

Chapter Twenty-One
[148] Edward Kamens, *The Buddhist Poetry of the Great Kamo Priestess: Daisaiin Senshi and Hosshin Wakashu* (Ann

Arbor: University of Michigan Press, 2020), p.85, p.143.

[149] Ibid, p.42.

[150] Ibid, p.89.

[151] This jar was acquired by Bernard Leach in Korea in 1935. He gifted it to Lucie Rie in 1943. Following Rie's death in 1995, the jar was purchased by the British Museum in 1998 (see Note 25 for the Museum Number).

[152] Susan Buys and Victoria Oakley, *Conservation and Restoration of Ceramics* (London & New York: Routledge, 2014), p.3.

[153] Fabio Rambelli, 'Introduction: The Invisible Empire: Spirits and Animism in Contemporary Japan,' in *Spirits and Animism in Contemporary Japan*, ed. by Fabio Rambelli (London: Bloomsbury, 2019), p.1.

[154] Satō Hiroo, 'The Dead Who remain: Spirits and Changing Views of the Afterlife,' in *Spirits and Animism in Contemporary Japan*, ed. by Fabio Rambelli (London: Bloomsbury, 2019), p.27.

[155] Anette Marfording, 'Cultural Relativism and the Construction of Culture: An Examination of Japan,' *Human Rights Quarterly*, vol. 19, no. 2 (1997): p.434.

[156] Ibid.

[157] John W. Barry et al., *Immigrant Youth in Cultural Transition: Acculturation, Identity, and Adaptation Across National Contexts* (Mahwah: Lawrence Erlbaum Associates, 2006), p.3.

[158] Akiko Hirai, *Akiko Hirai* (Uppingham: Goldmark Gallery, 2021), p.8.

[159] Ibid, p.5.

[160] Motokiyo Fukaya, 'Perspective on the Body in Early Modern Japan,' in *Materiality in Religion and* Culture, Saburo Shawn Morishita (ed.) (Zürich: Lit, 2017), p.74.

[161] Aristotle, *Physics Books 1–4*, trans. P.H. Wicksted and F.M. Cornford (Havard: Havard University Press, 1989), p.43.

Chapter Twenty-Two

[162] Jenny Chamarette, *Phenomenology and the Future of Film: Rethinking Subjectivity Beyond French Cinema* (Houndmills: Palgrave Macmillan, 2012), p.5.

[163] Sergei Eisenstein, 'A Dialectic Approach to Film Form,' in *Film Form: Essays in Film Theory*, ed. and trans. Jay Leda (New York and London: Harcourt, Brace & World, 1977), p.57.

[164] See Stair, 'From Precepts to Praxis,' pp.29–55.

Chapter Twenty-Three

[165] Charles Darwin, *On the Origin of Species By Means of Natural Selection, or the Preservation of Favoured Races in the Struggle for Life* (London: John Murray, 1873), p.104.

[166] Tony Birks in Anonymous, *Gabriele Koch* (London: Gallery K, 2000), n.p.

[167] David Attenborough in Anonymous, *Gabriele Koch* (Yeovil: Marston House, 1995), n.p.

[168] Tony Birks, *Gabriele Koch: Hand building and smoke firing* (Catrine: Stenlake, 2009), p.16.

[169] Darwin, *On the Origin of Species*, p.429.

Chapter Twenty-Four

[170] David Attenborough with Jonnie Hughes, *A Life on Our Planet: My Witness Statement and A Vision for the Future* (London: Ebury, 2020), pp.3–4.

[171] Greta Thunberg, 'Transcript: Greta Thunberg's Speech at the U.N. Climate Action Summit,' *NPR*, https://www.npr.org/2019/09/23/763452863/transcript-greta-thunbergs-speech-at-the-u-n-climate-action-summit?t=1633795933303. Date accessed: 9 October 2021.

[172] Miriam C. Dobson, Jill L Edmondson, 'Ugly vegetables are a major cause of food waste,' *The Independent*, 29 March 2019, https://www.independent.co.uk/life-style/food-and-drink/ugly-vegetable-food-waste-fruit-vegetable-a8825311.html. Date accessed: 9 October 2021.

[173] Sarah Clayton, 'Your Food Isn't Rubbish,' *Love Food Hate Waste*, https://www.lovefoodhatewaste.com/why-save-food. Date accessed: 12 October 2021.

[174] Thunberg, 'Transcript'.

Bibliography

Abram, David. *The Spell of The Sensuous: Perception and Language in a More-Than-Human World* (New York: Vintage, 1996).

Andrews, Malcolm. *Landscape and Western Art* (Oxford: Oxford University Press, 1999).

Animalu, A. O. E. *A Review of Oyibo's Grand Unified Theorum, With Realizations of a Hierarchy of Oyibo-Einstein Relativities*, http://www.math.buffalo.edu/mad/physics/Animalu_Alex_GAGUTreview1.pdf. Date accessed: 26 September 2022.

Anonymous. *Gabriele Koch* (London: Gallery K, 2000).

-----------. *Gabriele Koch* (Yeovil: Marston House, 1995).

Aristotle. *Physics Books 1–4.* Translated by P.H. Wicksted and F.M. Cornford (Harvard: Harvard University Press, 1989).

Aspden, Peter. 'Rules of Abstraction,' *FT Magazine*, March 18–19, 2006, pp.34–37.

Attenborough, David, with Hughes, Jonnie. *A Life on Our Planet: My Witness Statement and A Vision for the Future* (London: Ebury, 2020).

Azzopardi, Consiglia. 'Lacemaking in Malta,' *The Gozo Observer*, no. 16 (June 2007), pp.27–8.

Bachelard, Gaston. *The Poetics of Reverie: Childhood, Language, and the Cosmos* (Boston: Beacon Press 1971).

Barry, John W. et al. *Immigrant Youth in Cultural Transition: Acculturation, Identity, and Adaptation Across National Contexts* (Mahwah: Lawrence Erlbaum Associates, 2006).

Benjamin, Andrew. *Writing Art and Architecture* (Melbourne: re.press, 2010).

Benjamin, Walter. 'The Work of Art in the Age of its Technical Reproducibility (SecondVersion)'. In *The Work of Art in the Age of its Technical Reproducibility, and Other Writings*, edited by Michael Jennings, Brigid Doherty, and Thomas Y. Levin (Cambridge, Mass: Belknapp Press of Harvard University Press, 2008), pp.19–55.

Bhabha, Homi. *The Location of Culture* (Abingdon: Routledge, 2004).

Birks, Tony. *Gabriele Koch: Hand building and smoke firing* (Catrine: Stenlake, 2009).

Bloomer, Kent C., and Moore, Charles W. *Body, Memory, and Architecture* (Yale: Yale University Press, 1977).

Britton, Alison. 'Alison Britton.' In *The Maker's Eye*, edited by Crafts Council (London: Crafts Council, 1981), pp.16–19.

-----------. 'Use, Beauty, Ugliness and Irony'. In *The Raw and the Cooked: New Work in Clay in Britain*, edited by Museum of Modern Art Oxford (Oxford: Museum of Modern Art Oxford, 1993), pp.9–12.

-----------. *Seeing Things: Collected Writing on Art, Craft and Design.* 2nd edn (London: Occasional Papers, 2022).

Brook, Peter. *The Melodramatic Imagination: Balzac, Henry James, Melodrama, and the Mode of Excess* (New Haven and London: Yale University Press, 1976).

Buys, Susan, and Oakley, Victoria. *Conservation and Restoration of Ceramics* (London & New York: Routledge, 2014).

Chamarette, Jenny. *Phenomenology and the Future of Film: Rethinking Subjectivity Beyond French Cinema* (Houndmills: Palgrave Macmillan, 2012).

Clark, Garth. 'How Envy Killed the Crafts'. In *The Craft Reader*, edited by Glenn Adamson (Oxford and New York: Berg, 2010), pp.445–53.

Clayton, Sarah. 'Your Food Isn't Rubbish'. *Love Food Hate Waste*, https://www.lovefoodhatewaste.com/why-save-food. Date accessed: 12 October 2021.

Cooper, Emmanuel. 'The Clay of Life: The Ceramic Vessels of Magdalene Odundo'. In *Magdalene Odundo*, edited by Anthony Slayter-Ralph (Aldershot: Lund Humphries, 2004), PP.9–55.

-----------. *Contemporary Ceramics* (London: Thames & Hudson, 2009).

Crafts Council. *Pandora's Box* (London: Crafts Council, 1995).

Crawley, Greer, 'The Archive'. In *Sediment*, edited by Mariele Neudecker (London: Anomie, 2021), pp.99–101.

Darwin, Charles. *On the Origin of Species By Means of Natural Selection, or the Preservation of Favoured Races in the Struggle for Life* (London: John Murray, 1873).

De Waal, Edmund. *Bernard Leach* (London: Tate, 2014).

Derrida, Jacques. *On Touching – Jean-Luc Nancy*. Translated by Christine Irizarry (Stanford: Stanford University Press, 2005).

Dobson, Miriam C., and Edmondson, Jill L. 'Ugly vegetables are a major cause of food waste,' *The Independent*, 29 March 2019, https://www.independent.co.uk/life-style/food-and-drink/ugly-vegetable-food-waste-fruit-vegetable-a8825311.html. Date accessed: 9 October 2021.

Dormer, Peter. *Elizabeth Fritsch in Studio* (London: Bellew, 1985).

-----------. 'The status of craft'. In *The Culture of Craft*, edited by Peter Dormer (Manchester and New York: Manchester University Press, 1997), pp.18–9.

-----------. 'The Language and Practical Philosophy of Craft'. In *The Culture of Craft*, edited by Peter Dormer (Manchester: Manchester University Press, 1997), pp.219–30.

Drucker, Joanna. 'Affectivity and Entropy: Production Aesthetics in Contemporary Culture'. In *The Craft Reader*, edited by Glenn Adamson (Oxford and New York: Berg, 2010), pp.588–95.

Eisenstein, Sergei. 'A Dialectic Approach to Film Form'. In *Film Form: Essays in Film Theory*, edited and translated by Jay Leda (New York and London: Harcourt, Brace & World, 1977), pp.45–63.

Eliade, Mercia. *The Forge and the Crucible* (Chicago: University of Chicago Press, 1978).

Foster, Hal. *The Art-Architecture Complex* (London: Verso, 2011).

Frankel, Cyril. *Modern Pots: Hans Coper, Lucie Rie & their Contemporaries* (London: Thames & Hudson, 2000).

Fukaya, Motokiyo. 'Perspectives on the Body in Early Modern Japan'. In *Materiality in Religion and Culture*, edited by Saburo Shawn Morishita (Zürich: Lit, 2017), pp.73–80.

Gaskell, Peter. *Artisans and Machinery: The Moral and Physical Condition of the Manufacturing Population* (London: John W. Parker, 1836).

Goffman, Erving. 'Symbols of Class Status,' *The British Journal of Sociology*, vol. 2, no. 4 (December 1951), pp.294–304.

Graves, Alun. 'Ben Nicholson's Designs for Foley China,' *The Burlington Magazine*, vol. 140, no. 1143 (June 1998), pp.386–90.

Gray, Laura. *Contemporary British Ceramics and the Influence of Sculpture: Monuments, Multiples, Destruction and Display* (New York and Abingdon: Routledge, 2018).

Greenhalgh, Paul. 'The History of Craft'. In *The Culture of Craft*, edited by Peter Dormer (Manchester and New York: Manchester University Press, 1997), pp.20–52.

Harrod, Tanya. *The Crafts in Britain in the 20th Century* (Yale: Yale University Press, 1999).

Hazlitt Holland-Hibbert. *Barbara Hepworth: Drawings from the 1940s* (London and New York: Hazlitt Holland-Hibbert, 2005).

Hillis Miller, J. 'Touching Derrida Touching Nancy; The Main Traits of Derrida's Hand,' *Derrida Today*, vol. 1, no. 2 (2008), pp.145–166.

Hirai, Akiko. *Akiko Hirai* (Uppingham: Goldmark Gallery, 2021).

Hiroo, Satō. 'The Dead Who Remain: Spirits and Changing Views of the Afterlife'. In *Spirits and Animism in Contemporary Japan*, edited by Fabio Rambelli (London: Bloomsbury 2019), pp.17–28.

Houston, John. *The Abstract Vessel: Ceramics in Studio* (London: Bellew, 1991).

Hunt, Tristram. *The Radical Potter: Josiah Wedgwood and the Transformation of Britain* (London: Allen Lane, 2021).

ICA. *Fast Forward: New Directions in British Ceramics* (London: ICA, 1985).

Irwin, Sally. 'Forced Labour in Tea farming'. *The Freedom Hub*, https://thefreedomhub.org/blog/ending-modern-slavery/forced-labour-in-tea/. Date accessed: 26 April 2022.

Jones, Owen. *The Grammar of Ornament* (London: Bernard Quaritch, 1868).

Kamens, Edward. *The Buddhist Poetry of the Great Kamo Priestess: Daisaiin Senshi and Hosshin Wakashu* (Ann

Arbor: University of Michigan Press, 2020).

Kant, Immanuel. *Kant's Critique of Judgement*. Translated by J. H. Bernard (London: Macmillan, 1914).

Kharpertian, Theodore D. *The Menippean Satires of Thomas Pynchon* (Cranbury, London and Ontario: Associated University Presses, 1990).

Lambirth, Andrew. *Elizabeth Fritsch* (London: The Fine Art Society in collaboration with Joanna Bird Pottery, 2008).

Lane, Peter. *Ceramic Form: Design and Decoration (Revised Edition)* (London: A & C Black, 1998).

Leach, Bernard. *A Potter's Challenge*, edited by David Outerbridge (London: Souvenir Press, 1976).

-----------. *Drawings, Verse & Belief* (London: Jupiter, 1977).

-----------. 'Towards A Standard', In *Ceramic Art: Comment and Review, 1882–1977*, edited by Garth Clark (New York: E.P. Dutton, 1978), pp.59–85.

Lucie-Smith, Edward. *Elizabeth Fritsch: Vessels From Another World* (London: Bellew, 1993).

Marfording, Anette. 'Cultural Relativism and the Construction of Culture: An Examination of Japan,' *Human Rights Quarterly*, vol. 19, no. 2 (1997), pp.431–48.

Margetts, Martina. 'Metamorphosis: the Culture of Ceramics'. In *The Raw and the Cooked: New Work in Clay in Britain*, edited by Museum of Modern Art Oxford (Oxford: Museum of Modern Art Oxford, 1993), pp.13–15.

Maton, Karl. 'Habitus'. In *Pierre Bourdieu: Key Concepts*, edited by Michael Grenfell (London: Routledge, 2012), pp.48–64.

Mayer, David, and Gamer, Michael. '(Un)making a Monster: Melodrama, *The Satirist*, and the Cartoons of Sam De Wilde,' *Nineteenth Century Theatre and Film*, vol. 48, no. 2 (2021), pp.122–42.

Merleau-Ponty Maurice. *Phenomenology of Perception*. Translated by Donald A. Landes (London and New York: Routledge, 2012).

Metcalf, Bruce. 'Craft and art, culture and biology'. In *The Culture of Craft*, edited by Peter Dormer (Manchester and New York: Manchester University Press, 1997), pp.67–82.

Morphy, Howard. 'Art as a mode of action: Some problems with Gell's *Art and Agency*'. In *Museum Objects: Experiencing the Properties of Things*, edited by Sandra H. Dudley (London & New York: Routledge, 2012), pp.344–62.

Morris, William. 'The Lesser Arts of Life'. In *Ceramic Art: Comment and Review, 1882–1977*, edited by Garth Clark (New York: E.P. Dutton, 1978), pp.3–27.

Muthesius, Hermann. 'Art and the Machine'. In *The Craft Reader*, edited by Glenn Adamson (London & New York: Berg, 2010), pp.111–14.

Nicholson, Ben. 'Extract from letter to Lilian Somerville, March 25/26 1954'. In *Ben Nicholson: A Studio International Special*, edited by Maurice de Sausmarez (London: Studio International, 1969), p.57.

Odundo, Magdalene et al. *Magdalene Odundo in Cambridge* (Cambridge: The Fitzwilliam Museum, 2021).

Oyekan, Lawson. 'Lawson Oyekan, Interview with Sarah Tanguy'. *axisweb.org*, https://www.axisweb.org/p/lawsonoyekan/. Date accessed: 29 September 2020. Last updated: 23 March 2007.

Oyibo, Gabriel. 'The Grand Unified Theorem (Full Lecture),' *YouTube*, https://www.youtube.com/watch?v=g_1-2Q5EI68. Date accessed: 28 September 2022. Last updated: 1 March 2014.

Perry, Grayson. 'Climbing Everest Without Oxygen'. In *The Pre-Therapy Years*, edited by Catrin Jones and Chris Stephens (London: Thames & Hudson, 2020), pp.58–64.

Préaud, Tamara et al. *The Sèvres Porcelain Manufactory: Alexandre Brongniart and the Triumph of Art and Industry, 1800–1847* (New York: Bard Graduate Center for Studies in the Decorative Arts, 1997).

Rambelli, Fabio. 'Introduction: The Invisible Empire: Spirits and Animism in Contemporary Japan'. In *Spirits and Animism in Contemporary Japan*, edited by Fabio Rambelli (London: Bloomsbury 2019), pp.1–16.

Rose, Gillian. 'Looking at Landscape: The Uneasy Pleasures of Power, from Feminism and Geography: The Limits of Geographical Knowledge'. In *The Cultural Geography Reader*, edited by Timothy Oakes and Patricia L. Price (London & New York: Routledge, 2008), pp.171–75.

Rothwell, Sarah. 'Capturing Decorative Art – The Work of Frances Priest,' *The Decorative Arts Society Journal*, vol.45 (2021), pp.9–21.

Sainsbury's Centre for Visual Art. *Lucie Rie, Hans Coper, and their Pupils* (Norwich: SCVA, 1991).

Schechner, Richard, and Brady, Sara. *Performance Studies: An Introduction* (London & New York: Routledge, 2013).

Searle, G.R. *Morality and the Market in Modern Britain* (Oxford: Clarendon Press, 1998).

Seitz, William C. *The Responsive Eye* (New York: The Museum of Modern Art, 1965).

Shakespeare, William. *The Life of King Henry V*, edited by Barbara A. Mowat and Paul Werstine (New York: Washington Square Press, 1995).

Sjöholm, Jenny. 'The art studio as archive: tracing the geography of artistic potentiality, progress and production,' *Cultural Geographies*, vol. 21, no. 3 (July 2014), pp.505–14.

Slivka, Rose. 'The New Ceramic Presence'. In *Ceramic Art: Comment and Review, 1882–1977*, edited by Garth Clark (New York: E.P. Dutton, 1978), pp.131–142.

Slobodkin, Louis. *Sculpture: Principles and Practice* (New York: Dover Publications, 1949).

Sparkes, Brian. *The Red and The Black: Studies in Greek Pottery* (London & New York: Routledge, 1996).

Stair, Julian. 'From Precepts to Praxis: The Origins of British Studio Pottery'. In *Things of Beauty Growing: British Studio Pottery*, edited by Glenn Adamson, Martin Droth and Simon Olding (New Haven: Yale University Press, 2017), pp.29–55.

Sterling, Charles. *Still Life Painting: From Antiquity to the Twentieth* Century, 2nd edn. (New York: Harper and Row, 1981).

Thorpe, Ashley. *Contemporary British Ceramics: Beneath the Surface.* (Marlborough: The Crowood Press, 2021).

Thunberg, Greta. 'Transcript: Greta Thunberg's Speech at the U.N. Climate Action Summit'. *NPR.* https://www.npr.org/2019/09/23/763452863/transcript-greta-thunbergs-speech-at-the-u-n-climate-action-summit?t=1633795933303. Accessed: 9 October 2021.

Treggiden, Katie. *Urban Potters.* No pl.: (Ludion, 2017).

Turner, Frank M. 'Gladstone: A Political Not a Cultural Radical'. In *William Gladstone: New Studies and Perspectives*, edited by Roland Quinault et al (London and New York: Routledge, 2016), pp.15–30.

Turner, Victor. 'Liminal to Liminoid'. In Play, Flow, and Ritual: an essay in comparative symbology,' *Rice Institute Pamphlet – Rice University Studies,* 60, no. 3 (1974), pp.53–92.

Turner, Victor et al. *The Ritual Process: Structure and Anti-Structure* (London & New York: Routledge, 1969).

Ullman, B.L. 'Satura and Satire', *Classical Philology*, vol. 8, no.2 (April 1913), pp.172–94.

Van Hensbergen, Gijs. *Gaudi* (London: Harper Collins, 2001).

Varnedoe, Kirk. *Cy Twombly: A Retrospective* (New York: Museum of Modern Art, 1995).

Walvin, James. *Sugar: The World Corrupted, from Slavery to Obesity* (London: Little, Brown Books, 2017).

Yanagi, Sōetsu. *The Unknown Craftsman* (Tokyo: Kodansha International, 1976).

Acknowledgements

My sincere thanks to all the ceramicists featured in this volume, who have taken time out of their busy schedules to meet with me, read and comment upon my writing, and help with the sourcing of images. Such support means the world to me. Thank you.

I would also like to thank everyone at MAAK Contemporary Ceramics and Marsden Woo Gallery for their generosity in providing images and liaising with artists on my behalf. In this regard, special thanks to the photographer Philip Sayer for generously providing so many examples of his work. Thank you also to Alexander Brattell and Alick Cotterill.

Thank you to The Crowood Press for believing in this second volume. Sincere gratitude to Greer Crawley, who has been wonderfully supportive in helping me consider ideas, suggesting readings, passing on books, and proofreading the text.

Finally, thank you to my parents, who have patiently listened to essay drafts over the kitchen table, and whose love and support means more than words can say.

Image Credits

Front cover image: Flection Vessel (2018) by Sara Flynn (photograph by Stuart Burford, courtesy of Erskine, Hall & Coe). *Back cover images:* top left, Flaming June (2014) by Chun Liao (photograph by Phil Sayer, courtesy of Marsden Woo Gallery); top right, The Moon Jar (2016) by Akiko Hirai (photograph by Akiko Hirai); bottom left, Scalloped Vessel (2021) by Nico Conti (photograph by Matthew Warner); bottom right, Detail of The Ecstasy of St Teresa (After Bernini) (2008) by Nicholas Rena (photograph by Phil Sayer for Jerwood Foundation).

All interior photographs are by the author with the exception of the following. Maak Contemporary Ceramics: pp 8, 11, 26, 29, 30, 31, 60, 76, 169; Alex Robson for Lyon & Turnbull: p 23; Mike Abrahams: pp 33, 34, 35, 37, 38, 225; Julian King-Salter: pp 40, 41, 42, 43, 44, 45, 221; Karen Smith: pp 49, 50, 51, 52; Dan Kelly: pp 49, 51, 53, 221; Shane Enright: p 50; Colin Mills: p 54; Bertie Fritsch: p 58; Alexander Brattell: pp 59, 60; S. Hall: pp 62, 63, 64, 65, 66; Michael Harvey, courtesy of Erskine, Hall & Coe: pp 69, 70, 71; Glenn Norwood: 69, 70, 219; Stuart Burford, courtesy of Erskine, Hall & Coe: pp 71, 72, 73; Andy Stagg, courtesy of Erskine, Hall & Coe: p 72; J. Paul Getty Museum, California: p 74; Julian Stair: pp 77, 78, 79, 225; Jan Baldwin: pp 80, 81; Corvi-Mora, London: p 81; John Taylor: pp 85, 86, 87, 88, 89, 157, 158, 159, 161; Agata Pec, courtesy of Vessel Gallery, London: p 87; Matthew Warner: pp 91, 92, 93, 94, 95, 128, 129, 226; Paul Scott: pp 97, 98, 99, 100, 101, 102, 104, 105, 106, 107; Frode Larsen, The National Museum of Art, Architecture and Design, Norway: pp 100, 102, 105; John Pollex: p 104; Michael Holohan: p 110; Tony Richards: pp 111 (courtesy of Manchester Metropolitan University Special Collections Museum), 114; Joel Fildes: pp 111, 112, 115; Stephen Dixon: pp 113, 115, 219; Alison Welsh: p 116; Shannon Tofts: pp 119, 120, 121, 122, 125, 224; Alick Cotterill: p 127; Nico Conti: pp 128, 131; Matthew Rose: p 129; Ho Lai: pp 130, 218; Dewi Tannatt Lloyd: pp 136, 138, 139, 140, 219; Toni de Jesus: pp 137, 141; Jason Jacques Gallery and Gareth Mason: pp 142, 143, 145, 146, 148, 153, 155; Sarah Purvey: pp 162, 163; Phil Sayer: pp 166, 167, 168, 169, 170, 171 (all courtesy of Marsden Woo Gallery), 175 (for the Jerwood Foundation), 177 (Lynne Strover Gallery), 224; Browse & Darby: p 173; Nicholas Rena: p 174; Hélène Binet: p 176; Rachael Rena: p 177; Mark Woods (Cross Lane Projects, Kendal): pp 179, 182; Tiwani Contemporary: p184; Akiko Hirai: pp 186, 188, 189, 190, 191, 192, 193; Tim Copsey: 197, 198, 199, 200, 201, 218; Kelpie: p 203; Lutz Krainhoefner: p 203; James Champion: pp 203, 205, 206, 207; Harald Brekke: p 206; Márek Líška: pp 210, 211, 212, 213, 214, 215, 217; Adrian Sassoon: p 220; Sam Hall: p. 220; Philip Sinden: p 220; Rowan Rothschild: p 221; Chun Liao: p 222; Ben Boswell: p 222; Cristian Barnett: p 223; Louise Winter: p 223; Claire Newman Williams: p 224; Anne Renwick: p 225; Russell Sach: p 225.

Index

First published in 2023 by
The Crowood Press Ltd
Ramsbury, Marlborough
Wiltshire SN8 2HR

enquiries@crowood.com
www.crowood.com

British Library Cataloguing-in-Publication Data
A catalogue record for this book is available from the British Library.

ISBN 978 0 7198 4242 9

Cover design by Nick May/www.bluegecko22.com

Typeset by Envisage IT
Printed and bound in India by Parksons Graphics